Praise for *River of the West*

"A visionary and revisionist history of the Columbia River. . . . A unique historical experience—gorgeously written."

—Gretel Ehrlich, author of *A Match to the Heart*

"An original and vibrant account of the Columbia River's hold on the imagination of individuals and cultures. . . . Clark weaves an often mystical, sometimes tragic tapestry. . . . [A] valuable addition to the body of works on the Columbia River region."

—*Kirkus Reviews*

"Clark not only writes vividly . . . but also lyrically. . . . Clark's fine prose enlivens his sensitive look at a particular portion of Northwest history."

—*The Seattle Times*

"Clark has produced an outstanding literary tapestry. . . . This book's glory rests in Clark's writing, which is as fluid as the river he explores."

—*Library Journal*

"Clark presents no less than a visionary chronicle of the exploration and history of the Columbia River. Full of richly textured prose . . . Clark's finely etched portraits create a vivid account that devotees of history and Americana will read and savor."

—*Booklist*

RIVER *of* THE WEST

STORIES FROM THE COLUMBIA

ROBERT CLARK

Picador USA ✹ New York

RIVER OF THE WEST. Copyright © 1995 by Robert Clark. All rights
reserved. Printed in the United States of America. No part of this
book may be used or reproduced in any manner whatsoever without
written permission except in the case of brief quotations embodied
in critical articles or reviews. For information, address Picador USA,
175 Fifth Avenue, New York, N.Y. 10010.

Picador® is a U.S. registered trademark and is used by St. Martin's
Press under license from Pan Books Limited.

Library of Congress Cataloging-in-Publication Data

Clark, Robert, 1952–
    River of the west : a chronicle of the Columbia /
Robert Clark.
        p.   cm.
    ISBN 0-312-16987-6
    1. Columbia River—History.   2. Columbia River—Biography.
I. Title.
    F853.C54   1997
    979.7—dc21   97-20839
                                                    CIP

First published in the United States by HarperCollins Publishers

First Picador USA Edition: October 1997

10   9   8   7   6   5   4   3   2   1

F O R   C A R O L I N E

*A*ll the events which make up the annals of the nations are but shadows of our private experiences. Suddenly and silently the eras which we call history awake and glimmer in us, and *there* is room for Alexander and Hannibal to march and conquer. In short, the history which we read is only a fainter memory of events which have happened in our own experience. Tradition is a more interrupted and feebler memory.

The world is but canvas to our imaginations.

—Henry David Thoreau,
A Week on the Concord and Merrimack Rivers

*O*ut of his place, pushed by the hornéd flood,
With all his verdure spoiled and trees adrift
Down the great river to the op'ning gulf,
And there take root an island salt and bare,
The haunt of seals and orcs, and sea-mews' clang:
To teach thee that God attributes to place
No sanctity, if none be thither brought
By men who there frequent, or therein dwell.

—John Milton, *Paradise Lost*, XI

I forget the names of towns without rivers.
A town needs a river to forgive the town.
Whatever river, what ever town
it is much the same.
The cruel things I did I took to the river.
I begged the current: make me better.

—Richard Hugo, "The Towns We Know and
Leave Behind, the Rivers We Carry with Us"

Contents

*N*o one remembers the river's coming. It has been among us so long that it scarcely bears thinking about, a presence as enduring as dust. No one asks why the river came. The river requires only itself: it moves over the land, as God is said to have moved over the waters, for no other reason than it pleases itself to do so. The river is powerful and unknowable, and is spoken of in stammers and fragments, never with confidence or total comprehension: Does the water shape the river or does the river shape the water? Or is the river neither water nor riverbed, but the force of water falling down between its banks?

Put a boat into the river. Let it float out to the water's heart, equidistant from either shore, and boat and river become one motion. After a time, it sometimes seems they halt together, and the land on either side flows away behind them while they stand still, an island in a stream of hills and cliffs running eastward to oblivion.

In central Washington, at a hard and waterless place called Dry Falls, a person can stand in the scrub beneath the lip of a cataract three miles wide and nearly four hundred feet high—more than twice *the height and three times the width of Niagara Falls. About fifteen thousand years ago, a glacier blocked the path of the river and the river turned its course down what is now known as Grand Coulee. The water running over this precipice was two hundred feet deep. After a few thousand years the glacier withdrew, and today the falls are inundated only by absence and silence. The river has taken its business elsewhere.*

This has been the nature of things ever since islands emerged from the Precambrian ocean and knit themselves together to make this corner of the continent. Sixteen million years ago, lava began seeping out of cracks in the earth and covered eighty thousand miles of what is today Oregon, Washington, and Idaho. It formed a crust of basalt up to two miles thick and a carapace so heavy it sank beneath its own weight and created a basin through which the river could flow. The river followed the path of least resistance, and farther west the river cut a deep gorge straight through the rising peaks and volcanoes of the Cascade Range to the Pacific. The river takes its time, choosing its battles carefully; neither toiling nor sleeping, the river finds a way.

Throughout its twelve-hundred-mile course, the Columbia River drains 259,000 square miles or 180 million acre-feet of water each year—enough to cover both Oregon and Washington knee-deep. It is the second-largest river system in North America and the largest to empty into the Pacific. The river begins in the snows and glaciers of the Rockies in Montana, Alberta, and British Columbia. It carries away not only their melted waters but, pebble by pebble, the mountains themselves. The river serves to bear away land and water alike to the ocean that gave birth to the continents, to empty the world of solids and heights. But the river consists neither of water nor of earth; it is not a substance but a process, an endless belt that obliterates both time and space. It is like a wind or a ghost, unraveling the land, doing eternity's work, carrying the sea its due. It is the world before we knew the world and the world as it shall be, unseen beneath our waking, rolling through our dreams.

CHAPTER 1

Out of the Flood

1.

*I*n a time no one remembers, about twelve thousand years ago, the Columbia Plateau was both colder and wetter than it is today, a rolling grassland bordered to the north by the Cordilleran ice sheet that extended to the river's northern verge. Mastodons, saber-toothed cats, mammoth beavers, shaggy white bears, and giant condors ranged this land, their existence marked by bones buried in the river's alluvia and in the strata of myth, legend, and dream. A race of people lived along the river then, fishing for salmon and hunting in the milky light.

Near Wallula Gap, where the Columbia River meets the Snake River, someone had a knife, perhaps seven inches long and two inches broad, chipped from a slab of basalt. On a day not so very different from any other, the wind began to blow and the air filled with dust. After the passing of a night, the sun shone as dimly as a dying ember. Within hours, there was a noise, at first like a distant storm, then like thunder and wind mixed together, and finally like a rock slide of all the stars and moons in heaven.

The flood that came upon the knife, the knife maker, and his people could not be outrun. It swallowed them under five hundred feet of water, rock, and floating ice—ice from a glacial dam near the Bitterroot River in present-day Montana that held back a lake two hundred miles long and two thousand feet deep, enough water to fill half of Lake Michigan. When the dam broke, it released into the Columbia 380 cubic miles of water that reached depths of one thousand feet and a speed of fifty miles per hour and the Columbia's flow was ten times that of all the rivers in the world today. The river abandoned its customary channel and spread itself across two hundred miles of the plateau, scouring the earth and the river course clean of soil, hills, and life.

When the deluge had exhausted itself, the glacier moved southward yet again, damming the waters that then collected behind it for fifty years until they once again breached the ice. And so flood succeeded flood, some forty of them over the course of two thousand years until at last the sun grew stronger and drove the ice away. With the floods, the river ended one world together with its creatures and people and prepared the ground for another. Of that earlier time, it left not much more than the knife, which it carried downstream and buried in a gravel bar hundreds of feet high until it was uncovered in the autumn of 1953 by an archaeologist from the University of Oregon.

After the flood, time moved like rain—from the sky to the earth to the river to the sea and thence to the sky again—or as the salmon do, voyaging from river to sea to river in circles, deeper and deeper into the same course, laying down their dead and their children in the gravels of the river.

The salmon are a race apart, immortal voyageurs who pass beyond the world of the river into a realm so distant that it must have seemed to be the land of the dead; from the river to waters deep and black beyond dreaming. That they see such things as that place possesses and carry themselves back fattened and mighty to where they began might well be judged a miracle. The salmon begins life as an egg laid in the gravel of the river or one of its tributaries. Once hatched, the newborn salmon or alevin lives in the gravel sustained by its yolk sac, beginning a series of transformations in which it is reshaped and hammered into whatever form its habitat requires.

When the nutrients of the yolk sac are exhausted, the salmon takes on a form with fins and tail and wriggles up out of the gravel like a snake. It feeds on plankton, aquatic larvae, and caddis fly, and is nurtured as much by the forest as by the stream; by cedar, Douglas fir, and hemlock that shelter the banks and keep the waters cool and foster the insect life upon which the salmon depend. The infant salmon—called fry at this stage—shuns the light while it grows to adolescence in its home waters for a period of up to two years, prey to birds, snakes, and larger salmon. The salmon then begins its migration to the sea, lingering for a quarter year in estuaries where the salt water blends with the fresh, growing still larger and adapting itself to the ethos of the ocean and feeding on its creatures. Of the thousand eggs a single salmon lays in her nest or redd, perhaps one hundred will survive to this point. When it at last reaches the open ocean, its body, once a greenish forest hue, will shimmer like burnished metal, like clouds under a new moon.

For the next three to five years the salmon will travel thousands of miles in a counter-clockwise circle around the North Pacific in a great pilgrimage of fish, feeding on shrimp and herring and attaining a weight that can reach one hundred pounds and a length of three feet. It swims continuously at a speed of about ten miles per hour, until the urge to return home comes upon it, an insistent, irresistible voice from the river. Once the salmon enters the river, it swims thirty to ninety miles a day through slack water, cataracts, and cascades, and it eats no more. Rather, it consumes itself, burning its own flesh as it beats its way home. According to its species, its flanks turn red, its back swells upward into a hump, and the placid dignity of its face devolves as its jaws bend and hook into an agonized mask as willful and fiercely magnificent as a god.

When the salmon reaches its birthplace, perhaps a thousand miles upriver, it finds another salmon of its kind, and the female begins to dig with her tail in the gravel, excavating a grave for herself and a cradle for her children. She labors in this way for days, spent beyond endurance, her body already decomposing. When she is done, her mate swims beside her, brushing and mingling their tattered, unraveling flesh, and together they face the flow of the waters and shower down eggs and milt into the river bottom. They do this again and again until they have nothing left within them, and then they stop, still at last and, to most lights, dead. The larger animals of the place, eagle and bear, the salmon's only peers, gather their remains, and leave both what they do and do not eat of the fish in the forest for the earth, for the insects, and for the cedar and its fellows, who will feed the river, and with it the salmon's young. The salmon children that survive will do nothing more or less than their parents: they will know when it is time to leave the river and they will remember the way back, bearing themselves up its course and recovering the place that is theirs alone.

The Klikitat—one of the peoples who came to the river after the flood drowned the knife maker and his world—have a tale they tell of a time when the salmon ceased to feed them. It was not that the people did or didn't do something, but that they forgot those things that belong to and must be accorded to the salmon. The salmon returned only through the intercession of Rattlesnake, who ruminates upon his bitter thoughts among the stones and who alone of all creatures was able to bring the salmon back to life. In remembrance of this, a membrane inside the back of every salmon bears the form of Rattlesnake. What the people had forgotten is what every salmon knows; perhaps the only thing it knows: that in all the turnings of the world, to remember—to know how the story must be told and how and where it ends—is the highest and most singular necessity.

2.

Six thousand miles to the east, a quarter turn of the globe, there are also salmon, cousins to the fish of the river. They live much as Pacific salmon do, but because they are able to return to the sea one or more times after spawning, they die in the manner of men; not by the self-immolation of coupling and begetting but by old age, disease, and predation. But the people of ancient Europe honored them in much the same way as the people of the river did, and among the Celts it was said that the salmon was the wisest of creatures; that it lived in a well surrounded by trees upon whose fruit it alone could feed. From that food, the salmon came to know all the knowledge of the world and lived in a kind of paradise from which people were excluded, knowing things people were not permitted to know.

In 1492, when an Italian named Christopher Columbus took possession of some islands in the west of the Atlantic Ocean on behalf of the king and queen of Spain, he believed he was somewhere near Asia. But as Asia evaded him, the marvels of the place in which he had found himself increasingly impressed themselves upon his mind: fish glistening like gems in a turquoise sea, beaches of virgin-white sand, trees and plants bearing sweet fruit, and a benign climate that commended nakedness. He came to feel that he must be in the vicinity of the earthly paradise he had read about in the Christian Bible—a paradise from which humankind had been exiled by God, but that the geographers of his day maintained still existed at the head of four great rivers blocked by rapids and swells, their banks inhabited by monsters, cannibals, and

Amazons. Surely he was near the frontier of Eden, close to the temperate verge of riches beyond fathoming, and of secrets known only to angels.

As Columbus's certitude increased, he grew bolder in the conviction of his own knowledge and set about recording it. Every creature, people, and landform he observed, he described on paper, and in the writing of the thing, it seemed that he knew the thing, that he pulled the thing free from its place in the world, disembodied it and remade it in words, no longer the thing itself but an image in letters. Once recorded and reconstituted, it could be joined to other things with which it had originally no relation; spliced, woven, and queued with them, and made the ground of deductions; the proof of speculations; the fulfillment of prophecies; the culmination of histories; and the justification of a thousand deeds and desires. Everything Columbus saw, he wrote down and made his slave. His mastery over them made him akin to a god, for writing—the power to set things apart from themselves—seemed to allow him to perceive the universe and the ideas and forms that underpin it as God himself must do.

His journals filled with knowledge until it seemed they must overflow and the words flood out upon the page like molten gold or surge into the air as a flock of ravishingly plumed birds. He sat in his cabin aboard ship or onshore beneath the palms, and felt the bottomless youth that Adam felt in the Garden, and he began to name things. He renamed peoples, islands, villages, bays, and rivers, obliterating the words by which their inhabitants knew them. He gave them the names of saints and Spanish nobles, as though he were baptizing them. With his pen he placed a seal upon their lips to still the murmurings of what this place had been before he came to it. It was a kind of willful forgetting.

In the end, he renamed himself, stripping away the quotidian meaninglessness of "Christopher" and "Columbus" to lay bare his name's letters and roots. He styled himself "Christo-ferens," the Christ-bearer. And who was he, this man who carried Christ, as though on wings over the water? In Latin, "Columbus" signified the dove that showed Noah where he might find land when all the world was water, that descended on the Jordan River when Jesus was baptized and received his godhood, and that is manifest whenever the Holy Spirit comes—the dove through whom God "will pour out my spirit upon all flesh and your sons and daughters shall prophesy, and your young men shall see visions, and your old men shall dream dreams."

Columbus carried like a cross his knowledge and his power to redeem the world he had found. Within a few years, people began to say he had lost his mind. But even after he was dead, he gave his name to many things, not least among them the river to the northwest called Nch'i-Wana.

In the England of 1570, blessed by providence with a wise and beneficent queen, men of enterprise and imagination, and the envy and fear of her neighbors, surely no one knew more than John Dee. Born of Welsh parents, Dee was a man of breathtaking intellectual attainments, a graduate of the universities of Cambridge and Louvain, and a master of every secret of art and science the universe contained. At age twenty-three he astounded the scholars of Paris with his lectures on Euclid. Within a few years he had discoursed and written upon philosophy, law, medicine, astronomy, rhetoric, and navigation; counseled three sovereigns; and supped with the noblest persons and most learned minds of both Britain and the continent. With some four thousand printed and manuscript volumes to his name, he owned one of the largest libraries in Europe. He wore a gown and a long beard, and with a mind so capacious and a demeanor so wise, he was called Doctor Dee. But he was more than that; a magus, less a scholar or a scientist than a high priest of knowledge, the master of ineffable secrets.

Some called Doctor Dee a sorcerer. As a student, he had devised stage machinery for a play that seemed to cause the actors to fly across the stage in a manner that bedazzled and, many felt, bewitched the audience. He had cast horoscopes for Queen Mary and her court, passed on what he learned to her sister Elizabeth, and only narrowly escaped burning at the stake on charges of sedition and "enchanting the queen." He denied being a witch or a conjurer, although it was true that he delved into magic; not black magic but natural magic, the knowledge of higher forces and laws that was vouchsafed to the ancients and, through the rediscovery of lost texts, was being revived by a few select men in Renaissance Europe.

Chief among these ancient philosophers was Hermes Trismegistus, an Egyptian of shadowy history for whom God was "the sacred word," the knowledge that spoke its own name to itself, and who in that divine self-regard so loved what it perceived that it reproduced its own essence in man. Man, therefore, was in his soul divine, and his rightful business was to reclaim that birthright: "If you do not make yourself equal to God," Hermes was said to have written, "you cannot know God." In the Hermetic universe, all knowledge emanated from the divine, and there were accordingly no distinctions between science, art, and what some might call the occult. But in the estimate of Dee and his fellows, the practice of the occult was simply an attempt to control hidden but very real natural forces—a kind of mystical but rational humanism that sought to wrest by knowledge the power of nature and harness it for the benefit of humankind. Man was nothing less than an utterance of God, the master of the earth as God was master of the universe.

Dee, therefore, brought his mind to bear not only on the traditional intellectual fare of the universities but on alchemy, astrology, numerology, clairvoyance, and prophecy. Since human beings were only angels sundered from their wings, he invoked the angels themselves, who by telepathy revealed their secrets to him.

They steered him like helmsmen through the mind of God. He felt himself a being without limits and so became a creature of limitless enthusiasms, which extended beyond his own ambitions to encompass those of his country and its rulers. He made it his business to prove by historical deduction that the Tudor dynasty descended from the founders of Rome, and that Queen Elizabeth was therefore destined by blood to build an empire.

That empire surely lay to the east in Asia, which had riches enough to suit Elizabeth and her merchant courtiers, and mysteries and secrets enough to enthrall Dee. But a sea lay between England and Asia, and lands within it sufficiently large to thwart easy passage. Columbus and his Spanish successors had found no way through them during the past sixty years, nor had John Cabot's English-sponsored voyage discovered a route to the north. Since then, neither French nor English ships had penetrated Asia nor had anyone uncovered the wealth the newfound lands must contain.

But to Dee it was clear that these lands across the Atlantic were islands rather than an overarching continent. Subsequently there must be a way around them. The islands were remnants of Atlantis, of whose existence and destruction Plato had told; an island subsumed by flood but now rediscovered, like so many things, by the renascent European quest for knowledge and mastery of the world. Moreover, they were clearly the same islands in the Atlantic and Arctic that both King Arthur and the Welsh Prince Madoc were said to have explored during the infancy of British civilization; the same archipelago through which St. Brendan had voyaged only a little later. But even if America—or what Dee insisted on calling Atlantis—was one enormous island, it was an island all the same, and there had to be a passage, north and northwest, around or through it.

Even before Dee took up the matter, others had sensed the truth of it. Robert Thorne, a Bristol shipping merchant, attempted to bring it to the King's attention in a letter of 1527, writing:

. . . after they bee past the pole, goe right toward the pole An-
tartike, and then decline toward the lands and Ilands situated
between the Tropikes and under the Equinoctial, without
doubt they shal find there the richest lands and Ilands of the
worlde of Golde, precious stones, balmes, spices, and other
thinges that we here esteeme most. . . .

Thorne had never sailed much beyond the English Channel,
but that was immaterial. He based his assertions on words alone,
words from seamen's tales, from ancient authorities, and from
books: Plato, Marco Polo, *Mandeville's Travels*, Peter Martyr's
Decades of the New World, Castaneda's *Voyages to India*, and Roger
Barlow's *Brief Summe of Geographie*. Speculation hardened into
belief, and belief to fact. Books were their own justification, each
dividing and metastasizing into more books, engendering worlds
no one had ever sailed or walked.

By the mid-sixteenth century, maps followed from books,
their quadrants brimming with unseen islands such as Estland,
Icaria, Drogeo, Buss, and Hy-Brasil. Maps begot more maps,
each new chart unquestioningly accreting details from the last.
One of the more influential was that ascribed to the Zeno brothers, Venetian explorers of the new world who had in fact never
sailed nor ever lived. But all the maps—beyond their faith that
the pen, the type font, and the engraver's steel set to paper incarnated a reality more compelling than experience—incorporated one feature: a way around or through North America,
variously called the Northwest Passage, the Strait of Anian, and
the River of the West.

In their margins, the maps revealed what their worlds must
contain: monsters, death's-heads, Amazons, cannibals, and beasts
as well as gold, exotic fruits, and cities of pearl. In the new world
there was nothing of the old, nothing of the ordinary or the
known; it was composed solely of nightmares and dreams. It in-
cited men's fears and fed their curiosity, and while riches and em-

pire impelled most voyages to sea, some sought only to sate the imagination, to partake of marvels. Thus, in 1536 the *Trinity* and the *William* left Bristol with a cargo of thirty gentlemen tourists with the express purpose of viewing the wonders of Newfoundland. When their food supplies were exhausted, they fell to eating the sparse grasses and herbs that grew on the shore, and, in the end, each other.

The fascinations of the new world attracted not only the curious and the high-minded but also promoters, scoundrels, and confidence men. Chief among these was Sebastian Cabot, who claimed to have learned to measure longitude by divine revelation and had a largely fabricated résumé of North Atlantic voyages. His fame was such that the organizers of the Willoughby expedition of 1553 hired him as an adviser, and he gave them the benefit of his wisdom on the treatment of the natives they might encounter:

> . . . if you shall see them weare Lyons or Beares skinnes, having long bowes, and arrows, be not afraid of that sight . . . for as much as our people, and shippes may appeare unto them strange and wonderous, and theirs also to ours: it is to be considered, how they may be used, learning much of their natures and dispositions, by some one such person, as you may first either allure, or take to be brought aboord your ships . . . to the intent that he or she may allure other to draw nigh to shewe the commodities: and if the person taken may be made drunke with your beere, or wine, you shal know the secrets of his heart.

Cabot himself preferred to remain in England as a consultant and enjoy the fruits of his reputation. But despite his assurances of the voyage's success, Willoughby's three ships suffered a fate similar to that of the *Trinity* and the *William*. The vessels and their crews of desiccated, gelid cadavers were recovered a year later, drifting in the Arctic sea.

Such events muffled enthusiasm for more voyages of discovery, often for decades at a time. But nothing discouraged John Dee, the nation's supreme authority on navigation and the tides, as well as a confidante of the world's most eminent mapmaker, Gerardus Mercator. He also had the ear of Queen Elizabeth and her court. In 1570 he urged that exploration for a northwest passage be revived; that from it ". . . might grow Commoditye to this land chiefly, and to the rest of the Christen common wealth, farre passing all riches and wordly Threasure." Although Dee's own interest continued to lie primarily in Asia's much vaunted store of mystic and scientific knowledge, he was adept at enlisting men with more practical aims. Among them was Michael Lok, a speculator and financier supported by his wife's fortune, who as a leading member of the Muscovy Company had been a backer in efforts to discover a passage to Asia northeastward across the top of the Russian Arctic. This venture had proven a failure, but neither Lok's fervid belief in a passage nor his ability to fuel the imaginations of potential investors in such schemes was quelled.

Using Dee's prestige and encouragement, Lok signed a Yorkshireman named Martin Frobisher to captain an expedition to the northwest. Frobisher's stature as a seafarer was built in large measure on his career as a privateer, but he aspired to the glory that traversing the passage might bring; "the only thing in the world," he would later write, "that was left undone, whereby a notable mind might be made famous and fortunate." In 1576 he set off on the first of three voyages, and returned to England with an Inuit he took captive above the entrance to what would one day be known as Hudson Bay. London was tantalized by this savage clothed in fur, whose appearance suggested he was Asian. But the Inuit would not speak: he had bitten his tongue in two upon his capture, as though to prevent the English from seizing his words along with his body. Transplanted to Britain, he quickly withered and died, but the English made a series of illustrations of his corpse—"pictures in ink and paper," Lok says—one dressed in his native clothes, one in those of an English gentleman, and one in his nakedness.

Frobisher had also returned with some black rocks he insisted contained gold. Two assayers found nothing of value in them, but a third, an Italian of dubious reputation whose services were secured by Dee, was willing to support Frobisher's claim. On the strength of that corroboration, Frobisher was promoted to high admiral and he made voyages to the northwest in 1578 and 1579, carrying back another Inuit and two thousand tons of ore, which proved to be worthless. Frobisher's "gold" was eventually used to pave a London street.

Frobisher himself deftly escaped the fury of the voyage's investors, who turned instead on Lok and threw him into debtor's prison. In his cell and upon his release, Lok fulminated in letters on "the abuses of Captayne Furbusher against the Company" and fabricated maps depicting a clear passage emptying into the Pacific between what he dubbed Elizabeth's Land and Lok's Land, but he found few friends or supporters. The onetime pirate Frobisher was meanwhile celebrated in George Best's *A True Discourse of the late voyages of discoverie, for the finding of a passage to Cathaya, by the Northweast* with a map showing a channel called Frobisher's Straits giving on to the Strait of Anian and thence to China. Elsewhere, Frobisher was memorialized in verse as "A hector stout . . . on land, Ulysses on the seas" and was himself moved to draft a poem commending further explorations of America:

> *A pleasant ayre, a sweet and firtell soil,*
> *A certaine gaine, a never dying praise:*
> *An easie passage, voide of loathsome toile,*
> *Found out by some and knowen to me the waies,*
> *All this is there, then who will refraine to trie:*
> *That loves to live abroad, or dreads to die.*

With Lok disgraced and Frobisher reaping the benefits of his celebrity, John Dee was as intent as ever to promote a northwest passage. He formed an alliance with Sir Humfry Gilbert, a knight and warrior born of a monied Devon family. Gilbert was a favorite at court and something of a hero for his merciless suppression of native uprisings in Ireland, a strategy based on the butchering of women and children and the impaling of rebel heads on pikes for public exhibition. But, like Frobisher, he was on the whole a high-minded man: he suggested the lands on either side of the Strait of Anian might be settled with criminals and vagrants, noting the country had already been explored by eminent navigators too diverse to mention; and its historical pedigree had been vouched for by Plato and Aristotle (although "what moved these learned men to affirme thus much, I know not"). He volunteered to undertake its final discovery not for riches—"gold, silver, precious stones, cloth of gold, silks . . . grocery wares"—but as a patriot: "He is not worthy to live at all, that for feare, or daunger of death, shunneth his countrey service, and his own honour, seeing death is inevitable, and the fame of vertue immortall."

With a charter from the Queen, Gilbert laid his plans for a voyage, but on his first attempt was driven back to port by winter storms. In return for further counsel, he granted Dee all lands in North America above the fiftieth parallel—the bulk of modern Canada—and set sail in September 1580 with three ships, the *Delight,* the *Golden Hinde,* and the *Squirrel;* when the *Delight* wrecked off the coast of Newfoundland, Gilbert retreated to the *Squirrel,* which sank on the return voyage, drowning all hands, including him.

Dee, now an old man, organized what was to be his final attempt on the passage, The Colleagues of the Fellowship of the New Navigations Atlanticall and Septentrional for the Discoverie of the North-West Passage, with Sir Humfry's younger brother Adrian and a Devon master mariner, John Davis. Davis made three voyages in the 1580s, which were successful insofar as few lives were lost and much knowledge gained of the North Atlantic Arctic. But there was no cloth of gold, only the unremitting sun of summer upon the ice and borderless white. The strait had eluded Davis, who died maintaining that "the northwest passage is a matter nothing doubtful, but at any tyme almost to be passed, the sea navigable, void of use, the air tolerable, and the waters very deep."

Dee's neighbors at Mortlake meanwhile grew restive. One evening in 1583 while the doctor was abroad, they surrounded the house whose arcane and dreadful secrets they could but speculate upon and fear. Their numbers multiplied, and at last as one soul, they forced their way in. Carrying torches, they flooded through the house and penetrated to its heart and the heart of John Dee—the library and its books, to which they set fire.

On the other side of the new world, the Spanish had crossed Mexico and discovered the Pacific, and, in their fury at the obstruction that lay between them and Asia, they obliterated its people by slavery, torture, and the Spanish God's ensanguined machinery of redemption. They searched the coast north and south for Asia, golden cities, mythic islands, and magic rivers but were distracted by enemies. Spain feared nothing so much as England, the upstart Protestant island that harried her ships, falling upon them like a cloud of mosquitoes. The worst of the guileful, barbaric lot was Sir Francis Drake, the elusive pirate and scavenger.

In 1579 Drake had rounded Cape Horn into the Pacific and pillaged his way up the South American coast, following secret orders from Queen Elizabeth. For the Spanish, the nature of Drake's mission and his whereabouts were a source of mounting apprehension and irritation. Within the year, reports had placed Drake in California. This latest news was cause for alarm: the Spanish were as interested as the English in a northern passage across the new world, if only to block its western outlet, the Strait of Anian, and thus deny their enemies access to the Pacific. Now Drake was said to have sailed north of California to the forty-eighth parallel, and in that region to have espied a break in the coast beyond which was a large body of water, trending north and east.

Although this news confirmed many of their worst fears, the Spanish were slow to launch counterexpeditions. In 1595 Sebastián Rodriguez Cermeño reached Cape Mendocino on the northern California coast, but his galleon sank. Seven years later in 1602, Sebastián Vizcaino attained the forty-third parallel "where the coast turns to the northeast, and where the entrance to the Strait of Anian seems to begin." But he sailed no farther north, and the Spanish concentrated their North American efforts on California, continuing to believe in the reality of the strait, while wishing it only a fantasy.

In fact, Drake's passage on the northwest coast had never been anything more than a rumor upon which Vizcaino based a surmise of what lay north of him. But it was a rumor whose roots were now well established and whose ever-broadening foliage overshadowed the dull and inconclusive facts of verifiable events. Meanwhile, in London, Michael Lok was busy rehabilitating his reputation and seeking support for a fresh attempt upon the passage. He fashioned a new map, incorporating the latest cartographic intelligence that had come into his hands, and dedicated it to Sir Philip Sidney, one of the Queen's leading advisers. It retained the strait between Lok's and Elizabeth's Land but added to it an enormous inland sea that gave onto the Pacific, based on Drake's supposed voyage to the northwest coast.

The map attracted little attention and no investors, but Lok's obsession brooked no obstacles. In the mid-1590s he began circulating a story he said was told him in Venice by an old Greek captain named Juan de Fuca. With a map laid across the table between them, Fuca traced with his finger a voyage north from Mexico and along the coast of California to the forty-seventh parallel, where, he said, his ship had entered an inland sea and sailed for some twenty days, withdrawing only for fear of the natives.

They were "clad in Beasts skins," their land "very fruitful, and rich of gold, Silver, Pearle, and other things."

Lok attempted to raise money based on this story, but his efforts yielded only more stories, which circulated in taverns, drawing rooms, letters, and books. There was the voyage of Lorenzo Ferrer Maldonado, who was said to have sailed from the vicinity of Frobisher Strait in the North Atlantic Arctic through a channel from which he exited into the Pacific around the fiftieth parallel. Another tale recounted the passage of an Admiral Bartholomew de Fonte into a lake or sea situated on the northwest coast, where he met a ship sailing in the opposite direction that had set off from the Atlantic side of North America. This story and others of its ilk were no more than words, and there was no reason to believe the claims they made. But the words were spoken in a steady stream, like a long exhalation of breath that bolsters a dying fire, causing the flames to leap to life and their light and warmth to draw men near.

The things that could be proved were the things that were harder to believe, and so men threw themselves and their ships against the North American continent, as though its rock and ice were an illusion, a veil of chill air that might be parted by a ship's prow. They envisioned gold in the snowy wastes of Labrador and fruit trees beyond the ice floes. Over the horizon they saw before them, there must be a waterway flooding into the Pacific between the forty-fifth and fiftieth parallels; perhaps it was a river. The words bubbled up from the bottom of the sea and floated among them like wreckage.

It was not that they saw only benignity in this indifferent land. It held terrors, most of all that of cannibalism. But such cannibalism as there was arose not in encounters with the natives of the place but with the place itself; when the land gave nothing to eat and the starving crews turned upon their own flesh. They beheld themselves as though from a distance, not as the incarnation of God's word but as carrion, and they ate.

In 1611 Henry Hudson discovered the only inland sea to be found in North America, but his food stocks ran out and his crew set him and his son adrift to die. When those mutineers who survived reached England, the truth of what had passed came out, but they were not, as custom would demand, put to death for their treason. What they knew about the geography of the Arctic and its bearing on the discovery of the strait was too precious. In 1619 a Dane named Jens Munk led an expedition back to Hudson Bay, but his sixty-one men died when reduced to feeding upon sea wrack and shore scrub. Yet only six years later a map published in London promised that Hudson's Strait provided "a fair entrance to the South Sea." The promise of the word is more substantial than flesh, more enduring than stone.

By 1670 the English dream of a strait was for a moment dormant and the nation's energies were focused on settling colonies on the North American Atlantic coast, less to mine any imagined riches than to create an extension of England; a place in which farms and villages like those back home might be fashioned in a land called New England. Farther north, the country around Hudson Bay at last yielded something of value to the Europeans: furs. A royal charter granted the Hudson's Bay Company the better part of the lands once consigned to John Dee, who had now been in his grave for sixty years. The company's mission was the practical exploitation of a resource, but it was also an instrument of British imperial policy, and so included "the discovery of a new Passage into the South Sea."

The company also received instructions regarding the native peoples, that "it being both for the honour of the Crown and of the Protestant religion itself, that all persons within our territories, though never so remote, should be taught the knowledge of God, and be made acquainted with the mysteries of salvation." In practice, the company confined its business with its Indian trading partners to business, and to defending its territory from the French, with whom England was at war from 1689 onward. The company's officers were content to cling to the shore of the bay and collect the furs the natives brought from the interior. They responded as seemed necessary to the French men-of-war that now and again found their way to the company's posts, sometimes exchanging volleys of cannon, sometimes surrendering. With the 1713 signing of the Treaty of Utrecht, the company finally turned its attention to the interior and stationed a septuagenerian trader named James Knight to command its post at Fort York.

Knight sent a lieutenant to explore the country to the west, and he returned with a band of Chipewyan Indians bringing tales of "Western Seas" reachable by water from the bay, and of a "Yellow Mettle" that could be found there. The Indians drew Knight a map, a matrix of westward-flowing rivers, and he returned to London and convinced the company's directors to authorize an expedition "to find out the Streights of Anian." In 1719 Knight sailed with two ships and a crew of twenty-seven, and not one of them was ever seen by a white man again.

Over the next three years, masts, anchors, chests, and chains were recovered from the north shore of the bay, and at last a company officer named Samuel Hearne extracted an account of Knight's fate from some Inuit natives: how twenty-two perished after being shipwrecked and spending the winter onshore; how the then eighty-year-old Knight died, and only two men remained alive. The pair "frequently went to the tip of an adjacent rock, and earnestly looked to the South and East, as if in expectation of some vessels coming to their relief. After continuing there a considerable time together, and nothing appearing, they sat down close together and wept bitterly. At length, one of the two died, and the other's strength was so far exhausted that he fell down and died also, in attempting to dig a grave for his companion."

Samuel Hearne would himself prove in 1772 that there was no navigable passage leading west from Hudson Bay, but in the interim the corpses of Knight and others had little impact on the English search for a route to the Pacific. Arthur Dobbs, an Irish member of the British Parliament, took up the mantle of John Dee and Michael Lok. He published *An Account of the Countries Adjoining Hudson's Bay,* as well as maps illustrating a strait. In 1745 Dobbs lobbied Parliament to offer a reward of £20,000 for its discovery; when the Hudson's Bay Company asserted that its most knowledgeable explorers could find no such passage, he accused it of deceiving the public.

Meanwhile, the French, excluded from the northern reaches of Canada, began pressing toward the Pacific from the head of the Great Lakes in search of a passage the Indians called the Oregon, and the French (and later the English and Americans) called the River of the West; a river the natives said "flows straight toward the setting sun, and which widens continually as it descends." At best, the river could be reached through a chain of lakes and smaller streams; at worst, by a short portage over the "Shining Mountains," which the French renamed the Montagnes des Roches (or Rocky Mountains). Even Dobbs came to accept this view, and in 1766, as Governor of North Carolina, he sent mapmaker Jonathan Carver west to test it. Carver got no further than the eastern edge of the Sioux country of Minnesota but was nevertheless moved to write the influential *Travels in the Interior Parts of North America,* an overview of the entire geography of the continent.

In Carver's scheme, the Rocky Mountains formed the vortex of four rivers: the Bourbon flowing to Hudson Bay; the St. Lawrence to the Atlantic; the Mississippi to the Gulf of Mexico; and the Oregon or River of the West to the Pacific. The image of a passage through the new world formed a quarter of a millennium before had undergone a considerable metamorphosis: what was once an open sea became a strait that had now become a river. But in its features, it was in one respect the same: in a lofty, shining place, four rivers flowed down to four compass points around which God had ranged his earthly creation. It bore the face of paradise.

3.

The native people who came after the flood (and who still live along the river today) say that Coyote once had a knife, and with it slew a monster that lived at Celilo Falls. Celilo was to become the river people's greatest fishing ground along the Columbia— which they call Nch'i-Wana, or simply "the Great River"—and by killing the monster Coyote prepared it for their coming, just as he did the rest of the river. In the memory of the people of the river, it was a time that both preceded and mirrored their own time; a time peopled by creatures who possessed both human speech and the qualities of their animal namesakes. They wielded supernatural powers but were not so much a race of gods as a set of human essences bound to natural ones. Thus was Coyote clever but not wise; Rattlesnake was irascible; Bear brutishly strong; and Eagle noble but pitiless.

In the protoworld of the river, all these creatures interacted with or foreshadowed the lives of the people to come. But it was in Coyote—in his impetuousness, ambition, and capacity for self-delusion—that the river people found an intercessor, a being to mediate between them and a world indifferent to their cares. They say there was a witch at the river's mouth, where even today the great Columbia Bar menaces ships, and Coyote fastened her to a board of the kind the people would carry their infants upon and pushed her out to sea. He traveled up and down the river, an-nouncing the coming of the new people to the great animals of the place—Bear, Eagle, and Salmon—for whose passage he cleared the waters of obstruction that they might swim each year to where the people would live.

When he was done with these things, Coyote caused Crane to build a canoe and therein to bear the new people across the water. When they had come he gave them mouths with which to speak and sing and tell tales, and eat. He gave them food: he brought bitterroot from Grand Coulee, camas from the plain east of the river, and berries from the flanks of the mountains; and he taught them to hunt elk and to catch salmon with dip nets, spears, and weirs set in the river. Neither he nor they were granted dominion over nature; rather, Coyote mediated a covenant in which nature adopted the people of the river as its children and served as a guardian who would protect, instruct, and, when necessary, discipline them.

The world, they learned, must be thanked for its blessings, it must be listened to and obeyed, and the covenant between it and its children remade each season. When the first salmon was taken from the river in the spring, the people gathered to feast and to thank the salmon for coming again, honoring it together with the other foods that give themselves up to them; that die so their death might be thwarted. So too did every child, when he or she approached adulthood, go into the forest or some other wild place for three days and wait for the world to speak. The child would make a circle of stones and wait within it for a creature to come— perhaps a bear, a wolf, or a bird—and that creature would become the child's guardian and teacher. From the creature's nature the child discovered his own nature; the tale that was to be his from among the numberless tales that swam through the world like salmon. After the vision came, the child painted or scratched an image of himself and his creature on a rock or a cliff, although some say the pictures were made by the spirits of the forest. To pass through the woods and see such an image conferred great blessings on a child, but an adult that beheld one, it was said, would meet a swift and intractable death. Only children, it seemed, might freely travel there—might ferry the river to the country where the spirits dwelt, or, sitting on the riverbank, sifting rocks and sticks like bones in a reliquary, chanting their aimless litanies, hear its voice.

The Klikitat people lived just downstream from Celilo and took their name from the talking of the gulls that herded the first salmon upriver at Coyote's behest. Living among them was a slow-witted, tongue-tied, and clumsy girl named Gray Squirrel, who passed her days alone under a cedar. She knew nothing and did nothing and the tree took pity on her. It sent her to the mountains to gather the grasses that grew nowhere else. When she obtained these, the tree taught her to dig up and strip its finest, most delicate roots, and with these and the grasses to weave baskets. Her first baskets were plain and unadorned, and Rattlesnake proposed that she weave the pattern from his back into her work. Then she copied the silhouette of Mountain's peak. Her baskets were now beautiful, but Cedar cautioned her against pride. The last and most important thing she must learn, he told her, was to weave the fibers of her baskets as closely as skin, as taut and impenetrable as stone, so that they might contain water without so much as a drop escaping. She spent a long time under Cedar's boughs, and at last finished a basket of great beauty—a basket upon whose face Rattlesnake seemed to crawl and Mountain's cone to float. She took the basket to the river and filled it and walked up the bank's clattering stones, carrying the river back to her people.

4.

On August 11, 1775, Bruno de Hezeta, captain of the Spanish ship *Santiago*, passing forty-nine degrees north latitude on the Pacific coast of North America, received a note from his second-in-command:

> The sailors [are] getting so sick that only a few were able to serve on watch; and of these most are scurvy-ridden and

unable to attend working the ship; and thus . . . the ship and its crew [are] . . . exposed to the risk of perishing.

Hezeta's orders were to explore and lay claim to the coast north to the sixtieth parallel in the company of the *Sonora*, under the command of Juan Francisco de la Bodega y Quadra. As they had been for the previous two hundred years, the Spanish were anxious about foreign competitors intruding on their sphere of influence. Of late, Russian ships had descended from the Bering Sea and, it was rumored, reached as far south as Cape Mendocino.

But with his crew so afflicted, Hezeta faced the possibility of disaster or mutiny, and so turned his ship southward and beat his way down the coast. Six days later, on the clear afternoon of August 17, the *Santiago* passed 46°7' of latitude, and Hezeta saw a large bay he named Bahía de la Asunción. Its water was turbid and warmer in color than the surrounding sea, and the currents around its entrance were so tangled and fierce he dared not enter. That evening in his cabin, he wrote: "These currents and the seething of the waters have led me to believe that it may be the mouth of some great river or some passage to another sea." He drew a map showing two steep, low capes separated by an expanse of water he estimated to be perhaps a mile in width. The following day, he left the bay behind, sailing south with his malnourished and sea-battered crew.

The English knew nothing of Hezeta and his Bahía de la Asunción, nor did anyone else for nearly seventy years: Hezeta's voyage was a secret of the Spanish Crown, and his diary was hidden in a hydrographic office in Madrid. But the English were aware of the Russian presence in the North Pacific, although it was not the principal reason they sent Capt. James Cook to the Pacific in 1776, a year after Hezeta's voyage. Cook's orders were by now familiar to British mariners:

Proceed northward along the coast as far as latitude 65 degrees or farther . . . and explore such rivers and inlets as may appear to be of considerable extent and pointing towards Hudsons or Baffins Bays.

Cook made a circuit of Hawaii, the entire coast of Alaska, and the Bering Strait, where he met ice "as compact as a wall and . . . ten or twelve feet high at least," an observation that seemed to deflate any hope of an Arctic Northwest Passage. Nor did he find evidence of a Strait of Anian or the River of the West.

The British, however, were loath to abandon the idea of a passage, and anxious to wrest the northwest coast from the Spanish and Russian interests who sought to control the lucrative trade in furs that was beginning to flourish there. In 1791 the Admiralty outfitted a comprehensive expedition to the northwest coast under the command of Capt. George Vancouver. His primary task:

> [T]he acquiring [of] accurate information with respect to the nature and extent of any water-communication which may tend . . . to facilitate an intercourse for the purposes of commerce, between the north-west coast, and the country upon the opposite of the continent . . . it would be of great importance if it should be found that, by means of any considerable inlets of the sea, or even of large rivers communicating with the lakes in the interior of the continent, such an intercourse, as hath already been mentioned, could be established.

Carried to sea on this tide of words, Vancouver and the crews on his two ships, the *Discovery* and the *Chatham,* were skeptical of their superiors' instructions. Vancouver confided to his log, ". . . no small portion of facetious mirth passed among the seamen, in consequence of our sailing from old England on the *first of April,* for the purpose of discovering a north-west passage by following up the discoveries of De Fuca, De Fonte, and a numerous train of hypothetical navigators."

A year later, on April 27, 1792, Vancouver passed a bay in the vicinity of forty-six degrees north, and noted "the appearance of an inlet, or small river, the land behind not indicating it to be of any great extent. . . ." He continued:

> The sea had now changed from its natural, to river-coloured water; the probable consequence of some streams falling into the bay. . . . Not considering this opening worthy of more attention, I continued our pursuit to the n.w. being desirous to embrace the advantages of the prevailing breeze and pleasant weather, so favorable to our examination of the coast. . . .

North of this inlet, Vancouver met a vessel under the command of Capt. Robert Gray, an American from Boston. The infant United States of America had no particular agenda regarding the Pacific, and Gray's business on the coast was not exploration but the acquisition of sea-otter and beaver pelts he intended to exchange for tea in China.

Two weeks later, after a trading session with coastal Indians that ended with his crew slaughtering some twenty natives, Gray reached the inlet Vancouver chose to ignore. His log recorded:

> 12 [May]. N. Latt. 46°7' W. Long. 122°47'. This day saw an appearance of a spacious harbour abrest the ship, haul'd our wind for it, observ'd two sand bars making off, with a passage between them to a fine river. . . . the river extended to the ne as far as eye cou'd reach, and water fit to drink as far down as the bars at the entrance. we directed our course up this noble river in search of a Village.

Gray crossed the bar, where turbulent surf and rips made passage a feat of no little daring, and ascended the broad waters fifteen miles eastward. He collected 150 otter and 300 beaver skins from the natives, and commented in the log, "This river in my opinion, wou'd make be a very fine place for to sett up a Factory"—what the men of the fur trade call a trading post. Members of the crew had sexual intercourse with native women and pronounced them "very pretty . . . both *within* and *without*."

Gray named the river after his ship, which was christened with the name of Columbus, the *Columbia Rediviva,* or "Columbus Reborn." The name is a thing of grand lineage, a chain of letters linking this band of broad and earth-stained water to the sailor who became the Christ-bearer three hundred years before and who bore his new world like a crown of thorns. But Gray himself was a practical man of few words. He piloted the *Columbia Rediviva* through the bar to the open sea and on toward China on April 20, and in his private log wrote, "So ends."

Vancouver encountered Gray at Nootka and learned of the American foray into the river. It was not an achievement Gray set much store by, and he drew Vancouver a chart of the river. But Vancouver hastened south with the *Discovery* and the *Chatham,* captained by William Broughton, and on October 20 reattempted crossing the bar. The *Chatham* was successful, but the *Discovery* was forced back into the open sea, from where Vancouver contemplated a snow-shrouded volcanic peak hovering over the river to the east and named it Mount St. Helens "in honor of His Britannic Majesty's ambassador at the court of Madrid." Meanwhile Broughton made his way about one hundred miles upstream to a point where a large stream called the Multnomah (or Willamette) entered the river, casting names upon what he saw. He christened the place where the rivers met in Vancouver's honor and named the great mountain overlooking it from the south after Lord Hood, one of the voyage's sponsors.

After he had done these things, Broughton brought an aged chief from among the local Indians on board, and, according to the voyage's record, then "formally took possession of the river, and the country in its vicinity, in his Britannic Majesty's name, having every reason to believe, that the subjects of no other civilized nation or state had ever entered into this river before." The words drifted out over the water like dry leaves, and settled inaudibly into the flood. They may or may not have been rendered into the Chinook tongue to make them comprehensible to the chief, but he in any case "assisted at the ceremony, and drank his Majesty's health on the occasion."

Throughout this time, the fur traders of the Hudson's Bay Company and their Montreal-based competitors, the North West Company, searched the vast interior of North America for a path to the sea. In 1792 Alexander Mackenzie, an agent of the North West Company and the leader of an expedition to the Arctic coast three years before, set out from Lake Athabasca to reach the Pacific by land. He ascended the torrents and rapids of the Peace River to its headwaters in the mountains and found a westward-flowing stream a half-mile away that the Indians called Tacoutche-Tesse and said led to the ocean. Finding the southwest-running river and the wet and tangled forests on its banks impassable, Mackenzie turned west and bivouacked to the coast: "I now mixed up some vermilion in melted grease, and inscribed, in large characters, on the South-East face of the rock on which we had slept last night, this brief memorial—'Alexander Mackenzie, from Canada, by land, the twenty-second of July, one thousand, seven hundred and ninety-three.'"

Upon his return Mackenzie was a hero, the first white man to cross North America by land. In 1801 he wrote a book of his journeys, and, although he had found the Tacoutche-Tesse unnavigable, he continued to believe it was the upper stem of the Columbia:

> . . . the line of communication from the Pacific Ocean, pointed out by nature . . . the most Northern situation fit for colonization, and suitable to the residence of a civilized people. By opening this intercourse between the Atlantic and Pacific Oceans, and forming regular establishments through the inte-

rior, and at both extremes, as well as along the coasts and islands, the entire command of the fur trade of North America
might be obtained. . . .

5.

Thomas Jefferson, president of the United States, read Mackenzie's book, and in it saw what he saw at home in Virginia: the gentle rise of the Blue Ridge, the languid curves of rivers flowing to
the Ohio; a landscape that with a little effort was not so very different than the ordered, honey- and olive-laden country that
swaddled Virgil's Rome. Like Rome, the United States under Jefferson girded itself for great things; where liberty once sufficed,
empire beckoned, and with the purchase of Louisiana from the
French in 1803, Jefferson was eager to survey what he had purchased. He saw a nation reaching to the Pacific; a republic of
Monticellos astride a benign and unsullied land. And he was as
interested in a passage through the new land as he was in the land
itself: Jefferson had grown up with the lore of the Northwest Passage—indeed, perhaps no man in America was as well read as he
on the subject—and nothing excited him so much as the possibility of a direct route from the head of the Missouri to the Columbia and its Pacific outlet.

To that end, he retained Meriwether Lewis and William
Clark and initiated them into the literature and maps of the
northwest, and, in particular, into the now-accepted truth that
the Rocky Mountains might be bridged by a short portage from
the Missouri to the River of the West. Lewis and Clark left for
St. Louis in the spring of 1804 and reached the Rockies the following summer. They found no short portage but a whorl of waterfalls and rapids, and range upon range of mountains whose
heights and ruggedness would have been incomprehensible to Jefferson. When they at last sighted the Columbia on October 16,

1805, they were disillusioned men. Clark marked the day with a laconic entry in his journal:

> ... we Camped on the Columbia River a little above the point. . . . the Chief brought down all his men Singing and dancing as they Came, formed a ring and danced for Some time around us. we gave them a Smoke, and they returned to the village a little above, the Chief & Several delay untill I went to bead. bought 7 dogs & they gave us Several fresh Salmon & Som horse dried.

They ate the dogs and fish and gave Yellepit, the chief, a medal bearing Jefferson's image. The only goal of Lewis and Clark's weary party of twenty-nine was to reach the Pacific and return home. But both captains continued their assiduous recording of what they saw, and what they saw much of the time was a river that seemed as consecrated to death as to life: the rotting bodies of spawned-out salmon were a tide of putrefaction that lapped its banks; the natives who fished and wove here were frequently toothless and blind; and islands offshore harbored cairns of skulls and wind-shriveled cadavers wrapped in robes of wolf and elk. The width of the river narrowed from as much as a mile to perhaps a hundred feet downstream at the Dalles, a frenzied surge that flung itself off falls and through a funnel of basalt, shaking the very earth.

In the Klikitat and Wishram Indian country between the Dalles and the Cascades, the river's final set of rapids, Clark stopped to trade trinkets for more dogs and fish. In a house he observed "a British musket, a cutlass and Several brass Tea kittles of which they appeared verry fond." At a settlement where the Klikitat River entered the Columbia, the local chief showed him cloth of scarlet and blue, a jacket, and a hat, all apparently British or American in origin, as well as other prize possessions:

> [The chief] directed his wife to hand him his medison bag which he opened and Showed us 14 fingers which he Said was the fingers of his enemies which he had taken in war, and pointed to the s.e. from which direction I concluded they were

Snake Indians. . . . The Chief painted those fingers with Several others articles which was in his bag red and Securely put them back, having first made a Short harrang which I Suppose was bragging of what he had done in war. we purchased 12 dogs and 4 sacks of fish. . . .

On November 1, 1805, the party made a portage around the Cascades and observed the slackening of the river in the distance. They were at last within reach of the effects of tides, and the ocean was not far off. The river teemed with otters. The people here had pierced noses, and the women's foreheads were flattened.

As the expedition neared the ocean, it was enveloped for days in fog, out of which floated canoes of Indians, sometimes in native dress, sometimes in European jackets, overalls, shirts, and hats, bearing furs and fish to trade. On November 7 they paddled down the river's salt-tinged broadness, guided by an Indian in a British sailor's uniform, and the fog cleared. Clark wrote, "Great joy in camp we are in View of the Ocian, this great Pacific Octean which we been So long anxious to See."

Yet no sooner were Lewis and Clark encamped than the weather turned foul and remained so for the next four months: they cowered beneath thunderstorms, perpetually cold, wind-battered, and damp. They built rough cabins near the sea, hoping a ship might appear. But the horizon was an ashen bluff of cloud, as empty and black as an Indian's eye. They spent the winter eking out what subsistence the land afforded and repelling the predations of fleas and native thieves. Clark wrote, "It would be distressing to a feeling person to See our Situation at this time all wet and cold with our bedding et cetera also wet."

By spring, Lewis and Clark loathed this place and its people, and in his journal Clark contrasted an exquisite cedar war canoe, inlaid with shells, with the village of its makers: "the dirtiest and Stinkingest place I ever Saw in any Shape whatever." Throughout their time on the river, the Indians had for the most part kept their distance from the party except to trade. Then one day the natives refused to do even that. When Lewis and Clark failed to obtain a canoe by barter, they stole one. They left the mouth of the river on March 23, 1806.

They stopped for several days near the confluence of the Multnomah with the Columbia, and replenished their stores of game for the journey ahead. Here, as elsewhere, the Indians were reluctant to supply them with food, an attitude Lewis and Clark attributed to mean-spiritedness. But it was the hungriest time of year: the foods of winter were nearly spent and the spring runs of salmon not yet begun. They persuaded an old Indian to draw them a map of the Multnomah in the sand by the river, and in it they saw that this river might run all the way to California, or turn east and make the kind of easy portage across the Rockies the Columbia had refused them. Perhaps they could bring Jefferson this news of the Multnomah as a salve for his disappointment.

As they again mounted the river eastward, their irritation grew at what they took to be Indian cussedness, thievery, and duplicity: one stole a spoon from their tent and a few days later another tried to steal Lewis's dog. Near Celilo Falls, "the Great Mart of all this Country," Clark attempted to buy horses. But after the Indians "tanterlised me the greater part of the day," they abruptly canceled the transaction. When a saddle blanket disappeared, Lewis threatened to set fire to an entire village: "They have vexed me in such a manner by such repeated acts of villainy that I am quite disposed to treat them with every severyty. . . ." The blanket, which had fallen off the back of a runaway horse, was found and returned.

When they reached the place where the Snake flowed into the Columbia, the local chief, Yellepit, who had befriended the party on its way downstream, provided them with supplies and gave Clark a beautiful white horse. At night, a hundred Indians joined them in camp:

The fiddle was played and [my] men amused themselves with dancing about an hour. we then requested the Indians to dance which they very cheerfully complyed with. . . . one of their party who made himself the most Conspicuous Charecter in the dance and Songs, we were told was a Medesene man & Could fortell things. that he had foretold of our Comeing into their Country and was now about to Consult his God the moon if what we Said was the truth. . . .

That night, and the following night, their horses ran away, led, it seemed, by the white horse. But on April 30, 1806, they left the river for good at 11:00 A.M., their shadows cast behind them, sorrel on the desert earth.

6.

While Europe dreamt of a new world, a place where it might forget every limitation nature had laid upon it, the people of the river continued to remember. What they remembered was not so much a past but a present that contained everything that ever was and ever would be. Nothing was new; the world ran as the river ran, liquid, a ribbon of immutability flowing out of the sunrise into the sunset.

But by the early eighteenth century, when Europeans were establishing settlements on the Atlantic coast and the English foraged like cattle on Hudson Bay and filled their wordless mouths with their own flesh, time and change bore down upon the river people like a flood. The weather grew cold, then warm and dry, and then cold and wet again; the earth was bare and then fecund, then arid and rasping like the back of a snake; the fish returned in smaller numbers, or not at all. Familiar creatures seemed to flee, but others came in their stead that made men and women as swift as elk and as itinerant as geese.

Horses came to Native American peoples by way of the Spanish who occupied the southwest, and utterly transformed their lives. With horses, the tribes from west of the Rockies might join the bison hunt on the high plains and travel long distances to trade with their neighbors or to harry and subjugate them. And what one people possessed, their neighbors must have too, or risk perishing. So rode ambition, envy, and fear on the backs of horses, and goods to ease them and then urge them on again—iron kettles, cloth, ribbon, axes, glass baubles, and, not least, guns—until desire itself was at last sated by smallpox, measles, and other pestilences that could lay waste to a village like a slithering, unseen torrent.

Compared with their neighbors across the rest of the continent, these things came late to most of the river people, but the people sensed their imminence, a fleeting scent, an accretion of dust on their threshold. The earth itself uttered their advent, and dreams filled the sleep of the chiefs and medicine men like rising water. In 1782 members of the Yakima people fell ill and died in a way no one had seen before, their bodies and faces like painted scabrous stone, inscribed with pocks and marks.

Eight years after the *Columbia Rediviva* crossed the bar of the river in 1792, the mountain Vancouver's lieutenant Broughton had named St. Helens exploded. The ash coursed east and north above the river, obscured the sun, and fell like snow to a depth of six inches. The Spokane people believed it must be the snow that would fall at the end of the world; the snow that will never be succeeded by spring, when all the seasons save winter die and the flood returns. In their fear, the people at Nespelem near Grand Coulee forgot their fishing, hunting, and gathering and instead danced and prayed through the following summer. As a result many among them starved. A prophet told the Spokanes how it would be, how all remembering would be drowned: "Soon there will come from the rising sun a different kind of man from any you have yet seen, who will bring with them a book and will teach you everything, and after that the world will fall to pieces."

CHAPTER 2

The Astronomer

1.

Such sentiments as David Thompson owns do not paint themselves upon his face. He is a small man with a pug nose and a pudding-bowl haircut for his limp black locks, and is not given to idle conversation. Thompson is inclined to ironic casts of mind, to sarcasm and even belligerence, but also to piety. He has three books with him at all times and in all places: the journal in which he records his observations, a nautical almanac, and a Bible. In each, he considers much of the same matter: the magnitude and detail of God's creations; the places in which he has set stars, rivers, and peaks.

By 1810 Thompson has spent twenty-five years as a surveyor and cartographer to the fur trade—first with the Hudson's Bay Company and now with the North West Company—and he has seen the bulk of British North America. He has pioneered a route across the glaciers of the Rocky Mountains and crossed it three times. From any spot on earth, with only a hint of a star, he can determine his location within half a mile. Thompson reads God's creation like a book. And like Adam, he names and numbers its unnamed, unnumbered panoply in journals and on maps. He sees what God has vouchsafed to his people, and he sees a garden and a river running through it. Sometimes at night he settles next to the fire and reads a psalm in French to the Canadians who paddle his canoes, and repeats it for the Indians in the Cree tongue:

Il est un fleuve dont les courants réjouissent la cité de Dieu.

Seepea a yiskipak oche kitta mumatakoosemukun oo keche waskahikun Muneto.

There is a river, the streams whereof shall make glad the city of God.

The better part of the Canadians who make up his company are brutes. They each require upwards of eight pounds of meat or fish a day and a corresponding quantity of liquor. Their speech is putrid with curses and they are insensible to beauty or thought. The wilderness is the only home most of them have ever known, but they see no God in it. They are careless of their salvation, although Thompson has read about it to them and to the Indians:

Car Dieu a tant aimé le monde qu'il a donné son Fils unique.

Muneto a ispeeche saketat uske, ka ke makit oo pauko-Koosisana.

For God so loved the world, that he gave his only begotten Son.

The Indians seem bemused when Thompson talks to them about redemption. They shrug as though he proposes to trade them something they already possess. Perhaps they see too much God in this world to care about the next. For them, it pulses with innumerable spirits like a hive of bees.

Their creation hums, too, with stories, tales found in the trees and stars, under stones, and inside the very skins they trade. For every creature that yields itself to the hunter, and in its dressing and skinning, a story unsheathes itself. Thus, Thompson trades rifles and blue beads not only for furs but for stories, and then he gives back stories himself. Each story demands another to be joined to it, to be knit together like pieces of bark, patch by patch. Together the stories make a canoe that carries the world across the water.

The Old Testament tale of the deluge—the men, the women, the creatures, the boat, and the dove hovering over the endless plain of water—is a worthy story. Whenever Thompson tells this story, the Indians find it agreeable and give back a tale of their own: how the rivers and lakes rose and drowned every living thing, save for one otter, one beaver, one muskrat, and Weesarkejauk the Trickster, who fashioned an island from a clod of mud, from which the land and everything that lives upon it was reborn. For the Indians, the deluge was of little purpose, just another dispute between Weesarkejauk and the Great Spirit. But Thompson views the flood recounted in his Bible as a boon handed down by God to his favorite creatures, human beings, for whom he rid the earth of dinosaurs and other enemies by drowning them. When the floodwaters receded there was water, but the water was bound between the banks of rivers, whose courses were made to bear men and women in boats, to water their crops and cattle, and to slake their thirsts. Such a river ran honeyed with the balm of God's love for his creatures.

Thompson had heard and told tales of the flood years before, in the pine, lake, muskrat, and black-fly country between the plains and Hudson Bay. And it was not far from here, in the Piegan lands where the Rockies begin, that he learned about the rainbow. The Indians called the rainbow Peemahtisoonan Oochegun, the mark of life, and said it was a sign that the flood threatened by every rainstorm will not come, and that life will go on. When Thompson heard this, he responded with the rest of the tale of

Noah: The white people's God promised Noah and his children that there would be no more great floods and that henceforth everything in creation would fear and dread human beings and be meat for them. To mark this covenant, God made a bow among the clouds, a blade in the sky banded with the blood of his creatures: grasses, fish, and cattle, every one.

2.

People had not accorded Thompson much affection in his life, and he in turn had little use for people. He was a slight, fatherless Welsh boy who preferred the company of numbers, nature lore, and the tales of the *Arabian Nights*. At the age of six he had been taken in as a boarder at a London charity school. He showed such promise and seriousness of purpose that he was indentured by his masters to the Hudson's Bay Company in 1784, and put on board the RMS *Prince Rupert* for North America. He was fourteen years old.

In September they put him ashore at Churchill Factory, where the rivers of the Canadian plains and north woods drain into Hudson Bay. The light was blue and the shadows fell as heavy as iron. The wind beat against the luffed sails of the *Prince Rupert* and dissipated into the bare miles of emptiness that ranged out in every direction. Birds and waterfowl coursed southward like plumes of smoke. The sedge, muskeg, and such trees as there were had begun to color. All the earth was still, attendant, boreal and pregnant with winter. Thompson stood on the edge of the water and scuffed his shoes in the gravel and sand, and the stones rocked beneath him.

No doubt there were boys who would be apprehensive at being transported from the precincts of Westminster Abbey to the wastes of Hudson Bay and the society of Indians and polar bears, their solitude relieved only by the visit of supply ships once a year. But Thompson was not one of them. Hudson Bay suited him.

He copied ledgers, read, tracked the wildlife, and became an expert shot. He maintained a certain isolation from the other men at the factory, as the outposts of the Hudson's Bay Company were known, without incurring their suspicion or enmity. The others traded and inventoried skins, and devised such pleasures as they could. They kept beavers, bears, and martens as pets; took Indian women as their wives and sired children; and drank ferociously. But Thompson did not live as they did. He lived in his books and in the field, watching the migrations of the geese and the stars.

His superiors determined he had the aptitude to become a surveyor and mapmaker. They sent him north and west to study trail craft and cartography under a succession of ineffectual teachers, men who carried out the day's routines without words or rest, sustained by pipefuls of tobacco that they blended with weeds that grew about the place.

During this time, on a midwinter day, Thompson was alone in his cabin. He sat at the table with a checkerboard before him and the devil sat down opposite him. The devil's face was as dark as a Spaniard's and black hair covered his body. Wordlessly, he and Thompson played several rounds of draughts. The devil lost one game and then another, after which he arose and disappeared. This took place in the full light of day, and Thompson had to accept that what he had just experienced had truly occurred. This was not a godless place, but one so full of spirits, deities, and manitous that Thompson's God and his devil were but two among many.

In the autumn of Thompson's seventeenth year, the company gave him a blue-cloth jacket, leather trousers, and a bison robe and sent him west to winter with a party of six men. They followed the Saskatchewan River across the treeless plain where the bison took their pilgrimages, and after some weeks Thompson discerned the mountains in the west, looming dark and unformed like smoke from a far-off fire. A little farther along, near the place where the North Saskatchewan met the Bow River, they found the burned hulk of a massive, solitary white pine. It was the only such tree for miles in any direction, and it had been revered by the Piegans who inhabited the surrounding country. When the smallpox came, the Indians believed the tree would protect them, and they tethered horses to its trunk as an offering. But three-fifths of their people died. One warrior, who had lost his wife and all his children, lopped off the crown of the tree and set fire to its base, harrowed by grief.

Thompson and his party settled for the winter in a Piegan camp, with whom the Hudson's Bay Company enjoyed exceptionally good trading relations. The Piegans were warriors and plains hunters and allied themselves with other members of the Blackfoot nation. They were a lean and weathered people who had become expert marksmen, thanks to the guns and ammunition the company had traded them for furs. Few of their enemies possessed firearms, and they were feared on both sides of the mountains.

There was an old man at the camp named Sarkamappee, a Cree who lived among the Piegans. He was six feet tall, nearly ninety years of age, and the Piegans honored him. Throughout the four months of winter, Sarkamappee and Thompson talked and smoked every night, oblivious to the hour, and the Indian loosed his memory like a bound bundle of feathers and polished stones. He shared his stories with Thompson as a father does with his son.

His past extended into the previous century, and as he recalled it, it was as if he were reading from a scroll. But the present was less explicable to him, and he would sometimes sigh and say to Thompson: "What a stranger I now find myself in the land of my fathers." The smallpox, the lack of game, the madness that sometimes seized the spirits of both people and animals suggested the revenge of manitous whose anger he couldn't explain, but whose immanence was as heavy in the air as pine sap. The old stories that once explained how the things that are in the world came to be seemed to be losing their power and their medicine. The old songs and dances no longer worked as they once did. As for the white people's stories, they seemed to concern themselves with either the distant past, when their God made the world, or the distant future, when their God would unmake it. To judge by their stories, white people merely endured the present, and would prefer to be either dead or unborn.

Thompson listened more than he talked, and was less and less disposed to presume the truth as he had been taught it as a boy, save in the matter of salvation. By the end of his stay among the Piegans, Sarkamappee had commended him to Kootanneappee, the Piegan war chief. Kootanneappee observed Thompson with skepticism for several weeks—there was so much gravity in one who had lived so little—but at last promised him the permanent protection of the Piegans. They marked their friendship with a handshake, left hand to left hand, in the sign of Kootanneappee's people.

In the spring of 1788, Thompson returned to the muskrat country and was placed under the tutelage of Philip Turnor, the chief surveyor of the Hudson's Bay Company, who taught him the skills in astronomy, navigation, and mathematics that pertain to mapmaking. He learned to use the telescope, artificial horizon, chronometer, and sextant to plot his position with such accuracy that many of his readings would stand unchanged two hundred years later. By night, Thompson pressed his right eye so assiduously to the telescope and to his calculations that it became inflamed. By day, he recorded his observations of birds, fish, and mammals. He also examined the anatomies of mosquitoes and flies with a magnifying glass and derived a theory concerning the operation of their blood-hungry jaws.

Thompson took especial interest in the beaver. A royal charter of 1670 had granted the Hudson's Bay Company virtual dominion over all the lands draining into Hudson Bay (and thus the better part of British North America), with the specific goal of culling its furred wildlife. Every pelt—fox, lynx, muskrat, marten, bear, and wolf—had some value, but none was as prized as the beaver's, whose dense, impermeable fur could be pounded, rolled, and shellacked into hat felting of sublime quality. For two hundred years, a beaver hat marked its wearer as someone of consequence. The gentlemen of London and Paris crowned themselves with hats named Wellington, Beau, D'Orsay, and Regent, and emptied thousands of lakes and streams of their beaver. In Thompson's day, the Hudson's Bay Company or its rival, the North West Company, might trade an Indian a rifle for twenty beaver skins or a yard of calico for three pelts. The gun cost the fur traders a little more than £1, whereas the skins would fetch £25 in London. The transaction was not an evenhanded one, but with the hat, a man in Pall Mall might best his social betters and be remarked for it; with the gun, a man on the Bow River might vanquish enemies of a century's standing and feed his family bison through the long winter.

Thompson came to see the beaver as the Indians did. The Indians understood that just as the bear is stronger than they, the beaver is wiser. In their story, the beavers had once been land dwellers not unlike human beings but had so angered the Great Spirit that he drove them underwater. They retained their sagacity and prudence but were condemned to live and labor forever in the water, a fallen race.

At first the Indians trapped the beaver by demolishing its lodge and then impaling its family on pikes. But the white men brought iron traps and baited them with castoreum, the beaver's own irresistible scent, which alone could cause the beaver to forsake its judicious nature. The trap itself did not kill the beaver; rather, when it realized its foot was caught, it dove underwater to flee. But the wire the trap was fastened to only allowed the trap to move in one direction, and once the beaver was submerged, it was held there and drowned. The beaver died by water as it lived by water, gulled by the scent of its own essence.

It was not lost on the Indians that the white man had castoreum to destroy the beaver much as he had liquor to destroy
them. Indian acquaintances told Thompson that the Indian and
the beaver would perish together, forsaken by the Great Spirit.
The country between Hudson Bay and Lake Winnipeg was
largely trapped out; the lands east of the mountains were increasingly barren. Smallpox killed whole villages of native peoples. Crossing and recrossing the lake country and plains over
the next ten years, Thompson would pass through Indian encampments as silent as stone, befogged with a stench that could
make a man swoon, their tents furnished with swelling corpses.
In the grass and the forest duff between them were the torn bodies of children, their corrupted flesh tasted and rejected by dogs
and wolves.

For the Piegans, with whom Thompson's bonds grew ever
closer, the plague came at a time when they were at war with the
Snake River people. The war went badly and the Piegans plied
the Great Spirit with feathers, branches of trees, and sweet-
smelling grass, but to no avail. They believed the Great Spirit had
abandoned them. The sickness and the wars were an affliction
that settled upon them from the sky, covering and silencing the
people and their broken charms, dances, songs, and stories like a
fall of snow.

With the plagues there came other kinds of evil. Some creatures seemed possessed by manitous that transformed their ordinary natures: A grizzly bear entered a Piegan camp and killed two
warriors and started to devour them. When more warriors attempted to retrieve the bodies, the bear rose up and disembow-
eled one, crushed another, and ripped the thigh of a third. When
the bear was at last brought down, the Indians burned its corpse
until every part of it, even the teeth and claws, were ashes, lest its
spirit escape and wander among them again.

Drink might do to the native people what only a legion of er-
rant bears could accomplish, and many seemed to crave it as much

as they might guns and horses—not as a mere narcotic but as an inducer of something akin to dreams and visions. It seemed to Thompson that over the period of years he had spent in North America the Indians had become increasingly concerned with the future and what it might bring, as though life were now a succession of unforeseen and dissimilar accidents rather than a cycle of seasons and rhythms whose makeup varied more in degree than in kind. Having had so many mysterious incidents and calamities befall them, the Indians sought prophecies, visions, and dreams that might foretell the future. When they observed Thompson scanning the heavens with his telescope or sextant, they found unconvincing his explanation that he was determining his location on earth in relation to the stars. Instead, the word began to spread that Thompson was reading the future in the night sky, and thus the Indians began to call him the Star Man.

A Cree named Tapahpahtum came to Thompson in midwinter and asked him to foretell the future. Thompson responded that he possessed no such gift. But the Indian returned time and time again, and he stood while Thompson surveyed the stars in the cold clear night, the snow singing and squeaking beneath their feet. "My family is without meat. Give me a wind to cover my scent so I can go hunting," Tapahpahtum begged, but Thompson said he had no power for such a thing. He told him he must pray to the Great Spirit.

Tapahpahtum went home and beat a drum and sang to the manitou of the winds. He burned herbs on the fire, but the days remained cold and still. After three nights he came back and implored Thompson again to tell the Great Spirit to give him a wind. Thompson, now impatient, sent him away. By dawn, however, when Thompson at last left his telescope and retreated to his tent and his bedroll, the tops of the tallest pines began to pitch in a freshening breeze that by midday was a gale. Throughout the next week, Tapahpahtum killed three moose and other game. The story spread through the country about the Star Man and his powers.

Not long thereafter, Tapahpahtum and a friend, Wishakoo, began to share lodgings and drink together. Wishakoo abandoned the hunt and gave himself up to liquor, under whose enchantment he saw and heard disturbing things. He began to cry out, "*Nee weettogo*," which is to say, "I am the cannibal manitou—the spirit that devours men." When Wishakoo said this, the others around him became afraid and would bind him with cords until the trance passed. But it continued to possess him for three years and at last his people shot him and burned his body until it was a fine tilth of ash.

Throughout the following years and into the first decade of the new century, Thompson observed a ravenous appetite for drink, prophecy, and new dances, songs, and charms among the native people. At the same time the fur trade continued to move farther west and north to undepleted trapping grounds. Thompson's loyalties to the Hudson's Bay Company grew tenuous, and in 1797 he accepted employment with the rival North West Company. His duties there were confined to surveying and cartography, and he enjoyed near total autonomy and freedom from managerial and trading responsibilities. In his own métier he was becoming something of a legend, and when the great Alexander Mackenzie, the first white man to cross North America by land, made mention of "the astronomer," everyone knew he was referring to Thompson.

In 1799 Thompson married Charlotte Small, the daughter of a Hudson's Bay man and his Cree wife. She was not quite fourteen years old at the time, and she would bear him fifteen children. Thompson was by all accounts a dutiful husband and father, who grew more humble and pious with each year. Through all this time he seemed to seek a sweeter, unsullied world—perhaps a world that existed before ships first laid anchor in Hudson Bay, a time when man and beaver coexisted in peace. There had been a moment when surely it had been in his grasp.

On an evening in November 1792, Thompson, then twenty-two years old, had walked out to the edge of a lake in muskrat country with a Scotsman named Andrew Davy with the idea of shooting some beavers that had a lodge there. It was the beavers' custom to swim near the shore in the early evening as long as the lake was free of ice, and on this night there was a full moon whose disk magnified itself on the water like a pewter penny in a bowl of blue ink. A beaver swam through its diameter directly toward them, and Davy raised his gun to shoot it but found his bolt had jammed. The beaver swam a little closer, looking deeply at them, and at last slapped its tail on the water as though to acknowledge them and bid them goodnight. Then the beaver returned to its house. Although they could do no more hunting that night, Thompson and Davy lay in that spot until about 11:00, listening to the rustle of the woods and the silence of the lake pressing itself together into ice. Then out of the east there was a brilliant light whose form resolved itself into a round mass that they realized was a meteor. Its luminance and size grew until it obscured the moon. It seemed to come directly toward them and then, when it surely must singe the very hair on their heads, it crashed three hundred yards away. It sounded moist and heavy. In the morning they went out to find some sign of it, but there was none.

It was a country that was fat with things to see, things that were gone so quickly they might never have been, save in the tales they compelled people to tell. There were mirages that conjured domes of ice across the top of a lake; forests that walked and danced; and the aurora, which hung in the sky and sang with the voices of the dogs and the dead.

Following Mackenzie's march of 1793, which only seemed to underscore the inaccessibility of the Pacific by land, the North West Company did not take much interest in the country beyond the mountains. By 1806, however, the arrival of the Americans Lewis and Clark at the mouth of the Columbia River suggested that if the British fur trade were to maintain its hegemony in

North America, it had best establish itself there. In any case, beaver stocks east of the Rockies continued to decline, from 182,346 skins in 1793 to 92,003 in 1805. And then there was a new and lucrative trade on the north Pacific coast: the sea otter. This creature was blessed with a pelt as excellent as the beaver's, and its disposition was so trusting and childlike it almost seemed to offer itself to the hunter for slaughter.

The company's plans to send Thompson on an exploratory journey across the mountains were thwarted by Thompson's old friends, the Piegans, who had no wish to see the rifles and ammunition the company traded fall into the hands of their neighbors. In 1806, on his return journey from the Pacific, Capt. Meriwether Lewis shot two Blackfoot Indians near the Marias River just south of the forty-ninth parallel and east of the mountains. The following summer, the Piegans, under the command of Kootanneappee, joined their confederates to the south to avenge the murders. With his way no longer barred, Thompson and six men ascended the mountains in June and located a pass beyond the headwaters of the North Saskatchewan River. Thompson had never attained such an elevation before and he strained to describe it in his journal: ". . . Stupendous and solitary Wilds covered with eternal snow, and Mountain connected to Mountain by immense Glaciers, the collection of Ages on which the beams of the Sun makes hardly any impression. . . ." Storms and avalanches cracked and rumbled through the gelid silence:

> The rushing of Snows down the Sides of the Mountains equalled the Thunder in Sound, overturning everything less than solid rock in its Course, sweeping the Mountain Forests, whole acres at a Time from the very Roots, leaving not a Vestige behind.

On June 24, Thompson began to descend a creek's western slope, and with each day the portages grew more difficult and food in shorter supply:

. . . a current foaming white [that] the horses with Difficulty crossed & recrossed at every 2 or 300 yards, & the Men crossed by clinging to the Tails and Manes of the Horses, and yet ran no small Danger of being swept away and drowned. . . . Gave the men a large Dog for Supper for want of Better.

On June 30, they followed the creek—"a Torrent that seemingly nothing can resist"—through a canyon of white, layered, frangible rock, like curtains of oyster shell. Here, at last, it emptied itself, flattened and spent, into a broad valley braided and graveled by the channels of a large and fast-running river. Thompson decided this river must be the Kootenay, which Indians and traders had told him looped north, then south, finally draining into the Columbia. They made a camp and took what nourishment they could find, while Thompson scouted for a suitable location for a post:

> As I was this Morning searching for a Place to build on, we came to a wild horse that had been killed yesterday even[ing], and not knowing whence to get a mouthful for the day, we took a little of the outside Meat, the inside we could not touch as the horse was not embowelled and a strong taint pervaded the whole Carcase . . . so soon as we arrived at the Camp, we boiled it, and shared a small piece to every Man who joyfully ate it, in hopes of it being portable in the Stomach, hunger is an excellent Sauce, we found the Taste tolerable good, and 3 of the Men set off to dispute with the wolves the rest of the Carcase of the Horse, of which they brought [back] about 100 pounds.

The meat wracked the entire party with sickness, and their condition was only alleviated by the local natives, the Kutenai, who brought them fresh elk.

Thompson began to build a post he called Kootenay House upriver. It was near the outlet of a large and placid lake that was eventually named Windemere because of its resemblance to its mountain-ringed namesake in the English Lake District. He sent some men back across the pass for goods on the other side of the mountains, and began to establish trading relations with the Kutenai and their neighbors to the southeast, the Flatheads.

Throughout the fall and winter, Thompson remained encamped here and took astronomical and cartographic observations and notes on the flora and fauna of the place:

> . . . the Kootanae River . . . is well wooded with a kind of Hemlock, 3 sorts of Fir, three of pine, with Aspens and Birch, and its sides are thick set with Alders-Willows and a few Poplar, About 20 miles above the portage are low points of fine white Cedars, the Red Cedars grow everywhere but seldom to any Size. Beaver seem to be plenty and the River, Islands, and Valley seem expressly made for them. Of the Animals there are a few bears and others, a few Red Deer and a small sort of Chevreuil, one of whom 10 men will very well eat in a meal.

Among the fish were Pacific salmon, which by Thompson's calculation returned to this place from the sea after making a round-trip of at least twenty-five hundred miles: "The largest weighed 26 pounds. They were tolerable good, but having come so far had lost all their fatness."

Meanwhile, the walls of Kootenay House rose by the river and the men crowned it with a chimney of river rock. Thompson himself talked business with the Kutenai and Flatheads and "collected every information possible from them":

> 2 of them were very old Men, they spoke much to the purpose on all questions I asked, and after drawing a Chart of their Country and from thence to the Sea, and describing the Nations along the River, they assured me that from this House to the Sea and back again was only the voyage of a Summer Moon. . . . I told them Beavers, Bears, Otters, et cetera were the Objects of our coming. They assured me they would all

make a good Hunt and see me next Spring with the rest of their countrymen. They traded 29 skins value, in Beavers, Bears, Cats, Otters and Fishers, with a little Sturgeon Oil and about a Bushel of Berries.

Now that he was so well situated within the log walls of his stockade by the river, with the wealth of the country waiting to be harvested, and the Indians eager to take whatever he might offer for their pelts, Thompson felt the Briton within him renascent. Perhaps the lofty, supple, straight trees might make masts and spars for the Royal Navy. He gazed out to the promontories on either side of the river. He named the peaks to the west for military heroes, and the highest for Admiral Nelson.

Thompson's serenity did not last long, however. A small band of Piegans arrived, sent by Kootanneappee to observe his activities. Thompson angrily denounced them as spies and drove them off. A month later, twenty-six more Piegans arrived, set up camp, and harried the Kutenai and Flatheads with whom Thompson was trying to trade. Thompson upbraided them each day, showing off the fortitude of his walls and the condition of his guns: "You intend to destroy us," he said, "but many of you will die before you do so. Go back to your countrymen and tell them so." The Piegans left as the leaves began to color, and Thompson waited throughout the winter, as snowflakes fell like ashes, and wondered what Kootanneappee would do.

By the spring of 1808, it was clear the Piegans had decided to do nothing. Despite the strong counsel of the civil chief, Kootanneappee persuaded the majority of the warriors that with so many enemies poised to do the Piegans evil, they could scarcely afford to divert their energies to destroying the North West Company post established by Thompson. In addition, no matter how stealthful they might be in their attack, there was no guarantee they would succeed in surprising Thompson. Kootanneappee reminded them that Thompson, the Star Man, was able to see the future: "What can we do with this man," he asked, "when our women cannot mend a pair of shoes but he sees them?" When Thompson heard about this later, he noted with some pleasure in his diary that "Kootanneappee, my steady friend" had prevailed, and "thus by the mercy of good Providence I averted this danger."

Through the rest of 1808 and into the following year, Thompson consolidated his work at Kootenay House and made a series of forays southward along the western slope of the mountains. He founded a post he called Kullyspell House where the Clark Fork enters Lake Pend Oreille, and another named Salish House farther down the Clark Fork in the Bitterroot Range. During his first summer here, he recrossed the mountains and delivered three hundred pounds of furs to the North West Company's chief backcountry fort at Rainy Lake, near the head of Lake Superior; during his second summer, in 1809, he took back twelve hundred pounds.

It seemed as benign a land as any in North America, moderate in climate if irregular in game, and free from the human and natural pestilences that afflicted the rest of the continent. The land yielded fur in promising quantities, and the native people were eager to trade. Yet there were portents of less-kind times ahead. On a journey to trade with the Lake people, who were members of the Kutenai that lived south of the forty-ninth parallel, he learned that the Piegans had crossed the mountains and stolen thirty-five of the Lake people's horses; they, in turn, had killed at least one Piegan warrior, and so now there was a war between them. The Lake chief promised Thompson his protection as long as Thompson brought him guns and ammunition.

To the east, in the country between Lake Pend Oreille and the Rockies, Thompson began trading with the Salish people, enemies of the Piegans whose skill with bows and arrows was legendary but who had no guns. Thompson agreed to supply them with rifles in return for pelts, and made them a little speech: he told them if they wanted to procure the advantages he was prepared to afford them, they must give up gaming and the leisure to which they were accustomed and apply themselves industriously to hunting and skinning beaver and other such creatures as bore fur in that country.

Thompson and his men returned to their post with seven geese, two ducks, an antelope, dried salmon, and camas roots. "And so we are rich," Thompson wrote in his diary. But this country could also be a fearful place. Above the river in the mountains, eclipses covered the sun, storms spun in the sky like whirlpools, and tame horses went wild. Thompson once shot a doe while crossing over the pass, where the snow lingered into July and the trees were bent and gnarled by the wind. His men had started beheading and skinning her when she raised herself up on her legs like a newborn fawn and stood for half a minute, blood pulsing from the stump of her neck dropping rivulets in the snow. The men said this doe must be the devil, and despite their hunger and Thompson's entreaties that they come to their senses, they abandoned the meat. With each month, it became more difficult to convince men, whether native or Canadian, to stay in this place, which was on the whole so mild and verdant.

When spring came in 1810, it appeared that the wars among the Indian nations could only multiply and that white men would soon be drawn into them. The Salish had met and defeated the Piegans during the bison hunt east of the mountains, armed not only with North West Company weapons but with North West Company traders that Thompson had posted at their sides. The Piegans and Blackfeet had in turn attacked American hunters east of the mountains on the Missouri River. The Americans were rash and reckless in Thompson's view, and their presence in the country could only exacerbate the confusions and ructions loosed upon the land these days. Moreover, they misunderstood the Indians and underestimated their abilities in war.

In addition to fur hunting, Americans with John Jacob Astor's Pacific Fur Country were pressing their nation's claim on the Columbia River. The North West Company had made attempts to locate the source of the Columbia and to take possession of it from its headwaters to the sea. Following the lead of Alexander Mackenzie, who wrongly believed he had found the source of the Columbia on his way to the Pacific in 1793, the company sent Simon Fraser over the mountains in 1808. Fraser found a river and followed its treacherous canyons for more than five hundred miles. However, the river did not exit at the bar to the open Pacific as observed by Gray and Vancouver; rather, it spilled into the Strait of Georgia running between the mainland coast and Vancouver Island. It was a mighty river, indeed, but it was not the Columbia. Thompson would name it the Fraser a few years later in honor of its first white explorer.

During the spring, the North West Company's directors learned that Astor's Pacific Fur Country planned to establish a permanent post at the mouth of the Columbia. So it was that when Thompson returned that summer on his annual journey to Rainy Lake, he was given orders to return west immediately to discover and claim the entire path of the Columbia and to arrive at its mouth in advance of the Americans.

As Thompson made his preparations to leave Rainy Lake House, a woman put the evil eye on him. This woman was known as a prophetess, a conjurer, and a reader of dreams, but Thompson remembered her as the consort of one of his men six years before, when she had been about eighteen. In the camps and in the canoes, she had sought to use her feminine snares to command attention, thereby agitating his men and disconcerting their wives. He could not permit such a woman to travel with his company, so he dismissed her. Since then, she had made her way in the world, as so many others had who preyed upon the Indians' desire to know more about the future. She carried a stick about four and a half feet long; one side of the stick was black and carved with birds, animals, and insects painted in vermilion, and the other side was red, with creatures colored in black. She gazed at him contemptuously. She spoke no words, but her face said she remembered everything that had passed, that she was now a person of some consequence, and that she had not forgotten how he had shamed her. He was in her power and he ought, therefore, to be afraid. Thompson knew she was the worst sort of charlatan, but as his canoe broached the water west from Rainy Lake, her eyes loomed in the forest above and behind him and settled upon his soul with scarcely a sound, like drips falling from the blade of a paddle.

3.

In October of 1810, David Thompson and three men are hiding atop a hill three hundred feet above the North Saskatchewan River in the foothills of the Rocky Mountains. The night is cold. They huddle in a grove of pines so dense that light can neither penetrate nor escape. Thompson's white lieutenant, William Henry, and the two Indian hunters are apprehensive. Thompson is afraid. His other men and canoes are missing and there are signs that the Piegans are nearby. He has heard shots and has come upon stones marked with blood.

Thompson knows the Piegans mean to find and kill them all rather than allow them to cross the mountains. Although he knows exactly where he is, for the first time in his life, Thompson feels utterly lost, seized like the sea between two tidal gravities. In the morning, the dawn light surrounds the grove of pines at the top of the hill like a blue fog. He sends a hunter and William Henry to look for the men and the canoes he is supposed to take over the mountains. The plan was to rendezvous near here two weeks ago, but there has been no sign of them. Thompson fears they have been taken by the Piegans. Above the trees, winter hastens nearer on long clouds like strings of beads, and drives fodder and game before it. The other hunter scans the meager food that remains in their store. "I have had bad dreams, dreams that this meat will never be eaten," he says, and he saddles his horse and rides off to the east.

Thompson used to swap stories with the Piegans, but stories are no longer his business. He has come here to write upon the land—to inscribe meridian and parallel lines upon it and to lay the lines of reason across it. A man with many stories has many friends, but a man who would write, who would make his mark, who would trade a story for history, is often alone. So Thompson is alone in the trees on the hill above the river. It seems as though the river is above him, roaring over him like a steady, gustless wind, and he is waiting to write—or waiting, perhaps, for some great hand to take him up and write with him.

After three weeks on the hill above the river, the food supplies are exhausted and Thompson is distracted to the point of dementia. To go back is to betray the North West Company; to go forward is to betray the Piegans. There is a kind of annihilation guaranteed by either course, prompting Thompson to remain fixed as though pinioned in the jaws of a trap, thrashing ineffectually in his dilemma. Alexander Henry, William Henry's cousin from Rocky Mountain House, had turned up on the hill this morning, and while not insolent in his bearing, seemed almost to contradict Thompson's assessment of the danger presented by the Piegans. When a band of Piegans appeared at Rocky Mountain House, Henry had given them liquor dosed with laudanum and, while they were passed out, sent Thompson's voyageurs and their craft upriver. In Henry's estimation, the matter is relatively straightforward: the entire party could rendezvous up there, and then the journey to the West could continue.

But Thompson could countenance no such thing. Henry was young and overconfident. He did not know this place and its people as Thompson did; he could not detect the viscous weight of bad faith in the air that the Piegans apprehended so clearly, the impending breach by Thompson of understandings that Thompson had once fostered. Thompson would at last cross the mountains, but only at a point far to the north, at the headwaters of the Athabasca River. Thompson heard some condescension in Henry's response to this, but Henry agreed to arrange for Thompson's voyageurs to assemble in the foothills to the north, whence they would make their way as Thompson saw fit.

It is the end of October when Thompson and his party begin their journey in earnest, and although the weather is tolerable, the way is continually choked with thick woods and deadfalls and they do not reach the Athabasca until November 29. It is too late to continue with horses, so they set about constructing sleds and snowshoes and laying up stores for the crossing. By night Thompson takes astronomical observations; by day he measures the temperature, which drops at times to thirty-two degrees below zero. In the last week of December, he writes letters. He begs a friend in Montreal to forgive him for not writing regularly and thanks him for watching out for Charlotte and his four children. "It is my wish to give all my children an equal and good education; my conscience obliges me to it, and it is for this I am now working in this country," he writes. Christmas is meager, sober, and cold, marked by Thompson reading from the Bible and little festivity. A few men desert to Alexander Henry's shelter at Rocky Mountain House, and Henry records their condition as "pitiful."

Three days before the New Year, Thompson and the remainder of his company begin to climb toward the crest of the mountains. Coté, Luscier, L'Amoreux, D'Eau, Vallade, Battoche, Pareille, and Du Nord drive dogsleds bearing 760 pounds of trade goods and supplies. Villiard and Vaudette guide horses carrying 200 pounds of pemmican, 35 pounds of grease, and 60 pounds of flour. Thomas the Iroquois, who has ascended the Athabasca before, serves as guide, and Baptiste is the hunter. Most of them believe, with some reason, that it is madness to undertake such a journey.

The country they pass through is considered the haunt of a creature resembling a mammoth, and nothing Thompson says dispels the apprehension the men feel. The temperature remains fixed between twenty and thirty degrees below zero, and without snowshoes a man sinks to his waist or his shoulders or deeper, risking drowning in the snow. They find fresh signs of a creature whose tracks measure fourteen inches by eight inches, and the men believe it to be a young mammoth, but Thompson says it's a bear. Most of the time Thompson stays ahead of the company, scouting the route with the guide and spending little time supervising his men. Du Nord, a Canadian Thompson dislikes more each day, beats a dog to death, and someone has to carry a load in the dog's stead. The party covers perhaps four miles a day, and the snow is becoming wet and immeasurably deep. There is no wood near the summit, thus no fire to warm or dry them in the night.

On January 10, 1811, they reach the summit of the mountains, and Thompson is exhilarated. He sees range upon range set before him, but the men see only desolation. Thompson contemplates an enormous glacier composed of a green and jewellike ice that stretches for miles. Among his men, it only inspires a kind of dread. Thompson goes to bed each night and sorts through the cache of ideas and reflections that fill his head; the men sleep shrinking from the cold that seeps into their bedrolls like ice water.

As they descend, the weather grows warmer, but the men remain dispirited. They reach an enormous bend in a river that Thompson believes must be the Kootenay. If that is the case, they are not far from Kootenay House, which should surely comfort every soul in the company. Thompson is concerned about his men, even though they are like children in their incapacity to see beyond the morrow, and he would give them some wisdom and some succor if he could. But four men have deserted, led by Du Nord. Others are sick or refuse to continue, and Thompson sends them with Thomas back to the Rocky Mountain House, along with letters he has written on wooden boards since there is no paper. He digs a hole in the snow by the river, which he roofs with cedar logs, and winters with Vallade and L'Amoreux at this camp he calls Flat Heart.

❀

Even in March this is an unyielding place, not in the obdurate manner of the eastern side of the mountains, but in a way that is insufferably resilient, wet, and ungainly. The ground and everything around it is sodden; the snow lingers as a kind of freezing, oozing jelly; and Thompson's ax, too puny for these preternatural trees, bounces off their bark. The days, too, are unyielding in their bleakness, and Thompson seems to walk in circles, surveying the woods, recording the temperature, scratching with his pen:

> March 5th Tuesday—6 AM 30+; 2 PM 33+; 9 PM 30+. A snowy Night & Day with squally easterly Winds and at times calm. I saw a White Headed Eagle. Writing Letters et cetera.

This land wants wringing out, and Thompson and his men begin to build a canoe that will carry them to some drier place up the river. But there is no birch bark, and so they fashion a canoe of cedar boards sewn together with pine roots and sealed watertight with sap. A party arrives from Rocky Mountain House, which will relieve L'Amoreux and leave Pareille and Coté to join Vallade. They labor for a month on the canoe, which is twenty-five feet long and a little more than four feet wide. When they lift it to put it into the water, the bottom splits, and so they begin again. While the men work on the canoe, Thompson recalculates measurements he has taken a dozen times before, and then he fashions averages, means, themes, and variations. He fills a page with arithmetic and then enters triumphantly at its bottom:

> The mean of the foregoing
> Observations is
> Latde 52°8'1" N
> Longde 118°18'18" W
> Variation 22° East

When the canoe is finished, it is exceedingly light and shipworthy, and on April 17, Thompson, Pareille, Coté, and Vallade set off, paddling against the current, a series of rapids, and day after day of blowing snow. Thompson continues to take notes in his book:

> Pray God to give us a good voyage. The Country everywhere is yet like the depth of winter, the Snow, full 3 feet to 3½ feet deep and no wild Fowl about. . . . The whole of this day the Rapids may be said to touch each other, & most of them dangerous, full of large Rocks & Stones, with cascades of water, very strong and the poling very bad. We came up leading the Canoe in excessive cold water, towing up with the line at the same time on Snow Shoes on full 3 feet of Snow & sometimes in the Water so that we were all wet & sadly benumbed, very bad work.

Other stretches of the river are frozen and compel them to drag the canoe across the ice. There are many tracks, but little game for the taking. They kill a pair of swans and loot the nest of its eggs. Vallade brings down a bird Thompson calls a Cormorant: "This had fine green eyes, the ball black, the Eye Lids mottled Blue like very small Beads to a Button Hole & the neck and Head a fine glossy light Black with a bunch of Side Feathers on each side of the back of the Head." In mid-May, they pass Kootenay House and at last reach the lake at the head of the river, 268 miles from their winter camp.

From here, Thompson plans to descend by water to the Clark Fork, Pend Oreille, and then to the Columbia. Along the way, he hires two Indians, a Kutenai to hunt, and Ignace, "an Iroquois to be Steersman of my canoe for 550 Livres & the ordinary equipment." They reach Salish House on May 27, but it is deserted:

> I examined the old House but found no letter nor writing of any kind to inform me what had become of the people who had wintered there. Wrote a few lines in Charcoal on a Board in case the Americans should pass, purporting that we had left the House on account of the War with the Piegans. Killed a Mare for Food. Killed 2 Rattle Snakes. I was near treading on one of them.

Thompson is told by the Kutenai in the vicinity that the

traders from the North West Company have established a new post on the Spokane River, so he now turns west. It is familiar ground to Thompson. He was the first white man to explore it, and to bring trade to its people, and he may take some credit for the things that have forever altered their lives. An aged Kalispel chief and Thompson share a pipe and a fire, and the Indian remembers when they were afraid of the Piegans, who came over the mountains and raided their camps and slaughtered their women and children: "We had no defense until you crossed the mountains and brought us firearms. Now we no longer need to hide ourselves, but have regained much of our country and hunt the bisons for food and clothing and have good leather tents."

When Thompson reaches the Spokane River, he is unhappy with the talk he hears around the camp. The Spokane people, together with their neighbors, the Sanpoil, plan to attack an unarmed people living to the west of them, the Okanagan, simply to test the new guns acquired from the North West Company. Thompson sends gifts to the Spokane chiefs, and when they receive him, he urges them to recall the war party, which is already on its way. He reminds them that they themselves were defenseless only three years before, hiding from their enemies and living on roots and fish, as the Okanagan are now. If the Spokanes and their allies are such brave and mighty warriors, why don't they attack the Piegans? The chiefs take Thompson's counsel and send fifty warriors east to aid the Salish and the Kutenai against the Piegans. Thompson and his party continue west, only a day from the Columbia. On the way, he records in his book how the soil changes to a rich, deeply colored loam as they near the river: it would make a grand place for agriculture.

On June 19, 1811, Thompson reaches the Columbia at Kettle Falls. Two waterfalls are set a few hundred yards apart here, and although neither is high, the water seems to boil. There is a substantial number of Indians, but the place belongs to and is consecrated to the salmon, upon whose backs a man might almost cross the river. The Indians fish with baskets shaped like pots, which may also be the source of the name Kettle Falls. Thompson has missed by a few days the ceremonies that greeted the arrival of the year's first salmon, but he sees the care the Indians take to be hospitable to the fish, keeping the shore spotless and throwing nothing into the water. In return, the Indians say, the salmon offer themselves by the thousands. As Thompson understands it, the salmon is the god of these people, and their days and seasons turn around its roseate flesh.

Thompson and his men spend two weeks here constructing a canoe, which they assemble by the riverbank, taking care not to breach any of the natives' strictures. Thompson is at first inclined to take the Indians' regard for the purity and sanctity of the river and its water as the result of some overscrupulousness and superstition. But one morning as they work, one of his men takes the bone of a horse and carelessly flings it into the river, and instantly the salmon flee and no more are caught that day until the afternoon, and only after the bone has been retrieved.

When the canoe is finished, it is reloaded with the goods Thompson regularly inventories: 12 pounds of beads, 858 buttons, 2,000 bells, 7½ yards of calico, 10 peacock feathers, 1 bottle of lavender and 2 of peppermint, 1,500 rings, 8 guns, 86 pounds of powder, sundry shot and balls, 141 pounds of tobacco, and 3 pints of seed corn. As they are leaving, they receive word of a trader who has drowned with his wife and four children on the Clark Fork. Thompson records this as an example of the mysterious and unpredictable ways of the waters west of the mountains, with their unseen, fatal whirlpools and eddies from which there is no escape. He climbs into the canoe with seven men and his goods, borne, it almost seems, on a tide of salmon against whose flood they stroke.

They travel seventy miles the first day, through open country that Thompson finds gentle and handsome to behold:

> The country always wears a pleasing romantic view, the early part of the day hills and valleys, et cetera, with partly wooded thinly, and partly meadow, the latter the most predominant. From about 11 AM . . . the river presented much steep rocks often in steps like stairs of 20 to 30 feet perpendicular of black grayish rock, reddened in places.

They come ashore that evening at a village of Sanpoil Indians, who present Thompson with salmon, berries, and roots. They dance and sing for him, as though his arrival is something they have long and joyfully anticipated; they regard him as though he were a marvel from another world, the fulfillment of a prophecy whose story they know well.

He gives the chiefs tobacco, and they bring him more food. He attempts to explain the trade he hopes to establish with them, and they echo each sentence he utters with a monosyllabic chant, as though he were a priest singing the litany and they were the respondents: "I took notice that good and bad news, life and death, were always pronounced in the same manner, and that the answer was also the same." They insist on dancing again for him:

> The song was a mild simple music, the cadence measured, but the figure of the dance quite wild and irregular. On one side stood all the old people of both sexes. These formed groups of 4 to 10 who danced in time, hardly stirring out of the same spot. All the young and active formed a large group on the other side, men, women, and children mixed dancing, first up as far as the line of old people extended, then turning around and dancing down to the same extent, each of this large group touching each other with closeness.

After a while, they stop, but then the dance begins again at the chief's command, this time "that we might be preserved on the Strong Rapids we had to run on our way to the sea." The dancing lasts another hour, until "the dust of their feet often fairly obscured the dancers though we stood only about 4 feet from them. . . ."

Thompson tells them about his plan to paddle to the sea, but they know nothing of the sea, or even of the river beyond "Strong Rapids," about forty miles downstream. They are poor save for the salmon in their weirs and they hunt deer by encircling each animal with hunters and bringing it down with stone-headed arrows. It is unlikely that they have any beaver.

Thompson leaves at noon the next day after taking sextant readings from the sun. When they reach the rapids, he decides to empty the canoe and make a portage with their trading goods around the worst of the rough water. They leave the canoe in the river, guiding it down the rapids with a rope.

> . . . but in doing this they ran too close to a drift tree on a rock which tore part of the upper lath away and struck Ignace out of the stern of the canoe, although he had never swam in his life he swam so as to keep himself above the waves till they turned the canoe around to take him up.

The party camps on the bank, which has grown less verdant as they have passed downriver, with rocks everywhere and nary a tree in sight. Thompson tries to create some comfort here for Ignace, who has sustained a number of injuries in the river. Thompson lances one of Ignace's veins to let a little blood and, as is their custom, they talk in Cree and French about God and his Book.

On July 5, 1811, the party comes to a village where they take shelter from a rainstorm with a people who call themselves Nespelem. Again, they are given gifts of salmon, berries, and roots, and dances and songs are made for their arrival and safe journey. Although "the land to us appears to be very poor white gray earth of a kind of impalpable powder mixed with stones," the people seem more prosperous than their neighbors upstream:

The women were tolerably well clothed, the men rather slightly, their blankets of bear, muskrat and black tailed deer skins, their ornaments of shells, whether in bracelets, arm bands, often their hair, on their garments or in fillets around the head.

Thompson has seen as much Indian dancing as any white man in North America, but with these river people he begins to see a pattern that is a little baffling:

> . . . all their dances are a kind of religious prayer for some end. They in their dance never assume a gay, joyous countenance, but always one of a serious turn. . . . The step is almost always the semblance of running, as of people pursuing and being pursued.

It is the same downriver with the Methow people and the Wenatchee, whom they reach on July 7:

> They put down their little presents of berries, roots, et cetera, and then continually kept blessing us and wishing us all manner of good [for] visiting them, with clapping their hands and extending them to the skies. When any of us approached their ranks they expressed their good will and thanks with outstretched arms and words followed by a strong whistling aspiration of breath. I discoursed with them and they seemed thankful for the good I offered them of trading their superfluities for articles they stood much in need of. A very respectable old man sat down by me thankful to see us and smoke of our tobacco before he died. He often felt my shoes and legs gently as if to know whether I was like themselves.

Thompson is gratified with the reception he is receiving here and elsewhere on the river. But can this deluge of thanksgiving and reverence that travels with him down the river truly be the result of the mere chance to trade skins for calico, beads, and guns? It is as though he is bringing them something much more vital than this, although it is not his nature to ponder what exactly this might be.

In the morning, Thompson can see mountains topped with

snow in the southwest. Ignace steers the canoe down the river as though descending deep into the earth. They have traveled about sixty miles per day since leaving Kettle Falls. Cliffs of gray rock shaded with green and brown rise up higher with each mile. The sky is cold and azure, the sun a milky ball. As they head south the country grows more desolate and waterless, and becomes an infernal land that supports only snakes, rocks, and brush. The Indians here, the Wanapum, have no berries or roots but give Thompson fat and delicious salmon. Near White Bluffs, a chief insists he meet a certain tribal elder:

> He returned with . . . an old white headed man with the handle of a tea-kettle for an ornament about his head. He showed no signs of age except his hair and a few wrinkles in his face. He was quite naked and ran as fast as the horses. We could not but admire him. I invited the horsemen to invite all their people to smoke, which they set off to do in a round gallop, and the old man on foot ran after them and did not lose much ground.

Thompson meets Yakima, too, who have beaver in their hunting grounds to the west. They tell a story about how, of all the creatures here, the beaver alone brought them fire from the sky when they had none. If they are industrious, Thompson tells them, the beaver will now bring them other things that they need.

On July 9, Thompson reaches the confluence of the Columbia and the Snake, where the river increases mightily in size and begins to turn west toward the sea. He takes observations at night and during the day, although his sextant has through some unknown happenstance come out of alignment and cannot be entirely relied upon. At the meeting of the rivers, he posts a piece of paper: "Know hereby that this country is claimed by Great Britain as part of its territories, and that the N.W. Company of Merchants from Canada, finding the Factory for this people inconvenient for them, do hereby intend to erect a factory in this place for the commerce of the country around. D. Thompson. July 9th, 1811."

That night, the Walla Walla Indians who reside here give him a feast and a celebration that is superior to any he has seen thus far.

The chief is distinguished in his bearing. He does not fawn or invite condescension. He shows Thompson a medal that has come into his possession. It has the likeness of Thomas Jefferson on it. He tells Thompson that trade is an urgent business for his people: "We must continue in the state of our fathers, and our children do the same, unless you white men will bring us arms, iron arrowheads, axes, knives, and many other things which you have and which we very much want."

The following day Thompson floats another thirty-two miles downriver. He passes villages of Indians that he tries to meet by inviting them to smoke with him. They are dirty and nearly naked, and they cower or run from him. In the afternoon he sees a mountain capped with snow. Through his telescope the snow looks whiter than clouds, as though it must be replenished every day, or remains frozen in perpetuity.

The country around them is still dry and inhospitable, although the heat is made bearable by the wind that blows each afternoon. On July 11, Thompson enters the first of a series of rapids, where the river narrows from one thousand yards in width to less than sixty, entrapped between steep, overhanging walls of basalt in a place called the Dalles. These rapids culminate in Celilo Falls, a cataract that transforms the river into something Thompson likens to a monster, "raging and hissing, as if alive." After successfully passing through the first set of rapids, he is ebullient and sets a fir tree afire at their camp that night. In the trunk he carves his name, the date, and the latitude and longitude of the place he has calculated from his celestial observations.

The next day he makes a portage around the falls, which house a salmon fishery even more fecund than the one at Kettle Falls. But beyond the falls the Indians are, Thompson believes, of a lesser character than those upstream. They greet him, but with obscene dances and vulgar English words that have found their way upriver from where ships have penetrated. He suspects that the Indian men are thieves, and the women offer themselves to members of his party. They know too much of this world. He hastens downstream.

On July 12, he nears the snowcapped peak on the south bank he had observed from upstream, and he can now see two similar mountains on the north bank, one behind him and one farther downriver. The Columbia cuts through a range of mountains here, and as they pass through them between sets of rapids, the banks of the river grow lush with trees of every kind. It seems they have left the desert and entered a garden.

A day later they cross the final rapids and camp at Point Vancouver. Nearby is where the Willamette River enters from the south, the easternmost point of the Columbia that has been charted. The chief there "jabbered a few words of broken English he had learnt from the ships" and invited Thompson to sup among his people:

> These people took us into their houses which were well arranged, very full of salmon, and so close as to be intolerably warm. . . . They speak a language quite different from the others, are of a squat, fat, brawny make, dark brown hair, the children light colored too, the women fat, brawny and naked, as are also the men, not so dirty as those at the Falls. Latitude 45°39'47" N.

Thompson knows he is within a day of his goal. The morning of July 15, 1811, is "a very fine day, somewhat cloudy. Stayed [in camp] till 6:25 A.M. shaving and arranging ourselves." Dressed in the best attire he can muster, he has a Union Jack mounted on the canoe's stern and sets off into the cottony light of the river's morning fog. When the company reaches Tongue Point, where Astor has threatened to establish his trading post, Thompson stands in the bow and prepares to lay claim to this place for his king and his company. But as the boat clears the point, he sees white men's cabins on the shore. They land, and he extends his greetings and congratulations as a gentleman should:

> At 1 P.M. thank God for our safe arrival, we came to the House of Mr. Astor's Company, Messrs. McDougal, Stuart & Stuart, who received me in the most polite manner, and here we hope to stay a few days to refresh ourselves.

Later in the afternoon, he takes his men to see the Pacific, a few miles away. The river fans out wider and wider and is lost in the sea, which clasps the horizon in every direction. Thompson tells his men that there before them stands all of Asia, five thousand miles ahead. They are unimpressed. They need a map to grasp the idea, Thompson decides. Despite his talk, however, his men remain disappointed. None of them has seen anything larger than Lake Superior, and few have seen even that. They require something that shouts out its majesty and infinitude. And this sea, it seems, is not so mighty, but flat and gray; and this land the river passes on its way here is not a garden.

Thompson remains at the American trading post, which its officers have named Astoria after their patron, for five days. The two chief Astorians, as Thompson dubs them, McDougal and Stuart, are former North West Company men, and any rivalry or suspicion they feel is tempered by that bond. When Thompson prepares to leave on his return journey on July 22, he exchanges one of his exhausted Canadians for a Hawaiian employed by the Astorians, and he agrees to travel with Stuart and another Scots employee, Alexander Ross, who want to go upriver to establish an inland post.

When they came down the Columbia, their passage was swift,

as though the river bore them on its back. On their return, however, they paddle against the current—the river is against them, and so too, it seems, is every creature that inhabits its banks. Scarcely have they left Astoria when a blind chief comes to them in a canoe paddled by two slaves. The chief tells Thompson he will bring him salmon, but he never brings the fish and the other Indians they meet that day act strangely. Thompson suspects an attack and keeps the canoes in the water at their camp that night, in case they must flee.

Near the first set of rapids a few days later, Thompson encounters a well-dressed young Indian armed with a quiver and bow, who asks Thompson to protect him and his wife, who accompanies him. As they talk, Thompson realizes that the young man is not a man but a *berdache,* a woman attired in the garments of a man; a woman he knew two years ago as the Kutenai wife of a voyageur named Boisverd. Her name was Ququnok Patke, "One-Standing-Lodge-Pole-Woman," and Thompson had banished her from Kullyspell House when her overbearing presence became disruptive. She returned home to her people among the Kutenai, claiming that Boisverd had performed a kind of medicine on her that transformed her into a man. Soon after, Boisverd was killed by a violent fall from his horse.

The woman began to have dreams, and out of the dreams welled up prophecies and powers to heal and to maim. She took the name Kauxuma Nupika, "Gone-to-the-Spirits," and she garbed herself in the raiment of a warrior. She wished to marry, but no maidens among her people would have her, and she vowed vengeance on them. She fixed her attentions on widows and abandoned wives, who became her lovers. It was said that in a fit of anger she pierced one lover through the arm with an arrow and then instantly healed the wound. It was also said that she performed heroic feats in war and that she had a penis fashioned from the hide of a bison. In the last year, she had taken a new wife and now traveled as a prophetess. Her prophecies are terrifying.

The two have traveled in this guise west through the Snake River country and down the Columbia, recounting the prophetess's dreams: the white man brings smallpox to destroy the people; giants shall come and plow up the earth, burying the people's lodges and villages; and all the people shall die. She has so frightened the Indians who have heard these predictions that they are determined to kill her and her companion. Now the woman throws herself on Thompson's mercy, and he agrees to carry her as far as the confluence with the Snake. This is a dangerous concession for Thompson and his men, for her presence incites hostility among the Indians, who already view Thompson's party with great suspicion: ". . . Had not the Kutenai-ess been under our immediate care, she would have been killed for the lies she told on her way to the Sea."

At their camps along the river, the Indians attempt to steal from them or extort goods in exchange for help they had rendered freely on their downriver passage:

> These people are a mixture of kindness and treachery. They render any service required, but demand high payment, and [are] ready to enforce their demands, Dag[ger] in hand. They steal all they can lay their hands on, and from every appearance only our number and Arms prevented them from cutting us all off.

Others come to Thompson in fear, asking him if the prophecies are true. He tells them the white man did not bring the smallpox, the Indian has only prospered through trade with them, and that the white man cannot destroy their people and their land. Thompson points to the stars, and even the people here know of his reputation as the Star Man. He says, "You ought to know that the Great Spirit is the only master of the ground, and such as it was in the day of your grandfathers, it is now, and will continue the same for your grandsons."

✿

At the rapids of the Cascades, at Celilo Falls, and up through the Dalles, the Indians refuse them any assistance or food, and as they pass through the several chasms of that place, warriors stand on the banks above aiming bows strung with poison-tipped arrows at them. They do not fire, but when Thompson emerges into the open river, the Indians chase them, while other natives curse and harry them from the banks. As they paddle eastward toward the Snake, villagers Thompson had once smoked with now hide from him or at best give him news of war parties pursuing him and then quickly retreat.

Farther east, the river is less populated and the threat of attack recedes. They are out of harm's way, and Thompson returns to his habit of noting the features of the river and its creatures. The rock is gray tending to black, rising in shafts but broken into horizontal strata, like shattered columns. He records the measurements of a salmon: four feet, four inches long and two feet in circumference. At Thompson's insistence, they land on an island that serves as a cemetery, where the Indians inter their people in sheds. Thompson wants to examine the sheds and their contents in detail and record his observations in his notebook, but his interpreter dissuades him. It would anger both the dead and their living relations. They continue on their way.

The land they now pass had seemed dry but hospitable on their downstream journey, but upon closer inspection it has a hellish aspect, and the banks of the river are a thoroughfare of buzzing snakes. The men take to throwing an oar ashore before they land, and each time a half-dozen rattlers scatter. The snakes secret themselves in bedrolls, and when they emerge hold themselves erect, inches from the men's faces. They are a kind of evil made incarnate that would drive the party away from this river, and Thompson grows to loathe them with an uncharacteristic and febrile hatred.

When he reaches the junction of the Snake and the Columbia, Thompson spends hours considering the geology of the place, which seems, like so much of what he has seen in the last month, to defy logic:

> The rock is rude black rock, often shows from 2 to 3 lines in the bed, the same strata almost always inclining to the westward and sometimes descending in a curve and then assuming a horizontal line. The strata sometimes 40 feet deep and many pieces stand isolated like tables and pillars et cetera. The pillarlike rock has always its chasms perpendicular and split in pieces as by accident, in every horizontal direction. It appears to be one compact bed having no lines in it that are not perpendicular and the depth of its bed is as far as 30 feet. One must say that the finger of the Deity has opened by immediate operation the passage of the river through such solid materials as must forever have resisted its actions.

Where the rock is riven, it is shattered as though by the blows of a mallet or a fist, and seems a kind of wreckage—tumbled pillars and tables—like a house through which a storm or flood has passed. It must be that God made this place and then thought better of it: When he originally spoke the word that created it, he did not say what he meant so he razed his own creation here and revised it. The work, it seems to Thompson, is crude, done in haste, even in frustration or anger, by brute force. It looks unfinished. So perhaps God is at work—speaking the words, weaving some new world—even as Thompson sits at the junction, writing furiously and confusedly in his book.

Thompson decides to forgo further travel on the Columbia, and instead continues east along the Snake and then by land to the Spokane House, which he reaches on August 11, 1811. The dreams and troubles that are afoot on the Columbia have not infected this country, and the Indians are pleased to smoke with Thompson and hear his stories of the river and the place where it meets the sea. He leaves six days later for Kettle Falls, where he will build a canoe and ascend the Columbia to its source, wherever that proves to be.

At the falls, Thompson meets the chief of the Salish and gives him all the ammunition he can spare, urging him to ally his people with the Kutenai and Spokanes to make war on the Piegans. The chief agrees. While they finish building their canoe, there is a death in the camp and Thompson is again intent on examining the body and the manner of its interment, and again is prevailed upon by the natives in his party to desist.

On September 2, they leave Kettle Falls accompanied by eight canoes full of Indians. They have to paddle against a strong current that persists for the remainder of their journey. The banks are rocky, narrow, and heavily forested in some places. The river broadens to become a lake, but as the days pass it narrows. On September 14, they reach a place that will be named Dalles des Morts, the fiercest and most unpredictable rapid on the Columbia River. By towing and carrying their canoes, they make their way through, and four days later reach an enormous bend in the river where the river's course changes from north to south. A little while later they reach a hut and the place Thompson recognizes as Flat Heart. The water is low and broad, with rocks scattered across its breadth half-submerged, like the backs of turtles. It moves slowly, carrying the first amber and blood-brown leaves of autumn, sounding a deep, undying chord like a cool, damp wind. It seems as solid and gray as a road that a person might walk down, just as Jesus walked on the sea in the Book. This river, which Thompson had dubbed the Kootenay, is the Columbia. He has been in its heart for many years, but had not understood.

The water closes over the furrow that Thompson's canoe cuts through the river, but his presence washes up to the bank and remains among the people there. Stuart and Ross travel up the river a week after him and find the natives full of talk about the Star Man, the man with the book. They dance for Stuart and Ross, just as they danced for Thompson. Near the White Bluffs and Priest Rapids above the great bend in the river, the people bring the white men the corpses of their dead children to be raised up. Stuart and Ross are moved to pity; they offer some gifts, and tell the Indians to bury their dead. They have no book; they do not speak with the stars. Their business is furs; trade is their book, the good news they evangelize in this desert for which God has so little love to give.

In 1812 Thompson ascends the mountains again and, from what he sees, speculates that there is indeed a monster that inhabits their crest. He goes south again, starting at the bottom of the lake from which the river wells, and sees how unstaunchable the flood of war is that engulfs the Indians—how the wolves and dogs gnaw at the bones of children, and how the chiefs wish to be at peace as they once were but are unable to put down the things they have taken up.

War breaks out between Thompson's country and the Americans, and he returns to the vicinity of Montreal, where he will live the rest of his life. Based on the sum of a quarter-century's observations, Thompson creates a map—larger than a man is tall—of all the country the North West Company has an interest in, and every point on the map is anchored to a star. The map hangs at the company's headquarters and is soon forgotten, just as the company itself is forgotten once it is merged into the Hudson's Bay Company. The directors of Hudson's Bay eventually find there is little fur left in their lands, and that the Americans are likely to succeed in taking possession of the northwest territory south of the forty-ninth parallel. Accordingly, they issue instructions to trap the country so exhaustively that not a fur-bearing creature remains in it.

When the northwest is seceded to the United States, Thompson is employed to establish the borderline, and when he writes

to the Hudson's Bay Company directors and to government officials and peers of the realm in London, he points this out together
with his other services and achievements. He wonders why he has
done so much and yet has so little, and he supplements the mea-
gerness of his pension by surveying lot lines and boundaries.
When he is old, he writes a book on his travels and explorations,
but no publisher expresses any interest. He watches his children
bear children, and he mourns the children he saw so little of when
he was on his travels and who died when he had scarcely returned
to them. He takes his Bible and in his fine, mapmaker's hand
records their names within it: "John, aged 5 years and near 5
months, a beautiful, promising boy. Emma, aged 7 years and near
11 months. An amiable, innocent girl, too good for this world."
God stole them away while he was with the river and thus with
his book he raises them up.

CHAPTER 3

Castaways

1.

Rain succeeds rain, and the river runs like smoke, its eddies and whorls curling tendrils. David Douglas built himself a hut of cedar between the bank and the forest, but by Christmas water broached the threshold and lapped the walls, the loose strands of bark floating on the inundation like ribbons on the wind. He writes by a burning taper on New Year's night, and the light is amber and resinous:

> Commencing a year in such a far removed corner of the earth, where I am nearly destitute of civilized society, there is some scope for reflection. In 1824, I was on the Atlantic on my way to England; 1825, between the island of Juan Fernandez and the Galapagos in the Pacific; I am now here, and God only knows where I may be next. In all probability, if a change does not take place, I will shortly be consigned to the tomb. I can die satisfied

with myself. I never have given cause for remonstrance or pain
to an individual on earth. I am in my twenty-seventh year.

Douglas is a dutiful young man. He does what the Royal Horticultural Society sent him here to do with little regard for his personal comfort or inclinations. He is not a botanist—a position his
lack of formal education and station as the son of a Scots stone-
mason could never afford him—but a highly trained collector, a
forager of plants whose work is much esteemed by his sponsors in
London. He has succeeded not only by industry but by assiduousness; he has the determination and single-mindedness of a
Lancashire cotton grandee. In the chaos of this place, he sees what
he needs to see, and by stem, blade, and stalk, he weaves it into
coherence, to a pattern comprehensible to English science, a ging-
ham of taxonomy. The people of the river have seen him on his
knees collecting, and they call him the Man of Grass.

Douglas is affable, uncomplaining, modest, and willing, the
sort of boy whose future older men promote, and through whose
success they make themselves a legacy, recasting their younger
selves in the unformed ore of a promising apprentice. He is a son
to his elders, a brother to his contemporaries, and an uncle to their
children. He is eager to please, to garner cuttings from every mind
he meets, but his company is never burdensome and people seek
it. Yet he has never come near to marriage and he has the habit of
sleeping alone, at some distance from the habitations and camps
of his fellowmen. He is a good companion, but a better solitary.
As a child, he was pushed out of school, not on account of stupidity, contrariness, or a wandering, dreamy mind, but because he
was so assuredly, tenaciously somewhere else beyond the reach of
anybody. He sat in the classroom mute as a headstone, drained of
speech, daydreaming about hunting, fishing, and scouring the
countryside for whatever animals, plants, and rocks it might yield;
then scraping its hides, plucking its feathers, and pressing its
leaves and flowers flat between quarto sheets and Bible covers.

When he was ten, he was apprenticed to the gardener in charge of one of Scotland's most horticulturally distinguished estates. For seven years he culled its grounds, and by night he taught himself mathematics and committed *Lee's Introduction to Botany, Donn's Catalogue,* and *Nicol's Gardener's Calendar* to memory. His unrelenting labor and curiosity brought him to posts at even more legendary estates and by age twenty, to the University Garden at Glasgow, where he came to the attention of the Royal Horticultural Society. For pleasure he hunted and pored over books of travelers' tales, and in particular *Robinson Crusoe,* which he fastened himself to like an opium smoker to a pipe. He pursued botany and the society of its leading men as a means to gain solitude, like a ship's passage to islands that he might master utterly alone.

On his voyage to the Columbia River and the sodden firmament through which it pours like a wound, he seemed for a few days to have held the very thing itself in his hand, just as he might have held the nest of a bird or an orb of aqueous glass. It appeared out of the northeast, a volcanic cone girded with trees to the very apex of its clouded summit: Juan Fernandez, Crusoe's island. In pursuit of fresh water, the captain ordered a crew ashore, and Douglas joined them. As the beach hoved into view, they seemed to see a hut with smoke rising from it. The boat was beached and Douglas and the crew investigated, but the hut was vacant. As they began to look for water, a bareheaded, frantic man clothed in rags sprang from the vegetation. He announced himself as William Clark, a mariner late of Whitechapel, London, who had been left here by his ship five years ago. He invited them into his hut, furnished with a bed of straw and a length of log for a chair. He took a dram of rum with them and Douglas perused his library: a Bible, *The Book of Common Prayer,* a volume of Cowper's poems, and a recent edition of *Robinson Crusoe.*

Under the influence of drink, Clark grew voluble; his tales bloomed and branched and Douglas heeded every one. When Clark was finished, Douglas surveyed the island's fruit trees; there were apples, quinces, peaches, and figs that must have been culti-vated by Crusoe himself. When the time came to return to the ship, Douglas left the island and Clark with the greatest reluctance. He gave Clark some seeds, and Clark gave Douglas a goat—perhaps a goat descended from Crusoe's very herd!—which was slaughtered and roasted on board ship a week later on Christmas Day.

Now, even here on the river, where the ground is dank, fun-gal, and teeming with fleas for two-thirds of the year, Douglas builds himself a solitude, politely refusing a bed and a broad-striped wool blanket in the Hudson's Bay Company's fort. He pitches a tent of damp, muddied canvas or, when he can, fashions himself a house of branches, deadfalls, and leaves and makes a bedroll of waxy, needled boughs inside.

In the new year of 1826, soaked to his skin and limping from a recrudescent wound on his knee received the previous summer, Douglas reluctantly sought a roof to sleep under. He took up lodgings at Fort Vancouver, the Hudson's Bay Company post overlooking the Columbia opposite its confluence with the Wil-lamette. He had been wary of imposing upon the company and its chief factor at Fort Vancouver, Dr. John McLoughlin, despite the latter's continuous, sincere entreaties to accept the fort's hos-pitality. In 1823 Douglas had gone on a short and successful col-lecting trip to the Atlantic coast of America, and when the Royal Horticultural Society sent him around Cape Horn to the Colum-bia country the following year, he was acutely conscious of his good fortune and of his dependence on the goodwill of others. The river and its territory were the domain of the company under its franchise with the British Crown, and he therefore remained here solely at its pleasure.

In truth, Douglas's presence suited the company in respects he could hardly understand. Since retaking Astoria in 1812, the British had occupied the northwest under an ambiguous form of joint occupation with the United States. In theory, the region was open to the nationals of both countries, with the final resolution of sovereignty put off to some later and undefined date. In practice, with few Americans interested in settling or trading here, the company enjoyed exclusive use of the river and its resources. By 1821, the region was yielding the company twenty thousand beaver skins annually, the biggest harvest of furs in its entire territory. Fearing that a now-quiescent United States might begin to press its claims more energetically in the future, the company set about consolidating its hold on the river and establishing the legitimacy of its presence there. When the day of reckoning came, any form of evidence—including the work of naturalists such as Douglas—that indicated a long-standing British interest in the region could be made to serve the company's purposes, whether it be strengthening its position in the eyes of the world or commending the continual possession of the northwest to Parliament and British public opinion.

Despite their eagerness to retain possession of the river and the country to either side of it, the British lived on it less as permanent settlers than as guests at a great English country house. Visitors were greeted by a piper in full Highland regalia and led into the fort's great hall where the chief factor dispensed roasts, puddings, and fine Bordeaux from his high table. Thanks to a steady stream of ships and an annual overland express of voyageurs from Hudson Bay, the men of the company were supplied with every requisite—from tea to choice Canadian canoe bark—and saw little reason to take up the undignified labor of agriculture. The fur traders were, in both the public's and their own imaginations, "the company of adventurers" and the "Caesars of the wilderness." Their business was not only lucrative, but imbued with a kind of heroism and romance. The wise and avuncular McLoughlin, crowned with garlands of white hair, sat enthroned at his table like Arthur, and his men would no more clear the woods and farm than would Lancelot and Gawain take up the plow.

Douglas had reached the mouth of the river on April 7, 1825, and he helped take the soundings as his ship transited the great and treacherous bar, a melee of waves and swells that clashed on an unseen field of sand and shoal. The ship fired its cannon to announce its presence but heard no response, and anchored in a bay on the river's north side. From the ship's rail, the river looked like a meadow loomed over by the titanic forest, a darkness into which the silver light of the river emptied itself. That night Douglas slept aboard ship, its constant pitching and creaking stilled for the first time in eight months. "With truth," he wrote, "I may count this one of the happy moments of my life."

The following morning was cold and rainy, and Douglas went ashore, his legs dizzy from an eternity at sea. The forest pulled him into its lightless, humid density. Shiny leafed salal lapped his ankles, ferns brushed his knees, and the thorn-studded stems and leaves of devil's club threatened to claw his face. Out of that understory erupted trees as straight as candles, and as broad as a man is tall. Their crests lay hidden hundreds of feet above him. He threaded his way among hemlock, studded with thousands of tiny cinnamon-hued cones, and spruce, their shafts the color of dried blood. In the wetter places, cedar branches hung with lacy foliage. Toward the edge of the forest, spindly groves of alder lurched at windblown tangents over a tangle of berry canes.

Douglas had never seen the likes of such trees. He had read about one species, *Pseudotsuga taxifolia*, in the journals of Vancouver's expedition. Now he stood beneath them, lost in their shadows, their unctuous cool penetrating his clothes. They had trunks about six yards around and the bark was stratified and furrowed with crevasses. They rose branchless for a hundred feet and showered down cones under whose scales bracts emerged like the tongues of serpents.

The forest was soundless here, the trees like petrified giants of a former age, removed from time and decay. And yet as Douglas stood there, what had seemed to him an immutable stillness began to pulse with the steady drip of water and the ceaseless sawing of rot and engenderment: the greedy parasitism of mosses, fungi, and lichens that transformed the fallen trees to humus and duff; the seedlings implanted and taking suck on the fallen trunks of their ancestors; and the ground, swollen and soft with detritus and the liquors of rain. The forest was the world's great bazaar of birth and putrefaction, death indistinguishable from life. It was a counterparadise, an Eden of eternally mindless, causeless, dumb-lipped recurrence, a garden of oblivion. It seemed to pull Douglas's feet down into it, roof out the sky, and press his body against itself until he could no longer hear the lappings of his breath or the footfalls of his heart.

Douglas left the forest and made notes on ship. He called the trees pines, although none of them belong to that genus, including the giant *Pseudotsuga taxifolia*. Eventually it would be named for him, and commonly known as the Douglas fir, although it is not a fir. Its Latin name translates as "false hemlock," and so it is defined by what it is not, a thing unlike its fellows, disposed to stand alone.

Within a few days, Douglas moved upriver to the vicinity of Fort Vancouver and built his hut. He went where the company's traders had business or where Indian guides in the company's employ were willing to take him. In May he ascended the river as far as the Dalles, passing from the duck's-head-green coastal forests to the gray granite gorge and at last to the ocher drylands east of the Cascades. At the Dalles, he watched all the immensity of the river force itself through a deep and narrow fissure in the earth. He found that this country suited him, its landscapes less oppressively congested with verdure and more blessed with sunshine than the country back at Fort Vancouver. Just upstream, the salmon climbed the thundering terraces of Celilo Falls; the Indians leaned out from flimsy platforms over the chasm of the river, scooping out fish with cedar-bark nets on poles of pine.

Douglas estimated that Celilo Falls was four hundred yards in breadth; the salmon were innumerable, and anything the region afforded was available on its banks. He traded tobacco for food and made himself dinners of tea and salmon "cooked under the shade of a lordly pine or rocky dell far removed from the abodes of civilized life." He contemplated the heights of the riverbanks and surmised from their erosion that the river at one time must have run thousands of feet higher than it did now. He suspected no one here had seen a white man before; that the Indians were hostile but cowed; and that the peaks before him might be snowy islands in a sea of light and flowers that had never been ascended. He vowed to master them.

In a few weeks, Douglas canoed back to Fort Vancouver, and accompanied two Indians and a Canadian voyageur to the coast to search for edible roots. He found no roots, but hunted, fished, and adapted himself to life along the river and the ocean shore on either side of it: "With a basin of tea, a small piece of biscuit, and now and then a duck, I managed to live very well." Beyond his own resources, he enjoyed the hospitality of Cockqua, a chief among the Chinook people, who fed him the choicest parts of a ten-foot-long, four-hundred-pound sturgeon just taken from the river. He showed the Indians his spectacles and the boiling tea he gulped at his fire. With one shot he brought down an eagle forty-five yards away. He noted the Indians' fear and bedazzlement in his diary, believing that the Chinook, many clad in brass-buttoned naval jackets and sailor hats, had never seen the likes of him. Douglas gave Cockqua tobacco, knives, nails, and gun flints, and the chief in turn pledged that his young daughter would make him some hats. Cockqua invited him to sleep in his lodge, but Douglas pitched his tent fifty yards away.

For the remainder of the year, Douglas traveled in ellipses that bent north and south from the river: down the Willamette as far as the falls, up the coast to the Chehalis River, across its portage to the Cowlitz, and, with a sail fashioned from his greatcoat propelling his canoe before the wind, down again to Fort Vancouver. He folded seeds and flowers into paper packets, and packed them into metal boxes and wooden cases for shipment to England. He killed bears, owls, elk, and birds of a dozen descriptions. Cones fell from the great conifers with a blast from his rifle and ducks tumbled out of the sky, five to a shot. The hats he received from Cockqua's daughter shielded his face from the sun and rain and cut him a fine figure, their crowns embellished with his initials in fine handwork. He tried and failed to scale the mountains on either side of the river's gorge at the Cascades. He drank tea and wrote letters home, and he pined for replies, though none arrived.

At a camp along the Willamette, Douglas heard of the huge, pendulous cones that produced sweetly flavored seed the Indians carried as trail food. The cones came from a pine south of the river, deep in the mountains above the Umpqua. He resolved to find and botanize this tree, and added its discovery to the things he must accomplish here. He decided he should stay on the river for another year, however much it might displease the Royal Horticultural Society. He could scarcely admit his affection for this nubile land, where there were things that must be done beyond his sponsor's imagining.

For the first months of 1826, Douglas remains sheltered from the unremitting rains, categorizing the animals he has observed: bald and brown-headed eagles, partridges, pheasants, owls, ravens and crows, four species of hawk, three of geese, ten of duck, elk, deer, foxes, lynx, mice, shrews, and rats. On the twentieth of February, Jean Baptiste McKay, a hunter for the company, brings him a cone from the pine he seeks. It is sixteen and a half inches long and ten inches around. The trees themselves are said to be twenty to fifty feet in circumference and close to two hundred feet tall. He pays McKay to find him twelve more cones and a quantity of seed. Douglas seals 197 packets of the seeds he has thus far collected in a tin box, and after receiving another thirty quires of paper, courtesy of Dr. McLoughlin, he sets out upriver on March 20. The country spreads out before him like a painting of iridescent colors underlaid by a ground of gold, framed by tumescent clouds and sublime precipices. Its fearful indifference falls away and it seems to speak to him in his own words, to let itself be seen as he wishes to see it, not as wilderness but as Juan Fernandez, a garden isle. He gathers the impressions that strike his vision as though they were seeds, and enfolds them in paper:

> The rainbow from the vapour of the agitated water, which rushes with furious rapidity over shattered rocks and through deep caverns producing an agreeable although at the same time a somewhat melancholy echo through the thick wooded valley; the reflections from the snow on the mountains, together with the vivid green of the gigantic pines, form a contrast of rural grandeur that can scarcely be surpassed.

At Celilo, he and his guide from the company face down a band of Indians who intend to rob them, and are saved by the intervention of a chief of the Cayuse, a tribe that is "great friends of the white people." Douglas rewards him with an ornament: "I bored a hole in the only shilling I had, one that had been in my pocket since I left London, and, the septum of his nose being perforated, I suspended it to it with a brass wire. This was to him the great seal of friendship."

At the company post at Walla Walla, Douglas secures permission to set up a base of operations there for the summer and then proceeds upriver. By canoe and portage, he arrives on April 10 at the junction of the river with the Spokane. "This part of the Columbia is by far the most beautiful I have seen: very varied, extensive plains, with groups of pine-trees, like an English lawn. . . ." He joins a company party traveling north to Kettle Falls and Fort Colville, led by John Dease, the factor there, and John Work, who runs the post on the Flathead River on the western slope of the Rockies.

Dease and Work have been with the company for years. They know every word of the stories that most people in these times can only half tell, piecing them together like shards of a broken pot. They know Jaco Finlay, who traveled with David Thompson; they know Ignace LaMoose at Flathead Lake, the same Ignace, they say, that paddled Thompson's canoe on his first descent of the river; they know, insofar as any white person can, the Kutenai *berdache* Kauxuma Nupika. Nowadays she and Ignace teach the white people's Book to the Flatheads; she heals the sick and is fond of strong drink. She expelled an illness from the body of the chief of the Kutenai, and he gave her a warrior's name, Qanqon Kamek Klaula, "Sitting-in-the-Water-Grizzly."

The flintlock of Douglas's rifle is broken, and he goes cross-country to see Jaco Finlay, the only man in the territory known to repair such things. The aged Finlay lives amid the ruins of the company's old Spokane House post, adjacent to a native burial ground. He and his family have nothing to eat except camas root and black-moss cake, and Douglas shares his provisions with them. But he and Douglas cannot speak to each other; Finlay speaks no English, and his half-breed–voyageur French is impenetrable to Douglas. Douglas gives him the gun, and he scans it with his tired blue eyes. The following day it is returned, all its parts renewed, its scars and afflictions healed.

Douglas returns to Kettle Falls and is besieged by back pain and a furious headache that he treats with pots of tea, "some salts, and then a few grains of Dover's powder." He descends the river during the first days of June in a fit of insomnia, resting on its infernal banks in ninety-degree heat, dispatching rattlesnakes and rewrapping his specimens. On his arrival at Walla Walla, he finds letters from England waiting. He has told himself that he has little need for communications from home, but their effect on him is profound and unexpected: "Never in my life did I feel in such a state; an uneasy, melancholy, but pleasing sensation stole on my mind." He reads and rereads the letters through the night and into the dawn.

He makes preparations for a trip into the Blue Mountains, south and east of the river's junction with the Snake, and attempts to rest up for the journey. Pack rats keep him awake through the night, however, one carrying off his specimens, another his shaving brush and razor, and, in the early hours of the morning, his inkstand. "I lifted my gun (which is my night companion as well as day, and lies generally alongside of me, the muzzle to my feet) and gave him the contents." Douglas departs the following afternoon with a Cayuse guide and the twelve-year-old son of a Canadian trader, who will act as his interpreter.

Douglas travels at a feverish pace, pulling the man and the boy after him like a sleigh of lead, and covers forty miles each day. When they are hobbled by the mountain snows and can no longer continue, he leaves them at their camp and climbs upward on his own. He attains a summit and "without the least difficulty placed my foot on the highest peak of those untrodden regions where never European was before me."

He contemplates the view for perhaps half an hour and is suddenly engulfed by bellowing winds, fusillades of icy, cutting hail, and peals of thunder and lightning, which "would appear in massy sheets, as if the heavens were in a blaze." He flees the mountaintop, and reaches his camp in the middle of the evening. In the morning, the man refuses to go on because the boy, Douglas would later learn, has convinced him that Douglas is a necromancer who will either kill him or transform him into a grizzly bear.

Douglas hastily returns to Walla Walla and obtains another native guide, "a knave" with so few expectations in life that he would perform whatever work was ordered. Douglas and the guide reascend the mountains amid more assaults of sheet lightning, and when the seeds that Douglas seeks have been gathered, they return to the river near the outlet of the John Day. While taking his midday meal, Douglas discovers that his knife is missing and offers a reward to the natives gathered on the bank. He sees the glint of the knife secreted under the belt of one of them, who, when confronted, denies having taken it. "When detected he claimed the premium, but as he did not give it on the first application, I paid him, and paid him so well, with my fists that he will, I daresay, not forget *The Man of Grass* for some days to come."

A few miles downriver he catches sight of a fire that he presumes belongs to a native band, but it is the camp of a group of company men, among them John Work and others from Fort Vancouver. They have letters for him, and again he feels overwhelmed and somewhat embarrassed by his reaction to receiving them; he should not need them so, they should not come so close to loosening his eyes to tears.

He leaves the following morning to ascend the Snake with the men from the company. The temperature is over one hundred degrees and he likens the Palouse country that surrounds the river to "the deserts of Arabia," save for its easy access to water. They eat one of their horses and Douglas gathers, dries, and wraps sixty-nine varieties of seeds. They cross overland to the Spokane River. The natives have constructed salmon weirs in the river, funnels of basketry that trap fish, and once caught inside they are speared by the hundreds. It is a process that captivates Douglas, even as he grows more disenchanted with the Indians because of their scant regard for property, their feuds and interminable peace negotiations, and their infinite rounds of dancing, chanting, storytelling, and speechmaking in camp.

At Kettle Falls he makes preparations to return to Fort Vancouver: "Packed one bundle of dry plants among my little stock of clothing, consisting of one shirt, one pair of stockings and a nightcap, and a pair of old mitts, with an Indian bag of curious workmanship, made of Indian hemp and eagles' quills, used for carrying roots and other articles." His belongings descend by water; he travels by both horse and canoe. On August 21, Douglas passes the Grand Coulee, "a most singular channel and at one time must have been the channel of the Columbia." The water is bitter and the night sky cracks with lightning. He loses his teapot, tea, and sugar in a rapid near the Okanagan and reaches Walla Walla exhausted.

Douglas leaves immediately for the Dalles. He smokes with a large group of natives by the riverbank, and one of them steals his tobacco box. He scrambles to the top of a rock and harangues them with epithets and threats: "I told them they saw me as only one blanket man but I was more than that, I was the *Grass Man*, and was not afraid." They sit impassively; the box is not returned. He reaches Fort Vancouver a few days later. He is dressed, fed, and feted, and yet despite this he is melancholy and listless. After his chests of specimens are secured for shipment to England, he sets off in search of the mammoth-coned pine.

Douglas heads south on the Willamette with a large company party headed by A. R. McLeod. McLeod has worked in the northwest fur trade since Mackenzie's time, and although his eccentricity and singularity of mind have retarded his advancement to any great position in the company, he is trusted as a man who can get things done in the field. His present task is simple: to cleanse the entire country south of the river of beaver and thereby discourage incursions into the territory by American trappers.

The party works its way southward to the head of the Willamette and then to the Umpqua. McLeod and his men kill beaver while Douglas botanizes and fills his notebooks with names reminiscent of noblemen's chaste wives and their unsullied daughters: Gentiana, Argemone, Castanea, Shepherdia, Clethra, Helonia, Myrtacea. But this is just a diversion, something to help pass the weeks while he climbs south and east to the place where the pine grows. When he is not collecting plants he hunts and shoots, although the party has several full-time hunters and there is an abundance of meat. It is in the nature of McLeod's assignment: the mountains ring with gunfire, traps clap closed, bellies are slit, viscera slip to earth. The men move from creek to creek on a crusade of slaughter.

Douglas breaks away from the main party to search for the pine, accompanied by a native guide that he can speak to only with gestures and signs. Douglas lives uneasily on the land, whose previous beneficence and succor forsake him. The weather terrorizes him: ". . . every ten or fifteen minutes immense trees falling producing a crash as if the earth was cleaving asunder, which with the thunder peal on peal before the echo of the former died away, and the lightning in zigzag and forked flashes, had on my mind a sensation more than I can ever give vent to."

The morning of October 26 is clear and cold as ice. Douglas awakes with a severe headache and a wrenching pain in his gut. His sight is clouded. He staggers with his guide to the lodge of some Indians, who share their salmon with him, and he forces himself to travel another eighteen miles before making camp. At dawn, he walks on alone. He ponders whether he is a fool: "That may be correct, but I know that such objects as I am in quest of are not obtained without a share of labour, anxiety of mind, and sometimes risk of personal safety."

About an hour out of camp, he sees an Indian standing before him, his bow drawn and raised. Douglas drops his gun and signals the Indian to come to him. Douglas removes tobacco and a pipe from his bag, and he and the Indian smoke together. With a pencil and a scrap of paper, he renders a crude sketch of the pine and its cone. The Indian rises and points to a range of hills about fifteen miles to the south. He motions the Indian to follow him.

At noon they stand in the grove. Smooth-barked trees encircle them, fifty feet in circumference, two hundred feet or more tall, suffused with sap the color of honey. Douglas grows agitated: he cannot reach the cones and begins to fire his gun into the crowns of the trees. Cones fall to the ground like dark, tawny pears. A group of natives, painted in the fashion of warriors, appears from the forest and surrounds him. He persuades them to smoke, but as the pipe transits the circle of Indians, he sees one draw his bow and another begin to sharpen his knife with a flint. Douglas backs away from the circle, his rifle in his right hand, a drawn pistol in his left. He faces them in silence for some minutes, and at last one of them signals him for tobacco. Douglas complies, and the warriors depart.

He flees back to his camp with a few cones and twigs. Fearing that his guide will betray him, he sends him away and lies in the dark, composing his thoughts and writing:

> Cannot speak a word to my guide, not a book to read, constantly in expectation of an attack, and the position I am now lying in is on the grass with my gun beside me, writing by the light of my Columbian candle—namely, a piece of wood containing rosin.

The guide returns two hours before dawn consumed by panic. Douglas assumes the Indians are close by, but the guide makes signs of a bear. Douglas waits for daylight and finds a grizzly sow with two cubs in a clearing nearby. The bear rears up and growls, holding her young before her. Douglas fires a shot, which penetrates the mouth of one of the cubs and exits through the back of its head. The cub falls dead and the sow rises higher on her feet. Douglas lodges a shot in her breast and she bolts for the woods with her remaining cub. The carcass of the other cub is a pathetic thing and Douglas offers it to his guide as payment for his services on the journey.

As Douglas rejoins the main party a few days later and works his way back up to the river and Fort Vancouver, the rain comes and fastens itself on the land for the next six months. Into the winter and the new year of 1827, he consolidates his specimens and organizes his notes. He makes two ill-fated trips to the coast to gather plants that have heretofore evaded him, but is thwarted by capsizes, illness, and storms. He leaves the river with the company's spring caravan for Hudson Bay on March 20. It has been a fine year for the company, and Douglas sits among bales of pelts in one of an armada of canoes. Day by day, the voyageurs' paddles cleave the river, and soon they climb the western flank of the Rockies. The river disappears behind them like an island receding into the sea's horizon. He has been rescued. At Hudson Bay, they put him on a ship for the place he once called home.

In London, Douglas was a celebrity. Few men of Douglas's quality had explored the interior of the northwest, and fewer still had returned to England to relate their experiences. He was inducted into the Linnaen Society, the Zoological Society, and the Geological Society and invited to receptions and dinners, an honor a lowly Scots boy such as himself could hardly hope to imagine. He was even interviewed by the Colonial Office for his opinion on matters relating to the British claim on the northwest.

Yet in this adulation, Douglas felt himself less a fellow of the people who sought him out than an object of curiosity, a specimen to be exhibited and observed. He sat uneasily for a portrait, his hair thin and rangy over his high forehead, his eyes distracted, and his small but full-lipped mouth poised in an expression of bafflement or as though ready to blurt out an impropriety. His characteristic affability evaporated over the year of 1828, and his once impeccable manners and courtesy gave way to sullenness, arrogance, and fits of ill temper. He attempted to organize his journals into a manuscript for publication, but he could not bring himself to lift his pen. People began to take note of his clothes and grooming. He was as unkempt as a castaway, and his bearing distracted; "quite a savage in his appearance and manners," someone said.

There was no remedy but to find a ship and an island. In October 1829 he took passage by way of Hawaii to the river and seemed to disappear into it. He severed his links to the Royal Horticultural Society and traveled to California, the interior of the Fraser River, and Puget Sound. He enjoyed the hospitality of the company at Fort Vancouver, but the neighborhood around it had become crowded. A few Americans arrived in 1832, ostensibly to settle but in truth more preoccupied with reaping fortunes from the fur trade. Douglas conversed with their leader, Nathaniel Wyeth, who had given up an ice business in New England to get rich on pelts. Wyeth had been welcomed by Dr. McLoughlin and shown every courtesy, but the company's larger purpose was to discourage him and his countrymen from coming here. George Simpson, the head of the company's North America office, had written that the loss of its Columbia operations "would be ruinous," although he suspected American occupation was inevitable. Therefore the company's immediate policy was to offer native trappers higher prices for their furs than the Americans could reasonably afford to pay, and thereby "damp their sanguine expectations of profit." With the Americans thus thwarted, the company could pursue its longer-term strategy of stripping the country of fur-bearing creatures. That approach was rapidly bearing fruit: within three years, for example, the Snake River region—the Americans' main locus for trapping—would yield a mere 378 beaver skins per annum.

As the seasons pass, these are matters of little consequence to Douglas. For now, the country outside of Fort Vancouver holds but a few dozen white faces, and beyond company trading posts there are no settlements. Still, Douglas seeks out wilder places and more phenomenal feats of exploration and self-sufficiency. Accidents and injuries befall him in increasing number. He gathers specimens and notes that are no sooner taken than lost, carried off down the river by capsizes and rapids, obliterated by rain and mold. He makes an attempt on the summit of Mount Hood. The sun on the snow burns his eyes like a caustic, and the mountain drives him back down its flank.

He is in no way discouraged by these events, and even as they render his body more and more frail, they restore him to himself. The few letters he now writes to England are ebullient, awash in plans and possibilities. He travels laden like a dromedary in a caravan, carrying an eagle in a cage and snakes in his pocket. His person has become an ark of plants and creatures. The sight of his right eye is utterly obliterated, and his left eye is waxen. Yet he can see, so it seems to him, farther and more clearly. He reels through the world of the river infatuated; he lusts for its benisons, its superfluities, its chastisements. It engulfs and contains whatever he needs or desires. And its banks close upon themselves and circumscribe an island that encompasses everything he wants to see and become.

There is less and less word of him in England, and his friends fear he is lost or dead. But Douglas has never been more alive, more sure of his place in the world. In the spring of 1834, he sails for the island of Hawaii to explore its two peaks, Mauna Loa and Mauna Kea. He climbs them both in a single month, each ascent beginning in the jungle at sea level and ending in the snow at over thirteen thousand feet. He is oblivious to pain, exhaustion, and weather. Hauling a load of instruments and attired only in light clothing, he maintains a pace his local guides cannot match.

His body is shattered. He sails to Oahu, but he craves more. The missionaries and British officials in the islands say Douglas is possessed by a mania, that he no longer knows reason. In a letter to the wife of the consul, Douglas explains himself:

A sight of the volcano fills the mind with awe. . . . The strongest man is unstrung; the most courageous heart is daunted in approaching this place. How insignificant are the works of man in their greatest magnitude and perfection, compared with such a place. I have exhausted both mind and body, examining, measuring, and performing various experiments, and *now, I learn that I know nothing.* . . .

In early July, he leaves Honolulu for the island of Hawaii to renew his explorations. The ship is bound for Hilo but is detained by weather at Kohala Point. Douglas insists on being put ashore. He will walk the hundred miles to Hilo through sparsely settled country. After two days of walking, he stops on the morning of July 12 at the house of an English cattle hunter. Years before, Capt. James Cook was supposed to have set cattle loose in the islands so they could be used as emergency rations by shipwrecked sailors and castaways. Hunters now trapped the feral descendants of these animals in pits camouflaged by leaves and branches.

Douglas inquires about the state of the path, which broaches the lower slopes of Mauna Kea on its way to Hilo, and is warned about the cattle traps on its periphery. He sets off, his sights on reaching Hilo by evening. Mauna Kea looms; trees and foliage swaddle him in his course. That afternoon, he is discovered in a pit where a bull has also found its unseen way. Douglas has been repeatedly trampled and gored, his face unrecognizable, his body a spectacle from which words must flee and eyes turn away.

2.

Her name was Narcissa, and like a flower she seemed to exist only to please, to garner the grace of others and let herself be shaped by it. She was as good as people's estimation of her goodness, and she therefore strove to be exceedingly good. She cast her love onto the still waters of the world, that the light of Jesus might strike it and bend it back to illuminate her face, to show her who she was. She was a serious child, born in 1808 to serious parents in Prattsburg, New York, in the Finger Lakes country. Her father, Stephen Prentiss, gave himself to business—his two mills and his landholdings; her mother, Clarissa, gave herself to her children and to God. God took over her life a few years before Narcissa's birth. It was a time when God found many people to bend to his purposes; not merely to observe the commandments and sacraments, but to make his work their chief occupation. When he found them, he turned them toward him and transformed them; he incinerated their pride and complacency in an agony of tears and cries. When he was finished, they understood that their previous lives were ended, that their only business now must be to engender in others the transformation he had effected on them.

God seized many souls in this way, and although the world was full of souls, most of them were turned away from him. In Prattsburg, however, God's word poured down in a perpetual rain of services, sermons, and meetings. It spread through the town like a fever that moved people to weep and moan; to burn with the pain of their sin and call out for the cool water of his mercy; to dedicate their lives and their children's lives to his service. What God brought to Prattsburg, Prattsburg must bring to the wilderness in the new world. It was what God required, and Clarissa required it of Narcissa.

Narcissa was drawn to music and the domestic arts that made a civilized and comfortable home. But she loved her mother in fact as she loved God in principle, and as a teenager she began to accept the idea of a life devoted to God's service. The cities and towns of America had countless unredeemed souls, but the calling of foreign missionary work exerted a special attraction to the children of Prattsburg. Unclothed, unwashed, and ignorant, the undifferentiated consciousness of a savage was an empty page on which God's word might be written without the need to erase or overwrite. It was conversion not from some other state, but out of nothing—the very manner in which God had fashioned his creation.

The life of a missionary was therefore a high but arduous calling. Savage people inspired pity in the breasts of potential missionaries such as Narcissa, even though their customs excited disgust and their habitations fear. The American Board of Foreign Missions published the *Missionary Herald* each month and its stated object was nothing less than the "CONVERSION OF THE WORLD." Its pages rang with both spiritual exhortation and harrowing adventure stories culled from the godless regions of the globe: Syria, Ceylon, the American plains, Africa, South America, Hawaii, and the South Sea islands. Not much was heard about the far west of North America except that California was in the hands of the papist Spaniards. And little was known of the northwest, save for the odd report from a ship's captain who claimed to have experienced life among the belligerent, infanticidal natives of its north coast:

> Their funeral ceremonies are these. A chief or chiefess dying, after being washed, dressed, and painted, is kept for a few days in their house. The head is then severed from the body, and put into a small box, and suspended upon poles, near, (commonly in part of) their hut; the body is consumed by fire, and the ashes buried. A common person is entirely consumed by fire. A slave is thrown on the beach, to be washed away by the tide.

In 1831, however, when Narcissa was twenty-three, a more extensive and less forbidding report on the northwest written by J. S. Green, a missionary stationed in Hawaii, found its way to the *Herald*. Green could not recommend the establishment of missions along the better part of the coast—the natives were either too dangerous or beyond redemption because of their exposure to liquor—but he believed at least one place held out some prospect of success: "Somewhere in the vicinity of the Columbia River such a colony, I doubt not, would find a salubrious climate, a fertile soil, and ultimately a country of great importance." Green had not, in fact, visited the river—his ship could not cross the bar due to the breaking swells—but he had credible information that its natives were "a superior race of men, and though savage, are less bloody than the tribes further north." Moreover, a mission on the Columbia might be of practical benefit to the board's well-established outposts in Hawaii, supplying them with fish, timber, and a place of retirement for missionaries "whose strength has withered under the influence of a tropical sun." It might, incidentally, further American claims to the territory. But Green outlined the crux of the matter:

> Here are fifteen thousand pagans, men possessing an unusual share of intelligence, capable of being benefited by Christian instruction, of being blessings to the world—now the slaves of every lust, groping in unbroken darkness their way to ruin, and who, unless they soon receive the gospel, will inevitably perish. Their wants are pressing, and they appeal to the hearts of all who know the worth of the soul, the evil of sin, the preciousness of Jesus Christ, and the utter insufficiency of all means to subdue the heat, save the preaching of the cross. . . . A flame might thus be kindled, which would penetrate the surrounding darkness, and dispel the mists of superstition and ignorance, which for ages have brooded over all this part of the earth.

Green's plea was heard, and the desirability of a mission on the river became a piece of the board's strategy, although it would take some years to accomplish. It was to be Narcissa's destiny: the fifteen thousand souls would call to her, as they had to Green, as though she might be their mother, as though they were children crying in a distant room in a house whose unfamiliar hallways she had now begun to tread. Many beseeched her from the grave, although she could not have known it. Through the early 1830s, a fever swept down the river each year, like a wind pulled from the sea where the white people's boats lay at anchor, and carried the better part of the river people the way of the beaver.

🌰

Narcissa was neither pretty nor plain, but she possessed a pleasant voice, and a ladylike and sometimes distant manner. She had no husband, nor for the moment did she want one. She had only recently spurned the proposal of one suitor, Henry Spalding, a would-be missionary himself but rather too rough around the edges for Narcissa's taste. She kept house for her mother, and from her goodwill she drew every comfort she required. She edged toward some larger commitment to the service of Christ but as yet did not know what form it might take. In 1833, however, a story began to make its way east. A group of Flathead Indians had walked from their country all the way to St. Louis to say they wanted a Christian pastor to come to their people. Three of the Flatheads were chiefs, and another was Ignace LaMoose.

It was the kind of story that changed its shape and color with each telling, like a salmon migrating from fresh water to salt water to fresh, but that was of little consequence. It prompted the interest of a minister named Samuel Parker, who immediately began to organize a party of missionaries for the Far West. In November 1834, he came to the Finger Lakes to raise money and recruit, and Narcissa heard him speak. Afterwards, she went to him and confessed her desire to join his party as a missionary.

The missions board had misgivings about Parker, who seemed too old to undertake such an enterprise and, in his rather overweening enthusiasm for it, less conscious of its practical difficulties than he should be. As for Narcissa, the board preferred that missionaries be married, and in any case it could not countenance sending a young woman among savages without the protection of a husband. Narcissa must marry and do so quickly.

Parker suggested she consider Marcus Whitman, a physician living not far from Prattsburg whose pursuit of his own missionary vocation had been thwarted by his lack of a wife. Whitman, who had been abandoned by his mother and raised by a succession of relatives, was hardly refined, but his energy and commitment to Christ's work were formidable. In February 1835, he and

Narcissa were engaged. And with that barrier removed, Whitman immediately left to join Parker on a reconnaissance of the West. Narcissa, at times apprehensive and at others oppressed by melancholy, waited at home.

In December she heard from Whitman, who had traveled as far as the Green River in Wyoming with Parker. He had met chiefs from the Nez Percé people who expressed a desire for a mission in their country near the Snake and Columbia rivers. In August, he left Parker to go his own way, and returned home to lay plans for a missionary party to the Nez Percé headed by himself and Narcissa, and joined by Narcissa's former suitor, Henry Spalding, and his new wife, Eliza. Narcissa and Whitman were married in February 1836; by the end of March they were on the Missouri with the Spaldings, carrying the gospel into the wilderness.

On September 1, Narcissa arrived in the country Whitman had determined would be their home. She wrote to her mother, as she had each day of the westward journey:

> Here we all are at Walla Walla, through the mercy of a kind Providence, in health and all our lives. What cause for gratitude and praise to God! Surely my heart is ready to leap for joy at the thought of being so near the long-desired work of teaching the benighted ones the knowledge of a Savior, and having completed this hazardous journey under such favorable circumstances.

She had considered keeping a diary but rejected the notion: the words had no place to go, no object to light upon and reveal the colors of her heart; it would be like speaking into an emptiness or an oncoming wind. Of course, any letter she might write would probably take a year to reach its destination, and any reply just as long. But it was only by addressing herself to others, to their needs and curiosities, and particularly to her mother, that Narcissa could know the contents of her own mind—not through her own words, but in their echo. Thus she wrote: "Now, mother, if I was with you by the fireside, I would relate a scene that would amuse you, and at the same time call forth your sympathies. But for my own gratification I will write it."

They had been cheered by the welcome they received from the company agent at Walla Walla, and Whitman decided they should go to Fort Vancouver to introduce themselves to Dr. McLoughlin and gather supplies and intelligence about the condition of the country. They boarded boats and Narcissa gloried in the river:

> The Columbia is a beautiful river. Its waters are clear as crystal and smooth as a sea of glass, exceeding in beauty the Ohio; but the scenery on each side of it is very different. There is no timber to be seen, but there are high perpendicular banks of rocks in some places, while rugged bluffs and plains of sand in others, are all that meets the eye. We sailed until near sunset, when we landed, pitched our tents, supped our tea, bread and butter, boiled ham and potatoes, committed ourselves to the care of a kind Providence, and retired to rest.

Above the Cascades, Narcissa at last encountered the people of the river to whom she was to minister: "Every head was flattened. These are the first I have seen near enough to be able to examine them. Their eyes have a dull and heavy expression."

Two days later, they arrived at Fort Vancouver, which Narcissa dubbed "the New York of the Pacific Ocean." She was enchanted with the warmth of Dr. McLoughlin and the civility of his establishment, with its luxuriant gardens, the tasteful arrangements of its quarters, and the variety and deliciousness of the fare served in its dining hall. Nor was the place without religion: McLoughlin conducted services in French for the voyageurs, and the newly arrived Rev. Herbert Beaver had just installed himself as the fort's Anglican chaplain.

For the Reverend Mr. Beaver, however, Fort Vancouver was less pleasing. Everything about it affronted him, including the high spirits of the voyageurs, their Indian "wives," and their lack of respect for him. Its shiftless, indolent natives appalled him, and the country itself was a wasteland about which there was little to learn:

> It is a correct observation, that the more the qualities of a mild disposition exist in the nature of a savage, the more he degenerates as a man, while, on the contrary, the more his behaviour merits his appellation, the finer become his animal powers. What volumes does this speak in favor of our better Creed, which, while it regulates the faculties of the mind, does not prevent the development of those of the body! I apprehend that there is nothing in Zoology on this Northwest Coast, which is not well known, and very little that is useful in Botany. There may be much, both useful and unknown, in Mineralogy and Geology, but it must remain unexplored, till the immense forests shall have been, in a measure, cleared by an increasing civilized population.

However much Narcissa was impressed by his Oxford accent and the gracious manners of his wife, the Reverend Mr. Beaver had little use for Americans:

> I fear the Americans will soon make a grand effort to oust us out of this place altogether, as they claim to be the proprietors of the soil to the forty-ninth parallel of latitude. In this case, they will act the part of the ungrateful snake in the fable. They could never have existed here a day without our assistance. It is bad policy to encourage them.

Dr. McLoughlin's unremitting hospitality to Americans was one of the many things the Reverend Mr. Beaver could not abide. When he learned the chief factor had allowed Narcissa and Eliza Spalding to teach in the fort's school, their vulgar evangelism in tow, his umbrage knew no bounds: letters flew between his quarters and McLoughlin's, only a few steps away. McLoughlin summoned the Reverend Mr. Beaver to explain himself. Beaver refused to come. McLoughlin insisted that Beaver submit to his authority. Beaver would do no such thing. The Reverend Mr. Beaver wrote indignant missives on the subject to the company's North American governor, George Simpson, and to its directors in London. By this time Narcissa had long since returned upriver.

By mid-October, Narcissa was in Walla Walla, awaiting the completion of the house Whitman was constructing at Wailatpu, a short distance above the Walla Walla River's junction with the Columbia. It had been agreed that she and Whitman would minister to the Cayuse people from this post, and the Spaldings would work among the Nez Percé farther east. She wrote letters and felt the first stirrings of the child that slept in her womb. She was swollen with expectation. Life here would be good and the savages would be turned to God and saved:

> O, what a thought to think of meeting them among the blood-washed throng around the throne of God! Will not their songs be as sweet as any we can sing? What joy will then fill our souls to contemplate the privilege we now enjoy of spending and being spent for their good.

By Christmas, the house was finished. Narcissa admitted it was little more than a rustic lean-to with blankets to cover the openings where windows would be set, yet it made her happy.

> . . . my heart truly leaped for joy as I alighted from my horse, entered and seated myself before a pleasant fire. . . . It occurred to me that my dear parents had made a similar beginning, and perhaps a more difficult one than ours. We had neither straw, bedstead or table, nor anything to make them of except green cottonwood. . . . [The house is] in a lovely situation. We are on a beautiful level—a peninsula formed by the branches of the Walla Walla. . . . The rivers are barely skirted with timber.

This is all the woodland we can see; beyond them, as far as the eye can reach, plains and mountains appear.

❀

On March 14, 1837, her twenty-ninth birthday, Narcissa gave birth to a daughter, whom she named Alice Clarissa. To the local people her nativity was a source of fascination. None of them had seen a white baby before, and they attended the news of her birth and the progress of her infancy as though it were a great and wonderful blessing to the country:

> Fee-low-ki-ke, a kind friendly Indian, called to see her the next day after she was born. Said she was a Cayuse-te-mi (Cayuse girl) because she was born on Cayuse wai-tis (Cayuse land). He told us her arrival was expected by all the people of the country—the Nez Perces, Cayuses and Walla Wallapoos Indians, and, now [that] she has arrived, it would be heard of by all of them. . . .

By Alice Clarissa's first birthday, Narcissa's kitchen had taken on the flavor of a nursery school, filled at most hours of the day with a dozen native children and their mothers. Alice Clarissa's physical and intellectual development outstripped that of Indian children twice her age, a phenomenon Narcissa attributed to insufficient nourishment and the native custom of keeping their infants strapped on their carrying boards for most of the day.

For all the chaos it caused in her household, Narcissa was eager to bring not only her religion but formal education and a sense of the value of work and thrift to the Cayuse's children. Their parents seemed happy to commit their children to Narcissa's care for storytelling and Bible lessons, but blanched when she assigned them chores around the mission: "They are so impressed with the idea that all who work are slaves and inferior persons, that the moment they hear of their children doing the least little thing they are panic stricken and make trouble."

The Cayuse adults to whom Whitman, now relatively fluent in their language, gave religious and moral instruction had similar qualms: "Some feel almost to blame us for telling them about eternal realities. One said it was good when they knew nothing but to hunt, eat, drink and sleep; now it is bad." To the Cayuse, there was a fundamental flaw in Whitman's way of thinking. Why should people till the earth when the river flowed with fish, the hills ran with elk, and the earth was pregnant with roots? Why did the Whitmans maintain that living on the earth was bad, when it was clearly so good?

The Whitmans were not well disposed to a life lacking regular productive labor, but in one respect they saw all too well what the future held. At about this time, their colleague Henry Spalding wrote:

> The Salmon will be arrested in their upward course by some measure which the untiring invention of man will find out & which is not necessary here to conjecture. That day will be the date of universal starvation of nearly all the tribes of this vast country, if they be not timely settled upon their lands and furnished with means of a substantial subsistence.

It was therefore a crucial part of the missionary program, in Whitman's words, "to point them with one hand to the Lamb of God which taketh away the sins of the world" and "to point with the other to the hoe, as the means of saving their famishing bodies from an untimely grave & furnishing the means of subsistence to future generations."

Thus far, the Whitmans had not had any great success in impressing these verities upon the Cayuse, nor could they, of course, speak to them of what they suspected the future would bring. Narcissa placed her hopes with the children she taught and took into her home, and wrote to her sister Jane of one promising case:

> One dear boy, who has been living with us little more than a year, gives pleasing evidence of a change of heart, and the

lispings of his desires to God in prayer are like the first prat-
tlings of an infant child. . . . He has recently heard that his
father is dead, which makes him feel very bad, and he cries;
then he goes to Jesus and prays, and feels comforted.

There were, however, few such examples Narcissa could put
before the world. She clung to her own child as the font of her comfort and optimism in this arid land, as her child clung to her while
she wrote her letters:

You see, Jane, Alice has come and laid her dirty hands on this
letter, and given it a fine mark. I send it as it is, so that you may
have some of her doings to look at, and realize, perhaps, there
is such a child in existence.

In the same year Alice Clarissa turned a year old, far away in
another part of the river people began to speak of the death of
Qanqon Kamek Klaula. She was riding with her Kutenai people
as a warrior when her party was ambushed by the Piegans. As
each Kutenai warrior fell and was scalped, the roof of the forest
echoed with the Piegans' war cries. One Kutenai was able to steal
away and hide himself in the brush, from where he watched the
slaughter. Qanqon Kamek Klaula had been shot several times but
remained standing. After killing all her tribesmen, the Piegans
surrounded her. They held her down and cut her breasts with
their knives, but the wounds healed as quickly as they were in-
flicted. At last, one was able to open her chest just below the ster-
num and, reaching upward, cut out her heart, and she finally died.
Then they stripped her body and lay it upright against a pole, like
Jesus in the white people's Book. Trouble followed the Piegans
for some time thereafter, and the body of Qanqon Kamek Klaula
decayed slowly, over a very long time, like a great tree that has
fallen in the forest.

That was all there was to say of Qanqon Kamek Klaula, although people would speak of her even a hundred years later. It was one death among so many; it was as though there were a great emptying out of the world and now it was abandoned and still, like a tree that a flock of birds forsakes, flying away from it in one motion. It was like that now, and it had been that way before. Long ago, the Kutenai said, there was a great sickness and all the people died, save for one young man. He said to himself, "Let me go around this world to see if there is any place where there is anyone."

He went from village to village, searching, but the lodges were deserted and the canoes sat empty, brushing the riverbanks. He was as alone as the sun in the sky and he wailed because he was the only person in the world. Then he saw two bears foraging for berries, but as he drew closer he realized they were two women, a big, older one and a young one. They cried when they saw him, because they too believed all the other people had died. The three gathered together and wept.

The man lived with the two women he had mistaken for a she-bear and her cub, and not long after the daughter was old enough to become his wife. They had many children, thus bringing the Kutenai into the world again.

By the spring of 1839, Alice Clarissa spoke and sang hymns in both English and Nez Percé, helped her mother set the table, and played happily outside the house. Her fears were few, but when Whitman took her swimming in the river by the house, she was afraid of the great expanse of water. The mission had expanded and possessed a printing press, and Narcissa had a helper, Margaret, to assist with the housework. One of the Cayuse that attended Whitman's meetings had exhibited a remorse for his sins that seemed consistent with genuine conversion. All these benefactions moved Narcissa to a kind of hope she had rarely experienced in her three years among the river people:

O, my dear Jane, could you see us here this beautiful eve, the full moon shining in all her splendor, clear, yet freezing cold, my little one sleeping by my side, husband at worship with the people within hearing, and I sitting in 'the door of the tent' writing, with my usual clothing except a shawl, and a handkerchief on my head, and before me a large comfortable fire in the open air. Do you think we suffer? No, dear Jane. . . .

A few weeks later, on the second Friday in June, Alice Clarissa overcame her fear of the river. She and Narcissa were working in a garden, from which she pulled a radish. Whitman saw her washing it in the river and was horrified to find she had made her way there unattended. He reminded her of the fate of a sick household dog named Boxer that he had drowned in the river a few weeks before. He explained how the water had killed Boxer, and could kill her if she were ever so careless again.

On Saturday night, Alice Clarissa wanted to sleep on a mat on the floor rather than in Narcissa's bed. On Sunday morning, Narcissa woke her with a kiss and they held each other for a while. It was the custom for Narcissa to bathe her on Sunday morning before church, but this morning she protested and submitted to the water with great reluctance. At worship, as she did every Sunday, Alice Clarissa selected the hymn. This time she chose "Rock of Ages." She was an enthusiastic chorister, and knew the lyrics to her favorite hymns by heart in English and Nez Percé. That morning she rose out of her chair and prompted Narcissa with the next verse: "Mamma, 'Should my tears forever flow?'"

After church, when the table was set and supper was being prepared, Alice Clarissa picked up two cups from the table and took them by herself to the river to fill them with the water. The river took her into itself, and when it was done, lay her facedown in a little eddy cut into the bank, so that she might not be borne away, but forever cradled in that place.

In the weeks after Alice Clarissa's drowning, Narcissa composed letters, many letters, as she might a quilt, patch by patch, from her shifting and amorphous memories of the incidents of that Sunday. She arranged them one way and then another, hoping to see some pattern or symmetry among them. She wrote her parents, brothers, sisters, in-laws, and fellow missionaries draft upon draft, yet what she sought remained ungraspable, as though clearly visible underwater but by a trick of the eye impossible to set one's hand on:

> . . . by the time I got to the river's brink, it flashed across my mind like a dream, that I had had a glimpse of her, while sitting and reading, entering the house and on seeing the table set for supper, she exclaimed with her usual animation, "Mamma, supper is almost ready; let Alice get some water." She went up to the table and took *two cups* that set by her plate and Margaret's (for we drank water instead of tea) and disappeared. This was like a shadow that passed across my mind, passed away and made no impression. Strange as it seemed to myself, I did not recollect it until I reached the place where she had fallen in. And now where is she? . . .

> We kept her four days. She did not begin to change in her appearance much for the first three days. This proved to be a great comfort to me, for so long as she looked natural and was so sweet and I could caress her, I could not bear to have her out of my sight; but when she began to melt away like wax and her visage changed I wished then to put her in so safe, quiet and desirable a resting place as the grave—to see her no more until the morning of the resurrection.

> Although her grave is in sight, every time I step out of doors, yet my thoughts seldom wander there to find her. I seem to feel she is not there.

Other children died in the vicinity of the mission that summer. Two Cayuse brothers died in a single evening and were buried in a single coffin. Narcissa had nursed them, and they in turn had confessed their love of Jesus to her. After their death, their people began to wonder if the medicine she had given them killed them. The story drew Narcissa deeper into her grief and despair: "All these things together made me feel as I never felt before—I seemed to 'sink in deep waters, where the floods overwhelmed me'—and at times lost sight of my Supporter, or rather had not the strength to cast myself upon Him."

Throughout the next year, she also grew more disenchanted with the Indians. Narcissa thought Alice Clarissa's death was perhaps not such a bad thing, since she was now in the bosom of the Lord, safe from "the contaminating influence of heathenism." The Cayuse continued to attend the mission's classes and services, and sat rapt whenever stories from Scripture were read. Yet they had no interest in taking the steps toward true redemption, which was the purpose of God's word. To them, the stories were sufficient:

> They love to hear something new and marvelous—scripture names and history, or any subject that does not touch the heart. These they will repeat day after day and night after night, as if their salvation depended upon it; indeed, they make it their religion and are displeased the moment you attempt to shake the foundations of their hopes.

There was more and more work to do around the mission, and Whitman was frequently away on the river. Narcissa felt greatly relieved when the missions board assigned a zealous and hardworking missionary with good mechanical skills, Asabel Munger, to assist them. The Indians, by contrast, still seemed to Narcissa to possess no sense of the value of labor: "They are supremely selfish and would compel you to do everything for them, if they could, without compensation." Moreover, there were new people coming into the country that needed tending:

> A tide of immigration appears to be moving this way rapidly.
> What a few years will bring forth we know not. . . . Instead of
> two lonely American females, we now number fourteen, and
> soon may be twenty or more, if reports are true. We are em-
> phatically situated on the highway between the states and the
> Columbia River, and are a resting place for weary travelers. . . .

Immigration to the Columbia country was now actively encouraged in the United States as a prelude to a final resolution of
the "Oregon question" with Great Britain. The Hudson's Bay
Company in turn did little to discourage it, provided the settlers
confined themselves to lands south of the river. In 1840 their
numbers were small, but their arrival prompted questions about
just whom the lands around the river belonged to. On more than
one occasion, people from among the Cayuse suggested that perhaps the Whitmans owed them some compensation for the land
the mission stood on, or that the native people should be allowed
to reoccupy it as and when they saw fit.

The Whitmans in turn became more impatient with the Indians and their misapprehension of what God required of them:

> . . . [My] husband tells them that none of them are Christians;
> that they are all of them in the broad road to destruction, and
> that worshipping will not save them. They try to persuade him
> not to talk such bad talk to them, as they say, but talk good
> talk, or tell some story or history, so that they may have some
> Scripture names to learn. Some threaten to whip him and to
> destroy our crops . . . to see if they could not compel him to
> change his course of instruction with them.

In the following year of 1841, more settlers came into the country and onto the river. Tension increased between the Whitmans
and the Cayuse over the incursions of whites and the manner in
which the Indians had adopted the Christian faith. The traditional

medicine men of the native peoples began to reassert their primacy and confronted Whitman and Narcissa in their kitchen with bows, arrows, and war clubs, but were dispersed without incident.

The Whitmans and the Cayuse could not see the same God, or perhaps could not see him in the same way. Nor could the missionaries themselves. In March, Asabel Munger proclaimed himself Moses the lawgiver, the agent of judgment day. The Whitmans tried to reason with him and pray with him, but he could not see the point of what they said, only the clear fact that he was Christ's chosen representative on earth. In May, he nailed his left hand to the fireplace with two spikes, and thrust his right hand into the coals and held it there. His agonies lasted for four days and then he died.

Narcissa lost herself in illness and doubt: To what end did these manifold and incomprehensible trials point? Were all her aspirations vanities, and if so, who was she? She wrote more letters to her sister and mother: "I find one of my most difficult studies is to know my own heart, the motive by which I am actuated from day to day, and feel more than ever to cling closely to the word of God as our *only guide* in this dark and dreary wilderness world."

Twenty-five settlers came through the mission in the autumn, in most cases exhausted and starving, and Narcissa made it her business to welcome and look after them. "Our little place is a resting spot for many a weary, way-torn traveler and will be as long as we live here. If we can do good that way, perhaps it is as important as some other things we are doing." The progress of those other things—the mission's work with the Cayuse—was rapidly deteriorating. The Indians grew bolder in their confrontations with Whitman over ownership of the land and the practice of religion: they struck him on the chest, threatened him with axes and war clubs, grabbed his ear and shouted their demands into it, and, above all else, told him to stop talking.

Whitman was compelled to write to the board and inform it

of this state of affairs. The board was already aware of the tensions among the missionaries themselves, and with this additional intelligence made the decision to close the mission entirely. When word of the board's action reached him in the spring of 1842, Whitman set off for the east to persuade its members to reconsider, leaving Narcissa alone with the two orphaned native girls she had adopted the previous summer. She forbade them to speak Nez Percé, and busied herself in creating diversions for them:

> Baked bread and crackers today, and made two rag babies for my little girls. I keep them in the house most of the time to keep them away from the natives, and find it difficult to employ their time when I wish to be engaged with the women. They have a great disposition to take a piece of board or a stick and carry it around on their backs, if I would let them, for a baby, so I thought I would make them something that would change their taste a little. You wonder, I suppose, what looking objects Narcissa would make. No matter how they look, so long as it is a piece of cloth rolled up with eyes, nose, and a mouth marked on it with a pen, it answers every purpose. They caress them and carry them about the room at a great rate, and are as happy as need be. So much for my children.

Still, Narcissa slept by herself, resting her tired eyes in the darkness:

> Jane, I wish you were here to sleep with me, I am such a timid creature about sleeping alone that sometimes I suffer considerably, especially since my health has not been very good. . . . My eyes are much weaker than when I left home and no wonder, for I have so much use for them . . . so much writing as we have to do, both in our own language and the Nez Perces; and, besides, we have no way to feast our minds with knowledge necessary for health and spirituality without reading, and here the strength of the eyes are taxed again.

Through the fall and into the winter Narcissa pined for her husband and her family, whom Whitman visited, and began to conceive a plan whereby they might all immigrate to the river. She wrote Whitman letters, not knowing when or if they might reach him:

> Read this letter, my husband, and then give it to my mother—perhaps she would like once more to take a peep into one of the sacred chambers of her daughter's heart—it may comfort her, seeing she cannot see her face again in the flesh. But my better self I hope she will be permitted to see, and delight her eyes and heart with the sight, to the satisfaction of her soul. . . .
>
> My husband, what more can I say to you tonight? I wish you sweet sleep and a quiet rest under the shadow of Almighty love and to more mercy, and may the calm smile of the Savior's presence cheer you, and a Sabbath day's blessing be your portion and that of your companion in travel. So prays
>
> Your ever affectionate wife,
> Narcissa W.

In Whitman's absence, the Indians grew ever more restive. One tried to break into Narcissa's room in the middle of the night, armed with a war club. Throughout the country the Indians increasingly were talking about the whites coming into the country with the intention of taking away their land, and they said war should be prepared for. In the missionary community, Narcissa grieved the six lives recently lost to drowning "upon these frightful rivers of Oregon." It was more than she could bear: ". . . even now while I am writing the drum and savage yell are sounding in my ears every sound of which is as far as the east from the west from vibrating in unison with my feelings." Narcissa abandoned the mission for the duration of Whitman's absence, and took shelter at Walla Walla.

Meanwhile, in the east, Whitman had finished his business with the board, which accepted his plea to keep the mission open, not only for the sake of the Indians but for the settlers who would inevitably be coming into the territory. In May 1843, Whitman crossed the Missouri at the head of a wagon train of nine hundred people, all destined for Oregon. He arrived at the river in October, and was reunited with Narcissa. Only the fact that virtually all the settlers were bound for the Willamette prevented a conflagration of native anger.

The anxieties of the previous year and a half had pummeled Narcissa's mind and body, and in December 1843, she fell seriously ill with a tumor. Whitman wrote her parents and apprised them of her condition. He also told them of his accomplishments and hopes:

> As I hold the settlement of this country by Americans rather than by an English colony most important, I am happy to have been the means of landing so large an emigration on to the shores of the Columbia, with their wagons, families, and stock, all in safety. . . . It gives me much pleasure to be back again and quietly at work again for the Indians. It does not concern me so much what is to become of any particular set of Indians, as to give them the offer of salvation through the gospel and the opportunity of civilization, and then I am content to do good to all men as I have opportunity. I have no doubt our greatest work is to be to aid the white settlement of this country and help found its religious institutions. Providence has its full share in all these events. . . . The Indians have in no case obeyed the command to multiply and replenish the earth, and they cannot stand in the way of others in doing so.

By the end of winter, Narcissa seemed recovered from her illness. People remarked on the robustness of her bearing, the matronly dignity of the new weight she carried on her frame. The year 1844 became 1845, like a snake noiselessly shedding its translucent skin. But her fears about the future of the mission and the safety of herself and Whitman had no end:

> We have had some serious trials this spring with the Indians. Two important Indians have died and they have ventured to say and intimate that the doctor has killed them by his magical power, in the same way they accuse their own sorcerers and kill them for it.

The Indians had threatened them before and even laid hands upon them, but nothing had ever come of it. It was something they did for show, a toy employed in argument, and not very different from their insisting that Whitman stop talking "bad talk" to them. Whitman had faced them down on numerous occasions. He had told them he was unafraid to die, and with that their game was up. By now, surely they understood he was in earnest.

In 1845 another three thousand Americans immigrated to Oregon, and in 1846 the matter of sovereignty was settled with a border established on the forty-ninth parallel. George Simpson of the Hudson's Bay Company had begun to transfer the company's northwest operations to Victoria. The entire Columbia department had netted only thirteen thousand pelts the previous year, and, in any event, the fashion for beaver hats had, like the beaver itself, at long last passed away. Dr. McLoughlin chose to remain on the river, and retired on its precincts to a life of impoverished obscurity.

Narcissa's spirits rose that year, her tenth season on the river. She had taken in seven emigrant children whose parents had perished on the wagon road the previous October. The house now held eleven children, and Narcissa lost herself in caring for, feeding, and educating them. She wrote more letters urging her family to join her in Oregon. She also felt a new flowering of faith within her in witnessing the death of a young emigrant from Illinois named Joseph Finlay. Finlay was riddled with consumption, and when his wagon train reached the mission, he was too sick to continue. He spent his final hours in a bed at the Whitmans':

> I asked him if he felt the Saviour present with him now? He said deliberately, "I think He is." Occasionally ejaculations like these would be heard from him as we stood watching around him, "Lord, help me now; Thy will be done.". . . . In a few minutes he looked at us with inexpressible sweetness depicted in his countenance, and said, "Sweet Jesus! Sweet Jesus! Sweet Jesus!" as if anxious that we should receive the evidence of his Saviour's presence with him and the token he had just received from Him. It was like a ray of glory bursting through him upon our minds. . . . After this the occasional uttering of these words, "Sweet Jesus!" led us to think that his communion was more with the inhabitants of the heavenly world than with us, although he was most perfectly conscious of everything that passed up to the last moment. A little after one o'clock he uttered "Sweet Jesus! Sweet Redeemer!" and then "Farewell, farewell, farewell!" and, indistinctly, "I am going!" and thus expired, sweetly yielding up his spirit into the hands of his Redeemer.

Narcissa took great inspiration from this, knowing that if living a Christian life were impossible in this land, dying a Christian death was not. This was not a heavenly, aerial place, but one of waters; waters that took her child and her friends and bound them to its own purpose; waters on which every conceivable happiness and malignance might arrive and just as quickly be borne away; waters the natives believed in more strongly than eternal life; waters that spun them stories as their rivers spun them fish; waters without redemption, only an endless going round and round.

But one could die here well. God had made a portal in this godless place through which a woman could see heaven refracted through clear water. This realization freed her: to be drawn down into the river's metallic currents was, by a slight shift of one's vision, to be borne up into the golden light, into the white flesh of His bosom.

Narcissa saw the Indians less and less, or, in truth, simply paid them less attention. She was thirty-eight years old, her health remained frail, and her eyesight grew steadily weaker. The winter of 1846–47 was bottomlessly cold; the world was immobilized in ice, its motions frozen like waves and ripples in glass. She did not hear many complaints from the natives these days, although many had suffered or died in the cold, and she supposed their silence represented contentment. In any case, she was too busy with the needs of settlers—seventy had spent the winter at the mission—and her adopted children to pay attention to the Indians:

> I feel distressed sometimes to think that I am making so little personal effort for their benefit, when so much ought to be done, but perhaps I could not do more than I am through the family. . . . I have six girls sewing around me, or rather five—for one is reading, and the same time my baby is asking to go and bathe—she is two years the last of May, and her uneasiness and talk does not help me to many very profitable ideas. Now another comes with her work for me to fix. So it is from morning until evening; I must be with them or else they will be doing something they should not, or else not spending their time profitably.

Narcissa longed for something new and particular. She fixed her heart on bringing her sister, Jane, her brother, Edward, and perhaps even her parents west to the river. She had received little encouragement from them about this possibility, but she clung to it, having gone so far as to arrange a passage for her sister with another emigrant couple the previous year. On April 15, 1847, she wrote to Jane, whose letter dated March 27, 1846, she had just received:

Oh! how we wish you were here now, this very moment. It seems to me as if you would be happier than ever in your life before. Perhaps it is because I feel that I should be so, which makes me think that you would be; at any rate, I have every reason to feel that you would be far more so than where you are now. . . . Why did you not come with Mr. and Mrs. Thornton? Had you not the means? Oh! if you could only get here in some safe way, we would be willing to pay almost any price for bringing you. . . . Even now while I am writing I feel that perhaps my dear Jane and Edward are starting, or are on their way here. Oh! if I might indulge this feeling. I do, notwithstanding the improbabilities, and that, too, perhaps, to be disappointed.

. . . it is true, Jane, I love to sing just as well as ever. From what I have heard of Edward, it would be pleasant to hear him again; as for you, *kala tilapsa kunku* (I am longing for you continually to sing with), and it may be, put us all together, . . . we should make music such as would cause the Indians to stare.

In the summer, Narcissa took in more children, two half-breed boys. She heard, as though from a distance, about many deaths among the Indians by an epidemic of measles, about a Cayuse war party that had been routed in California, and about the chief's son being killed by whites. She saw thousands of wagons pass during the summer, or, rather, she saw them dimly through the thunderheads of dust created by their ceaseless passage. She heard nothing of emigration from any of her family.

In October she wrote to Jane, consigning another letter across the chasm that was three thousand miles wide, and a year deep:

Two men are at this place on their way to the States. One of them, Mr. Glenday, intends to return to this country next spring with his family. I have importuned him, and made an arrangement to have you accompany them to Wailatpu. Now Jane, will you do it? I know you will not refuse to come. At least I feel that you must and will come. I wrote you last spring and told you that I was expecting you and Edward this fall, and I have been looking for you in every company that have passed. But I have not seen you. . . .

Jane, there will be no use in your going home to see ma and pa before you come here—it will only make the matter worse with your heart. I want to see her as much as you. If you will all come here it will not be long before they will be climbing over the Rocky Mountains to see us. The love of parents for their children is very great. I see already in their movements, indications that they will ere long come this way. . . . Believe me, dear Jane, and come without fail, when you have so good an opportunity.

Farewell,

N. W.

3.

By the time Paul Kane reached the mission on July 18, 1847, he looked liked a castaway: his red beard draped his chest like a bib of Virginia creeper, his hair—surmounted by a seaman's cap with a narrow blue brim—unfurled itself to the four winds, and his clothes had been pounded colorless by dust, water, and ice. He looked, by the lights of some of the women, a little ungodly, although his speech and manners were quite polished. His eyes darted from place to place. When they rested, they stared; he seemed to see everything.

Kane came from Toronto but was of Irish birth. He carried a box of oil paints—white lead, Prussian blue, vermilion red, a brown of hematite, and yellow ocher—pencils, watercolors, and sundry pads, the largest ten by fourteen inches, with a marbled cover. He had pockets full of questions, and under his thicket of hair, a skull brimming over with birdcalls and animal lore. He said he had vagabonded through Italy some years ago in order to teach himself painting by copying the works of the masters. He thought it would be a fine idea to paint the Indians of the Far West before they were utterly domesticated or extinct.

Under the aid and protection of the Hudson's Bay Company, he had left Canada two years before, and crossed the mountains the previous November via the Athabasca Pass. Along the trail, stumps stood fifteen feet high, beheaded at snow level during winter crossings by David Thompson and his successors thirty years before. The snow was already twelve feet deep as Kane snowshoed down the western slope. He reeled from bank to bank of the Wood River and staggered into Boat Encampment. He sketched in pencil the great turn of the Columbia—broad, flat, and as gray as the blade of a scythe, the peaks and ridges leaning into one another like a tumbled stack of slates.

On November 15, Kane began traveling the thousand miles to Fort Vancouver and arrived two weeks before Christmas. In the first six months of 1847, he sketched and painted natives in their villages, lodges, and hunting and fishing encampments from Puget Sound to the Willamette Valley, but principally along the river. He worked fast, roughing out a likeness before his subject was much aware of being rendered, then finishing it with watercolor or oils at his leisure. He was an assiduous, encouraging listener to both voyageurs and natives, people whose tales belonged to a prior age that the American occupation was busily erasing.

By summer, he had his own stories as well as some notions about the river. Of the watercourse itself, he wrote:

> This river exceeds in grandeur any other perhaps in the world, not so much from its volume of water, although that is immense, as from the romantic wildness of its stupendous and ever-varying surrounding scenery, now towering into snow-capped mountains thousands of feet high, and now sinking in undulating terraces to the level of its pellucid waters.

Kane's description of the river was of a piece with language that might as easily evoke an image of the Alps or the headwaters of the

Nile—nature as spectacle, a thing seen through a proscenium arch, as though from outside. Kane could paint in this fashion, posing Indian bands like coveys of Florentine dukes around oaks of European muscularity, dappled in chiaroscuro. But there were things about the river that were not so easily understood or represented.

In his notebook, he did a little arithmetic: "Accidents on the Columbia River: Drowned at the Rapid St. Martin 2 / Dalles des Morts 2 / Grose Point 11 / Rapide de Prate 5 / La Shute 1 / Little Dalles 26 / Grand Dalles 15 / Cascades 4 / Portage New 2 / Total 68." These were incidents recalled by voyageurs. They did not include Alice Clarissa Whitman or the missionaries.

On another page, he recorded what seemed an extraordinary number of suicides along the river. A Walla Walla chief lost all his sons save one, and on this last son he lavished all his goods and knowledge. When this son died too, the chief had himself buried alive alongside him. A warrior near Kettle Falls shot himself when he had no more property to gamble with. Two sisters, wives of one man and each jealous of the other, went deep into the forest and hanged themselves. That was to say nothing of white people such as Asabel Munger.

Kane collected such lore wherever he could find it and wrote it down. About twenty-five or thirty years ago, there was a voyageur who killed his companions near the Dalles des Morts and made pemmican with their flesh. A little later, several canoes capsized in a rapid near Boat Encampment. A young naturalist and his bride-to-be were in one canoe; they were found dead in an embrace so strong their arms could not be unclasped, so they were buried entwined together. A dog had also washed up on the bank nearby. He held his master's cap between his teeth.

Kane became possessed by a fascination with the Indian graveyards on the river and made it his business to acquire a skull from one of them. He stole in among the poles that supported the elevated litters the dead lay on, removed a fine specimen with a flattened head, and secreted it in his luggage. It seemed the perfect emblem of the river. No one saw him, but that represented another imponderable: there was so much blindness among the people here. It was as inevitable as rain that, just as their teeth would erode to the gum line, their vision would eventually cloud: it would first diffuse to a borderless wash of neutral pigment and water, and then, invisibly and soundlessly, like the river grinding a stone, to an opacity of white as pure as bone.

Kane spent four days with the Whitmans. He made a sketch of the mission, which now occupied about forty acres and was ringed by herds of cattle, giving the impression, Kane thought, of a prosperous ranch. The house was constructed of adobe and shaped like a T with an upper half-story, and was finished with a whitewash made from river rock. The doors were green with gray trim and the floors were painted yellow. The house was full of children.

Whitman took him to the lodge of a Cayuse named Tomahas. Tomahas sat naked before him with an expression of stoic belligerence. He seemed unaware that Kane was drawing him until the sketch was nearly finished, and then asked to examine it. Scanning the portrait, he asked Kane if he intended to give it to the Americans, whom he loathed and whose power he had no wish to come under. Kane assured him it would not fall into their hands, but Tomahas was not convinced. He thrust the drawing into the fire, but Kane wrestled it away. Tomahas's face colored with fury, as though the sun were setting on the surface of his brow. It was a wrath the likes of which Kane had never seen. He fled to his horse and galloped back to the Whitmans.

He drew a likeness of the Cayuse chief Tiloukaikt without incident. Tiloukaikt sat motionless and didn't speak a word, as if in expectation, as if resigned to unspeakable things. A war party had left eighteen months ago to avenge the death of his son in California. Nothing had been heard of them. Kane inscribed lines on his pad, then slipped away without a sound.

At the mission, he sketched the Whitmans themselves. Whitman stood looking over his shoulder at Kane, a soft-brimmed hat pulled down over his head, his nose hooked downward, his chin angular, his eyes cool. He drew Narcissa in ink, seated at a table, one arm outstretched before her, the other cradling her head, a frieze of shadow zigzagging along its bend. Her neck was long, her lips full but expressionless, and her eyes gazed upward and leftward, as though fixed on heaven or some blissful emptiness. He made her look beautiful. Then he rendered a careful study of her fan, a slender thing fashioned by the natives from eagle feathers and strips of hide, and fastened by a broach of shell.

Kane came back to Walla Walla on July 22, just in time to hear that a messenger from the war party sent to California had returned. Kane raced to the Cayuse camp to observe his arrival and stood on a log, watching over the heads of an enormous crowd of Indians. The messenger stood for a long time in silence and the people surrounding him began to wail. At last, he began to recount the party's misfortunes and those of the Cayuse people in general: the sicknesses, the killings, the lies and betrayals. He uttered the names and stories of the dead, one by one. With the first name, a cry came up from the people; with the second and the third, the women loosened their hair and flung themselves on the ground. By the time the messenger reached the thirtieth name, two hours later, Kane was weeping.

At Walla Walla, it was feared that the extent of the bad feelings among the Indians might lead to retaliation against whites in the area, and particularly against Whitman, who seemed to them the source of every ill and calamity. Kane took it upon himself to warn the Whitmans, and rode for three hours at night, reaching the mission at 9:00 P.M. He pleaded with Whitman to take shelter at Walla Walla, at least until the Indians' current hysteria had abated. But Whitman was immovable and maintained that after spending so many years with the Indians and after doing so much for them, no harm could come to him. Kane faced down Whitman's unyielding certitudes for an hour, and then spurred his horse back to Walla Walla in the deepening night. He feared he might be killed, too. At the fort, with his paints, notebooks, pads, and the skull he had taken from the graveyard, he had sheet upon sheet of native portraits—faces the river people believed he had taken captive. Kane thought this was a ridiculous superstition, but the Indians had a logic of their own. What foolishness, they thought, to believe, as the white people seemed to, that words had any life apart from the stories they told; that images could be sundered like skins from the creatures that gave them existence. To carry the words and images away was to carry the things themselves away. For it to be otherwise would cleave the world in two.

Kane was crossing the height of the mountains on his way home when he heard what had passed at the mission on November 29. Five thousand whites had traveled by the Whitmans' that autumn, and the diseases they carried with them killed half the Cayuse people in their vicinity. Whitman's remedies were not efficacious, and the story spread that his medicine was designed to speed rather than retard the effects of the epidemic, and that if he were not killed quickly the Cayuse people would perish entirely. Sixty warriors came to the house that afternoon, lead by Tiloukaikt and Tomahas, who entered the kitchen. They told Whitman they had come to kill him. He insisted they would do no such thing. Tomahas removed a hatchet from beneath his robe and split Whitman's skull with it. They said afterward that this was necessary to release the evil spirits that dwelled in his head and so Whitman might at last hear what the Cayuse people said.

Narcissa dragged Whitman's body across the kitchen floor and into the sitting room. She fled upstairs. From a window she watched the Indians dance and chant. They began to break the windows of the house, then they killed the miller and the school-master. The son of Tiloukaikt saw her from below and shot her, but she did not die. She made her way back downstairs, blood flowering across the bodice of her dress. The Indians came back into the house and mutilated Whitman's face. Narcissa staggered to a sofa and two warriors carried her outside where the Cayuse women danced and sang the songs of the dead. The warriors could not decide what to do with her. One beat her head with a war club. Others cut her chest with knives and hatchets. At the end, when her God took pity on her and she saw and felt nothing more, she was dragged by her hair to a wallow of mud and her body rolled into it.

By dawn the next day, fourteen white people had been killed. A Roman Catholic priest who was on good terms with the Cayuse was allowed to say a funeral service in Latin. The bodies were laid together in a shallow grave, which wolves soon opened, dismembering the corpses and carrying them off into the yellow-eyed night.

Kane reached Toronto in October 1848 with more than five hundred sketches. He set to work painting. He sold a dozen pictures to the Hudson's Bay Company and a dozen more to the government of Ontario. He found a patron who ordered one hundred canvases. He painted things he had seen—the vast and dark interiors of native lodges on the river—as well as things he had not, such as Mount St. Helens in a pyrotechnic eruption, its billowing incandescence illuminating canoes of Indians on the river.

In the northwest, the country around the mission was opened to settlement in 1848, now that the government had determined that the Cayuse had lost title to their land by "forfeiture." In the same year, Congress established the Oregon Territory, which encompassed the land on both sides of the river from California to the forty-ninth parallel. The governorship of the new territory was offered to a defeated one-term congressman named Abraham

Lincoln. He refused it. The Cayuse who had killed the Whitmans traveled as fugitives for two years. Then in 1850, Tiloukaikt, Tomahas, and three other warriors were tried and hanged in Oregon City next to the falls of the Willamette. There were now twelve thousand white people in the Oregon Territory to applaud their execution; the native population had dwindled from an estimated fifty thousand in 1800 to perhaps one thousand.

In 1853 Kane married, and in the next few years his paintings were exhibited at Buckingham Palace and printed as chromolithographs. He published an account of his travels in 1859, which he called *Wanderings of an Artist Among the Indians of North America.* He was by this time English Canada's first and most eminent artist. But his sight had begun to fail him years before—he told people his eyes had undergone permanent damage in the northwest—and he rarely painted anymore. Aspiring painters came to his house to ask for instruction. He opened the door wide enough to refuse them, then closed it fast. He retired to his library chair, his jaw wreathed in a scarlet beard now tipped with silver like a fox's pelt, and sat, surrounded by books full of natural and religious lore that he could scarcely read, and images that he could scarcely see.

4.

Hall Kelley had been to the Columbia River for just a moment, but that is of no consequence. Long before he went there, he drank down the river until he could taste its bones, and then the river drank him. The river was in his mind, and ran more deeply and broadly there than anyone could imagine. By the end of his life, Americans had traveled the river from the Snake to the sea, and they had made their homes on its verge. The Americans were there because Kelley saw that they ought to be there.

The gray tissues of Kelley's brain curved and twisted around themselves, like the gray band of the river itself—turning, wrapping itself into eddies and whirlpools, yet bent on one course. Like an idea that is too powerful to be grasped, no ordinary person could see this whole course from a single place or in a single moment. But Kelley saw it, and he was paid dearly in treachery and venom for his vision. Someone, like a prophet or an angel, had to utter the word that is the river and make it flesh. He was that man, and he and the word are one thing:

> I am Hall J. Kelley; that is my name; am what education, habits, and the *grace* of God have made me, and have a disposition punctiliously to perform every duty in life. *Stupid, ignorant and crazy;* I have often been spoken of in this way; not to my face, but in whispers, and where slander can best succeed in doing its work. These opprobrious appellatives were applied to me in public journals, and from the mouth of calumny, when all devoted to the cause of humanity; when planning and effecting great and good things for the people of my country. I will give a list of some of them. How far they indicate mental imbecility or derangement, the candid, who know about the *founding* of the *settlements* on the American shores of the Pacific, the system of fair and merciful dealing with the Indians of North America, devised by me, and my handy works on both sides of the Continent, at every place of my abode in New England, in the wilderness and on the Island of the sea, all along, from youth to old age, can judge.

Kelley must speak slowly, for he does not write these words, but dictates them to an amanuensis. His enemies have deprived him not only of his reputation, his worldly goods, and the affection of his family, but also of his sight, his capacity to speak clearly, and the balance of his mind. They have even insinuated themselves among amanuenses, who, under the guise of carelessness or inattention, warp his words. The world takes advantage of the befuddlement and frailty that has afflicted him, and yet the truth of things grows clearer each day. There is so much to tell.

It is 1866, and he is working on a volume called *A History of the Settlement of Oregon and the Interior of Upper California and of the Persecutions and Afflictions of Forty Years' Continuance Endured by the Author, Hall J. Kelley, A.M.* It is the third recitation of the facts of Kelley's life, which, briefly, are these: He was born in 1790 in New Hampshire and attended Middlebury College and Harvard University. He published a textbook called *The American Instructor,* which garnered him a comfortable income and the means to acquire land in and around Boston. Kelley devoted himself to worthwhile if ultimately unrealized public projects: the establishment of a Massachusetts Seminary of Arts and Sciences; the founding of the Penitent Female Refuge Society; and the provision of universal Sunday school education.

But in the early 1820s, he read Biddle's edition of the journals of Lewis and Clark, and his life was transformed. By the end of the decade, he was entirely consumed by the idea of an American settlement of the Columbia River country. He wrote letters to eminent people and lobbied officials in Washington, D.C., in quest of its furtherance, and in 1829 founded the American Society for Encouraging the Settlement of the Oregon. In 1830 he published the pamphlet *A Geographical Sketch of that Part of North America called Oregon,* which commended the region to settlers:

> The Oregon Country is well watered. Its rivers are numerous; some of them are large and navigable; nearly all of them unite their copious tributes to form the grand *Columbia.* This river is one of the largest in North America, and will become the most *valuable* on this continent; valuable, because it is conveniently interspersed with extensive and fertile islands, and abounds with fish of the best kinds; *valuable,* because it is in the center of the commercial and trading world—opens into a valuable country, connects every part of it, by natural canals, and is navigable for vessels of large burden, all seasons of the year, free of ice, or any other obstruction.

He had never seen the river, but he had read every word ever written about it, and the conclusions he drew from his reading were so obvious as to render direct experience superfluous. Surely no one knew more about the river. He scrutinized its texts and contemplated its mysteries like a monk in his cloister. He saw how its first name, "Oregon," came from China; how its inhabitants were descendants of the lost tribes of Israel; how repellently beautiful its women were; how, based on his study of the histories of Admiral Fonte and Juan de Fuca, the United States' title to the northwest was unimpeachable.

Within a year, Kelley wrote a circular inviting potential colonists to join an overland expedition to "the delightful and fertile banks of the Columbia River." He sought out "persons to fill the civil, military and literary rolls . . . persons possessing a scientific knowledge of the different branches of mathematics and natural philosophy," as well as shipwrights, carpenters, blacksmiths, tanners, hatters, and tailors. He enrolled five hundred would-be settlers and announced that the party would leave for "the most valuable of all the unoccupied parts of the earth" on January 1, 1832.

But the bulk of the party members abandoned their plans, and the expedition never set off. Articles in journals such as the *New England Magazine* suggested that the entire venture was dangerous and foolhardy, despite Kelley's apparent sincerity:

> When we consider the dangers and hardships which he, as well as those he may delude, must undergo; when we think of the risk he has run, and still runs, of being sent to the insane hospital; when we reflect on his certain disappointments, and the ridicule he will incur by it, we are constrained to believe that disinterested benevolence is his motive. We are informed that this excellent person has now a list of the names of many hundred persons who receive his dreams as oracles.

Elsewhere, the press was less kind. The *Old American Comic Almanac* published a cartoon portraying the Columbia as the "Salt River" and the country around it as "Kelley's folly."

But not all of Kelley's original party were dissuaded. A few, led by the New England ice merchant Nathaniel Wyeth, formed their own expedition and trapped furs in the Oregon country, but founded no real settlement there. Kelley himself reformulated his plans and organized a small group that left New York in November 1832. He wrote to the secretary of state to inform the government of his intentions and of the unswerving purpose to which he had set his mind:

> For this *object*, I have left to the care of friends, an affectionate wife and three small children. I have denied myself for a season all social and domestic enjoyments; and am the subject of suffering privations, and great hardships; and, finally, for this *object*, I now live, or if its accomplishment requires the sacrifice I am ready to give myself a martyr.

By the time Kelley reached New Orleans he had been robbed and swindled by two of his companions, Foster and Lovett, and he traveled on to Mexico alone by ship. He lost a great deal of his provisions on board, and still more to the rapacious Mexican customs authorities. The victim of more robberies, frauds, and attacks on the trail, he arrived in San Diego, Alta California, in April 1834.

That summer, Kelley joined a party bound for Oregon headed by a trapper and trader named Ewing Young, and he reached the river on October 27, 1834. He was treated decently at Fort Vancouver, but without Dr. McLoughlin's customary hospitality and warmth. McLoughlin had received a letter from General Figueroa, the governor of California, informing him of a band of horse thieves operating out of California. Kelley was supposed to be one of them. For the next four months, except when hospitalized in the company's infirmary, he lay sick in a cabin outside the walls of the fort. He was indignant, tired, and, insofar as his writings reveal, oblivious to the river he had sought for so long.

He returned to New England by way of Hawaii in the spring of 1835, and reached his home in 1836. Thereafter, Kelley devoted himself to the organization of another expedition to the northwest, but it came to nothing. He applied to Congress for land grants in the territory but was ignored. He put together proposals for railways and canals in New York State and Panama but found no supporters. He then retired from public life at his house in Three Rivers, Massachusetts. His wife had abandoned him and fled with his children.

In the 1840s, when American settlement in the Oregon Territory became a reality, Kelley petitioned Congress for some recognition of his role in the matter, and asked for a small stipend. But there was no response. He calculated he spent about $50,000 on his efforts to settle Oregon, and he wrote Daniel Webster in 1842 to see if Congress might award him perhaps one-tenth of that amount. But when his name was mentioned in public in the coming years, it was not as the Moses of Oregon. In 1847 *The Rambler* considered the impending resolution of the boundary dispute between the United States and Britain, and the dubious value of the lands to which the nation would now take title:

> Some twenty years ago, a crack-brained schoolmaster of Boston named Kelly [*sic*], got up an excitement about Oregon in the New England States. . . . We have not learned, however, that either Kelly or any of his believers have realized any part of their expectations. From all we can learn, we believe that not a man has emigrated to the Columbia who has not bitterly rued his folly.

The house at Three Rivers is by this time in a state of some dilapidation. It has never been a building of much elegance: the ceilings vary in height and lean crazily; the floors pitch at angles like the deck of a ship at sea; and boulders, unidentifiable species of apple trees, and poison ivy dot the grounds. As for Kelley himself, he is half-blind, his hands shake, and at times he can scarcely speak without his sentences shattering into an indecipherable heap of fragments and stammers. He is poor and bereft of family, friends, and reputation, but "I live on, like some aged oak, lonely, on some bleak summit, withstanding storms and tempests, and smitten by thunderbolts, a branchless trunk."

He can still respond "in tones of thunder" to his enemies and their calumnies, although every phrase is an exhausting labor, a summit to be conquered. It has always been this way: he recalls that, even twenty years before, "at times of mental excitement and nervous irritation, I almost lost the physical ability of speech and was scarcely able to converse or write upon any subject, however familiar." His trials in attempting to settle the river only made matters worse:

> As a consequence of it all, my head is confused, and that con-
> tinually; and I cannot help it. Thoughts at times enter the mind
> disorderly. That which should come first, comes last, and the
> last first. . . . Language is broken and diffuse, without imagery
> or beauty or any rhetorical embellishment. . . . I copy and copy,
> again and again, and sometimes the last copy is worse than the
> first. I think my head and heart are full of thoughts, original,
> great and good.

There is a light of revelation in it, and as the words overwhelm him they also illuminate the truth; it is as though they strike him dumb with their clarity. In the heat of the summer afternoon he can hardly think at all, and the amanuensis vexes him. But then the reasons for things open up before him like flowers, and he must race to find the words and get them down and make his book:

> The nervous affection has increased—am more slow of speech—
> more slow of apprehension. Have nearly lost at times the physi-
> cal ability to compose, and am more liable to inadvertent
> speaking. Can prepare no more than thirty or forty lines of
> manuscript for the press in a day. . . . Will pass over, for the
> present, particular mention of wonderful interpositions of Di-
> vine Providence, of deliverance from the hands of bloody men,

of hair-breadth escapes from the rifle, from the jaws of wild beasts, from the stings of scorpions, and from the fangs and venom of serpents. I say I must curtail this book, and haste to make it ready for the consideration of Congress and the people of my country.

From the late 1840s to the middle of the 1860s, Kelley sees more and more the way things were, and the truth pours out of him like a stream emerging from a chasm, spreading out pellucid and still onto the plain. He remembers himself as a boy, "serious minded" by upbringing and innate disposition. He began to leave his fellows and his pastimes behind, and to walk alone. He lost himself in books, and so began the affliction of his optic nerves that would destroy his sight. In college, he fashioned a machine that exactly traced the circuits of the moons, stars, and planets; he predicted the times and situations of eclipses; and he proved the impossibility of perpetual motion. And then came the revelation:

> [I was] divinely appointed to do the very things I conceived and did for Oregon. In the year 1817 "the word came expressly to me.". . . In my youth the Lord Jesus revealed to me in visions the lonely, laborious and eventful life I was to live; and gave me at the time of the visions, and afterwards, unmistakable signs that the revelations were by Him, and I have lived exactly that manner of life.

If only his plans had been carried out as he envisioned them:

> Oregon would have teemed with a population from our own blest country, and the whole wilderness between the parallels 31 and 54, dark as it was, ere this day, would have been changed to shining fields and flowery gardens; and society there would have been dressed in lovely attire, and robed in charms of moral beauty.

But it was not to be. As early as 1824, powerful men in the hire of the Hudson's Bay Company set out to destroy him with a secret fund of $800,000 at their disposal:

> To accomplish their designs, and prevent mine, and to make an end of my project, they raised an army in the city of Boston, and afterwards in '27 enlisted troops in the cities of New York and Washington, and in '29 raised a more bloody troop in the village of Three Rivers, to which place I had just removed my family. . . . They watched every movement of mine, pursuing me from city to city, laying every plan to vex and worry me, to alienate friends and turn them from and against me, and to discourage those who had enlisted for Oregon (several hundred had enlisted) and to turn them from their purpose.

When he at last thwarted the minions of the company and set off for the river in 1833, they sent Foster and Lovett, their confidence men, to dog him and do whatever was necessary to prevent his "heaven-planned undertakings." They played on his generosity, and as soon he had dismissed them, they begged to rejoin his expedition. Thus, they plagued him with robbery and fraud across the Gulf to the pestilences of Vera Cruz (where he saved hundreds of lives by dispensing medicine drawn from his own dwindling supply) and through the wastes of Mexico, conspiring with bandits to strip him of every possession.

If they could not kill him, the company intended to drive him insane by "overstraining the thalami of the brain," blinding his eyes, and addling his thought and speech with "persecutions as cruel as man ever endured, since the nativity of Jesus Christ." Yet when surely his hope must fail, he received comfort. In a camp with Ewing Young's hunters not far from the southern tributaries of the river in Oregon, "an angel came to comfort me," saying:

> "Cheer up, be not afraid. Balm and a physician are here. God is thy helper, and he will deliver thee." In the solitude of that wilderness, where none but Indians and hunters had roamed—

at that still moment, I heard from a short distance, that shrill voice, so often heard in *civilized lands*—even the voice of a cockerel, a *domestic* bird, a chieftain among his race, so wont to celebrate his own triumphs, now loudly crowing, as though exulting in the triumphs of my enterprise, and proclaiming, "Now it is achieved; now, *in this wilderness,* is fixed thy abode of *civilization;* now, and henceforth, my voice and the voice of the turtle-dove shall be heard in this land."

Kelley arrived at the river a few weeks later, and met the beast that was the Hudson's Bay Company in its lair. Dr. McLoughlin "was kept informed of my movements in the States. . . . The persecuting monster, anticipating my coming to the place of his abode, was ready, with sword in hand, to cut me down; and, I was treated, at and after my arrival, with every demonstration of inhumanity." He was confined to a squalid shack whose putrescent odor betrayed its former use as an abattoir.

He lay sick and delirious for months. Men from the company stole into his room and broke into Kelley's trunk of wild-bull's hide, making off with documents and maps that conclusively proved American title to the river. Others, under the guise of nursing him back to health, gave him pills, but the pills were poison and took their effect over many years, debilitating his health and clouding his mind. Kelley learned that the company was an old hand at such business. A sick Indian, on the threshold of death and no longer fearful of the consequences of revealing the company's secrets, was put in the shack to die and confided in Kelley: "He had been a clerk to the physician, and employed in compounding medicines—had made lots of pills—made two kinds, black and white. The former were for sick Indians and were fatal in their effects."

Kelley at last secured passage to Hawaii on a ship captained by a drunken, swinish lout under orders from the company to deprive him of every civilized comfort. His cabin was taken over by the captain and an Indian woman who indulged themselves in debaucheries without "parallel upon the pure waters of the Columbia"; sailors spat on his bed and clothes; and he was fed sturgeon from a filthy pot, cold salt beef, and "a pudding composed of flour and mashed potatoes, half-baked and clammy—all without plate, knife, or fork."

From Hawaii, he sailed to the United States on a China clipper around the Horn, but his trials did not cease when he arrived home. The company succeeded in alienating his wife and children from his affections, and in getting libels and calumnies against his character widely published. Now, even in his retirement, they seek to destroy his reputation and to diminish his accomplishments, including the discovery of gold in California and the subsequent immigration of Americans into that territory; the conception and planning of the transcontinental railway; and, not least, the settlement of the Columbia:

> ... the foundation of the NATION's EXCHANGE ... a structure to be of stupendous magnitude, whose lofty dome, ere long, reflecting the effulgent light beaming from the highest heavens, will be seen from the darkest and most distant parts of the earth.

They break into his house and steal his manuscript pages as soon as they are written and hide the documents he is working from. But such hindrances only force him deeper into his mind, where the pure ore of truth lies undisturbed and gleaming. And his trials, "without a parallel in the present age of the world," are joys:

> They have, indeed, reduced me to a very suffering condition—such as men, looking at external appearances only, and incapable of discerning things spiritual, would think indescribably deplorable—but I am not "distressed"—*have never been "distressed"*—I rejoice, rather than grieve, that I am made a partaker in the sufferings of Christ.

Jesus went into the wilderness to steel himself for his passion, to learn the ways of death in death's own habitation. Then he brought his truth to the wilderness of men's hearts, and they reviled him and killed him. Kelley walked that road. He went to the river to wrest it away from the wilderness, to illuminate it, and to convenant it to his fellows. But it was their darkness and blindness that destroyed him. Is there any wickedness in nature that can compare to the deeds of men and women? They are the authors of their own nature, and they follow its narrative to the inexorable ends they write for themselves. The wilderness—the forest and the river—supplies only the bare fact of suffering and death; it is men and women who shape and adorn it to their thousand purposes. There has been little peace in Kelley's life, and what little he did have was the gift of nature:

> During the sea voyage of six months on board the ship *Canton Packet,* every fair day and moonlight night, my attention was turned to explorations of the starry heavens, and the abstruse regions of science; and all the while continued to study the book of nature, and that interesting little book ever in my hand, open and read with intense desire to know God and his handiworks.

The house at Three Rivers was once like a ship, embattled, but the only bulwark Kelley knew. Now it is something else. It sags a little more each day, the doors heave imperceptibly in their frames, and the walls shed their paint. Outside, the garden unravels itself into a forest and presses against the windows, threading shoots and tendrils into the casements. Kelley is oblivious to this, or, rather, he has made oblivion his home. In his blindness, he sees, and he writes his book in this wilderness and inhabits it— a shelter built of words in the woods, a place fit to die in. In the winter of 1874, he is found paralyzed on the floor of his house, curling concave upon himself like a dry, fallen leaf.

CHAPTER 4

Priests

1.

A t Priest Rapids there was nothing but the river. Behind the village, the cliffs mounted up in overlapping pyramids, in dense ebony heaps like the paws and heads of sleeping dogs, blocking off access from the west. Across the river, there was a barren plain of sand. The banks sheltered only snakes, and the land beyond was a runeless slate. The people at Priest Rapids drank and ate from the river and built their lodges from the rushes that grew in its sloughs. And when they looked into the river, they saw the heart of the world. They called themselves the Wanapum: the River People.

Priest Rapids was not one rapid, but seven, a sacred number, and surely God made himself felt nowhere else on the river as he did here. Once, before he made land to float upon it like boats on the sea, there was only water. And so Priest Rapids was a window, a rent in the earth's garment through which creation's naked essence might be glimpsed, the artery through which its plasma coursed. The rocks, islands, and banks were an archipelago, stars in the indigo of an infinitude of water.

There was no starting or ceasing here, no rest or silence. The water made a roar, like a wind with no origin or end, and beneath it the sounds of a thousand motions were knit together: of rocks turning and shifting and grinding; of water purling and slapping; and the soundings of fish, the undulations of wings, the rasp of scales, the keening of coyotes, and waves of drumbeats and infant's cries breaking against the night. All life was in this chasm, its manifold psalms and lamentations, tumbling against itself and boiling over, chaotic yet entirely inflected in one direction westward.

Living here, seeing so many things so deeply, the Wanapum were a people apart. They had no use for war with their neighbors and they easily shared what wealth they had with strangers, Indian and white. They danced for David Thompson; and it was Thompson's erstwhile rival from Astoria, Alexander Ross, who named their home Priest Rapids after he saw a Wanapum holy man standing on the bank with people who were picking up rattlesnakes and stroking the serpents' heads. In their village, which they called P'Na, the Wanapum slept, sang, and cooked in lodges made of reed mats laid over frames, less the form of houses than of the hulls of ships, capsized and grounded on this fruitless and brushy shoal. But Priest Rapids seemed to abound with little wonders—not so much marvelous as incongruous—and, with every generation, brought forth shamans, dreamers, prophets, and teachers.

They say that not long before the whites—the *suyapos* ("the greedy ones")—came, there lived an old priest. It was a time of plenty among the Wanapum: salmon seemed to throw themselves, iridescent and fat, into fish traps or onto spears. Sated and lazy, the people ceased to be mindful of blessings granted them and of the acts of remembrance and thanks that were the earth's due. The old priest tried to warn them that their complacency jeopardized all this good fortune—that the animal people who inhabited the world before the Indians had perished in the flood through just such heedlessness—but, deaf in their prosperity, they did not hear him.

Perhaps being old and parched, the priest could not raise his voice loud enough to rouse them from their forgetfulness. In any case, only a little boy paid him any mind. The two sat on the bank, on the rocks whose dusky opacities gathered in the heat and chill of the seasons. The world thundered down the river. They talked through many moons, and the old man taught the boy everything he knew about the old ways. They talked through moons in which the salmon came up the river and spread themselves in tides of carrion along its banks, and ravens bustled and cursed among their heaped-up flesh; moons when geese flew overhead in arrow-headed streams, their bleats waning southward like the beats of a broken heart; and moons when the moon itself was a brooch of ice suspended in a sky airless with cold, the days glazed and frangible with breath condensed to mist, the people, shoulder pressed against shoulder, encircling the fire, like children to the breast.

By the time he was done, the old priest's voice had grown soft and desiccated, as though his stories had been wrung out of him until none were left. Then he died, and, as was their custom, the people buried him in a canoe, facing west on a bluff above the river, and covered it with stones. They set fire to his lodge, the flames amber, the smoke an ivory fog. With the priest dead, they had no medicine against evil, and so they moved the entire village some distance up the rapid, fearing that whatever took the priest might still linger in that place.

Soon the boy was a young man and already past the time when he was considered ready to make his vision quest. Traditionally, Wanapum children sought their guardian spirits and their power songs on Saddle Mountain, a long and lofty escarpment that traversed the river north of Priest Rapids. But the young man put a canoe into the river, and it bore him to the sacred island, the first land that God made when he took mud and made a woman's body that became the earth and which birthed every creature that lives under the sun.

The young man took no water or food. He carried rocks around the island until his muscles quaked and let the sun sear his flesh and lap the moisture from his mouth until he was faint. Then he waited. Out of the night, or perhaps through the curtain of heat that rippled up from the bank, a buck of enormous size waded ashore, its antlers cresting in seven points.

When the boy returned to P'Na he had what his people called "the power": He had songs, stories, and lightning in his bones. He could see into things, heal the sick, and summon fish to his people's nets and elk to their bows. He had a name now, too: Shuwapsa. And he became chief of the Wanapum. He taught his people to honor the salmon and the other foods as they arrived each year and to make those observances and memorials that would ensure their return in the future.

Shuwapsa had a pole erected outside his lodge on which it was said God left him messages on pieces of buckskin. Thus he saw the white men coming, first as wanderers through the land and then as hunters with goods to trade; next would come those who dealt in the white man's god, some dressed like traders, some in black robes. After that, the white god would surge over the land like a shoal of clouds bellied in ashes, and his people would follow in their thousands and suck the very marrow from the earth.

From the pieces of buckskin, Shuwapsa knew these things and more; visions that were now invisible, stories that were ineffable, but that his people would someday require. He entrusted them to his son Sohappy, who was to succeed him as chief. Then around the time the white fur hunters came into the country, Shuwapsa died.

Sometime later, Sohappy led his people into the mountains to gather huckleberries in the high subalpine parks at summer's end.

For safekeeping, Sohappy's wife hid the prophecies in some rocks near P'Na, but when the Wanapum returned, she could not find the cache. For months, she scoured the riverbanks and rummaged through her memory, as though sieving sand for a mote of glass. Finding nothing, she lost her mind for shame and grief, and hanged herself.

For a decade or more, the prophecies lay in some fissure by the river, and then like seeds it seemed they germinated and blossomed, and launched their spores and fruit into the wind and into every corner of the country: after the fur traders came white priests and shamans like Marcus Whitman, who headed processions of *suyapo*s and spread pestilences among the Indians. Despite that, prompted by other prophecies that ascribed great power to the white people's Book, many native people adopted the new religion, and those that learned the new stories and sang the new songs became known as "Book Indians."

For a time the Indians and whites tried to live together, to make sense of each other, and they traded words as they once traded beads and furs. But although they surely wanted the same things—food, health, peace—it seemed impossible to bring them about. Frustration turned to paralysis and thence to fury, and it was as though each realized they must destroy the other; as though the natives brought the flame and the whites brought the fuel and together they made a pyre at Wailatpu in 1847 and set it alight. The smoke swelled like the chorus of a hymn and beat itself aloft on ravens' wings, a plainsong of nullity.

Scarcely had the embers of the Whitman mission ceased to hiss and the bloated corpses been laid to rest when the whites insisted there be more talk. Amid the cinders and ruin of the mission grounds, a council was called to dissuade other Indian peoples of the region from joining the Cayuse, who were now in open war against the whites. The whites were determined that no other tribes rebel against them, and if talk failed, force would be applied. The Indians feared what might befall them, but they dressed in their finest clothes and painted their horses as though it were a great occasion. A chief of the Nez Percé, Tuekakas, whose son would be known as Chief Joseph, held aloft a Bible translated into Sahaptian by the missionaries and spoke:

> When I left my home, I took the book in my hand and brought it with me. It is my light. I heard the Americans were coming to kill me. Still, I held the book before me and came on.

Yet faith and the succor of the gospel would not suffice. The American military authorities explained that the white god required propitiation:

> The laws of God have been broken here on this ground. Look at those walls, see how black they are, look at the large grave. He is angry at those people who broke His laws and spilt innocent blood.

The chiefs promised to maintain their neutrality and there was peace for a while. Yet even those Indians who made no pretense of believing in him were given to understand that the white god was angry, and that his anger would justify whatever action his people decided to take. Like the *suyapos* themselves, he claimed to be a god of words, reason, and immutable law, but as deep as his capacity for utterance was his hunger, so manifest in his anger. He might, as the Book said, speak and in his love bring forth the world, but he might also consume it whole in his rage.

In 1853 and 1854, soldiers and government officials came into the river country to survey a path for a railway that would connect the upper Midwest with the Puget Sound. At first it seemed the white men required only a narrow right-of-way for the tracks. But the head of the surveying party was Isaac Stevens, a small, lupine man with a large head, who had also seized for himself the positions of territorial governor and superintendent of Indian affairs for Washington Territory. He had more in mind than a railway line. In the summer of 1854, he sent messengers to the major peoples of the territory—the Yakima, Walla Walla, Umatilla, Klikitat, and Nez Percé—to call them to a council for the purpose of making a treaty to buy their lands and to grant them reservations. If they agreed to conclude such a treaty, they would be treated fairly by the great father in Washington City; if they refused, their lands would be confiscated by force and without compensation.

Under the leadership of the Yakima chief Kamiakin, the heads of the tribes met beforehand in the Grande Ronde Valley in northeastern Oregon and devised what they believed would be a foolproof negotiating strategy: each chief would independently demand his people's entire traditional territory as a reservation. If every single chief stuck unswervingly to this course, there could be no transfer of lands to the *suyapos*, since all the lands would be claimed as reservations. The whites would be thwarted with their own rules.

Stevens, however, was more a man of words than the chiefs. He knew the art of negotiation as a warrior knows his horse, and he could turn words round in midgallop and bend them to his will; lay ambushes and feints with them; turn them from one thing to another; and call them forth from other men's mouths as though their tongues were under his command. They fluttered around him like birds and alighted on his hand in order that he might stroke their breasts.

Stevens had a spy among the chiefs at the Grande Ronde council named Hollolsotetote, a Nez Percé chief with such an affinity for cultivating white authority that he was known by the name Lawyer. By the time of the council at Walla Walla in June 1855, Stevens was fully apprised of the Indian strategy. His own plan was to say as little as possible, communicating through his subordinates, and when he did speak, to deal in honeyed generalities; to let a dearth of words where the Indians expected many to discomfit them; to let uncertainty undo the chiefs' resolve.

For a week they smoked and Stevens's surrogates palavered: the great father in Washington was anxious to make the Indians his children, to provide for them, to show his affection with gifts. Stevens had a log stockade filled with provisions and bestowed a ration of four pounds of beef a day on each chief. He sized up their resistance and made notes, describing Kamiakin's character as being both "the panther and the grizzly bear":

> His countenance has an extraordinary play, one moment in frowns, the next in smiles, flashing with light and black as Erebus the same instant.

When Stevens himself spoke it was as a supplicant who, having confessed his innermost thoughts and desires, only sought an equal measure of good faith and sincerity from his opposite number. With eerie skill, he adapted the metaphors and rhetorical colors of Indian speech to his purposes. Again and again he implored, "My brothers, we want your hearts today. Let us have your hearts straight out."

In truth, the chiefs had been told very little of substance, but before that fact could become too apparent, Lawyer arose as Stevens had prearranged with him and spoke an appeal to history: "Long ago, the white men passed through our country and became acquainted with our country and all our streams, and our forefathers treated them well, as well as they could." Turning to Stevens, Lawyer continued, "From the time of Lewis and Clark we have known you, my friends; we poor people have known you as brothers."

With that he declared he would sign the treaty and urged his fellows to do the same. Stevens addressed the room magisterially: "We have the heart of the Nez Perces through their chief. Their hearts and our hearts are one. We want the hearts of the other tribes through their chiefs."

Their plan was in disarray and the Indians could not comprehend what had happened. The chief of the Cayuse spoke:

I am blind and ignorant. I have a heart but cannot say much in words. This is the reason why the chiefs do not understand each other and stand apart. Although I see your offer before me, I do not understand it and do not yet take it; I walk as in the dark and therefore cannot take hold of what I do not see.

Indian superintendent Joel Palmer replied for Stevens:

We come to open your eyes, and you refuse the light. . . . We have not come to steal your land; we offer more than it is worth, because our great father told us to take care of the red people. We come to you with his message to try to do you good.

Palmer and Stevens's frustration was growing more evident as they tried to explain the inevitability of what they proposed. Palmer pressed the chiefs:

Can you stop the waters of the Columbia from flowing on its course? Can you prevent the wind from blowing? Can you prevent the rain from falling? Can you prevent the whites from coming? You are answered no! Like the grasshoppers on the plains, some years there will be more come than others, but you cannot stop them. Our chief cannot stop them. We cannot stop them.

Still, there was no movement among the chiefs. Was the Indian position the product of intransigence or ignorance, or was it some inscrutable ploy? But Owhi, a Yakima chief, confessed a misapprehension that went beyond misunderstanding; that surpassed mere perception and was rooted like some primordial mass deep in the foundations of the world; a story that seemed familiar to Stevens, yet had been transformed into something wholly alien to his purposes:

God gave us the day and night, the night to rest in, and the day to see, and that as long as the earth shall last, he gave us the morning with our breath; and so he takes care of us on this earth and here we have met under his care. In the earth before the day or the day before the earth. God was before the earth, the heavens were clear and good and all things in the heavens were good. God looked one way then the other and named our lands for us to take care of. God made the other. We did not make the other, we did not make it, he made it to last forever. . . .

This leads the Indian to ask where does this talk come from that you have been giving us. God made this earth and it listens to him to know what he would decide. The almighty made us and gave us breath; we are talking together and God hears all that we say today. God looks down upon his children today as if we were all in one body. He is going to make one body of us; we Indians present have listened to your talk as if it came from God. But God named this land to us—that is the reason I am afraid to say anything. I am afraid of the almighty.

The chiefs asked that the council be recessed, and during the days that followed they were plied individually by the white agents, who promised them tools, mills, houses, and annual stipends for each chief who signed the treaty. Some began to fear that if they put Stevens off, they would get nothing for themselves or their people even as they shared Owhi's concern that in signing they would commit a grave transgression. Stevens addressed them:

Owhi is afraid, lest God be angry at his selling his land. Owhi, my brother, I do not think God will be angry with you if you do the best for yourself and your children. Ask yourself this question, "Will not God be angry with me if I neglect this opportunity to do them good?". . . The treaty will be drawn up tonight. You can see it tomorrow. The Nez Perces must not be put off any longer. This business must be dispatched. I hope all other hearts and ours will agree.

Such cohesion as still existed among the chiefs melted in the night. In the morning, as the last holdouts were preparing to put their marks on the treaty, the Nez Percé war chief Looking Glass arrived and saw what had transpired. He howled in pity and betrayal: "My people, what have you done? While I was gone, you sold my country. I have come home and there is no place left where I can pitch my lodge."

It was to no avail. The last mark, that of a Klikitat chief named Sla-Kish or Slockish, was appended to the treaty. When the council was done, the Indians had given up sixty thousand square miles of territory in exchange for three reservations, $500 annual annuities for their chiefs, and the promise of wagons, plows, hoes, blankets, axes, bridles, and provisions whose value was put by the white officials at $650,000. Privately, Stevens had told the most recalcitrant chiefs that "if they refused to sell, soldiers would be sent to wipe them off the earth." In his report, he noted only that "The council ended in a most satisfactory manner."

By the summer's end the war had come, boiling up the river like a thunderbank from the Yakima country. White miners had raped native women and Kamiakin led an alliance of his own people together with warriors from the Sinkiuse and Klikitat in retaliation, killing a group of six miners and an Indian agent once regarded as a friend. When the white authorities responded, the Indians routed a company of more than one hundred infantrymen and its commanding general. Sensing their advantage, the Walla Walla, Cayuse, and Palouse threatened to join the rebellion, and the Spokanes and Nez Percé weighed their options. The response of the whites was divided: the army, believing that white settlement was untenable in such an explosive atmosphere, favored an immediate halt to immigration and a defensive strategy designed to encourage negotiation, including redrafting the Walla Walla treaties; Stevens, however, wanted the Indians crushed and confined to their reservations, and the country immediately re-opened to whites without restriction.

So it was when Kamiakin unexpectedly proposed a negotiated and therefore to Stevens, unacceptable, peace, he compelled Maj. Gabriel Rains, an army officer, to compose a response in words such as he might himself utter; uncanny twins to what a native might say, as though Stevens had enslaved and mastered the Indians' speech along with their lands:

> We will not be quiet, but war forever, until not a Yakima breathes in the land he calls his own. The river only will we let retain this name to show to all people that here the Yakimas once lived. . . . Your people shall not catch salmon hereafter for you, for I will send soldiers to occupy your fisheries, and fire upon you. Your cattle and your horses, which you got from the white man, we will hunt up and kill and take them from you. The earth which drank the blood of the white man, shed by your hands, shall grow no more wheat nor roots for you, for we will destroy it. . . .
>
> The whites are as the stars in the heavens, or the leaves in the trees in summer time. Our warriors in the field are many, as you must see; but if not enough, a thousand for every one more will be sent to hunt you, and to kill you; and my kind advice to you, as you will see, is to scatter yourselves among the Indian tribes more peaceable, and there forget you were ever Yakimas.

The annihilation came, albeit over many winters. The first was bitterly cold and forced both belligerents to retire to their camps. In the summer of 1856 and in the following two years, the white army gained control of the country, not by engaging the Indians in battle but by filling it with forts and troops whose numbers hemmed in the Indians and rendered their offensives pointless.

Neither side could conclusively win or lose, and the war did its work through a kind of erosion. It pressed, lightly and insistently, like the slow steady force of wind or water or weight, until there was neither peace nor victory, but only a stasis in which everything that birthed the war endured motionless, wreckage rusting at the speed of God's heartbeat. The Nez Percé, whose participation might have tipped the balance, remained neutral, Kamiakin fled into exile, and more moderate chiefs such as the diplomatically adept Chief Moses of the Sinkiuse rose in influence.

Other peoples, too small in numbers to be of much consequence to any of the antagonists, found the war sought them out and laid its breath on their mouths. The Wanapum had not attended the Walla Walla council, and afterwards refused to join Kamiakin in an offensive Sohappy believed must be doomed. Qualchan, the son of Owhi and a leading Yakima warrior, was Sohappy's son-in-law, and the chief's decision rent the solidarity of his family. Although the neutrality of other tribes was respected by the Indian belligerents, Wanapum horses were repeatedly stolen. In 1857, when the hostilities were largely in ebb, Sohappy went to the American colonel Wright, who promised him that provided the Wanapum remained outside the conflict, they would have the protection of the Americans. Moreover, their right to the lands at Priest Rapids would be held inviolate in perpetuity.

The following year, in June 1858, the fighting resumed. At a camp in the mountains Qualchan once again appealed to their mutual familial and tribal loyalties, but Sohappy again refused to join the war, citing his agreement with Colonel Wright. Qualchan furiously ordered that if the Wanapum themselves would not fight, at least their horses could be taken and used in battle. Sohappy led some of his people forward to stop the Yakima from seizing the horses, and was shot by another member of Qualchan's family. Sohappy lay dead and the Wanapum made no further resistance. Their horses were driven away and, despised and leaderless, they made their way down to the river again. In September, Colonel Wright tracked and killed Qualchan, who was in flight along the Snake River; a few days later, Owhi was seized and executed, and that was the end of the fighting.

At the end of the year, the Wanapum looked downriver and saw something enormous moving up the current. It was as big as a lodge, as tall as a cutbank, and smoke poured off it, above and behind it, like a fan of birds. As it moved closer, the air throbbed and intermittent shrieks rent the sky. There were stories of monsters on the river—ogres, hags, and giant creatures that devoured everything in their course—and perhaps this was such a being. In particular, there was a tale of a huge beaver, a wish-push, with ruby eyes and razor claws that killed everything on the river because it could not abide the sound of running water, and therefore it labored night and day with an unearthly energy to stop the current and thereby kill the river.

But it was not the monstrous wish-push. It was a steamboat, the first steamboat to reach Priest Rapids, and was under the command of Joel Palmer, the Indian superintendent and negotiator at the Walla Walla council. Palmer had retired from the civil service and aimed to make his fortune shipping goods to the miners who were rushing into the country north of the Okanagan. At Priest Rapids, above which the river was impassable, he unloaded his shovels, powder, and picks and packed them into an overland wagon train bound for the gold fields. The steamboat was called the *Colonel Wright*, after the officer who had promised the Wanapum his protection during the war. Here, in the loneliest bend on the river in Washington Territory, no one had ever beheld such a monster.

Thereafter, the world was not the same; not new, but different only in degree, in the angles of its shadows, in the hues of its decaying verdure and flesh, a husk of the old. How had it come to be? Where must it run? What story must be told to comprehend it; to sing it into existence; to make a basket that can contain it? Every story must be made in this way: light, round, pleasing to the eye, yet miraculously capacious and so tight that not a drop of water can escape. And when the basket can hold no more—when the water floods, when the world becomes unintelligible—a new one must be woven in which the old one and all its predecessors can nest, one inside the other, basket within basket, story within story, world within world, all the moons that have ever risen encapsulated like the rings of a tree; each newborn tale both the cradle of whatever understanding today's new necessity craves and the casket of its dead ancestor.

That was how it was after the war and this is the story people on the river began to tell: how Old-One made the earth from the body of a woman and from her flesh fashioned everything upon it. So the earth is sinuous and rich, rising like a spring from the moist nurturance of her womb, its creatures taking forage in her hair and gentling their thirst from her breasts.

At first, the world was inhabited by a race of animals who were like people in some respects. They could all speak, and each was wise, but only in one thing: thus might Fox be remarkable in cunning and Beaver in assiduousness, but foolish and selfish in every other way. The animal people perished, mostly by cannibalism and stupidity.

Then Old-One repeopled the world with men and women, the ancestors of the River People. He formed them from clay and kindled them into life with his breath. They were helpless, ignorant, and much oppressed by other creatures and people. So Old-One sent them his son Jesus, who was a priest, a spirit doctor, and a walker in the desert. Evil men seized him and crucified him and he returned to his father in the sky.

Old-One saw that Jesus hadn't made things much better. Mostly he had talked. He hadn't taught the people anything to make their lives easier, or make them wise, or destroy the monsters and evil creatures that plagued them. So Old-One sent Coyote down and Coyote slew the monsters, taught the people to fish, named them, and gave them language.

Coyote was clever, but in his power could also be foolish and proud. When Old-One saw that Coyote had done everything he could for the people on earth, he came down himself in the form of a ragged old man. He met Coyote, who said to him, "I am Coyote. Who are you?"

"I am chief of all creation," Old-One answered. "It was I who sent you to set the earth to rights."

"No, you never sent me," Coyote said. "I don't know you. If you are chief of all creation, take that lake and move it over there."

Old-One said, "No, if you are the wonderful Coyote, let me see you do it."

Coyote moved the lake, and Old-One asked him to put it back again. Coyote tried but could not. Then Old-One moved it back himself, and Coyote acknowledged that Old-One was indeed chief of all creation.

Old-One told Coyote, "Your work here is done. From now on, I will send messages to earth through the souls of people that reach me in the sky but whose time to die is not yet come. Their souls will return to earth and their bodies will revive, and they will tell their people their experiences. When these things happen and when the earth is very old, Coyote and I will return. Coyote will come a little before me, and when he and the animal people are seen again on earth, then the time is at hand. I will return and all the spirits of the dead will come with me. Then all Indians, living and dead, will be together with their mother the earth and there will be every happiness and everything shall be right."

They say it was an Indian named Umtippe who recovered the body of Alice Clarissa Whitman from the river. In gratitude, Narcissa gave him a shirt of velvet, deep and dark as blue water, and emblazoned with stars. Some years later, the shirt came into the possession of a man born at Wallula with the name Wakwei, which means "arising from the dust of the Earth Mother." He was never as other men: His head was large and his body wizened and malformed, as though creation had chewed it up and spit it out in disgust. His words came slowly, like drips from a dryland spring, and his eyes took in the world in an interminable, aching arc, like a body swinging from a gibbet. He made vision quests in the Rattlesnake Hills west of the river above the big bend, and drew spirit guardians and animal powers to his person like flotsam to a whirlpool. He was made to be a priest and he was given many names: Waipshwa, "The Rock Carrier"; Yuyuniptqana, "The Shouting Mountain"; and, most frequently, Smohalla, "The Dreamer."

After the war, the river was ablaze with priests, visions, and dreams. Among the Nez Percé, a woman named Wiskaynatonmay died and returned to her people to recount her experience and teach them how to live. She led them in dances and they spun like stones in a pothole. At Umatilla, Luls died and saw his people floating facedown on the clouds, like cadavers on water, their faces painted red and their braids trailing feathers. He came back to life and gave his people a song to chant. He could read the minds of people among him whose thoughts were evil. In the midst of the dancing, he would single them out and they would drop unconscious to the ground like birds impaled on arrows.

Liswhalite, who lived on the river at White Salmon, could see into people's hearts, too. After his mother died, he heard voices from the night sky. He stood before his people and raised up his hands, which were marked with gilded stars. They were yellow and blue, and were said to signify the gold and silver for which the white people would enslave the Indian. Nearby, a prophet named Skamia told how the *suyapos* would someday kill all the fish by stopping the river with earth and stones.

There was a woman at Celilo named Hunwe, who died and then rose up four days later from her bier. She had seen heaven, where the bad that people do is written in a book. Because she had forgotten to acknowledge one of the evil things she had done while she was alive, she was sent back to live among her people for another four years. During that time she taught them dances and songs she had learned from the spirits. When the four years had passed, she robed herself in buckskins pierced with quills, painted her hands and face yellow and red, and lay down and died.

At Wallula when Smohalla was a boy, there was a Hudson's Bay Company post and a mission of white priests, rustling, bowing, and bending like ravens in their black robes, their beads clicking, their fingers carving crosses in the air. Smohalla parlayed with them as he did with Homli, the head shaman of the place. But in time Smohalla had more medicine than any of them: he could foretell when the salmon would return or when someone was about to die. He urged people to turn their backs on the *suyapo*s and all their works and goods, and in these ways he made enemies at Wallula. Not long after the war, he made a flag from Umtippe's shirt and went upriver and settled with the Wanapum at Priest Rapids.

He was looking to be left alone, to remove himself and his family from the contagion of the white people by setting himself apart on the most isolate reach of the river, keeping company with the rattlesnakes and the hapless, despised Wanapum. But everything in earth and heaven found him out: he had more visions—birds carried him on their backs and showed him things high beyond the sunset, where the river is a distant braid of silver untangling itself into sea. He was a great priest now; he was fecund with power and knowledge. His sight pierced to the heart of things and it seemed as though there was nothing in creation that did not seek to shape itself to accord with his words.

Everything came to him unbidden, and then death came and took his daughter. For two days her body lay in the longhouse while Smohalla tried to bring her back, but the cold hung in her flesh like a fog. The Wanapum carved a trench in the riverbank with an elk horn and put her in it. Smohalla called her name but there was no answer, and so her name vanished into that silence and was never spoken again.

Within a few days Smohalla's grief turned him to stone and he himself died. His wives painted his face yellow and entwined his hair with otter fur and laid him out while drums and death songs rang hollowly against the walls of the lodge. Then Smohalla sat up. For a long time he did not speak, and then he summoned all the river people to meet him at a place called Moon, halfway between Priest Rapids and Wallula, where Nch'i-Wana's waters turned and whorled, as though falling out of the riverbed into the center of the earth.

When they were gathered, Smohalla told them he had gone to the land of the dead. White men had tried to bar his way, but their horses' hooves were rooted in the earth and they could not move. Smohalla saw his daughter in that place and he was given messages, signs, dances, and songs and sent back to Priest Rapids to tell the people how to live. He showed them a drum on whose face was painted the sun, the moon, and a yellow seven-pointed star. The drum was in the shape of the earth, he explained, and its beat was the sound of life, the breath of the world.

Then he showed them a bell and he rang it. It is the sound of the heart, he said. It calls you to the dance. Then he showed them the dance, and he chose the seven most learned men in the village to be drummers and the dancing began: the people flexed up and down on the balls of their feet, as though they might leap into the air and take flight; they held feathers and arced their hands to shape spheres in the air. Then Smohalla led them out of the lodge and into the sun, instructing them to turn in a complete circle at the door. He said the dance was like a flight up to heaven and the turning was a passage around the world. By the door, he had set a carved bird on the top of the pole. It was called Wowshuxkluh, "Knocking-Off-Berries-with-a-Stick," and it had spoken to Smohalla during his vision quests. Its wings were yellow and its breast was blue, and it turned on its pole and followed the sun through the sky and the seasons Smohalla had ordained: the cold moons of autumn; the winter solstice when the sun turns around; the time when ravens come; the time when small insects flock; the harvest of roots; and the late summer salmon catch. Next to the bird hung the flag Smohalla had made from Umtippe's shirt, buoyed on the wind like a gown adrift, its smocking turned to ripples, its pleats fanning out on the water.

Within a short while, Smohalla was known up and down the river. Although he never seemed to seek power, he had married into Sohappy's family after the chief's death and had become the de facto head of the Wanapum. Now his influence among other peoples was becoming a source of concern among their chiefs. Moses of the Sinkiuse became convinced that Smohalla intended to use his medicine to destroy him. He went to Priest Rapids, threw the frail Smohalla to the ground, beat him bloody, and left him for dead. They say Smohalla pulled himself down the bank and into a canoe, and floated down the river for many days until he reached the ocean. The canoe beached itself on the coast, and he wandered down the length of California and deep into Mexico. He walked like a ghost, day and night, unseen, renewing his sinews and powers, mounting up the might of his priesthood with the things he saw. He turned north again, circling back through Arizona and into Utah and Nevada. He watched the Mormons receive commands from heaven and passed through the deserts that hem the world beyond the river.

When he returned to Priest Rapids, they imagined he must have been dead, and so he was; or rather so flayed by the blows of the earth and so weathered by the gales of stars the heavens rained down on him that he was beyond dying. He took life up in his arms, like a rattlesnake to his battered, twisted body, and raised it above his head and told the people to sing its name. He devised a rite for that purpose and had a longhouse built at P'Na of driftwood from the river, a place for praising the gifts and creatures of the earth that give themselves over to people as food.

He took water and raised it up and said its name, "*choos*," and drank, and the people drank with him. Then he took up the salmon and raised it up and said its name, "*nasau*," and ate it, and the people ate with him, and it was the same with camas root, elk, eel, and berries. Then, when all the foods had been thanked, he ended as he had begun, taking water, which precedes, bears up, and will complete all things, and said "*choos*," drinking it down, drowning death with life.

In the spring of 1859, the Congress of the United States of America at last ratified the treaties negotiated by Isaac Stevens. President James Buchanan declared the Indians' title to the lands of Oregon and the Washington Territory null, and opened up the country to settlers. The Indians were in turn expected to immigrate to the holdings on the reservations allotted them and to take up Christianity, English literacy, and farming. In practice, large numbers of Indians did none of these things, either because they were not parties to a treaty or because they simply refused to accept the treaties' legitimacy. They stood on the side of the river, fishing, hunkered down in talk, or simply watching, as the droves of white people rolled by. They took nothing that anyone wanted, but their presence, their silent gaze and lack of motion that bespoke a world founded on changelessness and indolence, was a kind of reproach; a sullen curse on the turning wheels, the plodding oxen, the yards of calico, and the barrels of sugar and iron nails with which the whites settled themselves into the river country.

Such Indians as these, though they represented only a portion of an already decimated population, were deemed an obstruction to peaceful settlement and civic order. Although they did nothing more than continue to hunt, fish, and camp in their traditional places, white officials saw them as actively rebellious

and called them renegades. It was difficult to conceive why anyone—even an Indian—should want to continue a life of hunting
and gathering lived out-of-doors or in crude shelters, nor was it
imagined that the Indians were clever enough to calculate any
political or economic advantage they might gain by their non-
compliance with the treaties. Surely, then, renegadism was based
not on reason but on stupidity, cussedness, or, most likely, malign influence. In the early 1860s, white officials began to hear
the word *Smohalla*, but they could not determine whether it described a force or a form; a cult, a political faction, or the founder
of one or both.

In 1861 an Oregon Indian agent named G. H. Abbot wrote
his superior of "Smo-kol-lah . . . a bad character" whose longhouse was "a rendezvous for thieves and outlaws. . . . The peace
of the country depends on the capture of him and his party in my
opinion." But no white man laid eyes on Smohalla, much less took
him captive. Meanwhile, renegades along the river were being
rounded up or, as likely as not, simply hanged by the likes of Lt.
Marcus Reno, who would achieve some infamy at Little Big Horn
within a few years. At the same time, discontent mounted among
the heretofore quiescent Nez Percé, a faction of whom Lawyer
had recently persuaded to sign away 6,932,270 acres of their 1855
reservation. In 1863 Tuekakas, the Nez Percé elder and father of
Joseph, opened a chest in his lodge and removed from it a copy of
the 1855 treaty and a translation of the Gospel According to
Matthew. He took them outside, stood before his people, and
tore the paper and the book to shreds.

Something or someone called "Smohalla," "The Dreamers,"
"The Drummers," or "The Prophets" was behind it all, the whites
believed. But as yet, Smohalla was a rumor, a wave of heat rip-
pling like seaweed in the desert distance. At last, in February of
1870, the Oregon superintendent of Indian affairs, A. B. Meacham, determined to track down and thwart "a grand scheme of ras-
cality being hatched under the leadership of a head man of the

Walla Walla tribe who is also known as the Great Dreamer, alias 'Big Talk on Four Mountains' alias Smokeller."

It was Meacham's understanding that Smohalla's influence radiated out from Priest Rapids as far south as Nevada, yet Smohalla himself was hard to find. Meacham traveled upriver with soldiers, translators, and a load of gifts. Cliffs blocked their passage, and within fifteen miles of Priest Rapids a messenger appeared who told them that they would have to wait another day to see Smohalla. When they at last ferried over the river and reached P'Na, a blinding headache descended on Meacham, who found himself able to speak only in platitudes, as though bewitched into a bland idiocy. For his part, Smohalla, who had arranged to have an American flag hung by the longhouse by way of greeting, said little or nothing, collected Meacham's gifts, and dispatched the party downriver.

Meacham crept away befuddled, the sensation of Smohalla's eyes fastened on the back of his head like hot pitch. Over the next two years, Smohalla remained mindful of Meacham. Meacham's brother was inexplicably killed by a falling tree in Idaho. No sooner had the devastated family gathered to mourn than a delegation from Smohalla arrived to pay its respects and to suggest that the white people's god did not, after all, avail them much under such circumstances.

There were reports in the newspapers of Smohalla inciting Indian tribes as far away as California to war; that he was traveling through Idaho enlisting an army of dreamers; that four or five thousand Indians were gathered at P'Na. The Indians had long since learned to claim ignorance of their own numbers—since God knew, who else needed to?—the knowledge of which might aid white officials in gauging how many of them were living off the reservation or failing to send their children to school. Although the population at P'Na was perhaps a twentieth of the number rumored, the danger was real, as Meacham's replacement, T. B. Odeneal, grasped in 1872:

They have a new and peculiar religion by the doctrines of which they are taught that a new God is coming to their rescue; that all the Indians who have died heretofore and who shall die hereafter are to be resurrected; that as they then will be very numerous and powerful they will be able to conquer the whites, recover their lands, and live as free and unrestrained as their fathers lived. Their model of a man is an Indian; they aspire to be Indians and nothing else.

The Indians themselves could no more track Smohalla than they could track the wise and cunning tomfoolery of Coyote. But they said he could heal the sick and perhaps raise the dead; that he could hold burning coals in his hands and endure cuts and wounds without bleeding; that he conjured a pot of food as bottomless as a lake that no mortal could empty.

He predicted that on August 7, 1869, darkness would fall in the middle of the day, and so it did: blackness came rushing toward the river like a wave sweeping up the shore, and then all was dark, as though the world were underwater with only a lambent ring floating above it. Then the light returned in the same fashion as it withdrew. Smohalla had an almanac and was adept at using it. But even if he did not predict the eclipse in the strictest sense, he knew something much more important: that God, seemingly so single-minded and immovable, might set the end of the world in motion, and then relent.

People said Smohalla also forecast what happened in the night on December 14, 1872, when the very earth seemed to stand up and shake its coat free of every appendage and then collapsed in a sigh of dust and clattering bones. The earthquake was felt into Montana and north into Canada, and the aftershocks continued for weeks, and it seemed clear that just as the Creator had demonstrated his unhappiness in the sky, so did the Earth Mother shudder in her pity and grief. People flocked to Smohalla, who told them what to do.

By the autumn of 1873, white officials seemed no closer than before to extinguishing renegadism. The Indian agent for the Warm Springs Reservation glumly reported to his superiors that thirty-nine more natives had abandoned their allotments:

> They are believers in a superstition known as the Smohollah. This religion, if such it may be called, is believed by nearly all the Umatillas, Spokane, a great number of the Yakimas and many renegades of other reservations. The religion is like that of the Mormons and ministers and works on the evil passions. The main object is to allow a plurality of wives, immunity from punishment for law-breaking and allowance of all the vices— especially drinking and gambling. . . . Some provision should be made at once for placing all these outlaws on a reservation where they could receive the benefit of strict law rigidly enforced.

In September a special agent, E. C. Kemble, was assigned to look into the matter and summoned Smohalla and the other leading Dreamer priests and chiefs to a council. All demurred, and then sought a postponement until a later date. When the council at last convened at Wallula on September 22, Smohalla was nowhere to be found but had sent two observers who sat on the ground wordlessly. Kemble was furious: Smohalla had evaded him for weeks, but that had not prevented Kemble from forming a picture of the priest:

> . . . a little, withered, decrepid, "medicine man" who practices the same species of enchantment which a class of white men and women employ in the dark and disreputable business of the fortune teller, the spiritualist, juggler, and trance medium, a kind of "religion" as old as the days of Pharaoh's magicians.

Such chiefs and dreamers as did attend were less than cooperative, either keeping their silence or uttering mystic opacities. An Umatilla priest maintained that only Nch'i-Wana, the great river, could speak for them; it listened to them; their minds and its mind were one; where else could they ever think of living?

The council adjourned having accomplished nothing, and Kemble continued his tour of the reservations. He was moved by a schoolhouse service conducted for Christianized Umatilla Indians, and noted the presence of Dreamers wrapped in blankets, huddled like funerary monuments against the wall at the back of the room: "Our hearts yearned for them," Kemble wrote, yet nothing was to be done for them; they were for every Christian purpose enchanted and possessed.

In the newspapers of Portland, the Dalles, and Walla Walla, rumors and suspicion abounded: a small gathering of renegades at White Bluffs became hundreds of warriors massing preparatory to being led into war by Smohalla; trenches and flumes dug by Chinese miners working for gold on the upper reaches of the river transmuted themselves into fortifications and earthworks at Priest Rapids; on the coast of Oregon a story arose of an imminent "united slaughter of all whites which scheme originated from Smohalla, a medicine man of the Snake Indians." Elsewhere, native assertions of the Dreamer faith became more overt: an 1874 Idaho jury trying a white settler named Ott for the murder of an Indian brought an acquittal when Indian witnesses refused to take the oath on the grounds they could not make a pledge to a god they did not believe in. Ott's release eventually led to war.

That same year Kemble was succeeded by another special agent, William Vandiver, whose frustration exceeded even that of his predecessor. He, too, found Smohalla elusive, less an entity than a rumor, whose "teachings are pernicious, for he inspires a belief among his followers, that white people will soon disappear from the country, and that the Indians will then have it to themselves again." Of more immediate concern was that Smohalla "counsels them not to settle upon reservations nor to receive assistance from the government."

In 1875 the problem of what one agent called the "Smohallow dance" was considered sufficiently significant and intractable to be addressed by the Commissioner of Indian Affairs in Washington, D.C., in his annual report to President Grant:

About 2,000 Indians are roaming on the Columbia River, in Washington Territory and Oregon, under the leadership of a self-constituted priest, Smohalla by name, whose followers represent nearly all the tribes of the Territory and State, and whose influence extends even into Idaho. He has been able to inspire in his adherents veneration toward himself, and by his teachings, which are received with implicit faith, superstition is fostered, unbridled license is granted to passion, civilization is despised, and reservation Indians are looked upon with contempt and disdain. These Indians, in their present unsettled and unrestricted life, have no earthly mission beyond that of annoyance to settlers and hindrance to the opening of the country, and are a positive detriment to all other Indians. . . .

In the summer of 1876, Marcus Reno, onetime hangman and Indian hunter of the Columbia and lately attached to Gen. George Custer, met a kind of death at Little Bighorn in Montana; not a bodily death by bullet or arrow as did most of his fellows, but the death of his person by shame, his reputation and good name pierced, slain, corrupted, bloated, and buried by the words others chose to describe his deeds on the battlefield. He ceased to be the agent of his own identity: His country had uses for him. He was made an emblem of cowardice, of the unbelievable and humiliating proposition that a mighty republic could be brought low by an unlettered herd of savages; or perhaps he was fashioned into a lie, a foil for the unspeakable sensation that something heretofore unexpressed in the nation's destiny had risen up like a child in the night and slain its parents.

Gen. Oliver Otis Howard, commander of the Military Department of the Columbia, was, like Custer, a hero of the Civil
War (with the stump of an amputated arm for proof) and an Indian fighter. Unlike Custer, he was moderate in his instincts and
profoundly religious, and he understood that he faced a potentially
disastrous situation when certain bands of the Nez Percé, loosely
organized under the leadership of Chief Joseph, refused to give up
their traditional grounds in the Wallowa Mountains of Oregon
and settle on the reservation established for them in Idaho.

Believing that the crux of the Nez Percé's resistance was their
immersion in the Dreamer religion, Howard sought a meeting
with Smohalla in April 1877. Howard made camp at Wallula and
message after message crossed and recrossed the river, on whose
opposite bank Smohalla had lodged himself. Smohalla insisted
that Howard come to him; Howard in turn feigned a lack of interest in meeting Smohalla at all, flatly telling his envoys that if
Smohalla wished to speak with the general, he must come to him.
The following day, Smohalla crossed the river in a flotilla of canoes with a retinue of three hundred.

Smohalla was not, in Howard's estimation, an impressive figure: he wore a shabby gray suit with a floppy bandanna tied
around his head. As for the rest of him, he was "a large-headed,
hump shouldered, odd little wizard of an Indian . . . short and
shapeless, scarcely any neck; bandy legs, rather long for his body."
But his eyes shone clear and deep, like orbs of black glass.

In discussion, Smohalla proved to be "a strange mixture of
timidity and daring, of superstition and intelligence." He was
unequivocal in stating that his people would under no circumstances leave the river. Howard had intended to be firm, but
when Smohalla asked him about the status of the law requiring
Indians to take up residence on reservations, Howard inexplicably told him that he would write President Grant, suggesting
that perhaps there could be some flexibility in the matter. Howard also seems to have been swayed from presenting an ultima-

tum to the Nez Percé, and instead proposed that a council be held the following month.

The council, held at Lapwai, the site of the onetime Spalding mission, was dominated not by the Joseph and the Nez Percé political leadership as Howard had expected, but by Dreamer priests. Their formal relation to Smohalla was unclear. They possessed little of his serenity and were vehement in pressing their case. The Nez Percé priest Toohoolsote was particularly relentless in attempting to corner Howard in logical and theological ambushes: "What person," Toohoolsote queried, "pretends to divide the land and put me on it?" Howard replied that he himself did, in the name of the president of the United States, Ulysses S. Grant. Toohoolsote seemed to sneer: his own authority, he told Howard, came from God. The "Great Spirit Chief . . . made the world as it is, and as he wanted it, and he made a part of it for us to live on. I do not see where you get the authority to say that we shall not live where he placed us."

Howard was impatient with the Nez Percé penchant for protracted talk: "Let us hear it no more, but come to business at once," he urged. Toohoolsote responded: "We want to talk a long time, many days, about the earth, about our land." The priest talked on for four more days until Howard, by reputation a gifted preacher and debater, could bear no more: "Shut up!" he brayed at Toohoolsote. But Toohoolsote was defiant:

> Who are you that you ask us to talk, and then tell me I shall not talk? Are you the Great Spirit? Did you make the world? Did you make the sun? Did you make the rivers run for us to drink? Did you make the grass to grow? Did you make all these things, that you talk to us as though we were boys? If you did, then you have the right to talk to us as you do.

Howard had Toohoolsote thrown in the stockade and reached an understanding with the fragmented and confused Nez Percé chiefs: the Wallowas would be vacated and opened to white settlement, or the army would clear them out by whatever means necessary. To no purpose, Joseph continued to protest: "This country holds your father's body. Never sell the bones of your father and mother."

West of where the river cleaves the Cascades, the land is green; east it is tan and towheaded, rangy and spare like a sorrel horse. Then, where the plateau climbs into the Wallowas, it is blue, as though rising into a sea whose floor is the sky. The air is like clear, cold water; the grasses grow in pillows and islands among the wildflowers; the pines' bark is fractured into scales, like a snake shedding its skin—all its scars and bitter history—winding itself out of its cares, reborn in the peppery scent of its own sweet pitch.

It is a fine place to live and as fine a one to die in, and its inhabitants can no more forsake it than they can the sound of their own voice. Joseph and his people tried to leave in June as Howard had told them they must, but once homeless it seemed as though chaos and incomprehension beset them; their young men attacked whites and were in turn attacked. They fled east in a curious spiraling path along much the same course as Lewis and Clark had first traveled to the river, as though rolling up the white people's westward road onto a spool: through the Clearwater and Lochsa country of Idaho, up the Lolo pass into Montana, into the Big Hole Valley, south into Yellowstone, and north again across the Yellowstone, Musselshell, and Missouri rivers.

Despite his best efforts and the might of the United States Army, Howard could not catch them; when his forces met them in battle they were discomfited or simply outrun. It was not that Joseph was a great or cunning warrior and strategist; rather, the Nez Percé were propelled by something random and imponderable, as though a gusting wind were blowing a sheet from Old Joseph's gospel down a road, bearing it away each time it was about to be grasped.

In October, massed forces of the army caught up with and surrounded the Nez Percé near the Milk River, not far from the Canadian border, whose shelter Joseph had been seeking in imitation of his Sioux counterparts from Little Bighorn. Hungry, exhausted, and cold, 147 children, 184 women, and 87 men gave themselves up to Howard. One hundred and twenty had died on the way, while Nez Percé warriors had slain 177 soldiers and civilians during the past three months. The winter months, more than Howard, had caught up with the Nez Percé. In the Wallowas, winter came gently, like an accretion of feathers and leaves; in Montana, it snapped at the heels of summer and the snow blew hard and crystalline, scouring their faces, like grit ground from bones.

The exodus of the Nez Percé was a tragedy that Howard believed originated almost entirely with Smohalla and the Dream religion. When the Bannock and Paiute revolt of 1878 threatened to spread from Idaho and eastern Oregon into the Columbia Valley, he moved quickly to isolate Smohalla, fearing that he might form an alliance with Chief Moses of the Sinkiuse and take up arms. But the old enmity between the two was still strong, and Moses had calculated that he would in any case be better off currying favor with Howard for his people than joining his fellow tribes in an uncertain enterprise.

Events overtook both Moses and Smohalla in ways that Howard could not have foreseen. On July 10, renegades from the Umatilla Reservation killed Mr. and Mrs. Alonzo Perkins in rugged country west of the river. But local civilian officials responded by swearing out arrest warrants on Moses and Smohalla, who now embodied the summit of Indian savagery and evil for white settlers: newspapers reviled Smohalla as the most dangerous Indian alive, slaughtering hundreds of settlers' cattle for sport and commanding squadrons of braves ready to commit "murder, rapine, and pillage" at his whim.

Moses was captured and thrown in jail. In November, as winter fell, Smohalla gathered the Wanapum at P'Na and fled southeast to the backcountry of the Yakima Reservation, out of the reach of white posses. Convinced that both Moses and Smohalla were now effectively harmless, Howard recommended to the territorial governor that no proceedings be taken against either of them. The wars were ended and Smohalla, although he had no intention of remaining on the reservation any longer than necessary, had done the thing he said he would never do.

In July 1884, Capt. J. W. MacMurray sat in his barracks at Fort Vancouver and wrote his report, or rather inscribed it on sheets of tall, ruled paper. The letters, precise and steady in form, yet betraying a floridity perhaps unexpected in a military officer, queued up wedged and angular, like arrows aimed toward the right-hand margin:

> A bold rock projects into the Columbia River forming an especially desirable salmon fishery. Just below is a low island upon the head of which the spring freshets deposit drift wood for fuel and fencing as well as other simple construction. Along the edge of the slough is some arable land which the Indians have fenced and cultivated for years. It furnishes fish, fuel, fencing material and ground for their simple crops.
>
> Salmon Man had been in possession of this place with his family and had fenced and cultivated the ground along the slough. In March 1884, a white man named William H. Boyd filed a claim along the river front including the head of the island and the cultivated and fenced area. He filed and proceeded to take possession, driving the Indians off and threatening them with the law if they trespassed on his "homestead."

Salmon Man—a name that might apply to any Indian on the river, or all of them—and William H. Boyd—any settler could be a Boyd—were both epitomes, and their stories were similar to so many others. Captain MacMurray reported to Nelson Miles, commandant of the army's Columbia department, and was charged with investigating breaches of the peace between the Indians and whites and, where possible, resolving them. In theory, he had authority over neither whites—governed by civil jurisdiction—nor Indians, who were controlled by the Bureau of Indian Affairs of the Department of the Interior. His job was therefore to keep them apart. Although rival agencies might feel he overstepped himself, few were inclined to argue with the United States Army.

Salmon Man versus William H. Boyd: as in most such cases MacMurray had encountered, the injustice done to the Indian party seemed clear. As for Salmon Man, what he must write was self-evident:

> I was also informed by many of the best people in the vicinity that Salmon Man and his people were known to be honest, industrious and self-supporting and that they had always occupied the site taken from them.
>
> In view of the facts in this case, I would respectfully recommend, that the attention of the officers of the Interior Department be called to the manifest wrong to the Indians, to the end that Mr. Boyd's filings may be canceled and Salmon Man be given possession of his home. . . .

He signed it, the *J* of his first name overspreading four lines, billowing yet taut, as extravagantly arced as a bow.

R. H. Milroy was a military man too, a former general rapidly approaching his eightieth birthday who had secured the post of agent of the Yakima Reservation as a retirement sinecure. His opinion of his native wards was unvarnished: they were variously "barbarous," "savage," "vicious," and "animal" and to improve them was no more practicable than the extraction of "their color from their hides." He had bitter experience with their incorrigibility, particularly when under the influence of the Dream religion; at one time he had idly fancied marshaling "the Bible, and History, Reason et cetera, to try to get them to stuff up this barbarism" but had abandoned the attempt. Still, Milroy had hopes for the ameliorative effects of education on Indians, provided it was begun at an early age. And if there were a way to circumvent objections, he also believed the whipping post might be put to good use in discouraging a whole range of undesirable behavior around the reservation.

By and large, the Indians were unpredictable and infantile, and managing them was akin to forcing the idiot, spring-mounted cranium of a jack into its box and getting the lid slammed down before the next fusillade of mayhem erupted. It was a thankless, Promethean chore that fixed his jaw in a clench and made him despair of both work and rest, and he did not appreciate what he was hearing about the peregrinations of Captain MacMurray. In Milroy's view, every river Indian, whether his tribe was a party to the 1855 treaty or not, ought to be on a reservation. But in addition to upholding Indian demands to remain on the river, MacMurray was also proposing a new system whereby Indians could file claims on their existing homes without traveling long distances or securing white witnesses to corroborate their claims. Then word reached Milroy in August that at the Dalles MacMurray had promised—or the Indians believed he had promised—that they could remain in their original homes on the river in perpetuity and that the army was prepared to guarantee it. Milroy's colleague Special Agent Cyrus Beede quoted Skaamiah, the chief there, as saying, "This captain told us that a man would be sent out from Washington to order us upon a reservation, but for us not to go, but stay here; this was our land . . . and our lands would be given back to us." In Beede's account, the chief registered no consciousness of either the treaties or the law:

A long time ago it was understood that we should have this land. The whites were satisfied with this arrangement. The Great Father in Washington allowed the whites to see this land but not to take it. When they were allowed to come they were told the chiefs owned this land and they must consult with the Indians if they wanted to stay. . . . The whites first decided this ground was not good. But they had a bear's heart in them.

Beede also reported that he had discovered in late August that, not satisfied with sowing chaos at the Dalles, MacMurray had made a pilgrimage into the very sanctum sanctorum of renegadism and repeated his lunacies to its head priest:

On the 22nd instant I went to Umatilla and on the 23rd crossed over the Columbia River to Switzler's Ranch in Washington Territory. The Indians were nearly all gone to the mountains for blackberries, but two rather intelligent men of this band came to see me on the 24th instant. They said that "These military men had a council with Smo-hol-ly's band this moon, not a month ago, and told the Indians that in another month General Miles would come and give the Indians all the Columbia River, and would confirm title to them, and they should do nothing now."

Milroy's scalp prickled and burned, and his eyes seemed to spin in his skull.

MacMurray rode fifty miles in a wagon, and then the road disappeared. Several Wanapum were waiting for him, his aide, and his interpreter, and together they began to ascend a mountain. From the height of the trail he could see hundreds of miles, and far below him "the silver stream of the great river flowed . . . being broken and glittering at several points, where ledges of rocks tore the current into angry foaming rapids."

They reached a cliff of shattered, precipitous basalt that rose out of the canyon of the river, beyond which lay an interminable and dusky plain, a field of stone. The narrow path clung to the face of the precipice like lichen, and it took two hours to reach the bottom, where riprap and scree ran to the river's edge. Beyond a range of sand dunes and sagebrush lay flags whipping in the wind, and beneath them the lodges of P'Na.

Smohalla appeared: "Short, thick-set, bald-headed and almost hunch-backed, he is not prepossessing at first sight, but he has an almost Websterian head, with a deep brow over bright, intelligent eyes." Smohalla walked MacMurray down through the village. The path had been swept and watered to keep the dust down. It was utterly empty, "but from the mat-roofed and walled salmon houses there came forth the most indescribable sound of bell-ringing, drum-beating, and cat-surpassing screeches." At the other end of the village Smohalla had prepared a lodge of canvas for MacMurray, carpeted with newly woven mats in intricate designs. Knowing that white men did not care to sit on the ground, Smohalla also had had a bench of wood constructed, sending away ninety miles to the Northern Pacific railhead at Ainsworth for the nails. MacMurray was fetched as much freshly caught planked salmon as he could eat, learning that the word P'Na means "fish weir." If there were anything else MacMurray required, Smohalla would provide it.

At dawn, the drumming began as it would every morning of MacMurray's stay in P'Na. He watched Smohalla conduct services and speak to his people:

> He is a finished orator. His manner is mostly of the bland, insinuating, persuasive style, but when aroused he is full of fire and seems to handle invectives effectively. His audience seemed spellbound under his magic manner, and it never lost interest to me, though he spoke in a language comprehended by few white men and translated to me at second or third hand.

In his previous contacts with whites, Smohalla had traded

declamations—positions and debating points flung down like daggers in the dirt—but MacMurray asked questions, listened, and in his canvas lodge, wrote down what Smohalla said. Tell me about the flag, MacMurray said. Smohalla told him that in that flag—red, yellow, green, and blue with a white star—was everything there was:

> This is my flag and it represents the world. God told me to look after my people—all are my people. There are four ways in the world—north and south and east and west. I have been all those ways. This is the center. I live here. The red spot is my heart. Everybody can see it. The yellow grass grows everywhere around this place. The green mountains are far away all around the world. There is only water beyond. The blue is the sky and the star is the north star. That star never changes; it is always in the same place. I keep my heart on that star: I never change.

Smohalla then asked MacMurray how the white people saw the world, and in particular how it was they partitioned the land. MacMurray found a small checkerboard in his kit and explained how, seen from above, land might be divided into townships, ranges, and sections, like the black and white squares of the checkerboard; and how the Great Father might award alternate sections to the railroad and to settlers. MacMurray said the Wanapum, like any white man, could file for and homestead parcels, and this was the only way they might avoid being cheated or utterly displaced by the white settlers.

Smohalla said he had heard all this before, and it was preposterous and contrary to nature:

> I will tell you about it. Once the world was all water, and God lived alone; he was lonesome, he had no place to put his foot. So he scratched the sand up from the bottom, and made the land and he made rocks and he made trees and he made a man

and the man was winged and could go anywhere. The man was lonesome and God made a woman.

Many more men and women grew up, and they lived on the banks of the great river whose waters were full of salmon. There were so many people that the stronger ones sometimes oppressed the weak and drove them from the best fisheries, which they claimed as their own. They fought and nearly all were killed, and their bones are to be seen in the sand hills yet.

God was very angry at this, and he took away their wings and commanded that the lands and fisheries should be common to all who lived upon them; that they were never to be marked off or divided, but that the people should enjoy the fruits that God planted in the land and the animals that lived upon it, and the fishes in the water. God said he was the father and the earth was the mother of mankind; that nature was the law; that the animals and fish and plants obeyed nature, and that man only was sinful. This is the old law.

I know all kinds of men. First there were the river people. God made them first. Then he made the Canadian and then he made the Black Robe. A long time after that came the Boston Man and then the King George Man. Bye and bye came the Black Man, and last he made the Chinaman with a tail. He is of no account, and he has to work all the time.

All these are new people; only the Indians are of the old stock. After a while, when God is ready, he will drive away all the people except the people who have obeyed his laws. Those who cut up the lands or sign papers for lands will be defrauded of their rights, and will be punished by God's anger.

It is a bad law and my people cannot obey it. I want my people to stay with me here. All the dead men will come to life again; their spirits will come to their bodies again. We must wait here, in the homes of our fathers, and be ready to meet them in the bosom of our mother.

Over the coming days, MacMurray watched Smohalla perform ceremonies, preach, chant, and sit wordlessly while dancers moved around the longhouse. Sometimes the priest passed into a state that seemed to occupy a ground somewhere between sleep and death:

He falls into trances and lies rigid for considerable periods. . . . These trances always excite great interest and often alarm, as he threatens to abandon his earthly body altogether because of the disobedience of his people, and on each occasion they are in a state of suspense as to whether God will send his soul back to earth to reoccupy his body, or will, on the contrary, abandon and leave them without his guidance.

It is this going into long trances, out of which he comes as from a heavy sleep and almost immediately relates his experiences in the spirit land, that gives rise to the title of "Dreamers," or believers in dreams, commonly given to his followers by the neighboring whites. . . . I questioned him as to his trances and hoped to have him explain them to me, but he avoided the subject and was angered when I pressed him. He manifestly believes all he says of what occurs to him in this trance state.

Smohalla had a notebook, filled with symbols and letters, in which he was said to record dreams and prophecies. They were unintelligible to MacMurray. Then the priest brought out another book:

He showed me an almanac of a preceding year and asked me to readjust it for eclipses, as it did not work as it formerly had done. I explained that Washington made up new ones every year, and that the old ones could not be fixed up to date. He had probably obtained this one from the station agent at the railroad, now superseded by a new one, who had cut off Smohalla's supply of astronomical data. My inability to repair the

1882 almanac for use in prognosticating in 1884 cost me much of his respect as a wise man from the east.

After this incident, Smohalla seemed less inclined to speak to MacMurray about matters of consequence. But his principal adjutant, Kotiakin, the son of the Yakima war chief, Kamiakin, made himself available, retelling the same stories Smohalla had told, as though MacMurray had not grasped their import. Kotiakin was in mourning for one of his children, a daughter, and his voice bore the traces of grief.

Kotiakin began again to tell how God had been alone, with his solitude and all around him nothing but water; how he made the earth, its creatures, and a man. Then the man grew lonely, just as God had, so God made a woman to be his companion. The woman was given all the knowledge and skill to provide food, clothing, and all the necessities of life, just as the earth provides nurture and shelter for all its creatures.

God gave woman these things in her dreams and they were preserved for all her descendants, even to this day, in a little basket, which held his gifts within it and was, in its round and humble beauty, a gift in itself.

When MacMurray was preparing to leave, Kotiakin presented him with a basket to remember him by. Perhaps, Kotiakin suggested, his wife would enjoy it. It was, according to Kotiakin and by every appearance, of great antiquity, as though buried in the earth and uncovered in a state of perfect preservation. It was shaped like a drum and was only two and a half inches across, a child's basket, a toy. What thing it might ever contain MacMurray could not fathom or guess.

❀

MacMurray finished his tour of the river country in October and began to work on his reports. His immediate concern was the accounts he had heard from the Wanapum and off-reservation Yakima about what he would term the "tyrannical and brutal actions" of Milroy. Recently, the natives had told him, Milroy had taken to putting Indian parents in leg irons and imprisoning them on bread and water for failing to send their children to the agency school. MacMurray arranged to have Kotiakin come to the agency and give an affidavit of these charges to an interpreter. Outraged at MacMurray's presumption, Milroy responded with a tirade, shouting and slamming his fists on the table:

> My word is law. I will punish any man on the reservation as I see fit to do, when he breaks the law. They must obey me. They must understand that I never punish except for a breach of law. Making complaints to the military will do no good, as they are only punished when they do wrong. When they do well, I treat them well. I am going to do my duty to the best of my ability, as the government directs me, and as God lets me.

MacMurray had told the Indians that Milroy had been sent from Washington to help them, a proposition they found risible and bizarre under the circumstances. The captain himself found that his proposal for a less onerous land-claim-filing process had been dismissed out of hand by the Interior Department. In the new year of 1885 he discovered and reported to his superiors that Milroy had arrested and jailed another group of the off-reservation Yakima for failing to send their children to school. The agent also had Kotiakin bound hand and foot and confined for a week on bread and water. Milroy kept him jailed through the winter, removing his shackles only when he was marched outside each day to saw wood for the agency stove. In the middle of March, Kotiakin was able to pull up the floor of his cell and escape. The bulk of his people had already fled to P'Na, out of Milroy's reach.

MacMurray continued to agitate for Milroy's removal from the Yakima agency, and both the commander of the Division of the Pacific and the secretary of war came to concur in this recommendation. The Interior Department, however, defended its sovereignty in the matter, and Milroy, plagued by chest pains and faintness, remained in his post. MacMurray himself was transferred out of the area. On his return to the east, MacMurray gave lectures to learned societies on the beliefs of the river people and his experiences among them. He died fourteen years after meeting Smohalla, having attained the rank of major.

In the summer of 1885, Capt. E. L. Huggins, an officer of the Second Cavalry, decided to seek out Smohalla. He had no official reason for doing so, save curiosity—upon leaving the army he would become a journalist—but his assiduousness was remarkable. Two days' ride from Priest Rapids, he was told that he might encounter Smohalla that very evening at a camp of Indians a few miles distant. Huggins rode there and found men singing and dancing in the firelight, but Smohalla was not among them.

The next day he worked his way along the bank of the Columbia and found it "strewn with beautiful arrow and spear heads of obsidian and other translucent material." He met a band of Indians who told him that Smohalla was still at P'Na, and if he hurried he might find him there. He climbed the slope of the mountain leading up to the river's western flank and made a camp from which his mules wandered away in the night. In the morning, he took his horse and set off alone up the mountain through meadow grass and flowers to the precipice above Priest Rapids. He descended the treacherously narrow path down its face, knocking rock slides loose as he went, and at last came to the valley floor. Ponies grazed near the trail, looked up and saw him, and stampeded away, their hooves sounding an avalanche of stones on the riverbank.

P'Na seemed deserted. When Huggins finally located a villager willing to speak, he learned that Smohalla was away in the Kittitas Valley, some fifty miles distant. He returned to his camp on the mountain just before dark and the sky seemed full of smoke. The mules were still gone.

Weeks later, having abandoned and largely forgotten his quest, Huggins was resting on the upper reaches of the Yakima River. The alder and maple leaves were waxing amber and the shadows fell like lodge poles laid on the ground. Three Indians in vibrant red and yellow headdresses rode toward him, and the smallest and eldest dismounted and said laconically and quietly, "*Nika Smo-halla*—I am Smohalla." He was silent for a while, then added, "You wanted to see me," and gave a detailed account of Huggins's movements during the last month.

"Yes," said Huggins, "but it was for nothing special. I had heard about Smohalla and I wanted to make his acquaintance."

"Then you did not come about the land?" the priest asked. Huggins expressed ignorance, and Smohalla explained that white men were trying to take away his people's land at P'Na. Smohalla satisfied himself that Huggins was indeed sincere, and then railed against those of his fellow natives who had taken up white ways and whom he referred to contemptuously as Book Indians: "No one has any respect for those Book Indians. Even the white men like me better and treat me better than they do the Book Indians."

Huggins wondered if Indians nevertheless ought to learn to farm and labor as the whites did, since the country was filling up with settlers and surely change was inevitable.

Smohalla spread his hand before him in an arc, as though passing a feather over the ground. "My young men shall never work," he said. "Men who work cannot dream, and wisdom comes to us in dreams."

Huggins pressed him: Wasn't the frantic labor of salmon and root harvest work?

"We simply take the gifts that are freely offered. We no more harm the earth than would an infant's fingers harm its mother's breast. But the white man tears up large tracts of land, runs deep ditches, cuts down forests, and changes the whole face of the earth. You know very well this is not right," he said and looked into Huggins's eyes. "Every honest man knows in his heart that this is all wrong."

Huggins asked him about the tenets of the Dream religion, but Smohalla was reluctant to discuss it. Each individual must learn it on his or her own, and it cannot be put into words. As for Huggins, "You have the wisdom of your race. Be content."

Nor would Smohalla be drawn about the exact way in which he believed the world would end. Did that mean, Huggins asked, that he was unsure of what he believed or whether what he prophesied was true?

"How do I know spring will come?" Smohalla replied. "Because it is now fall. We must have help from a stronger power if we are to exist. Without it our case is hopeless. Therefore it is sure to come." He stared at Huggins intently. "Do the white teachers believe what they teach?"

Huggins responded noncommittally: "Who can read the heart of another?" and raised the subject of the priest's legendary enmity for whites. Smohalla insisted this was misunderstood.

"It is not true. But the whites have caused us great suffering. Doctor Whitman many years ago made a long journey to the East to get a bottle of poison for us. He was gone about a year, and after he came back, strong and terrible diseases broke out among us. The Indians killed Doctor Whitman, but it was too late. He had uncorked his bottle and all the air was poisoned. Before that there was little sickness among us, but since then many of us have died."

His voice grew soft. "I have had children and grandchildren, but they are all dead. My last grandchild, a young woman of sixteen, died last month. If only her infant could have lived. I labored long to save them, but my medicine would not work as it used to."

After that, the conversation seemed to falter, sustained between silences only by outbursts of tired grievance. Smohalla announced he must go and stood up. Huggins gave him two blankets, and the priest shook his hand with some warmth. As he mounted his horse he told Huggins, "If they tell you Smohalla hates all white people, do not believe it," and, as he rode away, added, "You will find your mules."

The following day, some of Huggins's men did indeed recover the mules. Huggins soon returned east, retired from the service, and worked as a newspaperman. In 1890 Milroy and Kotiakin died within a few months of each other, and a period of quiet began in the Yakima country: the people accepted some aspects of the white way of life; the new agent in turn tolerated their religious practices.

Smohalla's eyesight began to fail him and many of his people drifted away, leaving Priest Rapids for the reservation. It seemed to them that his prophecies must forever be unrealized and that they had waited with him long enough. Some people left P'Na in that way; others were carried off by death; Smohalla remained with the last of his wives, who led him through the village and along the bank like an old and sightless warhorse. In March 1895, when the river was frozen like a sheet of stone, he fell into his dreams, and God did not send him back.

Soon there was a railway along the Columbia. The line ran through the place where Sohappy was buried. Assisted by the handful of Wanapum still living at P'Na, the workers moved Sohappy's bones, and laid the rails up the river like serpents of iron, over the ground where the secrets, stories, and prophecies lay hidden and forgotten.

2.

Thus did death live on a little longer in that land. It had not always been that way.

Just beyond the Grand Coulee, where the river, frustrated by glacial ice, split a channel through the dry plateau like a maul through cottonwood, there was once a chief among the Sanpoil with a son and a daughter. At that time there was no dying: everyone lived forever. The daughter was living in the woods alone, in the puberty hut as was the custom among girls her age, and she thought about love and she said, "I don't know whom I shall marry. I don't know anyone good-looking enough—except for my brother." Her brother was thinking the same thing: "I'm beautiful and so is my sister. I should marry her."

The Sanpoil were a fastidious people and they bathed in the river each morning and sometimes at night and their children swam as insouciantly as seals. One night on his way back from the river after bathing, the brother came to his sister's hut in the woods and spent the night there, returning home at dawn and sleeping through the morning so deeply that his mother could not wake him. He did the same thing the following night and the night thereafter. In the morning as he lay in the lodge, his lips pursed in sleep, his mother noticed paint on his cheek like that with which she had painted her daughter's face. That night she followed him to the hut and listened at the wall. She heard her children laughing and touching inside, telling each other, "I love you. There is no one else as beautiful as you. We must be married."

Their mother returned to the lodge and told her husband, the chief, what she had seen and heard. What should they do? He knew the people would laugh if they heard. He knew he must kill his son. So he sharpened a piece of bone, and when the boy came home at dawn and had fallen asleep in the blue morning light, the chief drove the bone into his heart. No one had ever been killed before. He buried the body under the rocks at the bottom of a cliff along the river. He then told his younger daughter that under no circumstances should she reveal to her sister what had happened to their brother.

That night the girl waited for her brother to come to her, but he did not appear and she heard crying from her parents' lodge, far away through the trees. In the morning, when her sister came with food, she seized her and forced her to confess what had passed. She told her sister to tell her mother that she wanted to return to the lodge and that she wanted to bathe and put on her best white buckskin dress. Her mother brought the dress to the hut and they bathed together in the river. Afterwards, the girl said she must return to the hut for the dress. She pulled the dress over her head and belted it and loosed her hair, but instead of continuing to her parents' lodge, she ran back through the woods toward the cliff. The chief saw what she was doing and tried to stop her, but he and his people reached her too late. She threw herself off the cliff and fell to the rocks where her brother lay buried. Lying there, her body shattered and exhaling its last breaths, she taunted her father and his people: "We said we'd be together and now we will be, for good. In times to come, other children will do the same thing."

The chief implored his brother chiefs and priests to help him bring his children back to life. But Raven objected, and so the children lay dead on the bank. A few days later, Raven's daughter died, and he cried out in his loss for help, but the chief would not relent: "My children are already rotting. I can't have them back. So now there will have to be death in all the days to come." Thereafter Raven tended his grief, pacing, muttering, and crying, all his motions black futilities.

From then on and for as long as anyone could remember, Sanpoil girls went into the woods when their menses came. They ran alone and stood on hilltops, singing the call of the hermit owl. Their animal guardians came to them and some girls became spirit doctors, even the least among them. Once a crippled girl, ugly and shy, went into the forest and a handsome teal-headed bird spoke to her as sweetly and attentively as a lover. It was Mallard, and for a token he gave her the power to command the Chinook wind, the wind from the east that comes in the spring and dissolves winter into water.

Later, no longer children themselves, Sanpoil women went into the woods to bear their children. They made a bunting of deerskin and a cradle board of cedar, and fastened the baby's umbilicus to it, together with a skunk's tail, feathers, and the heart of a squirrel. Then they gave the baby a name, the first of several it might bear over a lifetime; initially something merely descriptive; then perhaps a name that reflected a trait of body or disposition; then one inherited from an elder; and perhaps there would be a name given by a spirit guardian, a name found in the woods that must never be told to anyone.

Everything in the world had been made and named by the creator chief, who then named himself Sweat Lodge:

> I'll have no body, no head, nor will I be able to see. Whoever desires to construct me will have the right to do so. The one who builds me may pray to me for good looks or whatever he may wish—the one who made me. I'll take pity on him, and I'll give him what he requests—the one that made me. When anyone is dying, he may come to me and I'll help him then also. I'll help him to see the next world. So in this world I am Sweat Lodge, for the help of human beings.

The Sanpoil had names for the light before dawn, for the dawn itself, and for the light just after, and a dozen or so names for shades of white, gray, and brown. They fished, swam, and played through the summer, and in the fall they hunted and sang death songs for the bears they slew. They hung the bones and eyes of deer in the trees. In winter there was no work and little play. It belonged to the spirit and sacred things. All winter, the Sanpoil danced, prayed, and listened to their priests and shamans. They sat in the sweat lodge, in the bosom of everything. Outside, their children took the disks of ice that formed in the tops of water baskets and threw them at the sun to drive the cold away.

In all seasons they prayed to the river, and in particular for the salmon's return. There was no position of greater responsibility than that of salmon chief, whose influence was envied even by the shamans. One, John Tom, who was judged the greatest of Sanpoil salmon chiefs, seemed to bear the world on his shoulders. Blackbird and Badger spoke to him on the riverbank and vouchsafed him the powers of a great healer and spirit doctor. A rock in the river gave him the name Resting-on-the-Banks. But he took the name he used for most of his life from a piece of driftwood he saw descending a set of rapids on the river: "Watch me," it said. "I'm just drifting by." It gave him a song and a name, Shwiwisha, which means "drifting by." One year, the river was low and no fish came:

> I went down to the river. There was nothing but water—only water, no fish anywhere. I was overcome. I wept. I wiped away my tears and called to my power. I sang my salmon song. Soon the water rose, the salmon came. Many, many salmon appeared. I speared a great many. Then the sun became so bright that I could no longer see. I went back to my people. After that many salmon were speared.

The shamans made their cures with water, loosing spirits from the body by taking them in their hands and submerging them in a basket of water. On the banks of the river, the children excavated channels and coves in the sand and laid out the walls of imaginary lodges with sticks.

The Sanpoil never made war themselves and war seldom visited them. One autumn a Nez Percé raiding party appeared. The older people fled into the woods and hills, but the children, scattered along the bank and in play and hiding places around the village, were left behind. The Nez Percé clubbed a boy to death and, together with a salmon, bound him to a lodge pole and erected it in the village. But even for this, the Sanpoil sought no revenge, and their sorrow ebbed away like rain puddles in the sun.

It was the Sanpoil who greeted David Thompson with such glee and wonder when he began his descent of the river from Kettle Falls in 1811. In addition to their pacifism, they distributed food and goods among themselves on the basis of need and elected their chiefs by a free vote of all the men and women of the village. They ate salmon and game, and, unlike so many whites, they considered feeding on dogs a repellent act.

They were devoted to matters of the spirit and gambled with abandon, summering on the riverbank playing dice and shell games with beaver teeth and deer bones. They fished with spears from cottonwood platforms overhanging the river and built weirs in the bends and eddies. They hunted in packs of dozens of men, herding elk into an ambush of archers, and brimmed their baskets with roots. When a daughter harvested her first food or a son brought down his first kill, they feasted. The world of spirit and daily survival intersected in one embrace: far from being taboo, it was a great privilege to slay and eat a species of one's animal guardian. Once at Whitestone, one of the larger Sanpoil villages, the people drove an entire herd of deer over the cliff and into the river, a cascade of tumbling antlers and limbs heaping up into a tawny rainbow's end in the shallows.

Thompson's rival and colleague Alexander Henry wrote: "The Simpoils seldom leave their own country, and, like their neighbors, the Spokanes, live upon the produce of their lands and the quantities of fat, well-flavored salmon which they take in the river." For their part, the Sanpoil initially believed the white men to be gods who had come "out of the water at the edge of the world." They came to know otherwise: the whites themselves were as devoted as any mortal supplicant to the hide of the beaver, to whose honor they consecrated a house upriver from the Sanpoil and named it Fort Spokane.

Oblivious to the need for rifles, the Sanpoil did little trading with the whites, but were nonetheless visited by epidemics of measles and smallpox. By the 1850s, their winter village of White-stone and their summer fishing camp, Enparailik, "Colored Like Cottonwood Leaves," held perhaps 250 people. They were not a party to Stevens's treaty of 1855 nor to the war that followed it. But through the next two decades the Sanpoil came under increasing pressure either to homestead their land or to abandon it for a reservation, notions that were not so much debatable as incomprehensible. In 1871 when the American Indian agent came to see him yet again to get an estimate of the tribe's membership and what it might take to secure its cooperation, their chief, Quetalikin, confessed himself dumbfounded:

> I am a child in knowledge. I have listened to what you have said. There are three things you have spoken of. First you want our numbers; second you desire to know if we have any religious teachings or wish to have any; and third you want to know what our wants and wishes are. The first I understand; the second I poorly understand, but the third, I don't understand at all. But the chief of us all, God, has numbered us and no man shall number us.

To the agent's ears this was an evasion, not an answer, but in truth Quetalikin was by no means an obstructor of white interests: when a Sanpoil stole goods from some whites, Quetalikin had him whipped as he would any other malefactor and ordered him to make restitution; and the chief also accepted a Bible from some missionaries. He could not read it, but that was of little consequence: he held it as he prayed to Sweat Lodge and chanted and conducted ceremonies over it.

Quetalikin took a firm line with the whites over the dispossession of Sanpoil lands, but the tribe's pacifism and egalitarian, decentralized politics left him without the means to defend his position in terms the whites would understand. Meanwhile, alerted by the success of mineral strikes just over the border in Canada, white mining interests and settlers insisted that Sanpoil territory be opened up. The American authorities unilaterally declared a reservation established between Kettle Falls and the Okanagan and just as quickly disestablished it when it was discovered that some of the most potentially valuable mining sites lay within its northern boundary. Quetalikin could do little but watch the cares and confusions of this new and ungraspable world pour down on the Sanpoil like winter into fall; and as for driving them away, he might as well fling ice at the sun.

Skolaskin was bent and hobbled and he walked with hands atop his knees or with a stick, like a cricket with a cane. People said he'd been thrown from his horse; churned up by the Hell Gate rapid in the river; or beaten to pemmican and trussed at the tendons by the husbands of the women he seduced. He was ugly and ridged as a sturgeon, but the women loved him. Despite his lameness and amphibian crimps and juts of limb, he could throw himself in the saddle like a thundercrack and ride like a snowflake on a gale.

Something malign had taken hold of Skolaskin when he was about twenty and clung to him for two years. Born at Sinakialt, "Brush-Spring," just upriver from Whitestone, he'd been an average boy, swimming and hunting as well as any, possessed of a middling spirit guardian. But the affliction had nearly killed him, and when it was done, he was folded up into himself like a moth stuck in its chrysalis, never able to stand erect, straighten his knees, or raise his arms over his head.

That he was alive at all was miraculous, but there was more. His voice was like a fire stick turning in its slot, rasping, insistent, smoking:

> I was dead. I died. I went so far to where dead people go. . . . I came to the gate to go through and there was a man standing

there watching the gate. When I got there this man says, "Where are you going?" I says, "I'm going someplace." And this man told [me], "You can't go through the gate, [you] have to go back. Go back where you started from. . . . You have to go back and preach." Well, I'm alive. I came to life. I'm going to get well and I will keep on [with] what I saw when [I] was in a trance.

At the start, there was no reason to pay him any mind: he was no one in particular from a village of no consequence; he traversed the ground like a toad, as raw and ugly as a bat's carcass. Moreover, there were other dreamers and priests in the surrounding country to contend with. One, Suiepkine, who had a following among both the Sanpoil and the Okanagan, was a spirit doctor of reputation who was also uncompromising in telling the Indian agents what they might do with their presidential proclamations and inducements:

There is [only] one thing I desire which is the breath of life. . . . I don't want the government to give me any farming implements. I was born without them. There is only one chief in the universe and he is God.

In contrast, Skolaskin had few acolytes and adherents, but he felt his spirit power beading up like bubbles in a pot on the verge of a boil. He flew into Suiepkine's camp on the back of a black stallion and proclaimed that Suiepkine was out of God's favor and that he would be punished for his abuses of power. As a sign, the earth itself would heave and shake. Skolaskin did not linger to hear the laughter and derision. He tore home up the river like a locust mounted on a panther's back and waited.

In the night of December 14, 1872, as the frost limned the clots of fallen leaves and powdered the river rocks and cold rubbed its flanks against the Sanpoil lodges, the world began to rock like a ball in a cradle. Cliffs lost their footing and fell into the river, and the river itself seemed to erupt through fissures into the recessed floors of the lodges. The earth screamed and clattered like a runaway train, and in the lodges, filling with water like sprung canoes, the people screamed with it.

When the dawn came and when over the coming days the ground shuddered now and again like a cough, there was no imagining what the world would come to: young women ran screaming into the woods, never to be seen again; old folks sat outside their thresholds and droned prayers. The people danced and sang through the winter, heedless of their responsibilities and labors, terrified of their fate, and lovesick for a savior. Skolaskin claimed their hearts like a bridegroom.

Skolaskin had a cylinder through which a man might look and see constellations, colored and turning like comets in a bowl, like spiders' nets of quartz, and in the center you could see the starry spoor of God himself. Skolaskin also had songs he taught the people: one for praise, the other for the dead. When the time came, the dead would not return to earth; instead, Skolaskin would take all the people to heaven to live and be gathered there with the spirits of their kin. He sat on a horse and one of his aides rang a bell as he rode around Whitestone. He explained how when he had died God had taken him apart and put him back together, leaving him a bit of a shambles as a reminder of his power. When it was time to go to heaven, his limbs would be made whole again.

Chief Quetalikin became an adherent of Skolaskin, as did the better part of the Sanpoil people, and followed his rules: no gambling, no drinking, no adultery, and no face painting or dancing on Sunday. He disciplined children for picking berries on holy days and punished young men and women for looking at their faces in the water; or rather, his aides did, for Skolaskin could not lift the whip himself. If Skolaskin was harsh, the growling earth on the one hand and the whites on the other were harsher still. People did as he said, or when the time came they might be left behind to suffer the firestorm with the whites and their chickens and cattle.

He loved women. When he was dead, God told him he would marry six virgins, and they were Ceeapeetsa, Chezet, Skoqwaele, Harriet, Quinspeetsa, and Suzanne. Suzanne was the head wife, although she wasn't a virgin when she came to Skolaskin's lodge. When she was fourteen, Suzanne had been sold to a stockman named Portuguese Joe Enos for flour, beans, and bacon. She got away when Portuguese Joe immigrated to the Azores, and after she betrothed herself to Skolaskin, she became a spirit doctor in her own right. A young Sanpoil named Kwilaminitsa had been stabbed and lay untreated until his wound was gangrenous and he himself was overcome by delirium. Suzanne poured water over him and then knelt and put her mouth on his side opposite the wound and drew out two pints of his blood. She mixed the blood with water, blew her breath across them, and then poured the two together back onto Kwilaminitsa's body. That night his eyes opened; in a week he was well.

A year after the earthquake, Skolaskin had consolidated his power to such an extent that the Colville Indian agent John Simms would write his superior of Quetalikin, "The chief is a well meaning man, but has lost his influence, and blindly follows the Prophet." The government was eager to open parts of the reservation both to white settlers and to other tribes, among them the powerful moderate Chief Moses and his Sinkiuse. But under Skolaskin's leadership the Sanpoil were immovable:

> They tell their followers that truth is revealed to them directly from heaven, and all that is necessary to secure their well being in this world, and happiness in the next is to obey them implicitly, and they do almost without an exception. A distrust of white men, and a disregard of their teachings and laws, seems to be the foundation of their faith, and no one is permitted to acknowledge any authority emanating from them.

Simms suggested that the only practicable course for the government was the arrest and imprisonment of Skolaskin and his closest lieutenants.

Skolaskin was an equal source of frustration to the Jesuit missionaries who had considered the upper Columbia their parish since the time of the Hudson's Bay Company. Skolaskin not only prevented the Black Robes from saying mass for their converts and baptizing their babies, but entirely forbade them to enter Sanpoil country. Meanwhile, tales of Skolaskin's seemingly bizarre and capricious ministry reached them: how he sold prophecies— obtained from an almanac—for a dollar; how he declared himself invulnerable to bullets; how he dreamt the end of the world was imminent and so ordered his people to destroy their dried fish stocks in preparation for it, only to reverse himself and condemn Whitestone to a hungry winter.

Hearing such things, Father Urban Grassi, a bull-faced Jesuit who had worked on the river for many years, became convinced that Skolaskin was an evil to whose "devil-sent" catechism Christ's priests must respond. Grassi reached Whitestone in June 1876 while both Quetalikin and Skolaskin were away. With little reluctance, the villagers explained their predicament to him:

> We do not hate you, Black Robe. You want to lead us to God and make us good. Our man of prayer wants to lead us to God and make us good. Both of you tend to the same goal, and how can we hate you? Both of you are equally dear to us.

Father Grassi returned in December of the following year. His guide was a Sanpoil adept in theological debate, as so many of the tribe seemed to be. Grassi made it his business to attempt to baptize any sick children in his vicinity that he received word of, lest they languish in purgatory. As they rode, the guide explained that he could not see the reason in this:

> See now how foolish you are. Do you think that God who

made the innocent babes is going to cast them off when they die? Where do you find parents who cast off their children?

At Whitestone, plumes of breath billowed from the mouths of young men sawing planks in the dusk. Around them were piles of timber, weighted with hassocks of snow. Skolaskin had ordained services in both the morning and the evening, and Grassi asked his guide's family if he might attend that night. They went to seek Skolaskin's consent:

He answered that I might go to their prayer if I wished, but that I could not speak. On hearing the bell, however, I went, and spoke too; but I spoke to the wind as far as I could judge; for the prophet interrupted me and told me I had spoken too much already; that they would not receive my prayers; that though he would not blame me for having adopted the prayer of Jesus Christ, I had no right to impose it upon others who had a different one.

After him several others spoke, even more vehemently than the pseudo-prophet; some arguing that the prayer of their prophet was the right one, others maintaining that baptism was of no use, as it was nothing but the power of understanding the word of God and doing it. Their speeches were often interrupted by vociferous applause. The speeches were followed by a prayer calmly said and devoutly, the bell being rung at different times; a hymn, without words, consisting only of an intonation of Ah, ah, ah, wound up the whole affair.

I remained two days among them, but with no fruit. I left them much astonished by telling them that they would never reach heaven by the prayer of their prophet.

Grassi took his mission down the river to its junctures with the Okanagan and the Wenatchee with more success. Fevers and influenzas beset the river in January and February, thickening in the lungs of its children like water curdling into ice. By Holy

Week, Grassi had baptized thirty infants, but he did not attempt to return to Whitestone.

Father Alexander Diomedi set off from Colville nearly two years later, on December 2, 1879. He was accompanied by "a pious Indian" named Edward and carried a sack of flour, a few pounds of bacon, a buffalo robe, and some tobacco to pay the ferryman for passage across the river. Six inches of snow lay on the ground when they left the mission, and they entered a forest dense with pine and fir, a winter forest as silent as ice. When they came to the river, no one would help them cross. They went to a village to try to persuade someone to take them over. A Sanpoil woman railed at Father Diomedi:

> Why have you come here among us? To convert us, I suppose! You are always preaching against our dreaming, but your own religion is worse than ours. I know how to read: I have been to Portland and I know that you priests are thieves.

Edward began to shout back at her, but Father Diomedi restrained him. They worked their way a few miles farther downriver and at last found someone with a canoe willing to take them across. They landed near Whitestone, where there was more than a foot of snow, and it was nearly the shortest day of the year. They made, as they did every day, three times a day, a gruel of flour and boiled water. In the morning they turned south into the Grand Coulee, planning to traverse the river's big bend by the overland route.

Within an hour they were in the desert of the coulee, a place without trees or forage, the dried carcass of the river's previous life. It began to snow and then a wind rose up and drove the snow into drifts, in which their horses foundered. The horizon dissolved and the air sang like a blinding swarm of ivory gnats. Father Diomedi thought he saw a wagon rolling in the distance, like a ship surmounting white swells. But it was a deer, robed in an alb of snow, and they followed it down to the river.

Edward went to Whitestone but returned to say that all help
had been refused him. Father Diomedi was unsurprised. Edward
had seen the stacks of lumber. The priest explained what they
meant:

> Skolaskin is a poor wretch who has greatly deceived his own
> people. He is a dreamer who sometimes shuts himself up in his
> tent and allows no one to see him. Then he comes out and tells
> his people that he has had a revelation from heaven during his
> seclusion.
>
> The revelation he had a few years ago was this: "There will
> be a great flood over the whole earth; all human beings shall be
> destroyed; but the Sanpoil Indians shall be saved, if they do
> what I command them." Then he told them to set to work and
> build a large boat in which they were to take refuge as soon as
> the flood began, which would be in the course of eight years
> from the time of his revelation. The people began to saw lum-
> ber with the whip-saw and had prepared about three thousand
> feet of it for the building of such a boat.
>
> He endeavored to persuade some Catholics to do the same;
> they informed me and I spoke several times to the people to
> caution them against such nonsense. Then he began to preach
> against priests and the Catholic religion, and has excited his
> own people so much, that at present it is impossible to do any-
> thing with that tribe, nor is it safe for a priest to go among
> them. When Father Vanzina went to visit them, Skolaskin,
> crippled as he was, took a knife and tried to strike him while
> he was preaching, seeing which Father Vanzina jumped on his
> horse and rode off.

The Sanpoil, he explained to Edward, were at least for now
beyond the reach of salvation.

Father Diomedi and Edward abandoned their plan to cross
the Grand Coulee and threaded their way downriver instead. At
the Okanagan, they met a band of Sinkiuse and a man named

Little Wolf. His daughter was ill and Father Diomedi implored him to permit her to be baptized: "Her soul will become as white as snow and if she dies, will enjoy eternal happiness." But Little Wolf would not allow it: there were no Catholics in the tribe and Chief Moses' consent would have to be obtained.

The child grew sicker, even as Father Diomedi grew fonder of her. He began to call her Mary, since she lacked a Christian name. He continued to press Little Wolf, and at last he agreed that if the child's condition became hopeless, he would allow her to be baptized:

> Finally, on Christmas Eve, the father said to me, "I give her to you.". . . So I called in my good Edward to be her godfather, and with as much solemnity as possible I baptized her. Six days later, the father sent a messenger to the mouth of the Okanagan, telling me that Mary was dead. Poor little creature! How much happier she is now than she would have been in her poor home! And how consoling the thought that the first flower of the Sinkiuse has been safely transplanted to a garden where it will never fade!

After Mary died, the winter became deeper. The sky blackened and boiled as though beaten by the wings of a thousand gray birds. The wind keened and tore trees out by their roots, like a madwoman harrowing her hair. The snow blew down in a hail of salt and ashes. Then the cold came, and seemed to halt the world entirely, like a wheel that rolls to a stop and freezes to the road. On the river, the ice advanced from both banks and reduced the current to a narrow channel down the middle. The Sanpoil River froze completely, as did the Okanagan and, finally, the Columbia—all their waters turned to stone.

In the forests and on the hill and plateau every creature that remained in the open perished. Those that survived took to dens and holes like anchorites. They were deaf as snakes and snow-blind; buried in the earth, they could do nothing but pray. And perhaps that was in the nature of winter's design: to insist on attention to the things of the spirit by stopping every other thing dead. It was as if Suzanne had gathered the world's water and blood and blown oblivion across their face with her breath, and the water turned to ice, the blood to rust, and the clockwork of life seized up. Or perhaps it was Father Diomedi's god who wanted to show how, when all the world is voiceless, still, and swaddled in snow, everything becomes one thing, as pure and white and distant as Mary's soul.

In January 1883, Robert S. Gardner, special agent of the Interior Department, completed a tour among the native peoples of the river with special emphasis on those living on or near the Colville Reservation. In an interview with a reporter, he discussed his observations and recommendations and reported one curiosity:

> The Sanpoil tribe numbers about four hundred Indians, and they all belong to a sect known as the dreamers. They are looking for another flood, which they expect soon to come upon the earth. In order to be prepared they have secured all the necessary material for the building of an ark, in which to sail off, as Noah did, when the flood comes. Among their material is 50,000 feet of lumber. The ark is to be 150 feet long, and about 50 or 60 feet wide.

Gardner proposed creating a permanent home near the Sanpoil country for Chief Moses and his Sinkiuse on the Nespelem River, where some of Moses' people had already settled. Skolaskin could not accept that Moses had any right to what he believed were Sanpoil lands, nor did he acknowledge the reality of the Colville Reservation—on which Whitestone was situated—or the government's authority to establish such a place.

Under Skolaskin's all-encompassing power, the Sanpoil treated the American authorities as if they did not exist, and their isolation from them was hermetic: Skolaskin refused to communicate with them, and to avoid trading with them or accepting government supplies, he sent as far away as Walla Walla for tools and nails to build his ark. In turn, the government reached an agreement with Moses—including a $1,000 annual annuity for the chief himself—without Sanpoil participation, and pointedly failed to invite Skolaskin when Moses and other local chiefs were brought to Washington, D.C., to be feted at the signing.

Despite Skolaskin's intentions to the contrary, the isolation and alienation of the Sanpoil both from the United States government and from other native peoples gave the American authorities more rather than less freedom to administer the Colville Reservation without regard to Sanpoil opinion and interests. Having used that country once as a catchment area for Moses, they now turned to it again as a solution to the problem of the Nez Percé.

The deleterious effects of the Sinkiuse settlement on the Nespelem had struck deeper than the Sanpoil pride: Skolaskin maintained in a series of protests to the Colville agency that drinking, gambling, and prostitution were making inroads among his own people due to the proximity of the white-acculturated Sinkiuse. Far from offering him any satisfaction on this count, the agent told Skolaskin to prepare himself for the arrival on the reservation of more than one hundred Nez Percé in May 1885.

As was their wont, the Sanpoil had held themselves neutral during the Nez Percé war of 1877, and they had not forgotten the stories of Nez Percé attacks against them in the past. After their defeat in Montana, Joseph's Nez Percé had been transported to Oklahoma Indian Territory where at least a third of them perished in the sweltering summers on a succession of temporary reservations. Yet at the same time, a favorable and somewhat romantic picture of Joseph himself was taking shape in the American national imagination—that of an essentially pacific and well-meaning chief ennobled by his inevitable defeat by white progress—and public opinion began to demand some kind of justice for the Nez Percé.

Logic dictated that they be settled with the rest of their people at Lapwai in Idaho, but the Lapwai Nez Percé—the remnant of Lawyer's band—were reluctant to take in their radical traditionalist cousins and, particularly, adherents of the Dreamer religion and its priests, among whom they numbered Joseph. Joseph and his core group of Dreamers were shunted to Colville.

But any religious affinities between Joseph and himself were lost on Skolaskin, who obstructed Nez Percé settlement at every turn: the Sanpoil blocked Nez Percé access to the farmland the Indian agent had assigned them and expropriated their cattle, driving them to Walla Walla to trade for nails for Skolaskin's ark. Meanwhile, Skolaskin continued to harry the Sinkiuse and to enforce his will among his own people with a personal police force that confined malefactors to a subterranean jail he ordered constructed at Whitestone. At this time, he also confessed to his people that God appeared to have changed his mind about the flood. The timber Skolaskin had ordered cut was bleached and weathered and scattered around the village like bones in a charnel house. It would now, Skolaskin decreed, be employed to build not an ark but a church.

In the summer of 1887, Richard Gwydir, the Colville Indian agent, decided that the government must intervene directly. He called a council to be attended by the Sanpoil, the Sinkiuse, and the Nez Percé, and arranged to have two infantry companies and a troop of cavalry standing by to enforce what was necessarily a predetermined outcome.

When Gwydir camped at Whitestone on July 21 on his way to the council site at Nespelem, a messenger arrived from Skolaskin requesting that he attend a meeting of Sanpoil to be held that evening:

After our horses had been picketed for the night, with my two companions I proceeded to the council, which was held in a crater-like enclosure, capable of holding 2,000 people. It was almost surrounded by a solid wall of stone and was well lighted by two fires of resinous wood, attended to and kept burning brightly by the old squaws. Excepting on a platform built against the wall at one end of the enclosure, there were no seats. The rough seats on the platform were covered with skins of the bear, cougar, lynx, wolf, and beaver. Never had I seen so numerous and great variety of wild animal pelts at one time.

Attended by fifty bonneted warriors, Skolaskin clambered onto the platform and scuttled to his seat. He spoke in a kind of song, like a priest at his incantations. He explained that this land was the home of the Sanpoil from the beginning of time and would be so until the end, when all the country from the river to the rising sun was once again a sea:

When God made dry land, when there was water, it was our land, and here our forefathers hunted the cougar, bear and deer, ages and ages before the white-faced race was known. Our medicine men prophesied to our forefathers of the coming of a new race with white faces like the snow, and warned us never to injure them, but to help them and be their friends. The white man of today is the race our medicine men prophesied were to come, and we have lived up to their advice, and have always been friends to the whites, and our boast that a white man's blood has never been shed by a Sanpoil is true.

It therefore especially aggrieved Skolaskin that the Nez Percé, who had attacked and killed whites, should be given lands belonging to a people who had never done them any harm whatsoever and who only sought to live quietly and support themselves by their own industry. Although the Sanpoil were pacifists, he could not countenance the forsaking of their lands:

The Sanpoils will not obey. They will not see their country, the country they have inherited and lived in since the coming of man, the country their children will inherit after them, be taken from them without a struggle for the future welfare of their children. The cougar, the wolf and the bear will fight for their young, and why not the Indian? Does he care less for his offspring than the wild beast does for its young?

Gwydir turned and faced not Skolaskin, but his people. They must accept, he insisted, that the whites were here to stay:

The sooner you Sanpoils fall into line the sooner your conditions will be bettered. . . . Whistelposum, chief of the Spokanes, Tonkasket, chief of the Okanagan, and Moses, chief of the [Sinkiuse], have taken this advice and their people have mills and schools, and are taken care of by the government until such time as they will be able to take care of themselves, while you Sanpoils, who claim ownership to all this land, and persist in refusing to listen to the Great Father, or take his advice, will be treated like disobedient children, who refuse to obey their fathers, and be punished according to your disobedience. When your chief, who should talk words of wisdom to you, says that you will oppose the will of the Great Father, he talks foolish. As well might a few trees on the mountain try to stop the avalanche as for you to attempt to oppose the will of the Great Father.

Gwydir continued on to Nespelem, putting off the opening of his council there until he was sure the troops were nearby. Then he positioned Joseph and the Nez Percé on his right, Moses on his left, and Skolaskin straight before him at the far end of the lodge. Gwydir announced at the start that his purpose in convening the meeting was to notify all concerned that Joseph and his people were to be permanently settled on the Colville Reservation: there was no negotiation on this point. In an instant, uproar consumed the lodge, with Joseph's and Moses' people applauding, and the Sanpoil dissenting vehemently. Skolaskin pulled himself up and initiated a stinging screed against the American authorities and their president, Grover Cleveland, who stole land from the Sanpoil to give to murderers such as Joseph and Moses.

Gwydir declared he could not tolerate such abuse being directed at the good name of the Great Father; and Skolaskin obliged him by turning his invective entirely toward Moses. Moses responded calmly: he himself had once viewed the whites as Skolaskin did, but at that time he was "as ignorant as a child and did not understand the ways of the Great Chief and the good he was doing for his Indian children." Now, he and the Sinkiuse, joined by his good friend Joseph and his people, pledged themselves to do "as the Great Father wished them to do."

Moses added that his people considered themselves blessed not to be ruled as the Sanpoil were because their chief was "a dreamer who could not make a talk without frothing at the mouth like a dog." Gwydir, who had thus far felt in command of the council, now grew apprehensive:

> At this point the Sanpoils became wild, but without orders from Chief Skolaskin, who sat stolid and impassive as a stone image, [they] could not make a movement. Seeing how critical the situation was, I stopped further talk from Moses, for it needed only a word from Skolaskin to start the fireworks, and I believed that he was debating in his own mind whether to give it. If anything started I would be held to blame by the Indian department for not using proper precaution and I would be the goat, for the department would have to have one. . . . But at that moment I heard the bugle call of the cavalry. The troops had arrived and not a moment too soon.

In the following days of the summer of 1887, Joseph and his people took possession of the plots allotted to them by the government, protected by American soldiers. Gwydir meanwhile urged his superiors to begin assuaging Skolaskin, perhaps by inviting him to Washington, D.C., to be received by the Great Father and to see firsthand the might of the United States government. But nothing came of it, and throughout 1888 Skolaskin continued to resist all cooperation with the authorities, especially in light of the rumors reaching him of plans to open all or part of the reservation to white settlement.

At the same time, disturbing accounts reached the Colville agency of capricious punishments being meted out by Skolaskin's lieutenants and of prisoners being held under appalling conditions at his Whitestone jail. For his part, Skolaskin declared himself beyond all authority: Skolaskin told his entourage that if the agent ever attempted to put him in jail, he would cause a wind to blow the door off its hinges and demolish the building; if the government tried to ship him off to prison, God himself would stop the wheels of the train when Skolaskin gave the word. Both the new Colville agent, Hal Cole, and his superiors were less inclined to diplomacy than Gwydir; Skolaskin's contempt could no longer go unanswered.

But before American officials could concoct a pretext for his arrest, Skolaskin supplied one himself. Skolaskin's police had arrested and jailed a Sinkiuse named Sqwielumpquen, who subsequently escaped. Sqwielumpquen was recaptured and rejailed, principally through the efforts of Kannumsahwickssa, one of Skolaskin's most formidable and ruthless lieutenants. It was common knowledge among the Sinkiuse that Skolaskin's police regularly arrested their people on false or minor charges for the purpose of extorting payments for their release from their friends and families. Sqwielumpquen had a cousin named Ginnamonteesah, who was also a nephew of Chief Moses. On hearing of his cousin's arrest, Ginnamonteesah became incensed and went to confront Kannumsahwickssa. He found him on a Sunday cutting hay in a field above the river, and struck him in the face. A few days later, Kannumsahwickssa ambushed Ginnamonteesah, shot him, and hid the body in a grave that was quickly discovered.

Both Kannumsahwickssa and Skolaskin were arrested but released when the district attorney for Washington Territory refused to prosecute the case, since it was an "inconsequential" altercation between two Indians. Through the late summer and early autumn, however, federal authorities evolved a strategy to employ the incident as the keystone in a dossier of charges designed to show that Skolaskin was a "pernicious influence" on the peace and well-being of the reservation. Under an obscure statute, such a person might be removed from and jailed at the secretary of the interior's pleasure.

On October 30, 1889, the Interior Department issued papers requesting the army to arrest and imprison Skolaskin as "a most dangerous and turbulent element among the Indians." On November 21, he was taken into custody and brought on the back of a mule to the stockade at Fort Spokane, thence downriver to Fort Vancouver, and to Alcatraz Island on the San Francisco Bay.

The sun shone every afternoon, yet it was the dampest place Skolaskin had ever been. The wind blew in frigid, clammy gusts and fog circled around the island. Everywhere, gulls shrieked, hectoring and ranting like a plague of mewling locusts. The birds sat on the island day after day, milling frantically, as though it were a carcass they were picking over. The guards let Skolaskin walk where he pleased, and sometimes he could see the city in the distance and the ships beating past with their plumes of sail and steam. But for the most part, he remained below ground in his rocky cell, and the island seemed a boat in whose hold he was chained, borne across the endless water that had inherited the world when God could bear man no more.

Ever since his arrival on Alcatraz, the military had been uncomfortable with his presence: he was not, strictly speaking, a prisoner since he had been neither charged with nor convicted of a crime. His status was more that of a detainee, habeas corpus notwithstanding, held in quarantine until the influenza of his power among the Sanpoil had remitted. Back at Whitestone, an elder named Celumkinlalalak succeeded to Skolaskin's chieftaincy with the support of agency officials. The government decided that Celumkinlalalak ought to have time to consolidate his position, and arranged to hold Skolaskin through the rest of 1890 and 1891. Agency officials were also proceeding with plans to open the northern half of the Colville Reservation to white settlers, and to permit miners to work the southern half. Skolaskin's return would not be a constructive force in implementing these measures.

There was other news of more personal interest. A group of Indians had tried to drown Father Grassi in the river by capsizing his canoe. As a result of this battle, he died of pneumonia. The agency began to build a sawmill at Whitestone, recognizing that the Sanpoil needed houses of lumber to replace their mat lodges and tepees of hides. As Skolaskin feared, drinking and crime increased in the absence of his authority, and lately some of his people had taken to robbing the "Celestials"—the Chinese—of the gold they panned in the district. And then sometime while he was at Alcatraz, Suzanne abandoned his lodge and ceased to be his wife.

In April 1891, after protracted negotiations with the military, a reporter from the *San Francisco Chronicle* got permission to visit him. Queried as to the basis on which Skolaskin was being held, the officer in charge said, "He is a ward of the nation and not a citizen of the United States, therefore the military authorities, with the consent of the Department of the Interior, have a perfect right to place him where he can do no harm." The *Chronicle* also reported that the specific grounds for Skolaskin's incarceration were his attempts "to stir up the Nez Perces to again go on the warpath, when his intrigues were foiled by his removal to the prison he now occupies."

The *Chronicle*'s reporter found Skolaskin sitting on a stone step at the end of a long corridor, his hair bound into four long braids. He spoke awkwardly in English:

> My heart is broken and I want to go home to my wife and my three children. I am all alone here and nobody to talk to and nobody to keep up my spirits. I am lame and cannot walk much, so that the freedom of the island which is given me does not do me much good. I am nearly always in my cell for pining for liberty. I do not know why they keep me here. I never did any harm. One time somebody killed a cow. It wasn't me that did it, but Chief Joseph, who hates me, wrote a paper to the old soldier chief at Vancouver, and the next thing I knew I was brought here.

The *Chronicle* drew an extremely sympathetic picture of Skolaskin: he had been confined "without ever having had a trial or having been convicted of any crime" and reduced from a warrior to a wasting husk of desolation:

> All of the native nobility which this specimen of the noble red man may have once possessed has evidently left him, for he is now a very crestfallen and mild-mannered creature. . . . The release so persistently denied him by the government officers will perhaps come to him in the shape of the silent reaper, and he will find reunion with his tribe in the happy hunting grounds of the beyond.

On June 22, 1892, a military interpreter named Arthur Chapman brought Skolaskin a contract for his signature:

> In case the authorities will permit me to return to my people, I promise to obey the Indian agent; to treat the employees of

the Agency well and make no threats against them; also that I will not make any trouble amongst the Indians nor between them and the white people, nor give any advice or talk to the Indians that will make them discontented or not willing to obey the agent.

Skolaskin inscribed a cross under the words and was told he could go home.

In his absence, the tribes of the Colville had, at Moses' urging, accepted cash payments for ceding the northern half of the reservation. Defying the American authorities, Skolaskin protested loudly against the agreement, but to little avail. The Sinkiuse, the Nez Percé, and many of his own people were ranged against him, and the new head of the Catholic mission, the Jesuit father Etienne de Rougé, had vastly increased his church's influence among them. Those who remained loyal to Skolaskin continued to eat their traditional diet and to refuse government rations and supplies, but their number dwindled each year. His other wives began to drift away. When the last of them, Quinspeetsa, announced that she too must go, he told her, "No, I need your help. I need somebody to get my firewood and cook for me." Quinspeetsa was unmoved, and Skolaskin said he would kill himself if she left. He took a rifle, hobbled outside where he could not be seen, and fired a shot in the air and waited. No one came. He pulled himself back to his lodge and discovered that Quinspeetsa had gathered up a blanket and a horse and ridden off.

By 1897 the lower half of the reservation was overrun by miners, who stole from the Indians, vandalized their burial grounds, and dynamited their fishing sites. The chiefs went to court to halt the white siege on their remaining lands, but in 1898 a federal judge ruled that for purposes of mining the Indian title to them was null. In short order, boomtowns and smelters were erected along the Sanpoil River. At the same time, a chief from a neighboring village named Nespelem George began accepting government supplies, and in return was recognized as the official chief in the area by the Colville agency. Skolaskin's power now scarcely extended beyond his own lodge.

In 1906 the government established an allotment system to dispose of the southern half of the Colville: those lands not claimed by individual Indians as their private tracts would be sold off as surplus, a process well under way by the end of the decade. Skolaskin was outraged and managed to collect enough money from such adherents as he still had to finance a trip to Washington to protest. The Colville agent telegraphed his superiors in advance of Skolaskin's arrival in the capital and urged them to refuse to see him. But when he arrived on January 7, 1911, he was received with what he felt was proper dignity at the offices of the Interior Department, although he was neither offered nor promised any redress of his grievances. But Washington, D.C., was like the heavenly cities in the white people's Bible, with towers thrusting up into the sky and stone corridors where his canes clicked and resounded like thundercracks. He went home satisfied, and not long after took an allotment for himself, which the agent recorded in the book as number S-1478.

Two years later, Suzanne reappeared in his life. She was sixty-four years old and bent; now she moved the way he had always done. Portuguese Joe Enos had died and left an estate valued at $200,000. Suzanne aimed to establish her identity as Joe's legitimate wife and therefore his widow. But that meant denying her ties to Skolaskin, who Joe's other heirs hoped to prove was her true husband. Suzanne maintained that she had done nothing more than cook for Skolaskin. During the trial her lawyers kept Skolaskin buttoned up in a Spokane hotel to prevent him from identifying Alice, the daughter he and Suzanne had conceived together, as his child.

Where they could not exclude Skolaskin's testimony, Suzanne's lawyers attempted to discredit him. Hadn't he claimed, they pressed him, to have spoken to God? Wasn't it he who compelled his people to build an ark on which he said they would all sail to heaven? Skolaskin said he couldn't recall saying such things. The jury ruled for Suzanne, but the judge and, on appeal, the Washington State Supreme Court upheld the heirs. That was the last he saw of her.

❀

Not long afterward, Skolaskin let Nespelem George cut his hair. His braids had reached his waist and now lay on the ground like lifeless serpents. His hair thereafter scarcely touched his ears and he wore brass buttons and shirts of cotton. But he kept his red saddle blanket with the wildflowers on it, and he always carried the corn-husk bag Suzanne had made for him many years ago.

In 1918 he spoke to Father Celestine Caldi, a Jesuit priest and rector of St. Rose's Church in Keller on the Sanpoil River. He is said to have simply told him: "I originated a religion. Conditions changed. I am the only one left. I want to be a Catholic."

Father Caldi taught him the things he must know to be received into the faith: how God destroys sin with water; how Jesus stood in the river and a spirit doctor poured water over him and he became like God; how he died but came back from the dead and spoke to his followers; and how in his dying on a cross he saved the world, carrying his people to heaven on wooden beams.

The winter of 1921–22 was as cold as anyone could remember, and Skolaskin was dwelling alone on his allotment on the river outside Whitestone. He did not live to see the spring; he died in the spirit time, as perhaps a priest should do, although he was no longer a priest himself. Three years before, on the feast of Corpus Christi in 1918, Skolaskin was baptized a Catholic and received the Christian name "Frank." They carried him to the altar rail and he saw Father Caldi's vestments and heard the rustle of the black robe beneath them. He heard some words in a language he could not understand, and then took the cool, white bread into his mouth. It was like paper, like something feathered alighting on his tongue.

CHAPTER 5

Emigrants

1.

Daisy rests in her cabin on the RMS *Empress of Ireland,* and the Mersey runs gray and green beneath her. At dusk, the river tinctures the sky and night glides in among the wharves of Liverpool like a vaporous, unseen ship. The *Empress* stirs and shudders, scenting the air with coal; pushes past huddled steamers, lighters, tugs, and tenders. The tide takes the *Empress,* clasps her keel, romances her, leads her like a dancer onto the Irish Sea.

There are lilies and violets in the cabin, and letters and telegrams from Nelly, Auntie Louie, Mrs. Dainty, and Daisy's mother, Mrs. Oxley. The cabin vibrates, the motion detectable even in the two berths, as though the world were not quite solid, as though it were still resolving itself into form. Through the port-hole she can hear the water caress the *Empress*'s hull, murmuring on the rivets and iron plates like the hiss and rustle of a linen sheet. Jack, Daisy's husband of just a few days, sleeps in the upper berth; Daisy, lulled yet discomfited by the *Empress*'s unceasing spasms, lies fitfully in the lower. They wester through the blue shoal of stars, veining it with a ribbon of smoke.

Jack—Capt. John Noel Phillips, late of the Lincolnshire Regiment and the King's African Rifles, wounded and decorated in the Boer War, veteran of Uganda and the Sudan—rises at 5:30 A.M. to reconnoiter the decks. Daisy wakes a little later and reads *Strand* magazine in her bed before joining Jack for a breakfast of minced veal and poached eggs, sausage and mashed potatoes, and steak and onions.

Then they walk together along the rail. The sea is turquoise, the swells napped with white. The wind snaps and blusters, and Daisy swaddles herself in blankets and burrows in a deck chair. She writes:

Canadian Pacific Railway,
Atlantic Service,
R.M.S. Empress of Ireland,

April 6th, 1912

My dearest Mother and All,

Here I am on board the ship and can hardly imagine it is really me. I thought of you all a great deal yesterday but all the same I felt glad that there was nobody to see us off. I got through it all right as it was but I am sure I should not have made such a good start. Jack's eyes simply were sparkling as he thought of being on "the wander" again, and so I managed to choke down my feelings.

Jack was thirty-seven and tall with a bemused, equine face and an oxbow mustache. She scarcely knew him: what a queer world it was, to have barely made a man's acquaintance not much after

Christmas and to be his wife by Easter! Daisy's mother, Mrs. Oxley, had taken an interest in Jack after his mother died; he and his father hadn't spoken in years, and when his commission expired he returned to England with no particular plans.

Under Mrs. Oxley's encouragement, Jack began to visit them at Windsor, where the Oxleys published the *Windsor and Eton Express* and lived comfortably if unluxuriously in the high street. Daisy was thirty-five and had never left home. She had dabbled in art, but never thought to call herself an artist. There were picnics and teas and shopping sprees, and outings on the river with her sister Freda, who studied painting at the Slade in London; her brothers went into business. As for Daisy, she hung about. There was a photograph of her in the parlor taken when she was perhaps three, seated on a swing, gripping the ropes—her boots crossed at the ankles, her bangs peeking out beneath a bonnet all scalloped and frilled—waiting solemn-faced for someone to give her a push.

Jack had a kind of perpetual forward motion about him, sighting his next destination down the pipe stem forever appended to his hand like a spyglass. He had scarcely spent a year in England since he was a child, and the dust of his peregrinations served to obscure the rather limited expectations life had afforded him: he had failed the examinations to enter Sandhurst but secured a commission by enlistment; now after a military career distinguished chiefly by doggedness, he was officially retired with a middling pension and some capital gleaned from off-duty ivory hunting in Africa. What else was there now for him but marriage and home? And what else for Daisy—prospectless, her every future avenue as unsure as the forever tentative expression on her face—but to be his wife?

Arrangements were quickly taken in hand. Daisy and Freda circuited the department stores and shops of Oxford Street, Piccadilly, and Regent Street like stations of the cross, seeking a trousseau and the domestic impedimenta that appertain to a married lady. Jack attended to the greater matter of how and where they might live, given their aspirations and income. In Trafalgar Square, overlooking Nelson's Column and Admiralty Arch, he found the offices of the Canadian Pacific Railway, and therein a brochure.

The paper was creamy and lustrous, the cover ivy green. It said "Windemere B.C." and above it was inset a watercolor of a mother and child in an orchard. Both were dressed in white. Both wore the kind of broad-brimmed hats one might don for a garden party. The child was perched on a ladder with an apple in her hand and an apple in her lap. The apples were green, gold, and crimson, and the branches they were suspended on seemed to enfold the mother and child.

Inside was a legend that read "Orchards, Sports, Homes" and a colored landscape that was a hybrid of Switzerland and the English Lake District: snowy peaks giving way to verdant hills; copses of trees and hedgerows; white villas with red-tiled roofs; lanes tumbling down to the lakeside where pleasure sloops heeled against a gentle breeze. There were other illustrations: cottages hemmed by gardens of pansies, pinks, sweet peas, dahlias, and roses such as might be inhabited by a family of Beatrix Potter mice; men casting fly rods into streams and tarns; orchards and cow meadows that seemed to belong not to farms but to plantations—dominions in Kenya or upland India where one grew coffee or tea.

The text, "The Story of the Happy Valley," was written by a self-described "old timer" who now styled himself R. Randolph Bruce, B.Sc., C.E., F.R.G.S. Bruce had come to the valley at the head of the Columbia River "away back in 1897" when that abundant but untamed land was peopled only by grizzled miners and shiftless savages. It was a temperate paradise, if lacking in amenities. Now, thanks to the labors of the brochure's publisher, Columbia Valley Irrigated Fruit Lands, Ltd., the valley was set to become not only a bountiful producer of orchard fruit and fine beef cattle but "the coming playground of the North American Continent": the railway was coming; so too was a motor road over the mountains; ferries and yachts would ply the rivers and lakes;

and irrigation works were under construction to enable effortless cultivation of fruit. The new settlers drawn here from the best corners of the empire by such progress bore little resemblance to the rugged prospectors of yesteryear:

> . . . a tract of land has been cleared for a polo ground, for a race-course, and for tennis and other sports, for of late lovers of polo have been drifting into the valley. A club has been formed, which will do much to stimulate the breeding of polo ponies as well as assist in increasing the social life of the country.
>
> In other ways the new settler is much better off than was the "old timer." He will get his mail three or four times a week. He will find companions who have been at Eton; he will find golfers who have played at St. Andrews, and in his hunts he will be joined by men who have shot tigers in India and the rhinoceros in South Africa. When he wants relaxation he can take the old prospectors' trail along one of the many creeks, which will lead him up amongst the glaciers, where he can get his "grizzly" and his black bear on the fresh green slopes in the month of May, or he can go up to the Duncan after a cariboo, or in the fall go over to the Kootenays and get a moose or sheep.

And how much might it cost a man to purchase one of the select forty-acre parcels that Columbia Valley Irrigated Fruit Lands, Ltd., was making available on application to its London agents, the Canadian Pacific Railway? Why only £1,000! Jack, who could scarcely hope to obtain a mortgaged semidetached house in Surbiton or Maidenhead, had £1,000 and now could afford a country estate and all its appurtenances. The logic of it, like the logic of their marriage, was irresistible. Jack and Daisy would marry at St. Gabriel's, Pimlico, board a boat train at Euston and—so quickly that the idea could scarcely be thought before it was already their fate—become emigrants.

By the second day at sea, the swells mount into peaks and valleys over which the *Empress* careens and rolls like a runaway train.

Daisy retires to her cabin, grips the gunnels of her berth, and feels her nausea pluck her off her feet and carry her away like a hydrogen balloon. Then the sea calms and now it is cold and she goes out on the deck and the sea is a forest of ice—frozen mounts and floes of an extraordinary number and size for the latitude and the season, so she hears.

Jack, who set his jaw as stiff as a bowsprit and rode out the storm unruffled, encourages her to walk the deck, and she records her circuits upon it and the daily round of life on the *Empress* in her letters—how it is a kind of circling, yet one never seems to come back to the same place: "As I sit here, I can hardly believe it is 'me.' In fact, I am sure 'me' is gone and it is a fresh somebody. . . . "

Daisy and Jack debark at Halifax in the night and leave by second-class train before the sun rises. In their berth, she writes her sister Freda. A curtain suffices for privacy. There are woodstoves at either end of the car for heat and for frying sausages and eggs. Every dozen miles or so, from St. John's to Montreal, towns and settlements shamble diffidently out of the woods toward the track and disappear again like apparitions. Then there is nothing:

I left off writing yesterday as the train was jolting so very much, and here we are again today, still moving on. We are nearing Lake Superior and the country is hilly, as it nearly all has been so far. It is more of the nature of the Chobham Common than anything else I can think of. There are fir trees everywhere, and what look like silver birch. No leaves yet, of course, and mostly brown undergrowth; though where there is grass it is "dirty" colours, and the snow is lying everywhere in patches. We continually pass rivers, very wide as a rule and all frozen, and many lakes; all of them are very broken in shape and have many little islands about. There are huge stone boulders of white and reddish stone in all the country we are now passing through. We

go miles and miles, with no sign of a hut or house and no people, but the sun is shining and the vastness of everything is
wonderful after the size of England. I am traveling in the train
quite well for me, and only get a little headache at times.

Happily, Daisy has found company on the train in the person
of a Mrs. Young and her three children who, it transpires, are also
traveling to the Columbia Valley to join her husband, a former
officer like Jack. Jack himself prowls the corridors, enraptures the
children with tales of the Boer War—of his exploits at Ladysmith,
Pieters Hill, and Pretoria, of the wounds that cratered and fis-
sured his body—and grows tetchy with the porters: "There are
black men on the train who make up the beds. Jack complained
he was not called early this morning, and the man said, 'I call you
early, Massa, but you was in dreamland!' "

Daisy is buoyed by the warming weather; by the opportunity
to walk the sidings in the forest where the train halts near lumber
camps. The men who work in the woods are "very weird," she
writes her mother in Windsor. "Some of them look quite wild."
They wear skins and furs and their faces are rough and brown as
bark, the sum of now uncountable, untraceable admixtures of
voyageur, Indian, and trader that have incarnated themselves in
this place since David Thompson last traveled this route—one
hundred years ago to the month.

Then winter seems to come again. The snow appears like a
wolf at the edge of a clearing and the woodsmen vanish into the
forest like deer; the air is the icy breath of a windigo. Daisy hears
that the Columbia is still frozen and, on the platform at Winnipeg, that the RMS *Titanic*, which left England a few days after
the *Empress*, has been lost with fifteen hundred souls drowned:

> In all probability it was some of the same icefloe or field. We
> realized that our ship suddenly changed its course and went
> right south. We were then only 400 or 500 yards from the huge
> icefield in which were many huge bergs, and we were many

hours passing it. The cold was intense, and I have never felt anything as icy as the wind.

There is a motherless girl traveling alone on the train and Daisy begins to help her dress each morning. She nurses another child with bottled chicken broth heated on the woodstove. The train runs out onto the prairie toward the ridge of the mountains:

> We left Calgary at 8 o'clock, and then I had one of the days of my life. The scenery through the Rockies is the most beautiful and glorious you can possibly imagine, and when you are passing through it all day at the rate of 40 miles an hour you simply cannot imagine the size and vastness of it all. . . . Switzerland is a tiny little place on a postage stamp after it all, and to think that this is where we are going to live.

The train crosses the divide—where the sky wheels through the winter and sows the ice and snow that births the river—in a tunnel; the railway carriages lope insouciantly over the crest of the Rockies like perambulators through Windsor Great Park. The track descends to the Columbia at Golden, and the valley is, indeed, beautiful: "You have snow-peaks on each side, and the country is like Chobham Common or Bagshot with the river running through as well, and the colours like Switzerland." Yet there are disconcerting surprises: the ninety-mile railway line to Invermere promised in Jack's brochure has not been constructed. They will have to motor to Invermere down a rugged, dusty track, nor will Daisy be able to bring all her wardrobe and accessories with her— and that is just the beginning. Daisy has never been more than a few miles from a railway station or a department store; never baked bread; never hauled water or coal; never washed laundry. It is doubtful that her mother has done so either, but Daisy queries her in a letter, if only to have her consult the family laundress:

> I shall have to wash, so will you see if you can find me a handbook, a small one, on the subject, and ask Mrs. Lakewood how

to wash handkerchiefs. I have soaked them but they will not come quite clean. Do you soak in cold or hot water, and do you use salt in the water?

The river is more ice than water and there is dust in her clothing and hair. The hotel in Invermere would scarcely pass muster as a boardinghouse in Windsor, and when the sun falls behind the Selkirks, the sunny valley turns as cold as ice water. Inside, there are disconcerting stories: how the irrigation projects, the clubs, the links, the canals, and the rest are unbuilt; how even if they were built the valley is too high, cold, and infertile to support fruit growing or farming; how R. Randolph Bruce, the "old timer" of Jack's brochure, is in fact the owner and promoter of Columbia Valley Irrigated Fruit Lands, Ltd., and a former mining engineer, land speculator, and untrustworthy bounder.

Yet Daisy refuses to find betrayal anywhere here. The valley bottom fills with night; there are sheets of gold and tangerine among the peaks; and every good thing this place can engender is a promise to which she has betrothed herself with all her heart. She writes her mother:

> We were only allowed a bag each so we had to leave all our boxes behind. But I am gradually altering all my ways, and by the time you next see me I shall be a very different person, I am sure! The process takes place slowly but surely, and you gradually find yourself altering.

At Toby Creek, where David Thompson built Kootenay House at the junction with the Columbia, the river is stilled to the rhythms of a lake. It idles north at the speed of a clock's pendulum; rushes and reeds muffle its susurrations; geese float like a fleet at anchor. On days such as the day Daisy first came here, they take flight without warning; as though wrenched from sleep, their wings tugged marionettelike by strings fixed to God's own fingers.

They grind upward into the sky; group and form themselves into lacework or a quilt of diamonds and lattices. They sing "Jubilate" or "Agnus Dei" or some other song of necessity.

"In Camp,"
Near Toby Creek
                                    Wednesday, the 24th April, 1912
My dearest Mother,
    If you could only see me here, sitting beside the tent surrounded by pots, pans and an out-of-doors cooking stove, I really think you would hardly know me! . . . We saw this plot of land on Sunday afternoon. It is about 3½ miles out of Wilmer (uphill all the way!), on a winding and dirty road or cart-track, you would call it. It is a 28-acre lot. Jack only wanted 20, but he liked this, and Mr. Bowden, who thinks he can help him, has taken the next big lot of about 80 acres and is working it with a friend of his who has just left the service, a Mr. Robinson. . . . Captain and Mrs. Young have got a lot, about ¾ of an hour's walk from here, and at present they are our nearest neighbours. . . .
    The place where we shall build the house overlooks Toby Creek and is on the edge of a sort of ravine. We look right up this to snow-clad peaks, and as I sit here I can count five snowy peaks and ten conifer trees. All the land is fir treed, and as we burn the wood in the stove it smells very nice. It is quite hot in the middle of the day but fresh and cold morning and night; in fact, more like Switzerland than anything else. Everyone is doing general farming about here at present as you cannot plant apple trees on virgin soil. In fact, we cannot grow much this year, as the irrigation system is not finished at present and this is a very dry place. Potatoes and rye, I think, will be all for a start, but the clearing and posting and fencing will keep Jack busy for some cosy time. . . .
    I walked over to see Mrs. Young yesterday afternoon while Jack went to Wilmer, and coming back I lost my way

and thought I should never find the tent. I took a wrong track and all this forest of firs looks alike; and of course I never met anyone to ask. At last I got back to the Irrigation Camp and asked if one of the men would take me to "Lot 22." I met Jack on the way back, in a fine state. He was on his way to the Camp to turn out some of the men to look for me! I still have not found my bump of locality. . . .

I am wearing my old brown skirt and golf jersey, and only wish the skirt was much shorter as the dust is so deep on the roads. This, of course, smothers anything in the hat line, so I am wearing my purple felt. Everyone here is living rough at present. The oldest residents up here are a General and Mrs. Poett. They only came last summer, and we met and were introduced to them yesterday. They have grown-up daughters who run the house. Servants cannot be had for love or money, and a Chinaman here gets £120 a year.

Any time a parcel comes, some water-softener would be a great gift as the water is so hard and I have to wash. I cannot get the stains out of handkerchiefs. What can I put in the water?

Much love, and looking for a letter soon.

Your affectionate child,

Daisy

She presses the pages into folds, and between them sets some flowers. They look like English anemones, red as holly berries, and they grow everywhere here.

Over the next two weeks Daisy's boxes, luggage, and parcels make their way upriver from the railhead at Golden, and they are cast around the camp among the larches, pines, and Douglas firs like cargo washed up on a beach. She and Jack sleep under an eiderdown on the tent floor and eat bread and marmalade and fry rashers of bacon. There are holes in Daisy's stockings and the pine needles stick to her bare heels. The birds watch her, songless. Then the silence is pierced by an explosion. Dynamite is the method of preference for clearing trees, and Jack says the sound is precisely that of a bursting artillery shell.

There is so much to need; so many things required. A recipe for bread to begin with and a book about poultry raising; copies of *Punch;* a fly rod; hair nets; gloves; cord, thread, and buttons; a ribbon corset; talcum powder; a pocketknife; notepaper for more letters, more requests, another list for Freda to take down to the Army and Navy Stores in Victoria:

> Dearest Friddles,
>
> Jack wants you to go to the Stores and ask them to send out to him at the above address 100 soft-nosed 303 cartridges and 20 soft-nosed 400/450. There are varying amounts of cordite in the latter. He is not sure of the amount of grains he wants for this but [Jack's brother] Kenny will send you the lid of one of his old boxes which will give it. In return for all this he sends you three 1d. and one ½d. stamp (which, by the way, are of no use to him), which will help to pay your bus fare from Paddington to the Stores!!

April turns to May. Another blast like a cannon; another tree falls. Jack aims to clear four acres this year. The barn is half finished, and the floor of the house laid out: a sitting room, a kitchen, a pantry, a den paneled in wood for Jack, Jack and Daisy's bedroom, and a spare room for storage. A covered porch will wrap around two ends of the house, the whole in a rustic "bungalow" style:

> We cannot afford a white painted house with a green roof, which looks so pretty here among the pines, so the house will just be brown stain, and the verandah made with peeled logs. And I think I shall have a bright green roof. The architect, who is also a carpenter and builds the house, says red, but I do not

think you will like red and brown when you come, and as several other people are having red, I want green!

Daisy wants Freda to visit—perhaps to settle. She is alone every day for three or four hours while Jack walks to town for supplies and mail. He wears his old khaki uniforms and walks with the tan dog and the dust glistens and billows in the sun and the two figures disappear as though into a honeyed cloud. He comes back with his shadow long behind him like a bride's train, with a potato sack of tinned food—peas, salmon, sausages, and milk— a loaf of bread, and onion sets for the garden. She waits to see what mail he has brought: a letter from Freda or Mother; a copy of *Punch;* perhaps the Madras muslin from the Stores for her curtains. Daisy's anticipation is like an ache, a hunger that builds and crests when Jack comes home around teatime. And then the next day, after lunch, he is gone again with more letters to Freda, which are like prayers:

> I am always wanting silly little things. When I looked in my boxes this morning and found all the things I have got I felt ashamed to ask for more, but please keep account and I will settle with you later. A ball of medium string will be very acceptable when the parcel of oddments comes. Canadian string is soft like darning cotton, and no good! Also, what I do want in spite of all my boots and shoes is a pair of shoes I can wear in the house and yet wear outside. I think perhaps brown ones with a strap across, but glacé is no good here, it cuts too soon. If not, a pair of shoes like I had and Mother used to have. (They have flat heels and broad toes and a strap across.) Perhaps they could be had with more pointed toes, and look more elegant but suitable for working about the house—but remember we are in the wilds of the country. . . .
>
> A few flowers enclosed, though I fear they give you no idea of the "real thing." The pink and white bell shape is the plant that grows everywhere. The others are a violet and the plant like the cyclamen, etc.

Daisy sets a table made of lathes with a checkered duster and arranges wild cherry blossoms in cheese and potted-meat jars. She drapes boxes with towels and Canadian blankets, their colored stripes broad as beaver tails. Jack sits in his African safari chair and smokes and together they plan the details of their house. They shall have the carpenter build a bay with a seat into the sitting-room window. She sees the window in her mind and frames it in words for her mother, and sees what David Thompson saw:

> There is a fine view of Mount Nelson, a snow peak, from the end of the verandah, and far below is a torrent at the bottom of the creek. We have the Selkirks on the one side and the Rockies on the other. . . . This is a grand country.

By the end of May, Jack has got it into his head to clear another two acres, and it is as though the forest is under bombardment:

> I love to see the men working on a tree with their double saws, then a call, a crash, and down comes the tree. . . . Then, when the felling is done, along comes an old boy, whom I call Guy Fawkes, who makes a hole with a crowbar and in goes some dynamite. You then hear the cry of "Fire" and you clear out of the way as quickly as you can and take shelter behind the largest tree you can find. The explosions are fairly heavy and up come these huge roots, and pieces and branches go up a tremendous height and very often fall at a great distance away. . . . Then all the branches that are lopped off are piled in bunches, and you have nice little bonfires all over the place.

Daisy writes in the rain while Jack is gone to town. The water drips through the roof of the barn in too many places to count. Outside it swamps the craters, furrows, and lacerations where the forest stood; where, with any luck, they will plant an acre of potatoes.

The Madras muslin has arrived in Golden. Perhaps Jack will return with it. The road is veiled in the rain and arcs down the hill, like Regent Street at Piccadilly. It is early afternoon and the world is napping:

> The house is at a standstill at present as they are waiting for window frames, but hope they will make another start soon. This is a country of waiting and possessing one's soul in patience, but it is very enjoyable all the same. . . .
>
> Two days ago Captain Young came over with his wagon and brought us two pillows, pillow cases and sheets. It was just lovely to feel a clean sheet under my chin, and not a scrubby gray blanket, but I don't think Jack appreciated it one little bit! . . . I went over to their barn and took my washing in a bundle under my arm and did my ironing there. Mrs. Young has *three* irons, and underclothes certainly feel much nicer ironed than not, I find, and certainly blouses *look* nicer. My Harrod's skirt is my chief joy as it is nice and short for walking in the dust, and just the thing for out here. My old brown is a sorry wreck and does for messing about in camp, but afterwards the only thing to do with it will be to *wash* it; of course, it is rather long for out here! I find my old mushroom the most useful and comfortable at present as it is so shady, but colours fade very quickly in the sun and my favourite green, I expect, will be the best suncolour. . . . Here comes Jack looking like a drowned rat in his Burberry! I must make some hot tea to try to warm things up.

Two days later Daisy takes up her letter to Freda again:

> I had to go to Wilmer yesterday afternoon for bread, and to my joy I found a letter from you and one from Mother, as well as *Punch* and the [*Windsor and Eton*] *Express*. You talk about the value of my letters home. You cannot picture what yours mean to me out here! It is so nice to feel we are more or less in touch now, and I am only about a fortnight behind everything you are doing. I love to hear all the little details of the spring-cleaning and the gardening, and who has been to

tea, and sit and picture it all when I get my quiet hour in the afternoon. . . .

This is a great place for studying natural history, and there are quantities of little gray squirrels about with lovely tails, and some other funny little things called "chip-monks" that are rather smaller than squirrels and have stripes on their backs. They are always playing about the lumber that is lying about the house, and there seem to be endless birds with a good bit of colour, and lovely dragonflies, some peacock blue and some with wings like gold-dust.

The Madras muslin from the Stores has arrived. It cost 2/- by parcel post, but we had to pay $2.85 duty, which is about 5/- in the £. But Timothy Eaton or Pryce-Jones are no good for anything like Madras muslin. The Canadians are evidently not people of taste, and all the old rubbish from England is shipped out to the Colonies. . . .

Ever so much love to you all, and to *you*.

Your affectionate sister,

Daisy

By the second week of June the wild roses are up, pink and low among the forest duff, fragrant in the sun. Toby Creek is at its height, and where it meets the Columbia it forms a broad and milky sheet in which snags and rocks tumble northward up the face of the world. It is, Daisy knows, the week of the Ascot races at home, the highlight of Windsor's social calendar. She feels very far away and worries that she is somehow lost—that she will lose England and thereby lose herself; that she will, not only without choice but without the knowledge of it, be borne away.

Moreover, she worries that her mother worries, and all week she writes letters home. She imagines herself assisting with the family's Ascot picnic—"I have been going through it all with you both helping to tie down those silly salt and mustard pots for the hamper"—and she thinks of the family maid Harbour, and of her brother Stanley. He has sent her a mirror and she looks into it:

> . . . I had not really seen myself properly out here until it came, as cracked and starred glass is not very interesting! I see now that I am very brown, and I think rounder in the face than I have been for some time. . . . Tell Harbour (if you like) that I often think of her when I am sweeping and washing up. If I ever come back to England I wonder if I shall be able to manage servants!
>
> In spite of my new surroundings I feel quite sure I have not altered and never shall. Jack will see to that for you, I am sure, and as to talking like a Colonial that will be quite impossible. At present I find my English is not perfect, and when I talk of "going to go" and that bacon *wants* mustard, he tells me the bacon does not want mustard, but of course *I* may (but this is "entre nous").

There has been a torrent of letters and parcels—magazines, summer-weight corsets for Daisy, Kipling stories and the army *Gazette* for Jack—and Daisy cries when she opens them. She tells Jack she cries because she is happy and she tells him she is a little preoccupied and he must be patient. She wishes there were another woman close by to talk with regularly, although she cannot fault her husband:

> Jack is always perfectly sweet and kind to me, and most unselfish in every way and ready to help me. I am a lucky girl and ought to be very happy. He is so proud and interested in the house as he says, and one hardly realizes he has never had a place he could call "home" since he was about twelve years old.

After years of silence, Jack had at last written his father only a month before. His brother Kenny wrote back to tell him their father had died May 30. Whether Thomas Phillips, old, bitter, and addled by drink, had comprehended the fact of Jack's marriage and emigration was unclear. There was a little money from the estate. Jack's older brother Francis had died in South Africa seven years ago, and now Kenny was the only member of his family toward whom he felt any affection.

Yet none of this touches his spirits, which rise through the summer and seem to pull Daisy up after them: the house is progressing nicely and the irrigation flume must surely reach their land soon. Daisy writes her mother:

> Jack is sitting resting in the shade as he has just come up from the potato field, reading the *Overseas Mail* which he dearly loves. He is covered in dust with a very dirty face, in an old flannel shirt, khaki breeches and puttees, and nearly black arms and neck he is so sunburnt. All the same, I really believe he is happy as a king, and very proud of his 28 acres. He is also drinking cold tea, which is his chief beverage . . . if you wait for us to come back to England I fear you will have to wait a very long time, as I don't believe Jack would ever tear himself away even if he could afford it.

The valley is the summation of all the places Jack has ever been or wished to be: Where the creek bends down into the river, he will exclaim, "That is exactly like the Congo," and the Columbia, in July an indolent spill across the table of the valley, reminds him of the Nile. He looks up the rise of his land into the Selkirks and imagines that the hill stations in India must be similar to this place, his place.

Jack corresponds with members of his old regiment, which is now serving in Gibraltar, but he is content here. His neighbors—Poett, Young, and Robinson, the partner of Mr. Bowden on the lot next door—are retired officers, veterans of India and Africa, and all companionable men. And as Daisy loves him—was she sure until now?—she learns to love what he loves:

> . . . I am very happy and I am sure Jack is. He came into lunch today from hoeing potatoes, exceedingly hot and dirty—we

had cheese and potato salad, scones, and strawberry jam, stewed prunes, milk, and lemonade—and said, "I do enjoy this life and no mistake," and I think he does.

As for herself, she tells Freda she has come to appreciate "the colonial life":

It is hard to a certain extent because it is all so different. But there are so many things that compensate, and in my case I am so well looked after I shall not come to any harm or grow lean and scraggy. Women are what Canada wants. There are such heaps of men, but all the same I hope bands of Suffragettes will not start coming out. *They* are not the sort that are wanted. . . .

The house is closed in by midsummer, and together they begin to unpack their things from England. So much is scratched or shattered or broken: tabletops are scored with marks and abraded; china and pottery tumbled to shards; joints and miters split and undone; picture glass crazed; and the whole coated and infused with dust. Other boxes and parcels, sent via Southampton rather than Liverpool, went down in the *Titanic*. It is all the life they left behind, the one Daisy pictured as clean, crisp, and pretty like the satin ribbon on a garden-party hat and took her comfort from these last four months. Now it is sullied, pathetic, and tawdry and it seems to mock her. It is people that matter, not things, and so she writes her mother:

Try ever so hard to keep [well], for my sake, so the next time I see you you will not have altered a little bit! I have no business to dictate to you . . . but this life out here has made me realize how silly I was to worry over silly little things that here I have to do without and do not really miss. I am sure when you come you will look and feel ten years younger, and when you think of me think of a slightly rounder face, very brown and freckled for me even. My hands have got harder and do not get half so rough or dirty as they used to, and I suppose the same with my

face, as my lips and skin used to peel. It is the dry air, and the
alkali in the air, whatever that may be.

Summer ascends into August. Daisy puts up plum jam under
the instruction of Mrs. Munsen, an Irishwoman who with her
husband does odd jobs around Toby Creek. Daisy in turn comes
to the aid of Mrs. Green, a new settler:

> She has been here a week and has two little girls, the baby a
> year old. She is horribly unhappy and does not like it a bit and
> begs her husband to go back. They came from Belfast and *he*
> was in the Inniskillens [regiment] and is very nice. Jack
> met him and then sent me to see "Mrs." and "buck her up"
> (slang) as she was a soldier's wife, and therefore no need of in-
> troduction but do what you can to help! She is a very nice
> woman, and evidently thought she was coming to Paradise!
> She thought there would be lots of fruit and eggs and milk.
> Finding only tinned varieties has been too much for her and
> she is frightfully homesick.

At night, Jack bellows hilariously as he reads silly poems and
sketches from *Punch* aloud to Daisy; Daisy swaggers round the
room and mimics the accents of Canadian speech, and Jack roars
with laughter but makes her promise she will never repeat these
performances in public. Every morning after breakfast she and
Jack cut down another tree to clear a view of Mount Hammond
for the verandah, one on each end of a crosscut saw. They plan the
orchard: an acre each of McIntosh and Jonathan apples to start.
Sometimes in the afternoon when no one is around Daisy bathes
in a washtub under the trees. She shampoos her hair, and the smell
of the soap, the sense of being for one instant immaculate, carries
her off. The roof of the house is painted green.

A telegram comes on the morning of August 16. Jack's brother
Kenny has been killed on his job in Staffordshire. He is survived

by Ada, his wife, and two children. There will be an inquest, and no doubt a settlement for Ada. Kenny had become entangled in a grinding machine and his body torn apart. Jack's ebullience vanishes with the day. He is listless and cannot sleep. Kenny's letters come for another two weeks after his death, like echoes that arrive long after the voice that made them has ceased. Beyond the trees and the barn, Jack stoops and digs potatoes, as though harvesting a field of cinders.

Jack and Daisy's view of Columbia Valley Irrigated Fruit Lands, Ltd., has grown considerably less generous over the months. The irrigation flume has ruptured and it is anyone's guess when water will come to their property—certainly not this year. Moreover, the completion of the house is being held up by the company's contractors. Daisy denounces its officers as "too greedy" and she and Jack pay a call on Mr. R. Randolph Bruce, the "old timer." Bruce explains he really has very little to do with the operation of the company, but he will see what he can do. He gives them some apples from his garden, and workers reappear at Toby Creek the next morning.

Jack meanwhile takes consolation from letters from his friends in the regiments and their wedding gifts, which continue to trickle through the mails. On the last Tuesday in August he returns from his errands, begins to empty his sack and announces to Daisy, "I have got a kitten in here somewhere," and extracts a blue-eyed tabby he has found in the village. Daisy is determined to develop it into a good mouser rather than a house pet, and fears that too much affection will spoil it. She wants it to sleep in a box, but Jack brings it into their bed and under their covers. By day he is no less attentive to it: "At present you see a lump near Jack's waist and go and feel, and find he has put the kitten inside his shirt because he thought it was cold! Or else you see a small head peeping over the top of his sweater as he walks about." They name the cat Four

Paws and he holds it and it restores some of his equanimity. It sits with him in his chair as he reads Kipling or stares into the night, weighing his duties and obligations—to Daisy, to his brother's widow and children, to his regiment—and smoking his pipe.

September comes, and they try to hunt grouse without much success. Each morning the ice in the water bucket is a little thicker, like a deepening clot of cream, and the snow line advances a little farther down the peaks toward the foothills. The trees begin to color. They are as gold, crimson, and ocher as Jack's battle ribbons: alder, aspen, maple, larch; Johannesburg, Ladysmith, Tugela Heights, Cape Colony. He bandages a boil on Daisy's left wrist and assures her, "I did heaps of this when I was in hospital." He never speaks of his wounds.

By the first of October, Jack and Daisy have at last moved into the house, which they name "Heston" after Jack's family home in Middlesex. Daisy walks through the five rooms again and again, lets her feet fall on dhurries and leopard-skin rugs, and when she is done sits down and reconnoiters it again in words for Freda:

> Now for a walk round the hall! Open front door, green, with top panel divided into four. Copper handle high up, over door inside two hippo tusks. Window on left with deep sill, on it Benares pipe bowl and Jack's father in brown frame. Jack's armchair in corner. Behind it stands the teatray and above it the Greuze picture from Paris. Bedroom door, small mat left-hand side of fireplace. My carved table (silver and curio table) cram full both shelves. Silver box from Khartoum, old repeater watch, magnifying glass, the barometer, and lots of little things. . . .

The canal through Panama is to be opened soon. Mother and Freda could be among the first to come that way, perhaps next summer—if they are not overtaken by events. Mother has officers to tea at home in Windsor, and sends reports of their talk to Daisy.

They speak of war as though it were a matter of "when" rather than "if"—as though it were a coming season whose signs can be read in the earth and the air. Daisy hopes they are wrong:

> I was so interested in hearing all the soldiermen you have had about, as you say, as long as it is not *real*, and now more than ever I pray, "Give peace in our time." If it was not, you know what it would mean for me. Jack spoke of it once on our wedding day and told me that duty would come first, but said, "Now, never think about it any more, but understand I am still a soldier." I have learnt to be so much braver here, but at times the thought will jump up. You understand, don't you? And now let us change the subject.

The parson came to call once to try to interest her in attending the local church. He was broad and dull in the Canadian manner, and save for reading some tracts her mother sends she has not practiced any religion since coming to the valley. The bungalow is not in any case without the fixtures of a moral education: the Greuze print— "The Father's Curse," "The Wicked Son Punished," "The Broken Pitcher," or some such thing—glares down from the wall. But her love and her faith are one thing, and they are bound up in this house with Jack, and they know no other expression or end.

When dinner is finished—roast veal, cabbage, potatoes, jam roly-poly; curry, blancmange, and stewed apricots; rissoles; cottage pie—and Daisy does the washing up, Jack attends to the fireplace. The wood from Toby Creek makes a fire as dusky orange as marmalade and the wood pops and hisses and shifts in the grates like a dog in uneasy sleep. By November, autumn yields to winter: the water barrel must be brought into the kitchen; the laundry freezes on the line; the mornings are clear and still. Then the snow comes: at first, ankle-deep and wet; then deep, high, and white as loaves overspilling their pans. The river slides through the valley like a stain of light.

Inside Daisy bakes and stencils Christmas cards. She packs a parcel of gifts for the Oxleys who still live in Windsor: moccasins made by the local Indians for Mother; genuine Canadian work gloves for Stanley; hat pins for Freda bearing the crest of Jack's regiment. Daisy's brother Arthur lives in Worcestershire and Stewart in southeast Asia, but surely, she writes her mother, there will be other holidays ere long:

> We must try to look forward to the Christmas not far distant when we shall all meet again from Malvern and Malaya and Canada, and join hands round a very large turkey and the largest Christmas pudding you have ever made! We shall spend the day very quietly by ourselves, I expect, go for a walk in the morning and come back in good time to boil the Christmas pudding. I am sure Jack will not be late!

Sometimes in December, when not so much as a drip falls from the eaves, the silence is so profound it gives her a start, as though she were napping, and it pulls her without warning awake into its emptiness. Daisy's iron sighs against khaki; the fire ticks in the stove; and at times Toby Creek and Heston are altogether altered into Windsor:

> The strange thing that happens to me out here are sounds. Suddenly I hear the parish church clock striking, or the bugles in the barracks, or a barrel organ playing, and it is so real I have to stop whatever I am doing and actually listen, even though my thoughts at the time were not in England. . . .

Yet when Christmas Eve came and night fell just before teatime, it was surely the same dusk whose shadow crept across Windsor High Street eight hours before; and a little later, past dinnertime, when Jack and Daisy began to open their presents from England, the stars that rose on Toby Creek and the Columbia must have been the same that were then bleeding into the dawn over the Thames. There were handkerchiefs, stationery, and pictures for Jack and books, a breadboard, and a battery-operated lamp for Daisy, and chocolates for the two of them; and for the house, a "Pandora's Box" of domestic oddments—pattypans for baking jam tarts, and curtain fabric, dried soup, tinned sardines, tea towels, Wright's Coal Tar Soap, skewers, and butterscotch.

In the morning, it is snowing lightly and cold. Jack and Daisy walk up the road and look out onto an adjacent hillside. Two wealthy Scots are building grand houses in the distance with barns and cottages for staff and laborers. They turn back down the hill, and the snow grows deeper. At home they change clothes: Daisy puts on a black velvet dress, and Jack his regimental colors. They write letters to the Oxleys, and Jack continues a note to Daisy's mother while Daisy works in the kitchen:

> It is now 3:15 P.M. The turkey is all ready, and is on the point of being put into the oven. Potatoes and cabbages grown on our own land are awaiting a saucepan which is already on the stove. Your Christmas pudding, safely received, is patiently awaiting another saucepan likewise on the stove. Daisy has already made six splendid looking mince pies from your mincemeat, two fine apples kindly given by Mrs. Munsen are on the sideboard with several of Mrs. Tull's chocolates, and both of us have good appetites.
>
> Thanking you and all the others ever so much for all the presents,
> I remain,
> Yours sincerely,
> John N. Phillips

In the days after Christmas, it remains cold and the snow falls light and fine as confectioners' sugar. Jack and Daisy have been invited to General and Mrs. Poett's for New Year's Eve. Jack has bought a sleigh but prefers to walk, and they allow an hour and a half to reach the Poetts' substantial home on the other side of a small lake, some miles up the hill. They walk with the aid of

Daisy's new flashlight as far as Captain Young's property and the main road. Then Jack switches it off, figuring they can see well enough by the moon, but when it grows too dark to go on without light, they discover the battery is dead. They obtain a Japanese lantern from another neighbor farther down the road. Jack has been told the most direct route to the Poetts' lies across the ice of the lake. He leads Daisy down the bank onto the lake, and the lamp catches fire and immolates itself.

Jack guides them across the ice by dead reckoning. There is no sign of the house. They edge their way forward for twenty minutes, past dark patches where the ice is thin or nonexistent. Daisy is as afraid as she has ever been since they have come to Canada and angry at Jack. Jack is stolid, unruffled, leading Daisy and her fear forward as if they were a rifle squad. The house appears as a glint of light on the far shore, then hoves into view like a liner casting gilded light onto the sea.

Inside, Daisy forgets their passage across the ice. Daisy cannot believe that such a party could be held in Canada. Mrs. Poett wears her diamonds and a velvet gown of deep red; the general has the bearing of a viceroy. The details fill pages to Freda:

> The drawing-room rugs were up and the floor polished for dancing. At one end the biggest Christmas tree, from floor to ceiling, all decorated with silver bells, balls, and tinsel, the real German things, sent from Dresden. . . . They have a gramophone and soon dancing began. The girls, who are all beauties in various ways, in charming white frocks with transparent necks. Oh, how I did enjoy it all and so did Jack—alternately minding the gramophone records and dancing. Then into supper—*such* a supper: prawns in aspic, salmon (frozen), rice (but fresh, not tinned), chicken mashed in white sauce, veal cake, lemon sponge, creams, mince pies, scones . . . and on the sideboard a huge iced cake made by Babs, the second girl. . . . Mrs. Poett has lived in India all her life and been waited on hand

and foot, but she is one of those wonderful hostesses and managers, and really I feel they are too good and charming to look at to be out here at all!

After supper they play games in the parlor with all the lamps put out. One is called Snapdragon and they pluck raisins from a bowl of brandy set alight. Their faces are lapped by the flames, orange and royal blue. Then they tell fortunes by drawing lead tokens from a box. Jack's is a riding boot; Daisy's a heart. At a quarter to twelve, the candles on the Christmas tree are lit and they toast absent friends. They sing "Auld Lang Syne," and at midnight the girls open the windows to let in the New Year.

Jack and Daisy walk home with a storm lantern in the first hours of 1913. Then winter comes in earnest. The mail is delayed, and Daisy thirsts for letters from home. The world is veiled in ice; the peaks stand austere and untouchable, and she confesses herself to Freda:

> I admire the mountains but I shall never love them. My heart, or really my true love, is and will be England! . . . Without a doubt *all* the men here love the life, but I think when any two women get together and talk from the bottom of their hearts the tears always shine in their eyes and they long for a "general" [housemaid] and a washerwoman.

The temperature remains at zero or less for weeks and then some time later, in the lee of the season, when Daisy has long forgotten the heart she received on the cusp of the year and the stone of winter is rolled away and the waters rise, she knows she is pregnant.

It was a pond near Toby Creek, but it could have been the sands of the Sudan. It could have been the frozen sea of the North Pole. You might bivouac it on your belly, as though under fire, or sled over it behind a team of dogs as the sun perpetually transited a tiny ellipse over your head. You might merely be walking home. Who knows what Clement and George Young, and Vivian Marples, ages seven, five, and eight, were playing? At any rate, the ice, such as it was in the first weeks of the winter of 1913–14, opened up beneath their feet, dark as an inkwell. The children flailed toward the edge of the break, which collapsed and withdrew a little farther every time they neared it, like a school-yard bully taunting them with a prized possession held out of reach. Then the cold made them sleepy as newborns and the water filled their lungs. It must have happened quickly and that was a kind of mercy.

In February 1914, Daisy had a letter from Mrs. Young, who had returned to England at the New Year with her husband (the captain) and their remaining daughter. They are looking for a farmhouse to let near Salisbury, but Mrs. Young admits her heart is, despite everything, still in the valley. Daisy tends the graves that overlook the river and the lake at Windemere and will bring flowers when the spring comes. She must do without Mrs. Young's company—and that of Mrs. Poett, whose family has also given up on life here—but now there are four of them at Heston: herself, Jack, Jack's old nanny Amelia, and Elizabeth, whom she calls Elizababy or E. B.:

> Like all babies, I suppose, happy in her cot kicking and cooing she is prettier and happier than anywhere else. I always have her up at odd minutes when I am free and every afternoon before dinner we have an hour's play. She clutches at her bottle now with both hands and has an enamel cup at teatime from which she drinks with furious energy! But plates and cups and saucers are pushed about so quickly I expect we shall soon begin to get smashes. She was five months last Monday and weighs one stone [fourteen pounds]. She has a tremendous voice and shouts with joy or temper. She does nothing by halves.

Daisy will go on at some length to her sister in this vein; when Jack writes Freda, he has other concerns:

Daisy is writing to Mrs. Oxley about the case of goods to come out to us so I will give you the details of my things at Ada's. There is an elephant's foot and two rhinoceros horns. The elephant's foot has been badly mounted and before coming out here I should like it to be sent to Rowland Ward's to be properly done up to act as a palm pot to stand on a table. . . .

The infant is quite fit now and we are trying to have her photo taken again to send you both a copy, but events move slowly.

Jack habitually refers to Elizabeth as "the infant," although whether this reflects any disaffection or is simply an example of his arid and sometimes bizarre sense of humor is unclear; on the back of a photograph of Amelia, Daisy, himself, and Elizabeth, he describes her as "the source of all my woes—the bacillus in white."

The house feels crowded, and Daisy records its not always pacific rhythms in letters to Freda:

[Elizabeth] is still a very good little girl but when her will is crossed she has taken to shrieking most horribly—it is wonderful that so small a thing can produce such a volume of sound without apparently any discomfort. Last night Jack really had to shake her and say "No, No," very strongly. She dissolved into tears, but she is so knowing that I think we shall have to take stern measures with her or she will be a terrible handful by and by. Amelia is irate at much of our treatment. "The Master always had *his* bottle *full*. The master was taken out in the brougham with the windows *shut!*"

Daisy and Jack despair of ever persuading Amelia to care for Elizabeth in the manner they would like. The old nanny fusses and cries when they correct her, and sits in the kitchen with her dentures out, wounded, stirring her tea. To have a private discussion, the Phillipses stand outside under the trees. Jack's involvement in raising Elizabeth is itself that of an executive officer delegating to his juniors: he scans the Liberty's catalog for prints and patterns for the baby that are to his liking, which Daisy then writes to Freda to order on their behalf. He is disinclined to handle Elizabeth when she is wet, fussy, or disheveled. Nor is he amenable to altering the routine of walks, outings, and social calls established before Elizabeth's birth:

> Jack wants to do things and make expeditions just the same as if there were no baby and if I say, "Let us wait until next year," he says, "Bother Elizabeth," so I just do my best. But she is so heavy in my arms when we are out all those hours and of course she *must* be good all the time.

When Daisy has a little time to herself, she walks. In the middle of May, she goes down to Windemere and plants flowers around the children's graves. The Youngs arranged for headstones, the only ones among the mounds in the crude pioneer cemetery. Daisy finds herself thinking, "Strangers in a strange land." Two weeks later, she hears that the *Empress of Ireland*, the ship she and Jack emigrated in just two years before, has sunk in the Gulf of St. Lawrence with the loss of more than a thousand lives. It is hot already, and she puts Elizabeth in the hammock on the verandah and pushes her back and forth, and the higher she goes, the more precipitous the hammock's arc, the more delightedly her daughter laughs and shrieks.

By midsummer, Elizabeth is beginning to speak and she calls Jack "Gaggey" and seeks him out in his safari chair. He puts down his Kipling or his *Gazette*, and recites her a silly poem. "I see Jack's heart is gradually softening," Daisy writes Freda. Jack is pleased with his life, and he is learning to incorporate Elizabeth into its routines:

> Sometimes he says, "What should I do all day in England, on our small income I could not afford to keep a horse or hunt or

play golf!" Living as we do all the time very carefully and economically cost us £240 last year, nearly all our income, but that was the cost of everything—sleigh, chicken feed, chickens, implements, etc.—this is entre nous.

As time goes on, they will become more self-sustaining, or that at least is the plan. But farming here is a highly contingent affair:

It is difficult to explain about the soil. With water one can grow anything, without nothing is successful. Watering with a can is no use as [the soil] is fine and [water] sinks through. The sun cracks the earth and it all evaporates, hence cultivation and running the water along in little trenches or ditches about once a week to thoroughly soak into the earth.

The irrigation system—which has finally arrived at Toby Creek—is already unsatisfactory, and the Phillipses are preparing with other settlers to bring suit against Mr. Bruce and Columbia Valley Irrigated Fruit Lands, Ltd. Yet the provision of the water only serves to blind them to other realities: with or without irrigation, Toby Creek is too high and its growing season too short for successful farming in general and orchard fruit in particular. With Elizabeth serenading them with gurgles and nonsense songs from her perambulator, Jack and Daisy plant their garden and their apple trees, strangers in a strange land, through the summer.

There is virtue in constancy; and so in devotion and duty. One might say they are all varieties of repetition, of events succeeding themselves in an ordered and reliable matter, almost in the manner of a machine. Of course there is no moral agency in a machine, but only infinite constancy, and does not constancy itself—the religious observance of routine and daily duty—instill a kind of morality? All this surely has some relation to soldiering, whose task is to ensure that life goes on undisturbed as it always has done. That, at any rate, is how Jack might see it.

Jack is a creature of habits; of repetition, some might say; of constancy, he would say, were he ever to address himself to the matter, which is exceedingly unlikely. What was good once will be as good twice, and perhaps improve with regular use. This is true of saddles, boots, firearms, anniversaries, grouse season, and books.

Take Kipling. Jack loves the poetry but hasn't much use for most of the prose, save for *The Light That Failed*. That will stand up to multiple readings, evening after evening; to pipe after pipe as the Selkirks flatten in the dusk and disappear. It's the story of Dick and Maisie. He's a motherless public-school lad who finds adventure and fame as a military sketch artist. She's a diffident would-be painter with an income. They played together as children, discharging into the sea a service revolver that Dick got ahold of. They grow up to be star-crossed lovers.

Dick builds a reputation for battle scenes from the siege of Khartoum, and returns to London in pursuit of Maisie. He takes her down the channel coast and proposes to her: they'll travel and paint and he'll go off to war once in a while:

> Maisie darling, come with me and see what the world is really like. It's very lovely, and it's very horrible,—but I won't let you see anything horrid,—and it doesn't care your life or mine for pictures or anything else except doing its own work and making love. Come, and I'll show you how to brew sangaree, and sling a hammock, and—oh, thousands of things, and you'll see for yourself what color means, and we'll find out together what love means, and then, maybe, we shall be allowed to do some good work. Come away!

But Maisie puts him off. She wants to find her own way as a painter. And if she changed her mind, who is to say that the need to be "on the wander" wouldn't seize him and draw them apart. His war-correspondent friends have a watch cry, "Trouble in the Balkans!" that is their summons to war, to their labors, and their true life:

. . . the go-fever, which is more real than many doctors' diseases, waked and raged, urging him who loved Maisie beyond anything in the world, to go away and taste the old hot, unregenerate life again,—to scuffle, swear, gamble, and love light loves with his fellows; to take ship and know the sea once more, and by her beget pictures; to talk to Binat among the sands of Port Said while Yellow 'Tina mixed the drinks; to hear the crackle of musketry, and see the smoke roll outward, thin and thicken again till the shining black faces came through, and in that hell every man was strictly responsible for his own head, and his alone, and struck with an unfettered arm.

Yet Dick is not the master of his own fate: he goes blind as the result of an old war injury. The sound of a regiment in the street reduces him to pity and self-loathing: "Oh, my men!—my beautiful men! . . . I could draw those chaps once. Who'll draw 'em now?" Maisie of course now offers her hand to him, but Dick wants no part of being nursed by her as an invalid. He connives passage to Egypt and thence to the front line in the desert where an enemy bullet strikes him down and he dies in the arms of a brother war correspondent.

The story loses nothing in rereading. Perhaps it gains. Perhaps it seizes the present circumstance, refracts it, reflects it back, sharper, deeper, truer:

There was no answer save the incessant angry murmur of the Nile as it raced round a basalt-walled bend and foamed across a rock ridge half a mile up-stream. It was as though the brown weight of the river would drive the white men back to their own country.

That might be said of this place. And as for the cry of the war correspondents, "Trouble in the Balkans!" that was rather a jest, if a well-taken one, for there is always trouble in the Balkans.

In July, Daisy fills the house with California poppies, and then larkspur and then chrysanthemums. Sometimes she closes her eyes and imagines the elms and oaks of the Long Walk in Windsor Great Park and she opens them and there are firs and larches, and it is not so much of a disappointment. Elizabeth's hair is beginning to curl and she sits on the floor with a doll they call "Judygaiter," into whose eyes she looks intently. She tries to pull the eyes out; and sometimes she talks to her, as though it were just the two of them in all the world.

On a Sunday, Jack and Daisy take Elizabeth thirteen miles up Toby Creek into the mountains. As the track climbs, the creek pours furiously through gorges and cataracts, writhing as though it were caught by the tail. At the top they can look into the alpine country where nothing grows. Falling rocks crack, thunder, and cannon down the ravines. The glaciers glint mistily in the sun and seem to swell and contract, as though breathing. Sometimes the wind shifts, and a gust comes off the glacier like an eclipse, and for an instant summer is entirely gone. It is like the breath of a prophet, cold and damp, scentless like ice.

On the eighth of August, four days after Britain declares war on Germany, Jack writes to Freda:

> This war will I'm afraid modify our plans very much. At any moment I may be called up, either back to England or to any part of the globe and during the uncertainty it is useless to go on developing so have cut down all our expenditure. Unless we are extremely lucky we shall, in the event of my being called on, lose most of the money we have put in here. Still, we both realize we have duties to perform, and if that is the only sacrifice we have to make for our share in a successful war we cannot complain. . . .
>
> You talk of your garden soil caking. In this very dry at-

mosphere our soil cakes immediately after rain or irrigation so perhaps our methods may not be out of place for you. To overcome this caking we plant everything in rows from one to two feet apart and the space between the rows is always kept constantly raked. . . . When we irrigate we never water the surface, that encourages a crust. We dig a deep channel with a hoe—say three inches deep between the rows of vegetables or flowers—and allow the water to run slowly for a night or so, then we turn the water off and rake again. . . . Never water your surface with a watering can, the hoeing of your trenches between the rows is a much easier job than it sounds. Have your trenches deep and narrow.

    Yours,

    Jack

It is a time of waiting. They go through the house and calculate what they might take, store, or sell; what windows and doors might be boarded up. If they go, will they come back? Every aspect of their future is out of their hands. They wait for a letter from Jack's regiment; they read every scrap of newsprint they can lay their hands on. Daisy writes Freda at the end of August:

We had the *Overseas Mail* yesterday. It was such a relief to get an English paper and see all that is going on. The Mother Country is just magnificent, I think, in the way she is facing things and an example to the world at a time of crisis. I am sure the Colonies can supply her with food and men to fight as well.

Jack idles the weeks away, unable to concentrate on either work or pleasure. He shoots a hawk out of the sky and dresses the wings, tail, and claws for drying. A month goes by, and September is at an end. Daisy can only wait on his waiting: "Jack wants to go badly, very badly," she writes Freda, "and chafes and frets."

October passes in the same manner. It is warm, and they enjoy the fruits of their garden. Fearing that word from his regiment may never come, he stocks the root cellar with food in case they remain through the winter after all. But by the second week of November, it is understood that Jack will receive his orders sooner than later. Meanwhile, they hang on to whatever war reports reach the valley:

> The rumour of news yesterday which came through on the phone was bad all round, but I suppose we cannot expect to go straight ahead. Right must conquer in the end and the day of reckoning for Germany must come, as Jack says. In the meantime we must steel our hearts and try to be brave.

Jack and Daisy decide to tour the valley one last time and visit the places they had always meant to see.

It is the anniversary of the drownings of the children. Jack drives the carriage to Windemere and the cemetery and Daisy tidies the plots and adorns the headstones with homemade wreaths. They spend the night at the hotel at Windemere. They sit in the dining room and someone plays "It's a Long Way to Tipperary" on the piano. They feel festive, as though they are at last part of the war effort.

In the morning they drive south, up to the head of the river:

> We then trotted on until five o'clock passing a ranch called Thunder Hill. The owner's wife was drowned in the Empress of Ireland and the poor husband was so terribly upset he nearly went out of his mind. He went to England for a trip and is now in Belgium or France fighting and some cousins are looking after the farm. We then reached a place called Canal Flats, very impressive (28 miles from Windemere). We passed the upper Columbia Lake which is very pretty. It empties itself there and is all sandy marsh.

It is the beginning of the river, and they come there late in the afternoon. The sun pours into the lake like copper and the surface of the water is perfectly still. It could be the place where every motion originates, itself motionless, the center of the world. But the world is not here; it is far away.

They sleep that night at a hotel in Canal Flats, and when they wake there are nine inches of snow on the ground. They leave for home, following the lake and then the river. Daisy drives the horse into the blizzard and Jack walks behind the carriage. The storm abates and they reach Windemere and the hotel. After dinner they visit Mr. and Mrs. Kingston, Canadians Jack met on a previous trip here:

> We had a very pleasant evening, Mrs. Kingston very chatty and Mr. Kingston somewhat like a ponderous pork butcher, though the biggest and best farmer here. . . . Linoleum-covered floors with plenty of rugs on top, a double sitting room divided by curtains—both large. A son of about 23, quite a nice youth, who owns a motor car, but they have no such things as good pictures or silver. We talked war, and Mrs. Kingston was busy making helmets and body belts. Mr. Kingston wondered if it was possible to collect money for a motor ambulance from the East Kootenay District, so you see the Empire does exist! Neither he nor she has ever been to England.

Jack and Daisy come home to Toby Creek the next day. There are letters waiting for them. General Poett has a brigade in Kitchener's army. Captain Young is missing in action. Jack's best friends in his regiment, King and Johnson, who retired with him, were called up six weeks ago. Now King is dead and Johnson wounded. Jack gets a telegram instructing him that he will be called up and to prepare himself to ship out at short notice:

> We only heard from King about five weeks ago. He was so excited at the prospect of going and now Jack is sending his sympathies to Mrs. King. But you know what Jack is. He just shuts up about anything he feels.

Two days before Christmas, Daisy writes Freda a last letter from Toby Creek:

> This is only a line to let you know we are very busy packing up. No pictures left on the walls, no ornaments, no silver—all packed in the box which locks! We do not know how long no-

tice we shall have, but Jack must be ready long before and it all helps to keep him going, he is so restless. . . . Jack is for throwing away everything about which there is a question, and I am giving various hats and blouses, also my white coat and skirt and my gray snowstorm tweed coat and skirt to the Turnor children. These clothes are five years old and Jack keeps impressing on me that an officer's wife must be well dressed at all costs. . . .

When Jack returns from the village with Christmas parcels, they are opened immediately. There is no point waiting for Christmas Day. Perhaps they will be gone by then. They sit amid the tea chests and boxes and open what Freda has sent: dried lavender, a 1915 wall calendar, and little Union Jack flags for the three of them. The room needs something to liven it up, Daisy decides, and hangs the calendar. Elizabeth clutches a Union Jack. On the following day it is the same as they empty the house and Daisy finishes her letter:

The calendar is the only picture on the wall, so is in its glory! E. Baby sat quiet, waving her flag for ages this morning.

There is a cross with Jesus hanging on it at a junction down the slope, and four roads flow away from him like the rivers of the world. They call the place Hill 60, three miles south of Ypres near the hamlet of St. Eloi. They have been under fire for some days. The war is neither a battle nor a truce. It goes on without ceasing, without thought, like a machine, and Jack is one of ten million souls it will take. Jack has been hit before, so he knows what has happened; the warm welling up from deep in his body like a spring that colors his clothes and spreads outward, an aureole of oblivion into which he then falls. It is April 4, 1915, three months after they left the valley, and he will die two weeks later in a field hospital in Boulogne.

If Daisy went to the coast—to the place on the channel where

Dick took Maisie and asked her to come away with him—she could hear the firing, like the throb of a factory far away. It is a foundry where they are grinding and hammering life into death, and when the work is finished nothing will be the same. Daisy will live modestly on her widow's pension in small flats and a little house in Oxford, working in a military hospital as a cook. Jack's friends from the regiment will pay for Elizabeth's education, and like her mother and aunt Freda, she will study art. When her mother dies in 1960, Freda will give her Daisy's letters from the valley. Daisy never returned there after the war, nor did most of the English emigrants: "Heston" was sold at a loss, and the green-roofed house was pulled down for scrap. R. Randolph Bruce became lieutenant-governor of British Columbia. The apple trees died and the forest grew back along Toby Creek.

2.

When she sang, Nora's voice encompassed all the sounds the prairie contained: the screech of wildcats; the keening of cyclones and train whistles; the seething of cicadas in the summer blaze; the rumble of Indian chants; the God-orphaned antiphons of the Negroes; the pallid laments of women betrayed and children dead. She sang lullabies, dirges, and stories, and her voice droned deep in her skull like a death rattle and buzzed in her nose like a snake, and sometimes she seemed to go so deep down into misfortune that people would beg her to stop, as though it pained their ears.

Nora had skin like a fall of white ash and eyes as cool and clear as water in a galvanized pail. She had a daughter Clara and a son Roy, and in July 1912 she and her husband, Charley, had another son. Charley was a figure of some consequence in the Democratic party in Okemah, Oklahoma, and they decided to name the child after the party's newly nominated presidential candidate. They named him Woodrow Wilson Guthrie.

Like many people, Charley believed Wilson would be the sav-

ior of the nation, a second Lincoln who would cement the progressive agenda firmly into the fabric of the republic. And a man
like Charley—who aimed to make a fortune in the land business
and become a power in local government—might ride on Wilson's coattails. Charley had an enthusiasm for every day of the
week, and was convinced of the good things fortune had in store
for Okemah: agricultural plenty, rising real estate values, and
maybe an oil boom. In the pursuit of his desires he was as persis-
tent and vociferous as a fly on a windowpane. He was unafraid of
a fight and was a good talker, too. He fancied he could sell bristles
to hogs if he put his mind to it. He had native blood in him and
spoke Creek and Cherokee—all the better to sweet-talk and swin-
dle Indians out of their titles and deeds. When he saw that the
local Negroes were voting in a bloc for the Republicans, he helped
arrange a lynching to put the fear of God into them and then got
them disenfranchised. Charley was no less ruthless with the socialists, who were more popular than he would have liked among
white farmers and laborers. He published essays in the *Okemah
Ledger* with titles like "Free Love the Fixed Aim of Socialism,"
"Socialism the Enemy of Christian Religion," and "Socialism
Urges Negro Equality."

Yet for all his smarts and push, Charley seemed to lose more
than he gained. His land deals went sour, he lost elections, and
trouble seemed to afflict his family: he built them a grand six-
room yellow house with a wraparound porch, a gym, and a music
room, and no sooner was it finished but it burned down. Nora
took it as a curse, and she pulled despair around her like a shawl,
and rocked, sang, and waited for the scourge to pour itself down
on them. She made lullabies for Clara, Roy, and Woody from tales
of lost children and grieving mothers, as though these would become their stories, as though she were reading their palms.

The deeper Nora went into her songs and stories—of widows
and jilted lovers wandering in the hills and forests; of abandoned
babies and disasters and floods—the more her memory of anything
else in her life withdrew. She would forget where she was and her

temper would erupt with fearsome suddenness. When Woody was five, she had another son, George, and people in Okemah began to talk of her as though she were touched: they said she chased the kids around the house with a broom and wrapped baby George in newspaper and put him in the oven.

But events bore Nora out. The Guthries were tinder for calamity: Charley would join the Ku Klux Klan and lose more elections and all their money. When Clara got to high school, she and Nora began to fight. In the spring of 1919, Nora ordered her to stay home from final examinations at school and help around the house. Clara refused; Nora grew angrier, and they circled each other in the kitchen like combatants in an arena, their fury spiraling. At last, Clara poured coal oil over her dress and touched a match to herself. She burned like a torch. Most of her skin was incinerated together with her nerve endings, and so she felt nothing afterwards. She talked cheerfully to Charley and the friends and neighbors who dropped by—she had only been trying to scare her mother—and was dead at the end of the day.

Nora had another baby, Mary Josephine, in 1922, and Charley ran for office again and lost. A year later, the Guthries were destitute, living on odd jobs and handouts. Charley's hands throbbed with arthritis and he kept the pain at bay with a jar of moonshine. Nora sobbed and railed against the world. She stopped singing altogether and sat in a movie theater all day when she could.

Roy and Woody kept the house and cooked and looked after George and Mary Josephine. Woody hung out with truants, Negroes, Indians, and vagrants. He was small and as scrawny as Christ on the cross, and at school the children teased him about his tattered clothes and wiry "nigger hair." He stayed away from classes, and taught himself to draw and play the harmonica.

In 1926 Charley sent George and Mary Josephine to live with his sister in Texas. Nora had become a specter in the shack they rented, silent save when a rage seized her and she threw crockery around the kitchen or threatened Charley with a kitchen knife.

Roy became a model of responsibility, tidy in his habits, thrifty, and industrious. Woody avoided home as much as he did school and cadged pocket money and meals playing his harmonica and drawing sketches around cafés and bars.

Charley quelled the dread and disappointment that had become his lot in life with drinking. One Saturday evening in June 1927, as he napped under his evening paper on the sofa, Nora set fire to him with a kerosene lantern, and watched him burn, her eyes huge and awestruck, as though the very apocalypse, lapping orange, pluming black, were consuming him. Charley staggered outside and rolled in the grass and then a neighbor rolled him in a blanket. Hospitalized and bandaged, he smoldered like a babe in purgatory for months.

Nora was committed to a state hospital for the insane, Charley moved to his sister's to continue his recuperation, and Woody, age fifteen, was alone in Okemah. Roy tried to look after him, but Woody preferred to sleep rough in a tin shack and later moved in with the family of a friend. He attended school often enough to excel in typing and geography. He visited Nora in the hospital, but she didn't know him anymore.

Woody took to the road, traveling among hoboes and visiting distant relatives and friends down into Texas and along the Gulf. When he got back to Okemah at the end of the summer of 1929, there was a letter from Charley. Charley was running a flophouse in Pampa in the Texas panhandle, collecting quarters from the oil roughnecks and hookers who bunked down there. There were other Guthrie relatives in the neighborhood and Woody could come and help him.

Woody went to Pampa without much enthusiasm and enrolled in the local high school. He failed most of his courses but found a close friend in a classmate, Matt Jennings. He and Jennings learned guitar from Woody's uncle Jeff, who also played the fiddle, and began to build a repertoire of cowboy and square-dancing songs. Within a year, Jeff, Woody, and Matt were playing—sometimes together, sometimes with other musician friends—for money at barn dances and rodeos around the panhandle.

In June 1930, Nora died in the asylum, and although Woody—now a wry and laconic eighteen-year-old—shrugged off her passing without much comment, it seemed as though she took half of heaven and earth down into the blackness with her. The next summer, locusts shrouded the skies and the land; the winter that followed was as bitter and white as lye. Spring rendered the frozen ground into gumbo, and by midsummer the baked and desiccated earth looked like a plain of shards, as cracked as Charley Guthrie's flesh.

Charley himself had lost his job, and was taken in by more Guthrie relatives. There was a story in the family that Charley's father, Jeremiah, had found a silver mine years ago in the desert near the Mexican border. With times so hard, it seemed like a good idea to go look for it, and Jeff, Charley, and Woody headed south. They didn't find any mine but they didn't look too hard either: they sat in the dead quiet among the brush and cactus, and sang and drank jars of corn whiskey and roasted a goat. The moon came up through the dusk like a quicksilver wafer, and drained the russet earth white. Coyotes psalmed the stars through the night, and in that riverless place called God to come home to them.

In Pampa, Woody continued with his guitar, learning Jimmie Rodgers songs and fashioning his personal variation on a comic Will Rogers persona. He was oblivious to money, an attitude that served him well. People had an appetite for the kind of music Woody and his friends were playing but couldn't afford to pay for it when they could scarcely put food on the table. They took comfort where they could. They read the Bible, listened to the radio, and believed in Jesus Christ and Franklin Roosevelt.

With so little to eat and so few of life's necessities within their grasp, people lived on faith instead of bread. They sang or spoke or imagined the things they wanted in words or pictures, as though their desires might gather mass like clouds out of an empty sky and fall like rain. They prayed and tried to heal themselves and the land. Charley took a new wife, Bettie Jean, who practiced a kind of spirit medicine she called electromagnetic healing. Few people in the countryside had electricity, just as in these drought times few had water, and it seemed that water and electricity were the right and left hands of God himself, of his mercy and power. Years before Émile Zola had written, "The day will come when electricity will be for everyone as the waters of the rivers and the wind of heaven." But for now, the earth was dark and dry.

Woody painted and drew Jesus, head after head after head, with representations of the "cops who killed him." He wrote songs to and about President Roosevelt: "If I was President Roosevelt / I'd make the groceries free / I'd give away new Stetson hats / and let the whiskey be." He got himself baptized in the Church of Christ, and dabbled in spiritualism. He wrote a credo—"May you see the non-reality of affliction and realize the allness of God. For God is truth, love"—and signed it "W. Guthrie—The soul doctor." Mostly, he read in the Pampa town library and played music, and wooed Matt Jennings's pretty little sister, Mary. In the fall of 1933, when Woody was twenty-one and Mary was seventeen, they married.

Then the wind began to blow. In 1934 and '35, in the panhandle and throughout the American Midwest, the soil was dry and fine as talc. When it took flight the dust was like snow—it stung faces and slithered across highways and mounded into drifts—but it was more like water; like a tide that penetrated over, under, and through every substance; that lapped, pooled, and formed ripples, bars, rips, and eddies. Shutters, windmills, and barn siding chittered and yawned like rigging in a gale. What did not blow away was inundated in dust. You could drown in it;

breathe it in and have your lungs fill with it and die of pneumonia. What had been loam and clay was now powder and sand; what had been solid was liquid; what had been dry land was a flood, and would bear them all away.

There seemed to be nothing to do but die or move on; "to cross the river," as Woody put it, one way or another. What nature wouldn't carry off on the wind, the bankers would haul away in foreclosure. It was time to be like Moses' people. Throughout Oklahoma, Kansas, Texas, Nebraska, and the Dakotas, farmers, laborers, and storekeepers became emigrants and pilgrims, and Woody went west with them.

Like most of the migrants, Woody went to California, where you could sleep outdoors all year and the water, in the words of a Jimmie Rodgers song Woody habitually played, tasted "like cherry wine." But California scarcely welcomed the migrants from the plains, collectively called "Okies": Police turned them back into the desert at the state border or arrested them for vagrancy. Agricultural labor brokers promised them five dollars a day picking peaches and avocados but paid them a dollar a week. They slept under bridges or along highways in hunger and squalor. Woody moved among them, from Los Angeles over the Tehachapi Mountains into the great Central Valley—as arid as the dust bowl save for irrigation—and his rootless insouciance heated into outrage.

The promised land was but another desert for the working man. For the past twenty years misfortune had followed on betrayal: Woodrow Wilson, whose very name Woody bore, sold out to the aristocrats and bankers of Europe and committed American boys to their insane and pointless war. His successors, Harding, Coolidge, and Hoover, let farmers starve and obstructed the trade union movement while allowing Wall Street to run amuck. Now the economy was a shambles and working people had nowhere to go—a roof to starve under, a place to lie down and die—even in California. That proved, as nothing else seemed to, that the capitalist polity was irredeemably corrupt and broken down, no longer capable of supporting even the robber industrialists and exploiters who had once thrived under it.

There was nothing—after the slaughter of the war, the capitalist hog's wallow of the twenties, and the scourge of the Depression—to believe in but the people themselves, and perhaps in Franklin Roosevelt. The apotheosis of wealth and good breeding, Roosevelt should have been everything working people despised, and yet he moved among them like Saint Francis among the animals, not a redeemer but surely a shepherd. He did not name the covenant he served—it seemed close enough to socialism by Woody's lights—but he knew where he wanted to lead them.

As long ago as 1920, when he was the unsuccessful Democratic candidate for vice president, he campaigned in the Pacific Northwest and mused aloud in a speech:

> Coming through today on the train has made me think pretty deeply. When you cross the mountain states and that portion of the coast states that lies well back from the ocean, you are impressed by those great stretches of physical territory, just land, territory now practically unused but destined someday to contain the homes of thousands and hundreds of thousands of citizens like us, a territory to be developed by the nation and for the nation. And as we were coming down the river today, I could not help thinking, as everyone does, of all that water running unchecked to the sea.

In fact, the harnessing of the Columbia River as a source of electric power or irrigation water or both became part of the Democratic party's platform that year. The most specific proposal had been conceived two years before by an Ephrata, Washington, lawyer named Billy Clapp and subsequently promoted by Rufus Woods, publisher and editor of the *Wenatchee World*. Clapp envisioned throwing a hydroelectric high dam across the river in the

Sanpoil country that would form a lake reaching more than one hundred miles back to the Canadian border. But the most ingenious and stunning aspect of Clapp's plan was to turn the Grand Coulee, the ancient dry course of the Columbia, into a massive irrigation storage reservoir by pumping river water from behind the dam up into its former bed. A heroically scaled project that might be likened to the construction of the pyramids, the Grand Coulee Dam would, Clapp believed, produce limitless cheap and clean electricity and transform the east central Washington desert from Priest Rapids to Spokane into an Eden.

In addition to Clapp and Woods, the Columbia Basin Project, as it was quickly dubbed, found its chief proponents in Nathaniel Washington, a direct descendent of George Washington's brother, and James O'Sullivan. O'Sullivan, the most tireless of them all, alone wrote fifteen newspaper articles in two months on behalf of the dam. At the start, O'Sullivan owned acreage that would be irrigated should the dam be built and therefore stood to gain a great deal from its construction. But both the slump that dogged American agriculture after the war and O'Sullivan's own bad luck diminished the value of his holdings; and his dedication to promoting the dam over any other work he might do did nothing to restore his fortunes.

People in and around Ephrata would surely prosper from the project, but from the start it was conceived to benefit the small farmer and the middle-class businessman or professional. The dam's opponents, the private utility industry, were of a different magnitude of power, wealth, and influence. Accustomed to lucrative monopolies, the "power trust" and its friends in government were quick to brand the Grand Coulee scheme, together with public utility ownership in general, as "socialistic" and "a colossal fraud" being foisted on the taxpayer by hicks and crackpots. Boosters like O'Sullivan portrayed the project as an exercise in democracy and a "square deal" for the little people, arguments that won little support in the 1920s.

In the election campaign of 1932, Franklin Roosevelt ran explicitly on a platform that not only supported the Columbia Basin Project but also opposed the power trust:

> . . . I state, in definite and certain terms that the next great hydroelectric development to be undertaken by the Federal Government must be that on the Columbia River. . . . And from there, my friends, . . . there will exist forever a national yardstick to prevent extortion against the public and to encourage the wider use of that servant of the American people—electric power.

In the summer of 1933, within three months of his inauguration, Roosevelt had authorized both Grand Coulee and another smaller dam at Bonneville, at the cascades of the lower Columbia. The city of Wenatchee held a "Carnival of Joy" to celebrate and the *Spokane Chronicle* reported that the rattlesnakes once so abundant at the dam site had disappeared, as though driven out by Roosevelt's decree.

The president returned triumphally in person in August 1934 and visited both Bonneville and Grand Coulee. He dreamt and reminisced: "I am reminded a good deal of another river . . . a river on which I was born and brought up—the Hudson." A century ago the Hudson had been connected to the rest of the continent via the Erie Canal and so became a great national highway. Perhaps the Columbia had the same fate, with navigation extending into eastern Washington, Idaho, and beyond.

Roosevelt admitted that these things—the dams and the other projects that might spring from them—involved an expenditure of federal funds that was disproportionate to the population of the Pacific Northwest, which contained 13 percent of the land area of the United States but at present only 2.8 percent of the population. But the region had a destiny that was larger than itself:

> In this Northwestern section of our land, we still have the opening of opportunity for a vastly increased population. There are many sections of the country, as you know, where conditions are crowded. There are many sections of the country

where land has run out or has been put to the wrong kind of use. America is growing. There are many people who want to go to a section of the country where they will have a better chance for themselves and their children. . . .

Out here you have not just space, you have space that can be used by human beings. You have a wonderful land—a land of opportunity—a land already peopled by Americans who know whither America is bound. You have people who are thinking about advantages for mankind, good education, and, above all, the chance for security, the chance to lead their own lives without wondering what is going to happen to them tomorrow. . . .

I know you good people are heart and soul behind this project and I think most of you are heart and soul behind what your government is trying to do to help the people of the United States. I wish I might stay here and survey everything in detail but, as you know, I have been on a long voyage and the sailor man does not stay put very long in one place.

He left them like a bishop, his blessings feathering the air like incense, and his train drew away along the river. He would come back and bring his other children with him.

In the dust-bowl years, unlike their counterparts in California, the people of the Northwest largely opened their hearts to the emigrants, who clutched tattered newspaper copies of Roosevelt's Columbia speeches. In eastern Washington they found signs that said, "Sure you're welcome—FDR says so!" Locals assured the water-obsessed refugees from the midwestern drought that while they didn't have much rainfall east of the Cascades, they had something better: the promise of irrigation, the steady, reliable provision of water when and where it was needed. Moreover, they would have cheap electricity controlled by the people, not the power trust:

water and power, by and for the people, the cornerstone of a square deal for the little man, symbolized by Franklin Roosevelt and his plan for the Columbia. A backwoods farmer settled near Bonneville told Richard Neuberger, a Portland-born journalist of liberal sympathies who wrote for the *New York Times* and *Life*, "That river belongs to us, not Wall Street." In 1936 at least ten thousand farm families immigrated to the Columbia country.

Where Woody traveled that year and in 1937 as one of 500,000 Okie migrants to California, there was neither welcome nor much water. He was on the highway alone: Mary, pregnant with their second child, stayed behind in Pampa with their newborn, Gwendolyn. Woody sang for drinks and meals in bars, cafés, and camps and the life he saw made him write his own songs: "Dust Bowl Refugee"; "(If You Ain't Got the) Do, Re, Mi"; and "So Long, It's Been Good to Know You." At the same time, like many Americans, he began to feel that Roosevelt's New Deal liberalism was an inadequate response to the injustice around him. He discovered the radical labor movement in the form of the International Workers of the World—Joe Hill's "Wobblies"—and their *Little Red Songbook*. In Los Angeles, where he and various relatives were gradually gaining an audience for their music, he began to attend Communist party functions.

In July 1937, Woody's cousin Jack talked the management of a left-leaning radio station, KFVD, into giving him and Woody an hour of unpaid airtime each day during which they sang hillbilly music and Woody spun stories and what he called "cornpone philosophy." In September, Jack dropped out and was replaced by a family friend, Maxine Crissman, whose on-air name was "Lefty Lou." The show began to attract a huge following among the homesick plains exiles in Los Angeles, and a nighttime broadcast was added that could be heard as far away as Oklahoma. They received a hundred letters a week and published a book of their favorite songs. Woody sent for Mary, Gwendolyn, and the new baby, Sue, although he forgot to pick them up when they arrived on the Santa Fe at Union Station.

In the new year of 1938, Woody moved to a new radio station and signed a contract for $75 a week. During his weeks off, he visited the refugee camps in the Central Valley, no longer a hobo himself, but a radio star. But he tried to wear his celebrity lightly:

> I'm just a pore boy trying to get along. The dust run me out of Texas and the officers run me in Lincoln Heights [jail in Los Angeles]. But they was nice to me. They had bars fixed up over the windows so nobody could get in and steal my guitar. . . . The Universe is my home, and Los Angeles is just a vase in my parlor. . . . I like pore people because they'll come out the winner in the long run. And I like rich people because they need friendship.

Woody still had little use for money, as Mary was only too aware, and he was determined to use his unique connection to "the people" in the service of social and economic justice. In "The Ballad of Pretty Boy Floyd" he expressed his preference for proletarian banditry over the politically sanctioned larceny of Wall Street and the bankers ("Some will rob you with a six-gun / And some with a fountain pen. . . . But . . . You will never see an outlaw / Drive a family from its home"). From a similar perspective, he transformed a popular hymn of Christian renunciation, "This World Is Not My Home," into a bitter socialist polemic: "Rich man took my home and drove me from my door. . . . My wife took down and died, upon the cabin floor. . . . And I ain't got no home in this world anymore." Although belied by his easy, self-effacing persona, Woody felt more and more convinced that he had a calling to speak both for and to the people.

Despite Woody's popularity and success, life in Los Angeles was not good for Mary. As often as not, Woody was absent from home; when he was there, he tended to ignore her. Mary suspected he might be having an affair with "Lefty Lou," and now openly said so. She took herself and the kids back to Pampa, and returned only when Woody agreed to dissolve the singing partnership, which was in any case running out of steam. When their third child, Bill, was born, Woody wasn't there to take Mary to the hospital.

With his radio career in hiatus, Woody deepened his political commitments: he performed at Communist party meetings and began to write a column in the *People's World* ("I ain't a communist necessarily, but I been in the red all my life"). Left-leaning Hollywood was quick to embrace Woody as an authentic proletarian, beside whom actor/singer friends such as Will Geer and Burl Ives appeared irretrievably bourgeois. He found himself performing for movie stars and celebrities by night, and by day defending in his column the Hitler-Stalin pact as well as Russia's subsequent invasion of Poland ("Stalin stepped in, took a big strip of Poland and give the farm lands back to the farmers"). While perhaps unsophisticated about geopolitics, Woody had the good sense to never formally join the party. Still, by the autumn of 1939, his radicalism was too well known for him to get much work in Los Angeles, and he decided to drop off Mary and the children in Pampa and try his luck in New York.

Woody got to New York in February 1940. He moved in with Will Geer and his wife, Herta, and after his somewhat lax standards of personal hygiene began to wear on them, moved on to Burl Ives's place on Riverside Drive. By February 23, he'd settled into a cheap hotel near Times Square and written some verses: "This land is your land, this land is my land / From California to Staten Island / From the Redwood Forest, to the Gulf Stream waters / God Blessed America for me." He would come back to them later.

Will Geer had arranged for Woody to sing at a "Grapes of Wrath Evening" he'd organized to benefit agricultural workers. Leadbelly and Aunt Molly Jackson, already well known by New York's radical community and intelligentsia, were on the program; Woody, on the other hand, was making his debut but, according to the *Daily Worker*, was "a real dust bowl refugee" who shouldn't be missed.

Woody took the stage of Broadway's Forrest Theater on March 3 with an aw-shucks manner as though he were working a barn dance in the panhandle. He said "Howdy," scratched his head, added something about how honored he was to be asked to play a few tunes in this "Rapes of Graft" show, and began to sing. The audience was enchanted; one member in particular, Alan Lomax, who archived folk music for the Library of Congress, felt that he had stumbled onto the anthro-musical Rosetta stone—a genuinely unspoiled purveyor of all the best of American folk traditions.

Lomax invited Woody straight down to Washington and recorded several hours of songs and conversation with him in the Department of the Interior's studios. Lomax also knew people at CBS, and in April got Woody a spot on a show called "Columbia School of the Air." That led to an appearance on "The Pursuit of Happiness," hosted by Burgess Meredith, and in May, a contract to record his dust-bowl ballads.

In the space of three months, Woody had become a near star in New York and on network radio. People could not get enough of him: outwardly an amiable hayseed, he sang with a droning but piercing conviction, spun enthralling stories, and played with words—double entendres, puns, spoonerisms, and all manner of syntactical inversion—like a three-card-monte artist. He was charming, and between Communist party ingenues and CBS secretaries, he developed and sated a formidable sexual appetite.

After the recordings were finished, Woody bought himself a new Plymouth and drove west with a young folk aficionado from Harvard named Pete Seeger. He intended to make up for his absence from Mary and the children by spending a long spell in Pampa, but only remained a few days. Instead, he visited union halls and refugee camps, and drove the leaders of the Oklahoma Communist party back to New York for the national party convention. Once they got to Manhattan, he gave them the car so they'd be able to get home.

Such acts of impulsive, eccentric charity suited Woody: he

knew enough of leftist mores to claim publicly that he was an atheist, but privately it was more complicated than that. He'd told people his two heroes were Will Rogers and Jesus Christ, and had in his own character fashioned what seemed to him a passable hybrid of the two. Woody's Jesus, however, was more an outlaw and revolutionary martyr than a god. He wrote a song, "They Laid Jesus Christ in His Grave," in which the Pharisees and Pilate were cast as bankers, tycoons, and Park Avenue aristocrats who killed Jesus for trying to help the poor.

By the end of the summer of 1940, Woody's record album, "Dust Bowl Ballads," was released to critical acclaim; however, sales were modest. But he landed a regular slot on a CBS show called "Back Where I Come From," and was deluged with offers for radio work. In November, CBS made him host of the Model Tobacco Company–sponsored "Pipe Smoking Time" at $350 a week. Naturally, it wouldn't do for him to go on writing the column he'd been doing for the *Daily Worker,* so he gave it up. He brought Mary, Gwendolyn, and Sue to New York where, awash in money, their marriage once again seemed to thrive: they went out on the town together and entertained in their apartment off Central Park while sitters watched the kids.

By the end of December, both family life and radio stardom had begun to sour. At home he felt trapped and laden down with obligations; at CBS he discovered he was wanted only for his folksy delivery of the Model Tobacco sales pitch—politics or even genuine folk music was strictly off limits. By year's end, he had more than he could bear, and loaded Mary, the children, and their scarcely opened Christmas presents into a new Pontiac and started driving west.

Mary thought Woody was crazy to walk away from everything he had in New York. They drove without stopping, tense and silent, Woody staring at the road like a pilot steering a ship into a gale. He got it into his head to visit a half-uncle in Mississippi named Lawrence Tanner. When they arrived on Tanner's doorstep, Woody mentioned they'd been eating mostly in Negro cafés. Tanner asked Woody how he'd like his daughter to marry a nigger, and Woody said he reckoned that would suit him just fine. Tanner threw them out.

Their next stop was at Mary's brother Matt's place in El Paso. Woody fought with Mary and got drunk and ornery. He stayed that way for some days, at one point throwing a brick through a store window with the observation, "Looks like a goddamn capitalist place to me." Having thus alienated his brother-in-law and oldest friend, they drove to California and settled for a few weeks in a ghost town called Sonora in the gold country of the Sierra foothills.

Woody figured they better go to Los Angeles and see if he could find some work. Down through the great Central Valley, the roadside camps and refugee squalor were largely gone, swept away by government programs and economic recovery. Woody felt a little lost. In Los Angeles, he spent most of his time filling notebooks with words, rhymes, and sketches while Mary cooked and washed and the children fussed. He worried that the people would get suckered into fighting the new war under way in Europe and get detoured off the road to socialism. Sometimes he wrote verses for the kids, as on the occasion when baby Bill knocked over a vase:

Ubangi, Ubanger, Youbangie, You
You bang Teeny [Gwendolyn] and Billy bangs Sue
Daddy and mommy are mad enough to kill,
Picking up the flowers what Bill did spill.

And sometimes he wrote as though he were making a gospel in his dime-store notebook:

When there shall be no want among you, because you'll own everything in Common. When the Rich will give their goods unto the Poor. I believe in this way. I just can't believe in any other way. This is the Christian way and it is already on a big part of the earth and it will come. To own everything in Common. That's what the Bible says. Common means all of us.

This is pure old commonism.

🏵️

Franklin Roosevelt returned to Grand Coulee in October 1937 for a picnic and a speech. The dam was half finished, and was, in Roosevelt's words, "the largest structure, so far as anybody knows, that has ever been undertaken by man." Nearly a mile long and 550 feet tall, its powerhouse would be the largest in the world and the 150-mile-long artificial lake backing up behind it the longest of its kind. The world's largest concrete plant would produce enough pour in its construction to build a highway around the perimeter of the United States. There were in excess of five thousand workers on the site—three score and more of whom would be killed during construction—earning from $0.90 to $1.62 an hour, and they were fed pancakes and turkey and were serviced in their off-hours by a dozen brothels and gaming parlors.

At the picnic, the president ate a ham sandwich and apple pie and licked his fingers clean. In the river bottom the water sluiced through the new piers of concrete like a downpour through a street grating. Over the next three years, the dam would rise atop them, poured block by block with grout pumped between the sections like frosting in a layer cake. Roosevelt spoke:

> Coming back to Grand Coulee after three years, I am made very happy by the wonderful progress that I have seen. And I cannot help feeling that everybody who has had anything to do with the building of this great dam is going to be made happy all the rest of his life . . . because we are building here something that is going to do a great amount of good for this Nation through all the years to come. . . .
>
> We look forward not only to the great good this will do in the development of power but also in the development of thousands of homes, the bringing in of millions of acres of new land for future Americans . . . that are going to be irrigated. There

are thousands of families in this country in the Middle West, in the Plains area, who are not making good because they are trying to farm on poor land. I look forward to the day when this valley, this basin, is opened up, giving the first opportunity to these American families who need some good farm land in place of their present farms. They are a splendid crowd of people, and it is up to us, as a nation, to help them live better than they are living now.

Not everyone in the country saw it that way, the president admitted. There were naysayers:

Most of the attacks being made . . . come from people who have never been out through the great west, come from people who do not understand the problem, for example, of the drought area. They are people who do not understand the obligation that the governments of the locality and of the state and of the Nation have to try to do everything they possibly can to make possible a decent living for the citizens within their borders.

Still, there were critics. On the left, writers for the *Nation* suspected land speculation must be rampant, although they could find little evidence of it. On the right, *Colliers* suggested the $400 million project was a boondoggle that would produce power nobody wanted or needed at taxpayer expense: "One of these days, science may evolve a method of producing power on a large scale for practically nothing—by 'cracking the atom,' for example"— but hydroelectric dams in the middle of nowhere were not the way.

Yet for the most part, the Columbia project was making a favorable impression on Americans, and even before its completion was attaining a mythic status in the public imagination. *Reader's Digest* spoke of "100,000 migrants from the dust bowl into the Northwest . . . [who] look to these new projects as the Israelites looked to Canaan." *Life* magazine, already renowned for the photojournalism that, together with Steinbeck's *Grapes of Wrath*, exposed the plight of the Okies, ran stories by Richard Neuberger

that portrayed the dam as a simultaneous triumph of technical ingenuity, populism, and the national destiny.

By 1939 the Columbia project had a full-time publicist: Stephen Kahn of the newly created Bonneville Power Administration (BPA). The BPA was set up to sell and distribute power from
the Columbia dams to both private and publicly owned utilities,
all at the same low rate, but its charter gave preference to public
systems. Without the need to return a profit to stockholders, public utilities were in a position to offer cheaper rates, a prospect
that alarmed the private power industry. When the bill authoriz-
ing BPA squeaked through Congress in 1937, the young Kahn—
Richard Neuberger's college roommate—worked as a lobbyist on
its behalf, having already organized an advocacy group called the
People's Power League of Oregon and spent time at the Ten-
nessee Valley Authority (TVA), one of the model projects of the
New Deal. A few months later Kahn was appointed BPA public
information officer.

Officially, BPA was nothing more than a government agency
charged with the prosaic business of shunting electricity through
power lines. But unofficially, as the private utility industry feared,
its agenda was the promotion of public ownership of power production and distribution. Staffed by Jewish liberals like Kahn,
BPA was portrayed by its enemies as an agent of socialism—"First
they'll socialize your electricity, then the grocery store, then your
wife," power company lobbyists liked to say. Privately, many at
the BPA would not have minded being called socialists: the agency
promoted not only the use of electricity and its provision to every
home in the region but, more surreptitiously, the acquisition of
private utilities by municipalities and rural cooperatives. Kahn
hoped BPA could be the foundation of a Columbia Valley Authority, which, like the TVA, would transform the whole region
not just with power and irrigation but through transportation,
economic-development, health, and cultural programs.

To that end, Kahn hired graphic artists to produce posters and advertisements exhorting the public to recognize "It's Your River!" He became adept at cultivating small-town newspaper editors. He was a master at transforming what were officially announced as hearings and informational meetings into public-power rallies by peppering audiences with supporters whose prepared questions would allow him to portray the BPA cause in the most favorable light. He created slogans and lyrics for inspirational songs. As tough and ruthless as he was idealistic, Kahn admitted he could move himself to tears with his own writing.

In 1939 he hired a film director named Gunther Von Fritsch to produce a documentary called *Hydro!*, a thirty-minute celebration of the river, hydroelectricity, and public power with professional narration and a dramatic original score. Kahn himself wrote the script, stressing "the untamed might of the Columbia, thirty million horses plunging relentlessly to the sea." Now at Bonneville Dam, "men forge their answer to the river's fury in concrete and steel," transforming the Columbia into "an oil well that will never run dry, a shackled giant."

At Grand Coulee—"the greatest thing man has ever done"— "The jackhammers thunder a call to arms against the desert: Water!" and create "a chance for the little fellow in the Big Bend country, an American destiny for a half a million migrants!" More prosaically but rather too craftily for the power industry, *Hydro!* contrasted cheap public power with private rates and sparkling electric ranges with sooty farmhouse woodstoves. In the end, it all came down to electricity—"Behind the American way of life lies hydro . . . power to make the American dream come true" as the nation "takes up the challenge of the Columbia, the saga of man's triumph over a continent!"

Kahn was pleased with *Hydro!*'s blend of patriotism and populism but thought the film—which consisted largely of panoramas of the river and construction activity at the dams—needed a more personal, human approach. He envisioned an on-screen narrator in the mold of a folksy storyteller and perhaps a score to match. He eventually reached Alan Lomax at the Library of Congress, who said he had just the man for the job.

As the spring of 1941 wore on, Woody had found nothing in Los Angeles to ease his boredom and discontent. Mary expected him to pack up and leave on one of his solo road trips. When he didn't, she considered leaving herself—she felt she and the kids were for all practical purposes alone already. Pete Seeger and some friends had formed a group called the Almanac Singers that was appearing with some success around the East Coast, and that only added to Woody's sense of failure. The automobile finance company wanted the three months he was in arrears immediately. When Gunther Von Fritsch turned up at his door, Woody was ready to go somewhere—anywhere.

Von Fritsch, however, was only considering Woody from a longer list of candidates he was interviewing. But Woody refused to accept that uncertainty: when a letter from BPA arrived informing him that a final decision would be some time in coming, he loaded the Pontiac and put the kids in. Mary, against all better judgment, got in too. Halfway to Oregon, they hocked the radio for groceries.

They arrived in Portland the first week of May 1941. The car looked like a kennel stuffed with squalling kids. Mary's blond hair was tangled, her expression flat as cold coffee. Woody was bearded, his nails like black crescent moons, his clothes tattered and soiled, and the aromas that rolled off his body ranged from sour milk to skunk fur to creosote. When he turned up at Steve Kahn's desk, the signs were not auspicious. But Kahn, for reasons beyond reason, wanted to do something for him. Woody had ignored hiring procedures, but maybe they could be sidestepped if the BPA director, Dr. Paul J. Raver, would agree to make a special case.

Raver was an owlish, orderly academic who was more interested in joining a good Portland country club than in changing the world, and Kahn sent Woody with his guitar into the director's office with faint hope that anything would come of it. He suspected that Raver, who looked away when Kahn tried to show him the Hooverville under the Grand Avenue bridge, would give Woody five minutes, if that. An hour later, Woody strolled out, signed his loyalty oath, and was a BPA employee with a one-month contract, to wit:

1. To narrate designated sequences of documentary motion picture, using both scripts furnished to him and scripts which he has assisted in preparing. . . .
2. To appear in designated scenes of film and accurately depict human experiences of man engaged in construction of Bonneville and Grand Coulee dams, erection of transmission lines, and other economic problems related to the federal development of the Columbia River.
3. To assist in writing narration, dialogue, and musical accompaniment requisite in the production of the above mentioned documentary film.

He would earn $266.66 for the month. He, Mary, and the three children got a room at the Bridgeport Hotel, and later moved to a walk-up on the southeast fringe of Portland. The finance company found the Pontiac and hauled it away. Woody figured he didn't want it anyway, he told Kahn.

Kahn gave him a desk in the basement of the BPA building, a typewriter, and some books on the history of the river: Thomas Jefferson, Lewis and Clark, the Indian wars. He gave him a driver, a Grange activist named Elmer Buehler. Elmer's father had lost everything on Portland Electric Company stock during the slump, and now Elmer evangelized for the BPA, projecting *Hydro!* to farmers and fruit and hop pickers inside church halls and outside under the summer moon. He drove Woody in a big black 1940 Hudson with "Bonneville Power Administration" in gold letters on the front doors. He kept the windows open on account of the smell. Woody sprawled his five-foot-seven-inch, 125-pound body across the backseat like a spill of dirty laundry. He and Elmer didn't talk much. Woody just played and sang this thing or that: "As I went walking that ribbon of highway / And saw above me the endless skyway / And saw below me that golden valley"—things that didn't seem to have much to do with the dams.

Elmer drove him to Spokane, Grand Coulee, Bonneville, Wenatchee, Yakima, the Dalles, Celilo Falls, and up and down the Willamette Valley, and Elmer wondered if he was taking any of it in. But the Northwest was making an impression, and the words were coming:

> I saw the Columbia River from just about every cliff, mountain, tree and post from which it can be seen. . . . It's got ridges of nine kinds of brown, hills out of six colors of green, ridges five shades of shadow, and stickers the eight tones of hell. . . .

At Grand Coulee, he watched the workers move in and out of the shadow of the dam—the biggest thing human beings had ever made, by and for the people—and he seemed to become one of them and it was all the work he had ever done and never sung:

> . . . I was there on these very spots and very grounds before, when the rockwall canyon stood there laughing around me, and while the crazybug machines, jeeps, jacks, dozers, mixers, trucks, cars, lifts, chains and pulleys and all of us beat ourselves down every day yelling and singing little snatches of songs we was too hot and too tired to set down with our pen and pencil right then while the thing was being built.

Back at the BPA, it seemed as though he was passing the time of day, joshing the secretaries and stinking up the office. Kahn wanted a half-dozen or so usable songs for the film, and he worried he wasn't going to get them. All Woody's melodies came from traditional sources, but that still meant there were an awful lot of lyrics to be written. Kahn considered standing over Woody with a whip.

Kahn thought you got ideas or saw things, and then laid them down in a row in words. He thought writing was like sawing wood, but for Woody it was like chasing something, and once you caught it you didn't know if it was pulling you or you were pulling it. It was like hoop snakes, mouth eating tail, cartwheeling down the hill; it was spiraling down, deeper and deeper, and finishing up on top again, only somewhere different; it was like Jesus, coming down and walking around and dying and going down to hell and coming back again and then leaving. It was the river, turning through heaven and earth.

How could he stop? He couldn't even sign a letter to Alan Lomax after it was all over; he typed:

Woody Guthrie
as per
Woody Guthrie
for
Woody Guthrie
and by god by
Woody Guthrie

and then wrote longhand, "Woody Guthrie."

Woody's typewriter thrummed like a turbine, and he wrote about twenty-eight songs in twenty-eight days, songs about the men who built the dam:

I worked in the Garden of Eden, that was in the year of two,
Joined the apple-pickers union and always paid my dues.
I'm the man who signed the contract to raise the rising sun
And that's about the biggest thing that man has ever done.

There were seven songs alone about the dam and its builders: "The Biggest Thing That Man Has Ever Done," "Grand Coulee Powder Monkey," "Jackhammer Blues," "The Song of the Grand

Coulee Dam," "Columbia Waters," "Guys on the Grand Coulee Dam," and "Ballad of the Great Grand Coulee":

> At the Umatilla Rapids, at The Dalles, and at Cascades,
> Mighty men have carved a history of the sacrifices made,
> In the thundering foaming waters of the big Celilo Falls,
> In the big Grand Coulee country that I love best of all.

> In the misty crystal glitter of the wild and windward spray,
> Men have fought the pounding waters, and met a wat'ry
>   grave,
> Well she tore their boats to splinters and she gave men
>   dreams to dream,
> Of the day the Coulee Dam would cross that wild and
>   wasted stream.

> Uncle Sam took up the challenge in the year of thirty-three,
> For the farmer and the worker, and all of you and me,
> He said roll along Columbia, you can ramble to the sea,
> But river while you're rambling, you can do some work for
>   me.

He wrote songs about migrants who will find irrigated farms by the river:

> Green pastures of plenty from desert ground,
> From the Grand Coulee dam where the waters run down,
> Ev'ry state in this Union us migrants have been,
> We come with the dust and we're gone with the wind.

There were songs about farmers without electricity ("My eyes are crossed, my back's in a cramp / Tryin' to read my bible by my coal oil lamp") and farmers whose land will blow away without ir- rigation. Sometimes there were songs about jobs, factories, the dam, government, public power, and the river, all mixed up:

> That Columbia River rolls right down the line,

And the Columbia Waters taste like sparklin' wine;
But the waters in the dust bowl tastes like picklin' brine.

The money that I draw from a workin' on Coulee Dam,
My wife will meet me at the kitchen door a stretchin' out her
   hand;
She'll make a little down payment on a forty acre tract of
   land.

We'll farm along the River and work from sun to sun,
I'll walk along the River and listen to the factories run,
I'll think to myself, Great Goodness, look what Uncle Sam
   has done.

But in the end, all the work, all the power, all the water came
down to the river itself:

Green Douglas firs where the waters cut through,
Down her wild mountains and canyons she flew.
Canadian Northwest to the ocean so blue,
Roll on, Columbia, roll on!
Roll on, Columbia, roll on,
Roll on, Columbia, roll on.
Your power is turning our darkness to dawn,
So roll on, Columbia, roll on!

He had never written so much nor, he felt, so well. After he
left his cubicle at BPA at the end of the day, he'd wander down to
the Hooverville under the bridge or sing for drinks in the skid-
row bars off Burnside Street. When they threw him out, he went
home and poured more verses and words into his notebooks.

It seemed as though he and Mary hardly saw each other. She'd
go out as soon as he'd get home. Each figured the other was stepping out with other people, and Gwendolyn, Sue, and Bill enter-
tained themselves in the yard behind the walk-up. And Woody
wrote something called "It Takes a Married Man to Sing a Wor-

ried Song" and then one called "The White Ghost Train":

> When a man and wife get married and are sleeping side by
> side
> Dreaming pretty dreams of heaven, into California glide,
> When the honeymoon it's over and they both wake up again,
> Well, it's tickets then for Reno on the same old White
> Ghost Train.
>
> Now the White Ghost Train is crowded and she runs
> around the world,
> The rich and stingy miser and the loving boys and girls,
> You can have your whirl at loving, and at trifling take a fling,
> You will pull in Hell at midnight on the lovely White Ghost
> Train.

When his BPA contract ran out in mid-June, he arranged to meet up with Pete Seeger and the Almanac Singers for a tour of the country. Now that Hitler had betrayed Stalin, it was time for the working man to get ready for war. Mary and the children stayed in Portland. She and Woody met up in Los Angeles that August, but somewhere, perhaps miles or years back, the will to go on together had dried up. Mary took the children to her family in Texas and that was the end of her and Woody.

It seemed a time for endings. Before he'd left Portland, Woody revisited the migrant labor and farm camps up and down the river. He sang wherever he went, but he began to think it didn't matter who sang the songs and he listened to the people in the camps sing. People should sing for themselves, he thought. Maybe he wasn't here to sing anyway; maybe it was for something else:

> I made it my business to go into lots of the tents and shacks
> this trip that I didn't make on other trips, and hear them all
> sing, the little sisters, brothers, yodelers, ma and pa in the old
> yaller light of a coal oil lamp, sittin in a rocker, or on the side
> of an old screaking bed, eyes about half shut, bottom lip

pooched out full of snoose, and they sang religious, hopeful songs and sentimental worried songs but hours on hour could sing and sing and sing. And I made a little speech in each tent and I said, You folks are the best in the West. Why dont you take time out and write up some songs about who you are, where you come from, where all you been, what you was a lookin for, what happened to you on the way, the work you done and the work you do and the work and the things you want to do. Your songs so far are not your songs, but songs that somebody else has put in your head, and for that matter, not your own life, not your own work, trouble, desires, or romances; why had you ought to sing like your rich when you ain't rich, or satisfied when you ain't satisfied, or junk like you hear on these nickel machines and over the radio? Every one of them would lean and look towards me and keep so still and such a solemn look on their faces, there in those little old greasy dirty hovels that it would bring the rising sun to tears. In a few minutes some young and dreaming member of the family would break down and say, I been a thinkin about that ever since I commenced a singin. And then the whole bunch would enter into a deeper religious conversation and decide that I was right. On more than one night, on more than one day, I've heard my Oakie friends ask me, Say Mister, you don't happen to be Mister Jesus do you? Come back?

3.

Grand Coulee Dam was completed in January 1942, a month after the United States went to war. By June, the 150-mile-long reservoir was full and then, like a veil of glass, water sheeted over the crest of the dam. Electricity coursed down the lines. For the opening ceremony, dam officials had gotten the Nez Percé chief from the Colville Reservation to throw the switch. He stood on the parapet, forty stories above the river, and felt how the whole huge thing vibrated and hummed as it sucked the river through it, drinking the blood of the world.

Within a year 96 percent of Columbia River power was going to the war effort. Aluminum mills—each of which consumed as much electricity in a day as did all the homes in Oregon—rolled out aluminum skins for bombers, which Boeing produced at the rate of sixteen per day. In Portland and Vancouver, Kaiser shipyard workers stitched plates together with electric welds and pushed a new ship out into the river every two weeks. James O'-Sullivan, Grand Coulee's most tireless advocate, had written Roosevelt and Churchill in 1940, urging that the dam's completion be speeded up in light of the contribution it could make to the war that was then inevitable. By 1942 both he and the dam were vindicated: what once seemed extravagant and wasteful was now proving vital to the war effort. Despite that, O'Sullivan himself became an obscure and impoverished figure in the swelling Northwest war boom: *Life* magazine inexplicably left him out of a photo of founding fathers of the Columbia Basin Project, and he and his family went without dental work and new clothes.

Woody, too, was finding neither money nor fame. The tour with the Almanac Singers had culminated in their appearance on a network radio spectacular called "This Is War!", singing Pete Seeger's "Round and Round Hitler's Grave," and they seemed poised for commercial success. Then the *New York World-Telegram* announced that "the Almanac singers have long been the favorite balladeers of the Communists and their official publications, the *Daily Worker* and *New Masses*." Other papers picked up the story: the Almanacs would not gain a mainstream audience after all.

Woody was hardly devastated: he was warier than ever of the blandishments of capitalism; moreover, he was in love. Living in New York, he'd met a dancer with the Martha Graham company named Marjorie Mazia. Born into a leftist Russian-Jewish family and educated in highbrow culture, sophisticated yet naive, exotic yet virginal, she was a far cry from Pampa. She was married, but that was beside the point. The very thought of her prompted sexual and psychic ecstasies that Woody poured into letters and notebooks. By June she was pregnant with Woody's child.

He was as happy as he'd ever been, but broke and not really getting anywhere with his writing and performing. When Stephen Kahn came to New York that summer to have Woody record the soundtrack for the BPA film—Kahn couldn't say when, with the war on, it might be released—Kahn gave him twenty dollars out of his own pocket to see him through the week. But then, thanks to yet another of Alan Lomax's contacts, Woody signed a contract with Dutton for a book called *Boomchasers*, a memoir of his life on the road. He arranged to have some of the advance sent to Mary in Texas. By the end of 1942 Woody finished the book, now retitled *Bound for Glory*, and on February 6, 1943, Marjorie gave birth to Cathy Ann Guthrie. Woody adored her as much as he adored Marjorie: she had her mother's dancer's legs and her daddy's curly hair. He nicknamed her "Stackabones" and drafted cartoons in which she announced, "I was elected to be sent out into the world to fight fascism."

In April 1943, *Bound for Glory* was published to reviews that praised its hard-edged agrarian realism and quirky style. Orville Prescott of the *New York Times* remarked, "There certainly hasn't been anything like it before, an ecstatic, breathless, jutting geyser of scrambled words." Dutton signed him for another book; interviewers and radio shows pursued him. At the same time Marjorie finally made a formal break with her husband. Woody rented a place near the sea on Coney Island and Marjorie and Cathy Ann came home to him at last.

In May, Woody received a notice from his draft board advising him that he would be called up for an induction physical the following month. His buddy Cisco Houston, a sometime member of the Almanacs, pressed him to join the merchant marine, where he could be among working men and travelers like himself instead of a grunt draftee in an infantry company. He shipped out in June on the *William B. Travis,* a supply ship bringing up the rear of a transatlantic convoy.

The *William B. Travis* plowed across the plain of the sea. The swells were dunes of verdigris or a cascade colored like paloverde bark, ruched out in every direction. They were at the nether end of the convoy, and sometimes they seemed to be alone, and at any moment a torpedo could take them down. Woody had never been to sea before, and sometimes he felt queasy—not in a seasick way but as though his mind were getting away from him like Nora's had; as though he were trying to imagine how deep the water beneath his feet might be, and could not begin to do so and then could see all too well.

In the fall of 1943, Willie Daniels was working in holes fifty and seventy-five feet deep, filling them with concrete. The windowless walls were eight hundred feet long, three to six feet thick, and one hundred feet high. They were the strangest, most enormous things he had ever seen, like kids' building blocks of stone set down in the desert, as big as skyscrapers laid on their sides. The insides were full of pits like giant sinks, forty in a row, seventeen-by-thirteen-feet, and twenty feet deep, each with a drain and a lid six feet thick. They repeated like cells in a honeycomb, and if you stood at one end of the building and tried to focus on the other, you'd probably see a mirage.

Willie didn't know what the buildings were, and wasn't supposed to ask. They just called them "canyons," and there were three of them. But they might have been ships, ships gray as river rock in the desert just south of Priest Rapids; ships like Noah's big enough to carry everyone and everything away. Sixteen men died building them.

People in the construction camp had stranger notions than

that: some said that every night the army people shipped bodies down the river under cover of darkness, the result of whatever they were cooking up with the professors and engineers. But the camp was awash in rumors, like whiskey vapors condensing out of the heated ignorance of too many people with too little information. Being colored and set aways off from most of the camp, Willie didn't know the half of it, which in any case was half of nothing.

Willie was by no means an ignorant man. He was born in Kildare, Texas, and went to the Negro college in Prairie View, and taught in colored-only schools around Texas. Come the Depression, he worked at a creosote plant: then on the railroad, bucking ties; then at a concrete plant making thirty-three dollars a week. When he heard from an uncle about the Hanford Engineering Works in the summer of '43—that it was paying a dollar an hour and desperate to hire all comers—Willie and his brother Vanis dropped everything and got a bus to Pasco on the Columbia River.

The bus tore down the narrow river road at a terrifying speed and Willie thought they'd drown in the river before they ever got to Hanford. Once they got settled in the barracks, the wind blew without a halt day and night. There was so much dust that within an hour of setting down your suitcase, you could write your name on it. Willie and Vanis bunked in the colored part of the camp and ate in the colored mess hall. Most of the men working with the concrete were colored. It was a rough camp: there was gambling, whores, and knife fights, but it was rougher still in the white section—mostly Okies and Arkies—where they had to use tear gas from time to time to settle the men down. There were fifty thousand workers at Hanford in 1943 to '44, which made it the fourth largest city in Washington State, and nobody knew about it or what it was, except that it was something for the war.

In April 1944, an Oregon congressman named Homer Angell told some reporters about something he called "the mystery load" that BPA was servicing: a project requiring vast amounts of power that would create "a new weapon of warfare, developed by new manufacturing processes that will turn large volumes of electricity into the most important projectile yet developed." The mystery load was fifty-five thousand kilowatts of Grand Coulee hydropower. All of BPA's public utility customers combined used perhaps forty-five thousand kilowatts. The army scrambled to get Angell's remarks removed from the news wires and by and large succeeded.

Willie left Hanford at the end of 1944, none the wiser about the "canyons," and went downriver to work in the shipyards in Vancouver. He'd made good money at Hanford—seventy dollars sometimes for a six-day week of twelve-hour shifts—even if there was no place to go and nothing to do and it was the driest, emptiest place he'd ever seen. For security reasons, you couldn't even say its name. It was a five-hundred-square-mile eddy in the Columbia, invisible as clear, still, silent water in an ocean of brush and river gravel, mute and unspeakable.

Down at the river there were intakes and outlets, drawing and discharging millions of gallons of water through pipes and tunnels, underground and aboveground, to the gray buildings and chambers Willie had helped make. On their days off, workers sometimes went swimming in the river, although the army had made even the Indians who'd lived and fished there forever abandon the site. Willie stayed away: the banks were snaky as anything in southeast Texas and, as he said to Vanis, folks had told him "That Columbia River don't give up the dead—No, sir."

By the summer of 1944, Woody had decided he wouldn't sign on for any more voyages if he could get away with it: he'd been torpedoed twice and Cathy Ann's infancy had slipped away while he wasn't looking, and he didn't want to miss the rest of her childhood. He also thought he'd better do what he could to help Franklin Roosevelt's campaign for a fourth term, which the Republicans and their candidate Thomas Dewey were setting up to be a plebiscite on socialism and the influence of the left on American life. The Communist Political Association put together a tour called "The Roosevelt Bandwagon" with Will Geer as master of ceremonies and featuring Woody and Cisco Houston among the performers.

Yet scarcely had Roosevelt been reelected when he died in April 1945. Woody had been critical of Roosevelt, but all the alternatives, in and out of the Democratic party, looked worse. As if to serve notice that a new order had arrived, the army sent him another induction notice. When he went down to the merchant marine hiring hall to try to ship out again to avoid being sent to boot camp, he was told that his name appeared on a list of people known to be involved with the Communist party. He was therefore no longer eligible to serve in the merchant marine. Woody was inducted into the army on V-E Day, May 1945.

They sent him to Texas for his basic training, and Mary brought Gwendolyn, Sue, and Bill to visit him. He hadn't seen them in four years, and he tried to act like their father. Woody and his children posed together in a photo booth at Woolworth's in Oklahoma City and he sang and joked for them. But they were figures he could barely make out, glimmers of hair and brown shoes and spindly limbs seen through water; they were far away across an enormous room like Grand Central Station; and even though he could swear his desire was moving him toward them, he could not reach out his arm or walk the span that lay between them.

Back at the base, the army put Woody in a teletypist class. On August 9, he was standing in the hall outside the classroom smoking during the break when he heard about the Nagasaki bomb and the Japanese surrender. The bomb was made of plutonium, produced and refined with Grand Coulee electricity and Columbia River water in the reactors and "canyons" on the banks of Columbia; dropped from a B-29 Superfortress fabricated of Columbia aluminum with Columbia hydropower; the gift and creature of the river; the river itself condensed to an instant of light, to a word beyond words.

Woody figured they'd discharge him right away, but they took their time. They made him barracks guard and had him sit around and then they made him a sign painter. He started singing and drawing sketches for the soldiers in the PX, wrote in his notebooks and worked up ideas for a novel, and masturbated like a caged monkey while he wrote Marjorie sexy letters. Mostly the letters were funny and conversational, but sometimes the writing was like a gyroscope, balanced and spinning, apparently self-sustaining and independent of anything outside itself. And then it would wobble and dip with a lurch that put his stomach on the roof of his mouth and spin away, untethered:

> Just dizzy. Woozy. Blubberdy. And scrubberdy and rustlety, tastlety, I was saying. Fantiffy, fantiffy, fantoy, fantoy. Poodle de poodle de dum dum. Doodle doodle dum. Cockle a doodle daylight, my old hen lays eggs for the railroad men.

And then it would be as it was before. And he'd think, "This is the soberest drunk I ever got on," and forget about it.

The army finally discharged Woody at the end of 1945, and he came home to Marjorie and Cathy on Coney Island and times were good. Their living room became the neighborhood center for political activists, nonconformist adolescents, mothers, and children. The joy Woody took in Cathy seemed to encompass all children, and he was tireless in lavishing them with singing and storytelling. He and Marjorie were as children among children in their happiness, and Woody knew he wanted to have another baby with her.

During 1946 Woody thought he would write a book about his life in the merchant marine and that fizzled out and then he started one about his childhood and that didn't go anywhere either. As for music, he had great hopes for a collective booking agency called People's Songs he'd started with Pete Seeger and some of the old Almanacs. After an initial burst of interest in People's Songs "hootenannies," however, the audiences started getting smaller. The music was too overtly political for the mainstream public, and even the unions—Woody's bread-and-butter audience—seemed to be losing interest. With the Depression and the war over, with Stalin turned from an ally into a villain and the gutless centrism of Harry Truman ascendant, it was as though people didn't have any use for social and economic justice.

Woody didn't take it lying down. He got more radical, more obstreperous, more shocking, and more offensive in his performances, mixing puns and sex jokes and political insults all together, figuring he could snap the world out of this lethargy it was nodding off into. But as often as not people thought he was just a boor or a weirdo. At parties and meetings Woody was acquiring a reputation for erratic behavior—silly, nonsensical talk and obnoxious high jinks like snatching somebody's cigarette holder and hiding it—that could be chalked up to drunkenness, except that it wasn't exactly clear he was drunk.

None of that really mattered to Woody though. The year 1947 was going to be even better than 1946. Marjorie was pregnant and Woody was working on a novel he called *House of Earth,* and he thought it was the finest thing he'd ever done: it was a simple and beautiful story about a destitute farmer in the Texas panhandle who wanted, against all odds, to build himself and his wife a home of adobe mud.

On the sixth of February, Woody and Marjorie celebrated Cathy's fourth birthday, and a few days later Woody went off to New Jersey to sing for a union meeting. Marjorie stayed home with Cathy, who insisted on wearing her new pink birthday dress, even just to sit on the couch and listen to the radio and nod her curly head in time to the music. In the afternoon, Marjorie went out for a few minutes to buy some fruit. When she got back, there was smoke inside the house. The couch was smoldering and Cathy was mewling softly, her dress and most of her skin burned away.

At the hospital, the only place the doctors could put the intravenous tube was into her foot and Marjorie held her foot and she thought Cathy was singing. Woody got home that night and found a note on the door telling him to come to the hospital right away. He came and saw Cathy and watched her and then he too held her foot—it was the only part of her anyone could hold—and by the morning she was dead. The firemen said it was the radio that started the fire: the electricity made a short or a spark and that ignited the dress. In the days that followed, Woody raged, but there was no longer anything in the world he could damn that was big enough to assuage him, and then he was quiet like the white dust of snow that iced the beach. In his notebook he paraphrased Job—"My roarings are poured out like the waters / For the thing which I greatly feared is come upon me"—as though he were a prophet unto himself, writing, "And the things you fear shall truly come upon you. . . ."

4.

Ralph Bennett was the kind of young man Steve Kahn liked to see working at BPA. His family had owned a newspaper, the *Optimist*, in the Dalles, which Bennett had taken over when he got home from college and which had been very friendly to the cause of public power. Bennett was smart, he was on the right side of things, and he understood the uses of publicity. BPA had scarcely hired him when he went out to La Grande, Oregon, and shook up the local private utility with an anti-power-trust brochure he put together on the spot called "The Man Nobody Knows."

Bennett had gone to Harvard—quite something for a boy from a little Columbia River town in Oregon. When he was a freshman in 1939, he was a grind, oblivious to everything but his class work, but then he discovered politics. He read Marx and Engels and joined the John Reed Club. He got on the editorial board of the *Crimson,* which like himself was passionately against America's entry into the war in Europe. Even after Hitler invaded Russia in 1941, Bennett remained antiwar, convinced that the theory of Marx and Engels and the practical experience of the 1914–18 world war showed that such conflicts served only the interests of international capitalists.

Pearl Harbor changed everything. Bennett wanted desperately to join the service but could not be inducted because of his poor eyesight. He went back to Harvard and finished his degree with a thesis on Engels's ideas about matriarchy in precapitalist society. Then his father died and he came home to run the *Optimist,* whose editorials proved vital in creating a public utility district in the Dalles. When the paper finally closed in 1946, BPA showed its appreciation by giving him a job in the public information office, working under Michael Loring, Steve Kahn's lieutenant. It was the best of all possible worlds: fighting Wall Street on behalf of the U.S. government while earning decent pay.

Folk music was part of the leftist ethos Bennett had steeped himself in, and he'd been moved by Woody Guthrie's records and his legendary stories of the American proletariat. When Bennett found out Guthrie had actually worked in this very place and written music here, he was awed. The river songs had been played on the radio and at meetings a few times, but the film *The Columbia* had been shelved during the war years and was still incomplete. Bennett figured the BPA should exploit its connection with Guthrie; moreover, he was eager to meet a man who was one of his heroes. When Bennett was assigned to work on a rural electrification conference being organized in Spokane, he persuaded Loring and Kahn that BPA ought to bring Guthrie in to entertain.

A week or two after Cathy Guthrie's death, Woody got a telegram from Ralph Bennett:

BPA INTERESTED IN YOUR SINGING COLUMBIA RIVER

SONGS AT NATIONAL RURAL ELECTRIC COOPERATIVE CONVENTION AT SPOKANE, APRIL 21 THRU 23. GOOD CHANCE YOUR SONGS TO COME INTO THEIR OWN OUT HERE WHERE THEY WERE MEANT TO BE SUNG. MIGHT ARRANGE OTHER APPEARANCES. ARE YOU INTERESTED? HOW MUCH BESIDES EXPENSES?

Bennett didn't hear anything from Guthrie, and figured it was unlikely he would want to come to Spokane. Meanwhile Bennett was preoccupied with plans for his wedding, which was set for March 30. Then word came from New York that Guthrie would appear for five hundred dollars plus a plane ticket to Spokane. Kahn approved and Bennett was ecstatic.

Bennett, married to his new wife, Anna Lou, for just three weeks, checked into the Davenport Hotel in Spokane on the appointed day in April. He asked the desk clerk if Mr. Guthrie had checked in. He had, indeed, Bennett was assured. He was in Room 1246. Bennett rode up to the top floor of the Davenport, and walked down the corridor toward Guthrie's room, his heart pounding with anticipation. The door was open. He entered and called out. No one answered. There was a knot of ripe, dirty clothes on the floor and the toilet was unflushed. Woody had been here.

Bennett found Woody a little later at a bar down the street. He had a guitar with the legend "This Machine Kills Fascists" slathered across the front and a sheath of songs in his belt. He'd been playing for drinks. He was runty and disheveled. But the way Woody talked, smiled, and joshed, he could have called Bennett a liar and a cheat and Bennett would have felt flattered.

Woody was in high spirits: he'd swapped the plane ticket for train passage and had cash left to spare; he'd zigzagged through the country and played at Communist party meetings along the way. He careened into Spokane and wrote Marjorie: "This is an awful nice hotel . . . just a little too fascisti to satisfy my higher ideals. But Spokane ain't that way at heart. . . . The folks out here

got a good shot of the old free and easy pioneer spirit in them
They still ride the tough grass and dig in the hills."

Back at the Davenport Hotel Woody found a telegram waiting for him from *People's World,* asking if he'd like to write about
his trip for them. He went straight to work, beginning with Ralph
Bennett—". . . a young man . . . [that] had just got married for
his first time a few days ago and was mentally still on his honey-
moon"—and their tour of Spokane:

> First place he took me was down to the padded room where
> the gents of the press was having a banquet. I had to sing be-
> fore they got started eating, but their knives and forks drowned
> me out. I took the old runout powder.
>
> He tried to get a mike so's I could sing around the mezza-
> nine but the big boss said no loud speakers was allowed in the
> mezzanine.
>
> He carried me down the street to the Masonic Temple and
> showed me a display booth where I would sing and play the
> next day. Then he looked at me with that newly wedded light
> in his eye and said he would stay over here in Spokane if I fig-
> ured I needed him to be my guide.
>
> I told him to guide it on out across them mountains to fin-
> ish up his honeymoon. . . .

The way Woody told it, Bennett left Spokane on the next
train. For his part, Bennett remembered Woody being confused,
sometimes almost incoherent, constantly forgetting the lyrics to
his songs. In any case, he'd met his hero and they'd talked about
the dust bowl, the migrant road, and Leadbelly. The trip had been
a bust for the BPA, if not for Woody: he invited the local Communist party chiefs up to his room for a bash and had a fling with
a woman. He drifted down the river and remembered the last
time he'd been here, and then he wrote about it in *People's World:*

> Way back in 1940 or '41, I made a fast walking trip up and

down the Columbia River and its tributaries, the Snake, the Hood, Willamette, Yakima, and the Klickitat, making up little songs about what I seen.

I made up 26 songs about the Bonneville dam, Grand Coulee dam, and the thunderous foamy waters of the rapids and cascades, the wild and windward watersprays from the high Sheliloh falls, and the folks living in the little shack house about a mile from the end of the line.

The Department of the Interior folks got ahold of me and took me into a clothes closet there at the Bonneville Power Administration and melted my songs down onto records.

In Portland, Michael Loring, Bennett's boss and another folk-music aficionado, set up a concert for Woody at Reed College. The students loved him, although he stumbled again and again over the words to his songs. At night, he paced and jerkily strummed his guitar like a windup toy. He offended the local union and Communist dignitaries with an acid portrait of their city in *People's World:*

> Portland is a place where rich ones run away to settle down and grow flowers and shrubbery to hide them from the massacres they've caused. Portland is the rose garden town where the red, brown, blackshirt cops ride up and down to show you their horses and saddles and gunmetal. Mentally, Portland is the deadest spot you ever walked through.

Sowing as much anger and confusion as delight, Woody arced up to Seattle and down the coast to San Francisco and Los Angeles. Then his ebullience and enthusiasm dropped away like the opening of a trapdoor beneath his feet. He felt low and lonely. By the start of summer he was home with Marjorie.

Ralph Bennett got letters from Woody that summer, asking with that funny penchant he had for tying words in knots, if the "weely nudes" had enjoyed their "money spoon" trip. But Bennett was preoccupied: the Republicans had taken control of Congress in 1946 and were now making themselves felt as their first budget came into force. The appropriation for BPA's public information office—which Oregon Republicans like Governor-to-be Douglas McKay saw as the nexus of leftism in a shamelessly liberal agency—had been drastically cut and in July Bennett was out of a job.

He wasn't worried: he wanted to help make a decent world and, more than anything, to become a writer, and something would turn up. He and Anna Lou moved into a place called Vanport down in the slough of the Columbia River between Portland and Vancouver, Washington. Vanport had been built by Henry Kaiser, a contractor for the Grand Coulee Dam, to house workers from his shipyards, and it was no less a miracle of construction than his fourteen-day liberty ships: in three months, from September to December 1942, five thousand workers built apartments, schools, and recreation and social facilities for forty thousand people. It was the second biggest city in Oregon and the largest housing development in the United States.

In 1947 there were only eighteen thousand people living in Vanport, but the only vacancy the housing authority could find for the Bennetts was in the colored section, which didn't bother Ralph in the least. As work in the shipyards wound down white workers moved on, but people like Willie Daniels remained behind. Blacks now made up a quarter to a third of the population of Vanport. Willie himself hadn't stuck around: you could scarcely leave the train station in Portland without seeing "White Trade Only" signs and he hadn't liked the work. After the war he'd gone back to Hanford and ended up working in a lab where they fed stuff from the reactors and "canyons" to sheep, goats, snakes, cows, rabbits, alligators, chickens, and lots of fish.

Ralph Bennett spent the remainder of 1947 idling in his Vanport apartment, still unconcerned about the future even though

Anna Lou was pregnant. He took a course in Shakespeare from a leftist professor at Reed, and felt that somehow this would lead to something, if only a clarifying of his own mind. He finally agreed to run the newspaper operated by the Vanport tenants' association, the *Vanport Tribune*. It wasn't the kind of writing he was aiming for, but he enjoyed knowing everybody and everything about the community. He sold ads and wrote all the stories, including child-care and nutrition columns. By the spring of 1948, the *Tribune* was selling six thousand copies a week and Bennett was beginning to think he, Anna Lou, and their newborn son, Mark, might be able to survive on the paper's earnings.

It had been a dreary winter. It seemed not a day passed without rain and the cold stayed through April. Then, in May, the sun came out, as though the weather were going to leapfrog spring and go straight to summer. It stayed warm, but the rains returned.

In the mountains—from the farthest reaches north of the Canoe River and Boat Encampment; around the ridge top of the Rockies and down through the Bitterroots and Yellowstone; from south of Snake River plain into Utah and Nevada; and along the Cascades—the world suddenly sloughed off winter, as though startled from a dream. The snows had been extraordinarily deep—drowning trees to their crests, mounting up in hummocks and cornices, obliterating every rough surface and relief—and now, loosed by sun and warm rains, they rendered themselves into water all at once, as though transmuted from substance to motion.

The river swelled from its farthest branches in Montana and British Columbia, and the authorities downstream were alerted and waited. It was like a train that had left from another country and would be arriving here in a week. There was concern, but not alarm. The Columbia rarely flooded, and few settlements were within its reach; moreover, to be afraid was askew from the spirit of the times. The river had been tamed and had in turn helped tame the massed forces of the Axis; and after the river, electricity, the atom, and every seemingly undoable thing—airplanes in days, ships in weeks, cities in months—had been accomplished. As if to drive the point home, the newspapers reported the very first delivery of Grand Coulee irrigation water on May 15 to a navy veteran from Indiana named O. V. Gillum, who had taken an eighty-five-acre farm near Pasco.

On Friday, May 28, Ralph Bennett got the copy for the next issue of the *Tribune* all the way to the printer before he realized something was missing. One of the Linotype setters asked him if he wasn't going to put something in about the flood threat. Bennett thought he'd better, if only to make a punchy headline. He had "River Flood Circles City" set in head type and then wrote some bland copy based on the official handout from the housing authority of Portland: Vanport is safe. The flood situation is being monitored and is under control. In the event of any change a siren will give residents ample warning:

REMEMBER:
DIKES ARE SAFE AT PRESENT
YOU WILL BE WARNED IF NECESSARY
YOU WILL HAVE TIME TO LEAVE
DON'T GET EXCITED

Sunday was Memorial Day. The war had ended less than three years before, and for most people the holiday for commemorating the dead was poignant, if not somber. The temperature was a perfect seventy-six degrees and the sun shone. Bennett had gone down to the enormous dike where the railroad line crossed the slough on Vanport's western edge. Water boiled up on the far side and siphoned through small fissures workers were patching with sandbags. The dike looked secure, although Vanport was now fifteen feet below the level of the river.

At 4:17 that afternoon there was a six-foot tear in the dike that expanded in less than a minute to sixty feet and then to five hundred feet. The water rolled through ten feet deep and jetted fifty feet in the air. When the water struck the first buildings inside the dike, it stove in their sides and spun them around and then they floated away on the tide.

The Bennetts had had friends over for lunch, and then about 4:30 P.M., they heard somebody yell that the flood had broken through. Bennett didn't believe it: there'd been no siren. But out on the street, there was enormous commotion, and in the distance a bank of something that looked like smoke. The surrounding sloughs took up much of the flood from the initial breach, and for some time the water spread through Vanport in a fan a few inches deep.

Bennett put Anna Lou and Mark in the car and told her to drive out and he'd catch up with them. He ran back inside and grabbed his movie camera, and shot film of the breach and rising water and got back to his family and car, which was now entangled in a massive traffic jam at Vanport's main entrance.

By 5:00 P.M., the water began to rise again in increments of a foot every few minutes. Two-story apartment buildings floated off their foundations and drifted away like arks, slowly turning in the whorl of the river. People were adrift on mattresses and tables, while rowboats berthed at second-story windows and took residents aboard. Walls crumpled and roofs collapsed, and household objects of every sort—toasters, radios, sofas, bushel baskets, stuffed toys, baseball bats, lamps, bleach bottles—were adrift together with leaves, tree limbs, boards, and trash, like a flock of birds in exodus. Telephone poles floated like lances on the water, battering the lines of cars fighting their way out. People clung to the running boards and pulled themselves across the trunks and fenders and tried to load the roofs with duffel bags and cardboard suitcases. In the distance, the transmitting tower of Portland's biggest radio station folded like a jackknife and collapsed in an efflorescence of blue flame.

In the morning of May 31, the river had sheathed everything in milky brown water. The peaks of a few of the tallest roofs were visible, and the water divided around them, lapped at their chimneys, and knitted itself together again and flowed on. The water was an opaque curtain laid over Vanport, and until the river pulled it away there was nothing to do but imagine what lay underneath it.

Most people knew they had lost everything, but wanted to know exactly what they'd lost, hoping that under the water where whole mountains of mud and silt from as far away as Wyoming were now settling, something—a wedding album, a service medal, a charm bracelet, a doll—might be intact. That took their minds away from the ineffable but irresistible conjuring up of friends and family who were missing. Mostly, people had simply become separated in the panic of the evacuation and were reunited within the following twenty-four hours. But with the water masking so many things, rumors accreted out of nothing, like ravens, suddenly glimpsed from the corner of one's eye, lined up on a bough. There was a five-story building with Romanesque arches and a grimy legend across the top that read Terminal Ice & Cold Storage Co., and people began to say it was full of bodies, sodden, cold, and stacked like cordwood, six hundred or more. Then they said that there were hundreds of corpses trapped inside apartments, bobbing against the ceilings. And somebody had seen a school bus full of kids get trapped in the flood and it was still there, still underwater, an aquarium brimming with children's bodies.

Eventually, the police recovered fifteen corpses in and around Vanport, although they couldn't begin to say how many might have floated away—maybe a few hundred. The place was full of transients, migrants, coloreds, Japanese, and people without relatives—people with no one to miss them. That led to accusations—particularly in the black community—that the police and the housing authority had been lax in preparing for and dealing with the flood; that if more of the tenants had been white or middle class or not emigrants, there would have been more warning and more escape routes. Or maybe Vanport would never have been built at all.

Ralph Bennett took Anna Lou and Mark down to the coast for a while before getting on to the business of putting their life back together. His BPA friends would come with some job leads for him: Steve Kahn thought there was a newspaper job up at Hanford; or perhaps one with Rufus Woods in Ephrata. Kahn was meanwhile making the most of the opportunities Vanport created for BPA. He had someone in an airplane shooting film of the flood scene as soon as the river broke through. The outcry over Vanport would create an atmosphere conducive to getting more dams built and perhaps at long last to the creation of a Columbia Valley Authority (CVA) to manage flood control, among other things. If nothing else, Kahn figured that the Vanport footage he'd had made could be incorporated into *The Columbia*, which he was determined to finish and get released.

Vanport figured in the political campaigns of 1948: a week after the flood, Kahn's old friend Richard Neuberger—now a candidate for the Oregon state senate—argued in the *Nation* for the CVA and dams on the Snake River; Paul Robeson came to the river in August on behalf of the Progressive party and its presidential candidate, Henry Wallace, and sang in the black neighborhood of northeast Portland. "Since I have been in Portland," he told his audience, "I not only saw the ruins of Vanport, but I have also seen what they have done with the people of Vanport." The housing crisis faced by displaced Vanport tenants underlined the need for a national housing policy of the kind being promoted by the Progressives.

Back in New York, the Communist party was backing Wallace—a fact that doomed Wallace's campaign once the general public perceived it—and so was People's Songs. Wallace—who'd enthusiastically shown *Hydro!* to Third World heads of state when he was Roosevelt's vice president from 1940 to 1944—adopted "Roll On Columbia" as one of his campaign songs. Woody, however, found Wallace insufficiently radical and couldn't work up much enthusiasm for performing on his behalf, despite entreaties from Pete Seeger and People's Songs. But Vanport stirred something up in Woody's mind. He wrote Ralph Bennett as well as Michael Loring of his concern for "the wartown of Vanport where so many thousands of families got their houses knocked down into kindling wood by the same old Columbia River I was singing so many good things about. I think the lack of flood control and power dams that caused this flood to break will give us all plenty to make up songs and to sing about for the rest of our native lives."

And so they did. By summer's end Woody had written "Vanport's Flood":

The radio and the handbills, they told us not to run.
These dikes and dams are holding, so stay inside your
    homes.
And if this dike starts breaking, we'll tell you so in time,
So you can pack your things and move, but everything's just
    fine
But all these waters, they broke in on us, not a warning, not
    a chance,
By this wild Columbia River, trapped and drowned just like
    rats.

We built our town of Vanport here to help us win this war.
At first I called it Kaiserville since Kaiser's plants are here.
I guess you could call it a wartown, I was working to win this
    fight.
But my folks didn't have a fighting chance when this river
    struck tonight.

Of all this world's wild rivers the wildest of them all
Is my snowfed Columbia when she starts to pitch and
    squawl.
Ten thousand towns like Vanport she'll snuff out like a
    match
If we don't shake hands and go to work and start in fighting
    back.

The Columbia, which Stephen Kahn finished at about the same time, used Vanport as its clinching argument for the creation of a CVA and the construction of a dozen or so additional dams. Kahn used much of the footage and rhetoric—"thirty million untamed horses racing to the sea"—he'd employed on *Hydro!* but with the framing device of Woody's songs, he transformed the BPA's vision of the river into a populist saga—the wild and mythic River of the West tamed by democracy in action to become "a river of hope" for the nation's destitute and displaced.

The Columbia dwelled on scenes of blowing dust and battered Model A's packed with emigrants crossing the desert; emigrants who, the film made it seem, when they reached the river, dropped their bedrolls, picked up shovels and picks, and built the Grand Coulee Dam as an expression of the national popular will. "Cynics scoffed," Kahn's script admitted, but the people persevered and "faced the fury of one million feet of water every second." When the war came, "in this hour of need, America looked westward to the Columbia" and its hydroelectric "lifelines of liberty, twenty-five hundred lines carrying a half-million kilowatts of power" to produce ships and planes, and to master "the magic of the atom."

Kahn portrayed the horror and tragedy of Vanport as a calamity visited on the very people who had tamed the river and won the war. Not to develop and control the river with more dams and the creation of a CVA was an insult to their trials and sacrifices, as well as an abjuring of what had been the nation's destiny since Jefferson.

It was powerful filmmaking in the service of ideas that were increasingly unpopular with the powerful: the election of 1948 seemed a repudiation not only of the left but of the New Deal in general. The Republicans strengthened their hold on government, and while they might favor dam projects that could serve private industry and agriculture, the hydro-socialism of the original BPA was an anathema. Michael Loring was told to track down Woody Guthrie and tell him to cease mentioning his connection to BPA in public. Ralph Bennett got a job as a newspaper correspondent in Ephrata, where he watched speculators and corporate and absentee owners start to take over Grand Coulee irrigated lands. In 1950 Stephen Kahn resigned and moved to California.

Only Elmer Buehler, Woody's driver, remained at BPA. They gave him a job as a janitor at a substation where he cleaned and tended the incinerator. In early 1953, shortly after the Eisenhower administration took office, they brought him all the copies of *Hydro!* and *The Columbia,* including the master prints. He was given to understand that Oregon governor Douglas McKay, the new Interior secretary, wanted them burned immediately.

5.

The years 1948 and 1949 were some of the bitterest Woody could remember. The left had not only been rejected but humiliated in 1948; abandoned and even denounced in congressional hearings by its onetime friends in labor, the arts, and government. At times it seemed that the people themselves had turned Iscariot, bent on destroying those who had worked for their redemption.

Woody took shelter on Coney Island with Marjorie and their new son Arlo and worked on a long novel, *Seeds of Man,* a sexually graphic story set in the desert border country of Texas. In the last few years, Woody had been writing not only erotic fiction, but letters, a penchant he developed in his early days with Marjorie and now shared with other women and even fans. In 1948 he sent three such letters to Mary Ruth Crissman, the kid sister of his old singing partner Lefty Lou, who became alarmed and passed them on to the U.S. attorney's office. Woody was charged with sending obscene materials through the mail, and, having refused to express regret to the judge, was sentenced to three months in jail. His lawyer got the sentence reduced—Marjorie was pregnant again and surely needed Woody at home—and he was released in time to spend Christmas of 1948 with his family and newborn son, Joady, named for Steinbeck's Tom Joad.

The words flowed out through the spring and summer of 1949, and the *Seeds of Man* manuscript grew to eight hundred pages. But Woody needed silence to hear his words, and the two children's jabbering and crying made him furious. One day he stuffed Arlo's mouth with sand to shut him up. In the fall, he sent his publisher, Dutton, the completed *Seeds of Man*. Deemed too long, too experimental, stylistically bizarre, and far too explicit, it was sent back. Marjorie was pregnant again, and in January 1950 had a daughter whom they named Nora, after Woody's mother.

Woody was drinking a lot; his extramarital affairs were undisguised and numerous; and his behavior grew more unpredictable by the day. Marjorie now feared what he might do to or around the kids and encouraged him to travel, while she considered what her options as a divorced mother of three would be like. It was 1950, and Woody hopped trains and hitched rides all the way to California and back, turning up on people's doorsteps like a whiskery, leering apparition of himself.

At home and on the road he plunged into more sexual encounters and masturbated himself raw and scrawled "seeds of man" on everything he owned, as though he could inundate the earth with his semen. He wrote his women letters, but the words in them went around and around and deeper down, like they were really addressed to themselves:

Since you come here and swum here the other night I've been

seeing what you might spiritually and soulfully describe as little shafty, shifty drafty drifty beams and rays and legs of lights and shapely shadows of old hopes too olden gone for any earthyling to have to even to try to tell or to describe to any other worldster.

Then he signed them "WWWW Gee Gee Gee Gee" and "WW Geehawker" and "Woodridge Duthridge" and filled their margins with his initials, like a filigreed picture frame, as though bounding himself with himself. He put his name on everything, as though he were Adam naming all creation "Adam."

Through 1951 and 1952, Marjorie threw him out, took him back, and threatened divorce, and Woody slept on sidewalks and in fleabags wearing five shirts at a time. He came back to Coney Island one night and cut the telephone line and came after Marjorie with a pair of scissors, his eyes as dull as shale. She somehow calmed him down and got him to go to the hospital to be looked over. When he talked it was like random spurts of machine-gun fire or a playing card buzzing against bicycle spokes. He moved in jerks and spasms, like a string of firecrackers. First the doctors decided he was an alcoholic and then, when it was clear that wasn't the root of the problem, they thought he might be schizophrenic. Later still, they speculated that maybe he was crazy in the way Nora had been crazy—afflicted in body, mind, and soul, like "St. Vitus dance, epilepsy, and mild insanity," Woody said—and it had gotten passed down in the family to him, like a keepsake. It was called Huntington's chorea.

There were times when he was like anybody else, and during one of those, in the fall of 1952, he got himself released. He went to California and moved into a cabin on Will Geer's property in Topanga Canyon near Los Angeles. Like most of the people Woody had known in Hollywood, Geer was blacklisted and unable to work in movies, radio, or television, and his place in Topanga was a nonconformist refuge for artists and activists riding out the McCarthy era. Woody flourished there and, resigning himself to a divorce from Marjorie, started talking about buying a piece of land and finding "wife #3."

Anneke Van Kirk was twenty, pretty, and bohemian. She had just gotten married, but she stepped into Woody's life in December and took charge. A month later, in January 1953, he was living with Anneke and her husband, and a month after that the husband told her to choose between them. Anneke left with Woody, and, by way of New York, they finished up living in a bus on some swampland in Florida owned by a friend. By June, Anneke was pregnant.

All this time Woody seemed pretty normal and in good spirits; good enough that he got back to writing, and took up where he'd left off with *Seeds of Man*. He was thinking about the time he'd gone down to look for Grandpa Jeremiah Guthrie's mine, and away he went:

> Cellar diggers gold, well drillers, toothy fillers, salty rivers, red-blood Indians, rootabaggers, back benders, heavy lifters, highway drifters, bums, hoboes, lobo wolfers, cradle robbers, gravey diggers. . . .

Then he was sending Marjorie and the kids letters, thousands and thousands of words long, trying to get everything that was in his head into them, like filling a hole that went right through the world. On June 10, while preparing his breakfast on the outdoor barbecue pit, he fed the fire with a little white gasoline and set himself aflame.

The burns weren't serious enough to endanger his life, but they wouldn't heal: they stank and throbbed and Woody felt like his very skin was in its death throes, only his heat-sickened brain still alive. As soon as they could, he and Anneke left for California, stopping in Mexico where Woody could get a quick divorce. Anneke then got her own divorce and the two were married at Los Angeles City Hall in December. Their relationship, however, had not endeared them to their California friends—who were friends of Marjorie's and of Anneke's husband as well—and they decided to settle in New York. On February 22, 1954, Anneke gave birth to Lorina Lynn Guthrie at Bellevue Hospital.

Woody was chipper when Anneke brought the baby home, and he got inspired to write again, this time trying his hand at drama:

WOODY (CARRIES GALLON TIN CAN FROM FENDER OF JALOPY): OUTTA MY DAMND WAY YOU BLATTY YOU BATTY BLIND BIRDS YOU BOTH OF YOU'RE SISSYS IN TH' FIRST DEGREE DONT EVEN KNOW HOWTA MAKE A WOODFIRE BURN . . . HERE STAND IT BACK GITIT OUTTA MY WAY OUT OUT OUTTY PLEASEY PLEASY PLEASY I'LL JUST DUMP MY LITTLE TINNY CAN RIGHT OFF DOWN HERE RIGHT ON TOPPA Y'R SMOKERY OLD FIREBOX AND YA'LL SEE'ER JUMPAT UP AND DANCE JUST AS PERTY AS YAD PLEASE AND JUST BLAZE AROUND AND JUST BURN AROUND AS PERTY AS YA'D ASK.

Nobody wanted to perform Woody's play, but he didn't care. At times he just lay there, apparently unconscious, and Anneke would come home and find Lorina crying, her diapers soaked through. One time Anneke got so mad she hit him, and a few days later he left.

Woody drifted out to California and back down through Texas, finishing up at Matt Jennings's place in El Paso and, at last, at Mary's. He passed out and urinated on her couch. He begged her to look after him: he didn't have anyone or anyplace to go. His daughter Sue, whom he hadn't seen in years and was now nearly grown, implored him: "Daddy, I've missed you very much and I love you, but Mom has made a good life for us here and it hurts her to have you stay, and so maybe you'd better just go."

Woody caught a freight home by way of Columbus, Ohio, where he was arrested and jailed for trespassing on railroad property. A few days after he got to New York in September 1954, he checked himself into the Brooklyn State Hospital and gave himself up to the words and to their god. He wrote Anneke: "I hear my words from Jesus run my crazified wards around my Brooklyn Stater place here a good deal more than I can hear the words of any of my other biggy doctors."

He went on like that and after a year and a half Anneke couldn't bear it anymore. She divorced him. Then Marjorie started checking in on him again, bringing the children to see him. But each day he was less among the people that came to see him, and more within himself. When he wasn't reading, he was writing, and the words were all going round and round. Sometimes he was just like anybody else, or pretty much the way he used to be, but most of the time he wasn't.

In December 1956, Woody's father died. Woody sent a letter to his sister Mary Jo to offer her some comfort and it was about the last thing he ever wrote:

Marjoree wrote to me that you wrote to her on the day after our dear father Charley Edward Guthrie passed on to his greaty goody everloving and heavenly and holy saintly reward as in the promises of my deary sweety Jesus M. Christo and so I say lets not be worrie eyedy weery eyedy nor tearyful eyedy nor now sorrowdy hearted down here on our lowlow earthful wordly planet to see him passy on up to the everlovin fingers of our good good lorde and our saver there Jesus my only goody earthyful boy to Jesus my only true hearted earthly man But I say to all of you I say to you all let's be gladdy let's be just be thankful let's all be really happy day for once in our earthly lives here to see our father go to his new earth and on into his new builty heavenly by gods very own hands and all of us struggle our bests to live such a godlyful kind of earthy life here we will each and all and everyone one of us here enter on in into gods great eternal glory at the day of our deathy. Amen Amen.

Woody lived another ten years. In 1966 the Department of

the Interior presented him with the United States Conservation Award. Marjorie and Arlo brought him the big framed commendation and he sat with it in his lap for a while, with a cigarette between his lips, drinking in the smoke. He had ceased speaking long ago. Sometimes his body jerked and his arms shot out, as if he were pointing out directions.

When Woody died the following year, the BPA named a substation for him near Hood River on the Columbia. The *Hood River News* declared the action "a sick joke" at the community's expense to honor "a 1930-vintage beatnik." The president of the chamber of commerce wanted to know, "What did this Mr. Guthrie ever do for our valley?"

In 1973 an Oklahoma graduate student named Harry Menig read about *Hydro!* and *The Columbia* in a magazine article by a journalist named David Johnson. Intrigued, Menig contacted Johnson and together they began to search for copies of the films. No one at BPA or the Department of the Interior could help them. Someone mentioned Elmer Buehler to them, and they tracked him down. Buehler told them what he'd been told to do in 1953, and he had indeed burned the films—all of them except two copies that were in his basement.

In 1986, in conjunction with the agency's upcoming fiftieth anniversary, two BPA employees, Gene Tollefson and Bill Murlin, began to research its history. Murlin was himself a folksinger and began to look for copies of the recordings of the Columbia songs Woody Guthrie had made in the BPA basement studio in 1941. None existed at BPA or any other government agency or library, and they were presumed destroyed. But Murlin eventually located Ralph Bennett, now a retired newspaperman in San Diego, who as a young Guthrie enthusiast had made copies of the original acetates in 1947. He still had them.

At the same time, Tollefson and Murlin tracked down Stephen Kahn. Kahn had become a wealthy man in California and lived in an enormous house in Carmel. He remembered exactly how it all had been before, when the river was his whole life; how he believed emigrants might come and become altogether new people. But no one is ever new; no one leaves the story that is the lot of this life, although they sometimes fancy it will end with their being saved from everything that has gone before.

He told them, "You realize the frailties of human beings, especially when they become older and more conservative and they say, 'Well, I've got to look out for number one.' Maybe I reached that conclusion, too."

They asked Kahn about a song, a kind of anthem he'd written himself back when he and everyone else were young. There was only one recording of it now, so distorted that you couldn't make out the words. Kahn said, "The old fire horse never forgets," and recited the lyrics, as though they were his own name:

We fought the cold Columbia from the Rockies to the sea
And we built ourselves a vision of a land that was to be
Of a land that men have dreamed of from the Grecian days
   till now
Where democracy is realized—Can Columbia show us how?

Then, for an instant, and against all inclination, the words touch him and pull him down, and conjure a memory that comes like a cold draft and settles tingly into the bone beneath his eyes, as if it were the first thing he ever loved. His voice cracks faintly, a riffle in the smooth flow of words, like an underwater sound, the creak of the rusted plates of a ship on the river bottom, sleepless in the down-running flood.

CHAPTER 6

Captives

1.

P eople said Kuni was born on a flat rock on an island in the
river, and so it seemed that from his first breath the river
flowed around and through him. His name meant "Holds
All Things" and he was born in 1855, the year the chiefs signed
the treaties. By the time the war that followed the treaty making
was over, his mother and the village women at Celilo Falls had
told him about the first white men that had come years before: the
Bostons and the King George fur traders, and the first of their
kind, the Star Man, David Thompson. The women told Kuni that
whenever the Hudson Bay men came over in their red jackets and
hats, the whole village sang, "Now the children of the stars have
come upon us." As they told Kuni these things, the women split
and boned salmon, hung it over the poles in the fish shed to dry,
and tended the fires. The smoke would rise up into the summer
sky like ladders to the sun.

Kuni liked the story of the white men in the red coats, and perhaps for that reason people began to call him Thompson, Tommy Thompson, and when he was elected chief in Celilo in 1875 that was how everyone knew him. As chief, he had charge of the longhouse and the salmon fishery at Celilo, the greatest on the river, and they were one labor: without the longhouse and the Washat or seven-drum rites prescribed by Smohalla, there would be no fish; and without the fish, there would be no longhouse, or any life at all.

Tommy had a vision once. He saw an orange light with yellow mixed in, and he knew it was the light that wove everything together, that gave the world shape in the way a basket shapes water. Then he carved a bird of cedar and mounted it on a pole outside the longhouse as Smohalla had done. It was supposed to carry messages to and from heaven, and there was some confusion about what kind of bird it was. Some people thought it was a raven, like a black-robe priest; some thought it was a dove, white like an angel, like Noah's pigeon; and maybe it was both, depending on how the light fell on it, depending on who was looking.

In the longhouse, Tommy conducted the salmon ceremony—where the water and the fish were remembered and thanked—and the feasts for roots and berries that followed it. He oversaw naming ceremonies, too: when the elders decided the time was right, a person took an ancestor's name to use for spiritual and tribal purposes, and then, by way of thanks, there was a giveaway of blankets and gifts. In fact, one way or another everything that happened in the longhouse had to do with naming, thanking, and fish.

At the river, Tommy was in charge of the fishing: He told people when they could start spearing and netting and when they had to stop. He saw to it that no one fished on Sunday or polluted the river or did anything else that might insult the salmon. Anyone who went against him was sent away. Tommy's rules worked and the fish always came and there was always enough: sixteen million salmon a year, of which all the native people on the river collectively harvested perhaps one fish in twenty. Celilo

Falls was the heart of the river, a quarter-mile-wide, horseshoe-shaped cataract that the bulk of the salmon passed through each year. A person could take five hundred salmon per day using a single net—and some of them might weigh eighty pounds—but no one needed that many fish.

More and more white people came to the river, but they wanted to be farmers: fishing was ignoble, undignified work, a job for dirty, lazy Indians, and there was no money in it. The treaties of 1855, which had been thorough in seizing every resource of interest to whites, left the fish to the Indians along with the "usual and accustomed places" along the riverbanks where the fish were caught. But then white people invented canning and they realized that cheap, plentiful Columbia River salmon would make good fuel for the factory and mill workers in places such as Chicago, Pittsburgh, and even Manchester, England. Money was the muse of *suyapo* ingenuity, and right there at the Dalles they invented fish wheels, gargantuan Ferris wheel–like contraptions that scooped salmon from the river by the ton. By the 1890s, 600,000 cases of Columbia salmon were being packed every year from an annual catch of nearly forty-five million pounds of fish.

Before that, white people's main interest in the river had been as a highway, a means to an end. They looked at the water and the banks, macadamized in stones and fish heads, promenaded by shrieking gulls and shiftless ravens, and saw a wasteland. But when the salmon became valuable, all that changed. By 1894 the Yakima Indian agent was complaining to his superiors in Washington that "the disputed fishing rights of the Indians along the Columbia has given me a vast amount of trouble"; "inch by inch" the canneries were forcing the Indians out of their traditional fishing places.

The Indians were legal wards of the Department of the Interior, and thus the federal government was obliged to defend them against white incursions on their rights, regardless of the sentiments of the government. In 1905 the courts in Washington State had upheld Winans Brothers Cannery in banning Indians from fishing sites on riverbank land it had bought. The federal government appealed the case to the United States Supreme Court, which found not only that the Indians were guaranteed access to their ancient fishing grounds under the 1855 treaty, but also that the treaty itself must always be interpreted as the Indians had originally understood it. In a tone suggesting that the justices were appalled at the disingenuousness of their brethren in Washington State, the court was unequivocal:

> The right to resort to the fishing places in controversy was a part of larger rights possessed by the Indians upon the exercise of which there was not a shadow of impediment and which were not much less necessary to the existence of the Indians than the atmosphere they breathed.

Assured that they had at least as much business on the river as the canneries, the Indians went back to fishing, some of them with as much enterprise and avidity as the whites themselves. A Yakima named Sam Williams built a fish wheel on the Oregon side of the river adjacent to the operations of the Dalles's biggest cannery, Seufert Brothers, which sued, claiming that the 1905 Supreme Court decision applied only in Washington. The Oregon courts found Seufert Brothers' contention eminently reasonable, but were swatted down by the Supreme Court, which reaffirmed its previous decision, noting that the Indians' fishing rights transcended and superseded state boundaries.

Sam Williams eventually got rich catching salmon. However, despite the fishing protections afforded to the Indians by the federal government, which some people thought gave them an advantage over whites, few other Indians became rich fishers. Maybe they just weren't lucky like Williams. In the winter, when Williams was a boy, his parents fell through the ice on the river and drowned, and it seemed as though he took his life's whole measure of misfortune in that one moment. He was raised in a Catholic orphanage and learned English and Latin, and when he was grown he could consort as easily with the cigar-chewers and bankers in the Dalles as with Tommy Thompson in the Celilo longhouse.

Williams had the blessing of money, and with it he built a new kind of church by the falls. Over in the western part of Washington, a native fisherman named Mud Bay Louie had been teaching a healing faith he called the Shaker religion on account of the way its adherents trembled and shook during their trances and visions. It was a cross between Washat and Christianity—it had drums and dreams and Jesus and his love, but without his cranky father or the white people's Book—and it gave Williams comfort in his old age. Through all his days, grace and fish poured down on him like syrup and huckleberries.

In truth, since the turn of the century, the salmon population had been dwindling, although nobody knew it yet. The fish were leaving the river like the light leaves the day at dusk, slowly like water settling into ice.

The prophets had said it would be this way at the end of the world. Then, in 1916 and 1917, while the *suyapos* gave up their children 500,000 at a time to the slaughter of war in the Somme and at Ypres, there was another sign. In Idaho in the Duck Valley, where the southernmost waters in its reach begin to find their way to the river, there were two Paiute Indians cutting wood in the deepest part of winter. From a distant hill they heard music, and when they went to look, they saw six men and six women dancing and singing.

The singers called them closer and the two Paiutes saw that they looked like ordinary Indians dressed in fine buckskins. But the singers explained that they were people from a prior world, when the animal people were on the earth. Now they had returned to tell the Indian people that the end of this world was imminent; a star was speeding toward the moon and when their paths crossed, the earth would be destroyed. The singers told the

Paiutes they must warn all their people. Then the singers were transformed into wolves who vanished into the brush like shadows and were gone.

That same winter, another Paiute, a trapper, found a coyote caught in one of his traps. Just as he was about to shoot the coyote, the coyote spoke and begged him to lower his rifle and listen to what he had to say. The coyote told him that he was one of the animal people and had come with a warning for the Indians. The white people were greedy and the Indians had forgotten the old ways. The Creator's heart was broken, and the world must soon end. The trapper released the coyote and then the coyote's body thickened and his coat silvered into the pelt of a great wolf and he vanished into the snow.

From Duck Valley the story came north and west to the Warm Springs Reservation in Oregon and thence across the river to the Yakima. In the longhouses of those few people along the river who still practiced the Dream religion it had the sure ring of truth, but they sent messengers down to the Paiute to be sure. When the runners returned and vouched for the veracity of the woodcutters and the trapper, they waited for the star to strike the moon, singing and dancing into the night for weeks. But months passed and nothing happened. Perhaps the animal people had been misinterpreted, or perhaps the Creator had relented. In any case, most everyone forgot about the warning, and the memory of it and the animal people vanished like most of the salmon, into the forgetting that enveloped the river.

2.

Sometimes, at the end of the day when their arms were tired from spearing and gaffing fish, David Sohappy's father would put aside his paddle and let the canoe drift down the river from below Priest Rapids to their camp at White Bluffs. David would throw his arms out over the bow and let his hands drag through the water and carve fantails and whorls in the flat, cold shallows of the river. The water was clear and there were shadows down inside it that moved like clouds suspended, like elk halting and darting into the forest. They were fish, and although he was only five years old, David was a fisherman.

David's grandfather, George, was a horseman who rode and tended cattle herds. The first Sohappy, David's great-great-grandfather, was killed on Naches Creek for his horses and because he wouldn't go to war over a treaty he hadn't signed. After that, David's great-uncle Smohalla led the Wanapum and taught the Washat religion. The Wanapum fished, hunted, and kept the old ways, and that was what David's father was teaching him now, as the fish hovered in the transparent gray of the water, as the river wove through David's fingers and bore the canoe downstream. It was the only thing for a Wanapum to do in life; the only way to keep hunger and death away—in a sense, to honor hunger and death in the hunt, in gathering roots and berries in the meadows, in fishing the river—and, when the world's end came, to secure a home in the next creation. It was the only thing worth having that the old could give to the young.

It was 1930, and that year, as in every year, the Sohappys migrated in a great circle from White Bluffs in the summer to the mountain country back of the Yakima Reservation for the fall hunt and then to Priest Rapids. In midwinter, the river purled and breathed under the ice, scarcely audible, like a bear in her den. David went out onto the frozen river and could make out the fish swimming beneath his feet. He chased their shadows as they tacked along the bank. He pierced the ice with stones and sticks; and, thrusting his arms into the water, chilled his hands to aching crimson trying to catch the fish.

There were piles of driftwood along the river, like mounds of bones and antlers, and they sparkled with frost. The reed walls of the houses and fish-drying sheds were the color of smoke, and the earth seemed thin and brittle, like a cast-off snake's skin. In the winter, the drums thundered day after day in the longhouse and David sat with the other Wanapum, who now numbered two dozen or so. He heard all the songs—for dying, childbearing, the hunt, the blessing of the horses, and the summoning and thanking of the fish—and his father told him the stories of the Wanapum.

One was about how the first white people came, the Star Man and the Hudson's Bay men, maybe 150 years ago. They only wanted to trade beaver skins. They said they didn't want anything else from the Wanapum. But they got a boy from the village to go with them and they took him to England and he lived there ten years. He didn't like it: the sky was always closed up as though hides had been laid over the sun, they didn't have roots to eat, the fish were scrawny, and the fires smelled like dirt and moss. He came back to Priest Rapids and didn't have much to say about it; he just went fishing.

David's father might have made up the story, or heard it from somebody who made it up. In any case, David didn't want to go to England; he wanted to go to Celilo, and in the spring of 1931, when he was six, his father took him. He'd never seen so many people or fish or so much water running so fast and hard. He could hear the noise from far away and it sounded like the idling motor of the whole world.

David's father showed him Tommy Thompson, maybe the greatest and oldest chief on the river, watching the fishing from the bank. Things were already getting away from him and the other chiefs who ran the fish council. The other tribes accused the Yakima—by far the biggest and most powerful tribe on the river—of overfishing; the Yakima in turn were suing the government for lost fishing rights; and the Dalles's city fathers thought it might be a good idea to tear down the old fishing camp at Celilo and build a "model" Indian village that could be a tourist attraction.

David didn't fish at Celilo. He was too small to go out onto the spindly platforms that overhung the chasm of the falls, and his people weren't dipnetters. They speared and pulled gill nets out from the bank. But around that time David caught his first fish, a one-foot salmon at White Bluffs. It practically pulled him into the river, and it was the happiest day of his life.

❧

Unless the fish were running thick, there was always as much talking and stories as there was catching fish, and David's father had told him about the Dreamers and the most famous, most powerful Dreamer of all, his great-uncle Smohalla. If he kept the old ways and observed the Washat, he would get dreams, too.

When the fishing season of 1931 was over, the Sohappys went back to White Swan on the reservation, where David's mother's family lived. One day David's father was backing up his pickup truck and he ran over David. David was badly injured, but he survived, and although he couldn't remember much about what had happened, he was convinced of one thing: after the accident, everything was different. David knew he had died and come back, like the Dreamers did.

His parents were broke and had to move around all winter, hunting and cutting wood, and it was time for David to go to school. He moved in with his grandmother. She didn't speak English and neither did David until he learned it at school. Grandmother was a serious and devout woman, and when she didn't have David working or listening to her stories and songs, she took him to services at the longhouse. He didn't get to play much, but sometimes, outside the longhouse, he and a little girl named Myra would play hunt-the-thimble or hide-and-seek, and the world was so wide that everything could be hidden, yet so laden with grace that everything could be found.

David still went fishing with his father, and by the fifth grade he had learned to read, write, and speak English, so he left school to hunt, fish, and work full time. But in 1937, they couldn't fish Priest Rapids anymore. The state of Washington passed a law requiring dipnetters to be licensed. Only Indians dipnetted. The game wardens told the Wanapum chief, Johnny Buck, that his people would have to start getting licenses and observing state regulations and fishing seasons. Johnny Buck wouldn't obey the wardens, but he wouldn't countenance breaking the law either, and told his people to stop fishing entirely.

David and his father went downriver to an old Indian fishing site called Cook's Landing, between the Cascades and the Dalles. But even that wasn't secure: the Bonneville Dam was under construction, although for the last five years the Indians had tried to stop it. There were hearings, and chiefs from up and down the river argued that the dam would be a clear violation of the 1855 treaties and threatened the native people's most fundamental sustenance. And even if it were legal to build such a thing, was it wise? An Indian from Celilo named Job Charley wrote:

> The Columbia River is like a big vein in your body. When they cut your main vein, what will happen? What will happen when they shut the river? The Bonneville Dam will hurt the people worse than the depression. This will be for all time.

But the dam could not be stopped, and in 1938, an Interior Department official confessed that he believed Indian fishing rights were "in dire peril." In 1939 the government agreed to provide six "in lieu" sites to replace the fishing places, tribal grounds, and ancient island graveyards dotting the river that would be flooded. Meanwhile, the states increased their efforts to crack down on what they termed fishing "renegadism." In 1939 a Klikitat named Sampson Tulee was arrested for fishing without a license and thrown in the county jail. Bureau of Indian Affairs lawyers took up his case, and argued that since Tulee was a federal ward under the treaties, the matter should be tried in federal court.

The government attorneys brought three senior chiefs from the river wearing full ceremonial regalia to the United States Court of Appeals in San Francisco. They pleaded with the judges and attempted to maintain their dignity. But even the most fluent of them found the language of *suyapo* law the most alien and impenetrable part of the white people's tongue. They became entangled in the words, flailing about as though their feet couldn't find a steady place to stand on the polished stone floor of the courthouse. The court told them their case must be processed at the state level before it would consider the matter.

The state of Washington obliged them with a series of guilty verdicts, and in 1942 the United States Supreme Court ruled on *Tulee v. Washington*. The justices found that the "treaty takes precedence over state law and state conservation laws are void and ineffective insofar as their application would infringe on rights secured by treaty." In short, the state could not require Indians to buy fishing licenses; it could, however, regulate fishing equipment and fishing seasons if there were clear conservation reasons for doing so.

None of this seemed to have any impact on the government's dam-building program. In theory, the government had every intention of compensating the Indians for the losses they might incur from dams, whether in land or in cash. In practice, however, it did very little indeed, and it took years to come to a settlement with the tribes, and even more years before delivering on its promises.

The Colville tribes occupying the country around Grand Coulee Dam would wait more than fifty years for a financial settlement. But in June 1941, they held a "Ceremony of Tears" in anticipation of the flooding of Kettle Falls by the lake filling up behind the dam. They danced and drummed for three days, and watched the *suyapo*s unmake their lives. Over their heads, cranes fastened sections of the new bridge that would span the waters burying the falls. There were twenty-seven hundred WPA workers camped nearby, stripping the valley's forests of timber before the water came. The salmon were already gone, their course blocked by the fifty-story-high face of the dam. Unlike Bonneville, it had been built without fish ladders, and so, in a stroke, salmon became extinct on two-thirds of the Columbia River, all eight hundred miles from its head in the Canadian Rockies to Grand Coulee.

The waters were scarcely lapping the crest of Kettle Falls before the Army Corps of Engineers was holding hearings to explore the idea of damming Celilo. Pearl Harbor had come and gone and every consideration bowed before the exigencies of the nation's security. An army colonel named Franklin Matthias came to see Chief Johnny Buck at Priest Rapids at the beginning of 1943. He told him the government was building something important at Hanford in the desert west of White Bluffs and they needed the river all to themselves. It was a secret and the Wanapum understood about secrets. Johnny Buck and Colonel Matthias reached an understanding: The Wanapum could stay at Priest Rapids, but they couldn't fish except when the colonel said it was okay. They had to stay out of the country where the government was building and be discreet about what they saw. If a Wanapum climbed up the black face of the mountain behind Priest Rapids, he might see what the colonel had built: huge gray longhouses, big as clouds.

Everywhere David Sohappy looked, the fishing was gone. He was eighteen. For the first time in his life he cut off his braids, and then he went to war.

At Celilo in 1943, Tommy Thompson took another wife. Her name was Flora, and she was a little younger than Tommy, who was already close to ninety. Flora thought he was still handsome, though. She said he had a light complexion and his hair was soft like a Frenchman's and it hung to his waist. Once he'd had twelve sweethearts at the same time, but now he just had Flora. He still had a man's hunger though: when he asked Flora, "How would you stand it if I had two or three other wives like I used to?" she told him, "I wouldn't mind it—I'd be getting some rest then."

Flora and Tommy were too old to have children, and maybe that was a good thing. Raising children was a trial, and losing them was worse. Flora knew a woman who miscarried four babies, and they came to her in a dream. They were in heaven, but from then on she couldn't stop imagining what she had done to lose them all, and they couldn't open their mouths to tell her. Had it been from hauling salmon up from the river to the fish shed or carrying wood on her back? The grief and the wondering took her down and she never came up.

The truth was, Flora had had a husband before, and a child too. He was some kind of shaman and he used to accuse her of stepping out on him with colored men. Then they had a daughter and she was the only decent thing in Flora's life. She used to sing all the Indian songs Flora could teach her, and even at four years old she could sing them better than most grown-ups in the longhouse. Then she died and Flora's heart withered like a dandelion and blew away.

Flora was a prisoner to her daughter's death for seven weeks, and then the child came to her, suspended in the air, and said, "Mother, I don't want you to be like that—you will never catch up to me in Glory." She told Flora to go look at herself in the mirror, and Flora saw her hair was all full of dirt and ashes. She took her black clothes off and gave herself a bath. She combed her hair and went down to the longhouse and told the people what had happened to her. Then Flora started to sing and she went on singing.

After that, she left her first husband and found Tommy, and everything she said made sense to him. White people don't understand the Indian religion, Flora told somebody once, "They think we worship the sun and stones and different images. But it isn't that. It's people that have died and are shown visions. That's how. The body lies in the center of the longhouse. When the body lies there, the whole center of the ground is our altar." What the dead teach and what the dreamers carry back with them is how to live right. When death takes a child away, nothing of this life adheres to her, but for an adult, deeds and history cling like burrs: "They go to heaven as clean as a fluffy feather, but we have got to suffer for everything we do and say."

When they were married, Flora and Tommy had a feast in the Celilo longhouse. The river poured down like Tommy's hair, and the dove on the pole outside carried Flora's songs up to Glory, up to her child who was waiting for her.

While their sons and grandsons fought the war, the chiefs fought the dams. Just before he closed down the *Dalles Optimist* and went to work for the Bonneville Power Administration, young Ralph Bennett wrote a story on the meeting between the Army Corps of Engineers and Tommy Thompson. It was held in the Dalles city council chambers, and Bennett was struck by the way "a gamy scent of the wild, of fish oil and tanned deerskin, permeated the bare, formal room." Tommy Thompson got up and spoke:

> The Great Fear came to me when I heard the white man was taking a step to build a dam below my fishing place. My heart seems to beat and tell me the white man is trying to destroy our food.

Downriver, Tommy's son-in-law, Frank Slockish, whose grandfather Sla-Kish was the last chief to put his mark on the 1855 treaty, was saying much the same thing. Now Slockish was the chief of the Klikitat and he was trying to explain that this fight was about food, and much more than that:

> We are making our story of our food for our children to remember after us, and our children will carry on the way of living on this mother earth. I don't remember when the white people came and took our food away from us red people and thought they were the sole owners of our food. We know that

different fish and food are our food. Same way with deer—our food. We know our roots of all kinds and the same with berries. What we remember is our food. This is my statement to you, my white friends, so you could see that some laws make me worry about my way of living. . . . The War Department don't know how bad we feel about all the boys in the war today, to protect that food and our country. I am begging your high War Department officials to help us red people, when we will be given power to do good, and we will then all thank you.

Slockish wanted to go on—he wanted to make sure the Washington and Oregon state governments wouldn't be allowed to go on interfering with Indian rights—but he was tired: "I could make more, but I am not feeling just right."

Slockish's boys, Wilbur and James, were scarcely home from the war when Slockish died. Wilbur had fought in the Philippines, with a wife and infant sons at home. James had been wounded in Europe and had been held in a German prisoner-of-war camp, and got a medal for heroism. Now they were home, grown men and fatherless. Their mother, Tommy Thompson's daughter, reminded them of what Tommy told her about how their people used to go up and down the river all the way from the Cascades to Celilo to fish and trade for those Hudson's Bay blankets with the colored stripes. Wilbur and James decided to go fishing.

They went up to the Klikitat River where the water thundered down to the big river like coal through a chute. They got arrested for fishing out of season and thrown in jail. The state hadn't forgotten about Sampson Tulee. The jailer gloated and welcomed Wilbur and James home to Washington State: "You're not wearing uniforms anymore—you're just a couple of dirty Indians again."

It was the same upriver at Celilo. Amos Switzler, an orphan boy raised in Tommy Thompson's home, told a reporter: "All we have to count on is those rocks and the fish we get here. When an Indian goes to school and then tries to get a job, he finds he is still just an Indian." Amos's friend Steve Boise had his ribs shot away in the Pacific and won the Purple Heart. He thought he had a fishing platform on the falls to come home to, but now he wasn't so sure. When the reporter persuaded him to talk, he went on about the 1855 treaty, hoping that if he said enough about it, perhaps what was printed in the paper would be true.

David Sohappy didn't get home until the autumn of 1946. He'd been in the Army Air Corps, and although he was quiet, people listened to him. By the time he was discharged he was a sergeant overseeing a group of men at Hickam Field in Hawaii. He figured he'd just fish after he was discharged, but the river seemed a different place, as though it had quietly changed course, and maybe changed him with it. His grandfather told him once, "If the white man tells you to move, and you do move, you'll never get back to where you were."

He found Myra, the little girl he used to play with at the longhouse, and married her and they started having children. He didn't fish: he fixed cars, he drove bulldozers and dump trucks, and he worked on fire crews. He knew the old ways were in decline: The longhouses were getting emptier every week. People stopped worrying about the traditional rules restricting fishing on Sunday. No one had even bothered to appoint a new chief when Frank Slockish died.

The native people were trying to negotiate with the whites on what they thought was neutral ground. But most of the time it was as though they had stepped onto a raft without knowing it and been carried downstream to another country whose very language and customs—writs, hearings, contracts, timetables, torts, invoices and indentures, and judgments—inevitably led deeper and deeper into the white people's world. It was a country full of men who knotted striped silk sashes around their necks and had papers from schools hanging on their walls with words that said they had mastered words so well that they could make up their own words and even decide what other people's words meant. One of them would slip on a black gown and sit behind a high table, perched like a raven on an oak altar, and decide whose words were prettier, and that was justice.

Sometimes it seemed to go the Indians' way: Tommy Thompson got an injunction against some small-time white fisherman who'd been fishing on an Indian site in the river, and thought maybe he could get something similar done about the dams. When some government officials and lawyers came to talk to Tommy about what it would take for him to feel all right about flooding Celilo Falls behind the Dalles Dam, he sent them away. He told them he was ninety-five years old. How old were they? Forty? Maybe fifty? They admitted they were. He told them he didn't make council with boys. They smiled and went away.

Tommy was a very wise Indian, but as a white man he was a fool. Short of having him hanged, the men he sent away could do pretty much whatever they wanted with him and his fish. While they were waiting to get their hands on Celilo, the Army Corps of Engineers went to work on a big dam upriver at the Umatilla Rapids they called McNary. The Indians tried to get the project halted so the impact of burying one of their principal fishing grounds under a giant lake could be assessed. The judge said "the damage would not be sufficiently irreparable to warrant granting an injunction."

It was the same way with the Dalles Dam. There were fewer and fewer fish all the time anyway. The white fishers on the lower river and out in the ocean were catching most of them before they ever got near Celilo, and the government's much-vaunted fish hatchery program was concentrated below Bonneville. Few people could get very enthusiastic about worrying about the fish that were left farther upstream.

Tommy finally gave up on the courts. When the appropriations bill to fund the dam went before Congress, he sang and prayed at the Celilo longhouse for three days to stop it. The bill went through anyway, and President Truman began to talk to the senators and representatives about building an aqueduct to California to divert all the river water that was being wasted and dumped into the ocean.

In April 1952, the Corps of Engineers started blasting for the Dalles Dam, reaming out the banks and punching holes in the river bottom to get at the rock that hadn't been touched by light since the flood of twelve thousand years before. The Smithsonian Institution evaluated the archaeological potential of the area that was going to be flooded and suggested it was worthy of investigation.

Luther Cressman was a specialist in the archaeology and anthropology of the American West. He trained as a sociologist at Columbia, was ordained as an Episcopal priest, and had been married to Margaret Mead. When he lost Mead to another man and forsook the priesthood, he came west to the University of Oregon to teach sociology. He started going on digs, and in 1938 he discovered a nine-thousand-year-old pair of sandals that proved that human beings had inhabited the Northwest much longer than anyone believed.

By 1952 he was the leading authority in his field, and when he heard about the Dalles project, he and his students arranged to spend the summer of 1953 excavating around the river. They found hundreds of specimens that collectively spanned a period of eleven thousand years, from Hudson's Bay Company buttons emblazoned with beavers to nine-thousand-year-old mortars, blades, and choppers.

In October, Cressman was digging at a site upstream from Celilo, well above the level of the river. He could work with a cigarette suspended from his lips and pass the time remembering the passages he still knew by heart from the prayer book, which were themselves about remembering:

For in the night in which he was betrayed, he took bread; and when he had given thanks, he brake it, and gave it to his disciples, saying, Take, eat, this my body, which is given to you; do this in remembrance of me. Likewise, after supper he took the cup, and when he had given thanks, he gave it to them, saying, Drink you all of this; for this is my blood of the New Testament, which is shed for you, and for many, for the remission of sins; Do this, as oft as ye shall drink it, in remembrance of me.

Then he found the knife, fixed fast in the earth by the flood of twelve millennia ago, like a fish entombed in ice.

❦

In 1954 the government and the tribes of the river reached a settlement over the flooding of Celilo, with the government agreeing to pay $23 million based on the enrollment of the various tribes. The officers of the Yakima Nation signed up every unenrolled Indian they could track down, including Grandfather George Sohappy and his entire family. The Sohappys, being Wanapum, were neither treaty Indians nor Yakima, but that made no difference to the tribe, which was getting $3,750 per head, with final payment due when the Corps of Engineers closed the floodgates.

That same year, someone vandalized the carved bird outside Tommy Thompson's longhouse. Flora thought it might have been the Corps of Engineers, but since they planned to put the whole village under fifty feet of water, why would they bother? Other people suspected disgruntled "Book" Indians, who might believe Tommy's Washat intransigence was hurting the future prospects of the more accommodating Indians on the river. Tommy had never backed down over the dam, and even the Oregon branch of the Daughters of the American Revolution declared that the treatment of the Indians at Celilo had been shameful. The Corps of Engineers brought Tommy a brass replica of the carved bird as a peace offering, which he accepted, but he never took his $3,750.

Tommy was ninety-nine years old that year; his great-grandson, Wilbur Slockish, Jr., was ten. He'd been born while his father, Wilbur senior, was in the Philippines, and like a lot of Indian boys, he lived with his grandmother or his aunt while his parents worked. They all lived up the Klikitat River, and ate the traditional foods—from salmon to eels to moss—and kept the old ways in the longhouse. Up the river, beneath the glacial snow-fields of Mount Adams, there were elk, berries, and roots. At home, the women knew all the songs and stories. The Klikitat were also the most renowned basket makers on the river, and the Slockish women were reputed to make just about the best baskets in their tribe.

That autumn, Wilbur moved with his parents to Wapato on the Yakima Reservation, and in many ways life there was less Indian than it was at Klikitat. Wilbur went to school and read the Sunday funnies and Reader's Digest Condensed Books. The next summer he and his older brother Leroy sneaked down to Celilo to see the fishing, which was continuing while the dam was being finished. They camped along the river and Wilbur talked his way out onto the platforms where the older men were fishing. The dipnetters stood on the ends of planks no more than a foot wide, sticking ten and twelve feet out into the river from the platforms. Tommy Thompson had always made people wear ropes around their waists, but there were drownings every year. Out on the planks, you weren't so much above the river as in it, staring down into a huge hole in the heart of the world where all its waters emptied out.

That winter, Wilbur woke up once at 3:00 A.M. and he heard a train, distinct but far away. In the morning, they told him Leroy had been hit and killed by a train, and he knew it must have been the one he heard, the one that woke him up in the night. After that, he was always hearing that train.

Later, he couldn't remember if he'd gone down to see the salmon run in the fall of 1956, the last one Celilo Falls would ever see. Indians from all over the river came to watch, not in any organized way as they had at Kettle Falls fifteen years before, but in ones and twos. That same autumn, the Sunday funnies in Northwest newspapers ran a comic strip serial featuring the adventures of Capt. Robert Gray, the *suyapo* discoverer of the river. After eight Sundays, Gray—exhorting the crew swabbing the decks of his ship, "Clean our *Columbia* proud, mates! She'll give her name to the great river of the west!"—claimed Nch'i-Wana for the United States. Then Gray was attacked by natives, who were stupid and bellicose, but easily cowed. They had no scruples about property: they even tried to steal the *Columbia's* anchor.

By that same autumn, bonds had been issued to build a dam at Priest Rapids, and another dam was planned upstream, to be called Wanapum. Colonel Matthias, who had run Hanford, was now a civilian in the construction business and would build it. He got together with his old friend Johnny Buck and swapped stories. Johnny's family got jobs working at the dam. As compensation for the flooding of P'Na village and the loss of its tule-reed homes and buildings, the Wanapum got Quonset huts and a new concrete longhouse on the west bank of the river out where the transmission lines climbed the black mountain.

Smohalla had said the sacred island where Shuwapsa had carried stones in his dream quest and where all the priests and chiefs were buried would be flooded at the end of the world. Skeptics used to say Smohalla's prophecies were vague—they could apply to any event at just about any time. But the engineers at the dam had this one scheduled right down to the month for 1962.

The Dalles Dam was finished in the beginning of 1957. It was one and a half miles long and it sprawled the river in a zigzag. It had a lock for ships, two fish ladders, and fourteen turbines. At the front were twenty-one floodgates, and they looked like teeth clenched across the river's band. It was so big and so unearthly that it could have been the work of the legendary monster beaver, the wish-push. Or maybe the giant hag who had barred the river in another age—chewing up canoes and men alike—had returned. Maybe the floodgates' teeth were her smile.

On March 10, 1957, at 10:00 A.M., the Corps of Engineers closed them tight. Six hours later Celilo Falls was underwater. The Indians had been told they needed to clear out by January 1 and were long gone. It was springtime and still cool and the rattlesnakes were sleepy. They ascended the bank, chased by the water, and lay stretched out and scattered on top, like strips of an unraveled basket.

On that day Tommy Thompson was 102 years old and was in his bed at a nursing home downriver. He was fitful under his blankets and Flora tried to ease him, but he wouldn't rest. He jerked about like a fish flung on the shore, and she had to call the orderly to settle him down. Tommy cried out to Flora, "Bring me more blankets. I can feel the waters rising. They are covering me up. I am shivering with cold."

3.

Tommy died two years later, and shortly after that Vice President Richard Nixon came to officially dedicate the dam. Flora gathered up Tommy's things—the old treaties, feathers, and stones—and put them in a bag for safekeeping, and sat with them in her house in the new Celilo village above the floodwaters of the dam. People there were trying to fish, but despite what the government had promised about hatcheries and fish ladders, there were fewer salmon above Bonneville than ever. Two months after the Dalles Dam flooded Celilo Falls, the states of Oregon and Washington closed the upriver Columbia to fishing, but the Umatilla, Warm Springs, Yakima, and Nez Percé bands fished anyway, and waited to see what the government would do. A month later the federal government issued regulations that forbade anyone to live at the "in lieu" sites it had granted the Indians in compensation for the flooded fishing grounds. Indians who fished had always lived on the riverbank, either year-round or seasonally. Now they were told to go live on the reservation—in some cases a hundred miles from the river—and commute to their fishing sites.

For the next seven years, the state and federal governments issued regulations and writs; the moderates who ran the tribal councils palavered and negotiated; and the fishers—now dubbed "renegades," like their ancestors who refused to take up allotments on the reservations one hundred years before—ignored them all. In June 1965, Oregon members of Congress implored the secretary of the interior, Stewart Udall, to put a stop to Indian fishing above Bonneville once and for all. Three months later, in the Puget Sound, conflict between fishers of the Nisqually tribe and state fish and game officers culminated in a melee of fists and clubs.

All those years David Sohappy had been working, and he knew he should have been fishing. He worked cattle and as an electrician, a mechanic, and a plumber, shepherding water, power, and oil for wages instead of gathering the food that had been put in and around the river by the Creator. It was as though the war and the world that followed after it had made him impatient, too preoccupied to attend what was already there, to wait for it, say its name, thank it, and take his life from it.

He heard there had been another prophecy circulating among those who still practiced the Washat. It wasn't written down—couldn't be written down—because it concerned things that were in the world before any words had ever been written. It had come down in 1956 with those last fish through Celilo, and it said to keep the old ways, fish, and wait—do these things and everything will be returned to you a thousandfold; forget them and you will perish with everyone else when this world is destroyed and the next one created.

These things were in David's mind for a long time, like a shadow fallen on his shoulder from a bird suspended high above him. In the early 1960s, he and Myra lost an infant son, Dean, to pneumonia. The rusting Desoto they drove wouldn't start and David couldn't get him to the hospital in time to save him. Then David got laid off from the sawmill where he'd been working. His brother Aleck and his friend Clarence Takheal were living and fishing at Cook's Landing on the river and he and Myra decided to join them. Cook's was an "in lieu" site where one or two dozen adults and children were always encamped in cars, trailers, and driftwood shacks in a landscape dotted with heaps of nets, firewood, tires, and fish-drying racks. Everything about the place was an affront to white government and decorum: the illegal habitations on the shore, the illegal fishing on the water, the contemptuous contentment of these people who—oblivious to phones, clocks, and credit cards—didn't want to do anything to advance themselves or their children.

Within a year David had built himself, Myra, and his eight children a house of driftwood—with a dirt floor and a woodstove—on the edge of the river. He was eligible for unemployment, food stamps, Aid to Dependent Children, and general assistance: he didn't take them. He had every reason to ease his cares with a drink and soothe his nerves with tobacco: he'd never touched them in his life and never did. He only fished, and taught his children to fish.

The authorities did not make it easy for him or anyone else at Cook's. Citations, writs, tickets, tags, and posters—pink, yellow, light blue, orange-on-white—fluttered down on them like an autumn without end. But the federal government couldn't quite bring itself to bulldoze Cook's or haul away its inhabitants in chains. The states of Oregon and Washington—goaded by sports and commercial fishermen and humiliated by the Indians' insouciant mockery of their fish and game professionals—decided that something had to be done, despite knowing that any number of

Supreme Court decisions forbade them from imposing controls on native fishing. But on March 4, 1966, the Oregon State Fish Commission announced that it would enforce its regulations on Indians and whites alike when the salmon came that spring.

Encouraged by white and native political activists familiar with the tactics of the civil rights movement and the student new-left, the people of Cook's responded. They announced the creation of their own "Columbia River Fish Commission," which declared a season that opened on April 4, a month before Oregon's. The commission laid down regulations forbidding fishing on Sunday and established conservation measures. Flora Thompson came down from Celilo and brought the bag with the treaties and Tommy's relics. She sang her songs and then the fishers of Cook's held a first-foods ceremony and put their nets in the water. "Eightball" Willie Tillequots was appointed game warden and posted himself on the riverbank with a .30-.30 carbine. Eightball fired a single warning shot across the bow of a Washington fisheries department motorboat that came too close for his taste. After that, fish and game officials stayed away.

The states waited until midsummer to respond to what the press had termed the "uprising" at Cook's. Washington authorities arrested David's brother Aleck and six other people from Cook's on July 27 for illegal fishing and for threatening state officials with firearms. One of them was Mitchem Tulee, a relative of Sampson Tulee, whom the Supreme Court had vindicated in 1942. He and Aleck Sohappy were each fined $250, with all but $50 of the fine suspended. Oregon seemed more vehement in the prosecution of Indian fishers, charging two Yakima with possession of out-of-season salmon and, a month later, various members of the Tulee and Takheal families with illegal use of nets.

Life on the river went on in that fashion for another year and nothing was resolved: citations were issued, fines were levied and suspended; law enforcement officers enforced and fishers fished in a familiar, symbiotic round, like a horse's tail swishing flies on a long summer's day. It was the Indians, and David in particular, who brought matters to a head. With advice from an organization called Survival for American Indians and legal support from a Ford Foundation grant, in May 1968 the Cook's Indians decided to get somebody arrested and pursue their case as far and as long as it took to settle the question of what rights native fishers had on the Columbia River.

The perpetrators were chosen with some care: David, in his forties, already possessed some of the sagacious gravitas white Americans associated with archetypal media Indians such as Chief Dan George. He would go fishing with his twenty-year-old nephew, Aleck's son, Richard. The "fish-in" would therefore be imbued with an ethos not only of the exercise of venerable native tradition but of blood ties, and there was something more: Richard was a sergeant on leave from the U.S. Army. He'd been wounded four times in Vietnam and in addition to four Purple Hearts had won both the Silver and Bronze Stars for valor. He was home on a recuperation leave. He'd already volunteered for another tour in Vietnam.

David and Richard were arrested by Washington fish wardens for illegal net fishing in June, and on July 1 were found guilty in Skamania County court. They were given thirty-day suspended sentences and $250 fines, with $200 of the fine suspended. That was the customary resolution of such cases and that was where it was supposed to end. This time it didn't. In addition to appealing to the state superior court, David and a roster of people that included most of the residents of Cook's Landing filed suit in federal court in Portland asking that the salmon seasons set by Washington and Oregon be suspended since they violated treaty rights. The case, which named Oregon fish commissioner McKee A. Smith as a defendant, went on the docket as *Sohappy v. Smith*.

Two months later the states retorted that Sohappy lacked "standing" as a representative of the Yakima tribe and tried to have the suit dismissed. The court was unpersuaded. Meanwhile,

Oregon continued to enforce its regulations, arresting seventeen more Indian fishers the following May. That summer they waited for the court to act on their case.

But where had they gone when they went to court? Maybe they had turned their lives over to some monstrous chancery, some star chamber that would hand back those lives recast in the law's own image: two things where there'd been one, sundered and seeking each other furiously—every question bifurcated, every answer gainsaid; every bond broken, every surety betrayed; every love riven, dragging its shattered hindquarters like a car-struck dog, like a shadow.

Richard was home from Vietnam on leave then, and one afternoon, sitting in Richard's car up on the highway in early June, he and David's eldest son, Alfred, got to drinking and then to talking about Vietnam. They drank some more—among David's children, Alfred was the only drinker—and then they took sides. Alfred said he thought the war was wrong, and that Richard shouldn't be there fighting in an unjust cause. Especially since he was an Indian, especially in a white man's war. Alfred might as well have spit in Richard's face.

The anger between them was like ice water down their backs, and then the hackles on their necks and scalps burned and prickled like their skin was being peeled off with a pair of pliers. Then they were fighting and their minds were so removed from time or place that it was as though their bodies were all mixed up together, limbs and hair and blood and hands and ardor. But when the motion stopped, Alfred didn't get up because he was dead.

Richard drove away, off to the Yakima Reservation. But the police brought him back and charged him with second-degree murder. The charge was reduced to manslaughter, and then the matter was forgotten, or at least no one spoke about it. David and Myra and Richard's parents, Aleck and Clara, circled each other dumbfoundedly at opposite ends of an ellipse that wreathed Cook's

Landing through the summer. In October, Aleck died, as though there were no place else for him to go.

On October 10, 1969, U.S. district court judge Robert Belloni ruled in *Sohappy v. Smith* that the states could not restrict the Indians' fishing except for clearly defined conservation purposes. That was in itself nothing new, but he also stated that they must regulate the fishery in such a way as to guarantee the Indians a "fair and equitable share" of the fish guaranteed them by the treaties.

The first part of Belloni's decision was a disappointment to state fish officials, but fundamentally only a restatement of federal precedent. The second part, however, provoked an apprehension that rumbled the plumbing of their guts: Indians represented perhaps 2 percent of the population of Washington and Oregon, but at the time of the treaties, perhaps half the inhabitants of the territory were Indian and those Indians were taking virtually all the fish. Did a "fair and equitable share" under Belloni's ruling therefore mean 2 percent of the fish, or could it conceivably mean more? Articles began appearing on editorial pages in Northwest newspapers speculating on the horror of taxpayer dollars being used to subsidize an exclusive reserve of fish for a tiny number of Indians. Advocates of sport and commercial fishing fretted and cringed.

David and the Cook's Indians didn't like the uncertainty of the Belloni decision any more than the whites did, which in any case hadn't done anything to alleviate the day-to-day confiscations of nets and issuings of citations on the river. They appealed to the secretary-general of the United Nations to send a peacemaking mission to the river and asked for financial aid to take the Indians' case to the World Court at The Hague. The council of Yakima Indian Nation, sensing that its own authority and interests were being eclipsed, unsuccessfully tried to get an injunction that would compel the Cook's Indians to obey tribal regulations.

The state people came to Cook's and offered David a special dispensation to fish all he wanted if he'd drop the matter. They also suggested that some kind of financial settlement might be reached.

David wasn't interested. He had a black footlocker he was filling with law books, briefs, and correspondence he'd started with people like the United States Commission on Civil Rights. He wanted this argument to be about his life and his religion—which were both nothing more and nothing less than fishing—but the government and the courts wouldn't let it be that way. So he had to master the white people's weapons while he and his sons went on fishing and Myra and his daughters ran the fish sheds. Myra had become a formidable and tenacious combatant in the fish wars in her own right. She was a small woman, given to wearing traditional clothes accessorized with outlandish hats and scarves. She had a way of looking deep into people's eyes with a little grin that made them feel she saw things they didn't necessarily want her to know about. She liked to stir things up and ask awkward questions. She had a thirty-five-millimeter camera and she'd follow the fish and game agents around, snapping their pictures and asking for their badge numbers. It was for her scrapbook, she'd explain.

Meanwhile, the question of what "fair and equitable" meant was settled elsewhere. Fishing activists in the Puget Sound, bolstered by *Sohappy v. Smith*, pressed the matter in federal court, and in 1974 Judge George Boldt ruled in *U.S. v. Washington* that half the catch destined for "usual and accustomed" fishing places must be reserved for the Indians, interpreting the treaties' boilerplate phrase *in common with* to mean fifty-fifty. Judge Belloni ruled later that year that the same rule must apply on the Columbia. White fishing interests were stunned and then outraged, and the federal government, the official plaintiff in the matter as the Indians' legal guardian, was stymied. It was reported that when Interior Secretary Rogers Morton was informed of Boldt's decision, he said, "Well, appeal it, appeal it!" and was informed, "We can't, Mr. Secretary. We won."

The task of undoing what became known simply as "Boldt"—whose author now found himself being burned in effigy by white Northwest fishers on a regular basis—fell to Slade Gorton, the attorney general of Washington State. Gorton, the thin-lipped, cadaverous heir to a New England seafood fortune, became the archnemesis of Indian fishing rights, if only because he labored so hard and so unsuccessfully to reverse them. Boldt was upheld by the circuit court of appeals and the Supreme Court refused to review the decision. In the Puget Sound, white and Indian fishers rammed each other's boats while on the Columbia, tribal and state officials tried without much success to cobble together a fishery management agreement. Finally, in 1978, the Supreme Court agreed to review Boldt. The patrician Gorton argued before the Court as though in his true element, but on July 2, 1979, the Court upheld Judge Boldt's original decision.

On the river and in David's heart, none of this seemed to mean anything. The court "decisions" didn't decide anything; they just led down one gyre of words and into another. What David knew was that he'd had a hundred nets confiscated since he came to Cook's and that, with grandchildren and relatives, he had twenty mouths to feed. He knew his black footlocker was abrim with paper, but he still wasn't being left alone to fish.

Meanwhile, Flora Thompson had died the previous spring. Her house caught fire and she and everything in it were consumed. Once before she had left a candle burning and the flame got hold of the flag Tommy flew outside his longhouse and burned it up along with the back part of the house. Maybe that had happened again. She loved to have candles burning, multitudes of them like they had in the Catholic and Shaker churches, the yellow tip of the flame lapping the air with a thread of black smoke like a song rising to heaven, and beneath it, in the middle of the light, the orange heart, egg-shaped like an unborn child. Everything in the house was melted into one charred shipwreck of black; Flora on the kitchen floor, tucked up into herself; the blankets and dresses; Tommy's things, feathers fused to treaty papers, flesh to words.

In 1979, while the Supreme Court was pondering its decision, David Sohappy made a decision of his own. He had a dream. He saw himself floating in the river out beyond Cook's, beneath the cliffs and the forest, on the gray choppy waves that angled downstream like the grain on a plank. He was facedown and he was dead.

He decided he wouldn't fish anymore. The boys could fish, with his second-born son, David junior, now the eldest, in charge. He would watch. He would wait for them. He would call out to them from the shore, and ask them how it was going, and if they hadn't got anything, he'd tell them where to put the nets. That's where the fish would be.

It was like a train exploding from a tunnel into the night, like a cannon or a door slammed far away. Then the sound shuddered up the river, a flight of ravens sheathing the sky. A little while later, the flume rose from where the top of the mountain had blown away. It kept rising all day, until it was a column of ash, steam, and fumes twelve miles high. And the white snow that had last fallen almost two hundred years before began to fall again.

On the mountain, the wind blew at seven hundred miles an hour and the temperature was close to six hundred degrees Fahrenheit. Boiling mud poured into the creeks and rivers. The forests were laid flat and the animals that lived in them were incinerated or their lungs were seared and they lay in the ashes like capsized statues cast in lead. Fifty-seven people died, almost all facing away from the mountain, their legs sprawled out behind them as though they had been running; and then, when they could run no more, as though they had been crawling, just before the flood of heat overtook them.

It was a Sunday morning in May 1980. Wilbur Slockish, Jr., was living upriver at Wishram, across from where Celilo Falls used to be, and as likely as not his head hurt. He was thirty-six years old, he had been married and unmarried, he'd been to California and back, and wherever he'd gone the drinking windigo followed him. Now he was married again and he and his new wife, Suzy, had ten kids between them. Maybe that was what turned things around or maybe it was getting off the reservation and back down to the river. Maybe it was the volcano and then getting arrested for fishing and doing sixty days in jail. Whatever the reason, by the end of 1980 Wilbur quit drinking and just went fishing.

He got enough fish to scrape by on, but not many more. The fish weren't coming. In 1900 forty million tons of fish had been caught on the river; in 1980, the catch would be two million tons. Nor, despite its confirmation by the Supreme Court, had the Boldt decision produced a "fair and equitable" distribution of fish. Native fishers were getting a tenth of the catch to which they were entitled; whites, on the other hand, were catching 89 percent of the fish allotted to them.

For the Indians, the reasons for the decline of the fishery were self-evident: the one hundred dams on the Columbia and its tributaries, deforestation, and the dubious policy of attempting to replace wild stocks with hatchery fish. Moreover, 80 percent of the salmon bound for the Columbia were being caught by commercial fishing fleets before they even reached the river. Above Bonneville, the salmon runs were so small the states had reduced the fall season to eight days. Privately, the state fishery agencies and their federal counterpart, the National Marine Fisheries Service (NMFS), had to admit that trying to maintain a salmon fishery above Bonneville was a nuisance. It would be simpler to let nature take its course and allow the fishery to die out.

The Indians felt differently, and the Yakima Nation government—until now committed to negotiation and compromise—sued the NMFS's parent agency, the United States Department of Commerce: the NMFS must honor its obligations under Boldt by compelling the states to protect the upriver fish runs and ensuring that Indians got their lawful share of the catch. This was not a course the newly elected administration of Ronald Reagan was inclined to pursue.

At Cook's Landing, the eruption of Mount St. Helens had told David Sohappy all he needed to know. Five more mountains would explode before the end, and then those who kept the old ways would go into the next creation; those who didn't would perish. It was time to get ready. David and Myra had been getting deeper into the Feather religion. It was the step beyond Washat; it was the eighth drum that came after Smohalla's seven drums. Mostly it was secret. But once you got the power, you could do healing with a feather, and that was where the name came from. And the power had something to do with spinning and "taking the water," with turning like a fire stick in tinder; like the salmon circling creation.

But to honor the salmon, David had to initiate himself into something besides the Feather religion, something just as arcane and to him much more alien. He opened his black footlocker and got out his books on treaty law and his *Black's Law Dictionary*, and he copied out passages longhand until they had stuck in his mind—definitions of "exercise," "inherent power," "prior right," "unalienable," and "poaching," which had to do with taking the king's deer. He read from the footlocker until he was dizzy.

People had always been willing to listen to David. His silences were like stories, and when he spoke all by himself, uninterrupted for half an hour, it was like a conversation. But he had to get good at talking to white people, and at talking and writing about the white people's law. The states and the NMFS might have obligations under the Boldt decision, but by the beginning of 1981 they were feeding stories to reporters with headlines like "Indians peril Columbia salmon master plan."

The reporters started coming to talk to David. He told them how he and the people at Cook's were just trying to keep the old ways—their fishing and their faith—and he gave them what they called "good copy": he'd talk about his religion and add, "There are lots of Christians around. They come and say God helps those who help themselves. I believe it. They help themselves to anything we have."

Myra was good copy, too. The state fish and game people were always driving in and out of Cook's at all hours to see if there were any wet nets around the place when there shouldn't be and to confiscate them if there were. They'd also post men with binoculars on both sides of the river to keep a regular eye on the Sohappys and, as they might put it, to keep the Sohappys "on their toes." In addition to the camera Myra took their pictures with, she got a radio scanner so she'd know when the fish agents were going to come calling, which might be any time of the day or night.

One time they showed up and Myra, maybe not entirely by accident, backed the family truck into a state warden's car and put a little dent in it. They arrested her for assault and took her off to jail. She needled, badgered, and harried them all the way there and through the bars of the holding cell until they couldn't take it. They called up David and told him to come get her. He told them, "You took her. You keep her." He figured that would scare them good.

But beyond getting in the newspapers, not much had changed in the fifteen years since David had come to Cook's Landing. Despite the court victories and the occasional respites from active prosecution they'd won him, the states were as intent as ever on getting the Cook's Indians off the river, whether by active enforcement or, as now, harassment. In August 1981, David thought he'd try another avenue of appeal and began to write to the United States Commission on Civil Rights:

First of all I'm David Sohappy. I live here on Cook's Landing in lieu site, practicing what I believe in, like my people of old have done, that believed in Indian ways.

Last Friday the last of July, that's 31st 1981, I set a net to catch a few salmon to take to our feast at Warm Springs,

Oregon, that's the first huckleberry feast, and on Saturday the first of August, when I went to get my net, the Dept. of Game was on the bank watching me and my son Sam So-happy getting our catch, which was one steelhead and one Chinook salmon that we were going to take to our religious ceremony. But the Game Dept. said I didn't have a permit for fishing. I told him I didn't believe I needed one for what I believe is our right. I pointed out to him that non-Indians are fishing on the Columbia, it's not closed to them, they've been open all the time since last spring. I told him the only time they can regulate me is for conservation purposes only and it seems to me there is no need for conservation, not when it's open to non-Indians all the time.

But it made no difference to him. He cited me and my boy for fishing on closed season. I have called the legal aid in Seattle and Portland. They in turn told me to contact our tribal leaders, which I have and my tribal chief said they would help me. I contacted our tribal lawyer and he told me he would not represent me because to do so would be against tribal interests.

So I thought I would write to you and tell you what the Indians here have to contend with, not only from the states, but from our own people.

I don't know where to go for remedy on religious rights that I believe in.

I have a newspaper clipping that I'm going to send over to you and a brief that I had my attorney prepare way back in 1976 where I tried to have my religious ways interpreted by the judge in district court in Portland. . . . I believe that you can get some idea of what we have to contend with—denial of my religious rights and exercise.

I don't have much more to say now—maybe later.

I remain,

David Sohappy

After he finished the letter, he had his sons put out another net into the river. In the morning it was gone, like a hundred other nets seized by the game wardens. He wrote another letter to the U.S. Commission on Civil Rights:

I believe I never reported all that is happening to me and others that's exercising what we believe in, mainly fishing for our subsistence and our way of life. Last night I set a net out here at Cook's Landing at about dusk and went back this morning to check, and found my net gone, same method of operation as in the past, done by the State Game Dept.

Even if I see them taking my net I never get a citation from them. I have asked in the past for a ticket, but to no avail—just plain steal my net and salmon with no way for me to prove it. . . . Over the years I have lost gear . . . all taken by state agencies, I figure over 135 nets all valuable, $300 at first per net to $600 per net now, most taken without no kind of citation, just plain stolen.

I have all the times and dates, and the [names of] the men who took them from me. . . . Hoping some day for redress for the irreparable damages done to me, like the Constitution says, no one shall deprive me of my possessions without just compensation.

Just some of the things that is happening to me and my family here in Cook's Landing, Wa. It's just some things that I felt that you might want to know. I have more I could say, but I'll save it for later.

I remain,
David Sohappy

David mailed the second letter and waited for the federal government under the new administration of President Ronald Reagan to look into his situation.

4.

On the night of September 13, 1981, in her room at the Meredith Motel in Hood River, Oregon, NMFS special agent Penelope Fields wrote up her notes for the day:

> At about 1210 hrs. Dick King and I went into Cooks, ostensibly looking for [a man named] George. While there, a beige Ford p/u truck, WA TT-2776, drove past us and left the area. We soon left as well, but had to wait approx 5 minutes for a train to pass. While waiting, we saw the Ford p/u parked across the road.
>
> At approx 1230 we drove across alongside the p/u, and began chatting with the driver, David Sohappy, Sr. He was accompanied by Mira Sohappy, Samuel Sohappy, Frank Sohappy (child), and a young female child—grandchildren of David. David began to tell us that, although the fishing season was closed, it was incumbent upon him to fish all the time—seasons made no difference. He said, in essence, that not to do so would be "conforming" to "them"—the state. He talked at length about the Indians right to fish in usual & customary places and how this right was higher than any law—federal or state—in the land. He told us that because of this he had the right to fish all the time—for him there were no seasons.

Special Agent Fields also noted that David Sohappy, Sr., told her and "Dick King"—the undercover name of ex–Green Beret and NMFS special agent Richard Severtson—that he welcomed the opportunity to be arrested and to confront the authorities in court, something he had been doing since 1968. Special Agent Severtson told David he was a fish broker with a company called Advanced Marketing Research and was interested in purchasing a large quantity of salmon. He mentioned a generous price. He had a buying station at a nearby ranch. Could David help him? David told him to come back the next day.

On September 14, Severtson and Fields took delivery of more than twenty-five hundred pounds of salmon taken from the river by David's sons the night before. Again, David talked repeatedly about his religion and what Severtson called his "idealogy." That night Special Agent Fields drafted a description of David Sohappy, Sr.:

> Beige jeans, lt. blue pull-over shirt, denim type jacket w/ camel collar—
>
> dk. green (olive) denim hat.
>
> Hair in 2 thin braids—1 yellow rubber band; 1 red rubber band.

The next day, Severtson and Fields returned to Cook's Landing:

> While S. A. Severtson accompanied Dave Sohappy, Sr., and his daughter to the undercover ranch site to buy fish, I stayed at Cooks Landing, chatting with his wife, Mira.
>
> The Sohappy's have lived there on the river for 15 years. They live in a rambling shack located right down at the dike. One large area of the shack, about 20 × 25 feet, is devoted to use as a drying room. In this room Mira Sohappy cuts up, dries & packages salmon and steelhead for retail sale.
>
> During the conversation with Mira it became very apparent that the Sohappys are a very militant Indian family. For instance, Mira expressed her views that the Indian children should not have to go to schools provided by white people. She said she and her husband try to tell the other Indian families that, in sending their children to school "almost as soon as they can walk & talk" they only learn to become taxpayers and work for the government. She also commented that her husband tried to explain to the others that they should not buy the subsidized housing available to them. While they say they will own a house in 30 years, David tells them that all they will be is a

taxpayer. She said she and David argue with their people constantly, telling them they must not conform to non-Indian rules and regulations. Mira also commented that, in their opinion, the Columbia River belongs to the Indians.

Myra told Special Agent Fields about her children, and about the two that had died: Dean, whom pneumonia drowned with the waters of his own infant lungs; and Alfred, who died on the river. Alfred's cousin Richard came home from his last tour of Vietnam full of bad dreams and trouble, and he took Alfred out on a boat and Alfred never came back. It hadn't happened that way, but that was the way Myra told it to Penny. Myra had a notion about Penny she couldn't put her finger on quite yet.

Special Agent Fields asked if she could see the salmon drying shed. Myra said that if Penny was really interested, she would explain everything to her. Myra guided her through the shed and showed her how the fish were cleaned, filleted, hung, smoked, and stored, more or less the way women on the river had been doing it for five thousand years. It took a long time, and that night Special Agent Fields wrote down the parts of it she could remember.

Over the next two weeks, Special Agents Severtson and Fields spent more time with the Sohappys and bought more fish from them. But on October 2, Myra gave them a scare. She turned up with her camera and starting snapping shots of Severtson and Fields. Special Agent Severtson asked her, "Why are you taking pictures?" Myra smiled a quizzical half-grin and said, "What's the matter—do you have a badge number on your chest?" Severtson laughed, and told her, of course not—he was just curious. Then David and Myra gave him some fish and Special Agent Fields sneaked behind the shed and took some pictures of her own of the transaction. But then David and Myra drove off without collecting a check for the fish, the evidence needed to legally implicate them. Despite that, Special Agents Severtson and Fields were confident of their case. But there was a technical problem that meant they needed to keep the Sohappys trading with them for a few more months: the law the NMFS was planning to charge them with violating wasn't on the books yet.

After they drove away, Myra told David she had a vision about the man she knew as Dick King: "I was looking at his chest and I could see a badge on it. He's a lawman."

David told her, yes, he knew that.

A month and a half later on November 16, 1981, President Ronald Reagan signed H.R. 1638/S. 736 into law. The bill created an amendment to the federal fish and wildlife regulations known as the Lacey Act. Specifically, the amendment made it a federal crime to catch fish in a manner that violated either state or tribal regulations. The bill was sponsored by Slade Gorton, the newly elected junior senator from Washington.

The undercover operations of Special Agents Severtson and Fields were begun at the request of the Washington State Department of Fisheries in anticipation of the amendment to the Lacey Act. By early 1982, the state had also commenced a program to influence public opinion. A series of articles appeared in the *Vancouver Columbian* that described how Indian poachers threatened the salmon population on the Columbia River; how thirty thousand salmon had mysteriously disappeared each year for the last two years; and how Indian activist fishers—including David Sohappy, "an Indian mystic who lives where he wants, fishes where he wants, and ignores tribal agreements with state and federal agencies"—openly flouted the law and threatened fish and game officials with firearms. The story was reprinted in newspapers around the Northwest, complete with photos of David Sohappy pictured at his Cook's Landing "no-man's-land."

By April, the spring salmon run was under way, and Special Agents Severtson and Fields were back on the river buying fish not just from David Sohappy but from dozens of Indians drawn by their attractive prices and their willingness to buy any and all fish available. People on the river were calling Severtson "King Tut" on account of his deep pockets and generous buying policies. They dubbed the perky, telegenic Fields "Penny the Weather Lady." One day, Fields drove into Cook's Landing and David's daughter, Barbara, casually remarked to her, "Oh yeah—we heard you were coming on the scanner," alluding to the constant monitoring of law enforcement frequencies the Sohappys had inaugurated years before in response to a decade of police harassment.

Discomfited by such passing remarks, Severtson and Fields could not figure out whether the Indians remained ignorant of their true identity or were simply oblivious to it. In any event, they accelerated their efforts to bring their operation to its desired conclusion. They'd hoped to draw David Sohappy—as the clear leader and mastermind of the river's renegade Indian fishers—deeper into "Advanced Marketing Research" as a kind of partner. But Sohappy was elusive: he appeared happy to sell them fish, but evinced little interest in becoming more involved, regardless of how lucrative it might be. But Bruce Jim, a member of the Warm Springs band living at Celilo village, was both credulous and avaricious, and he liked bantering with "Dick King" about building a fish-buying empire on the river that could net both of them millions.

This was a role they'd envisioned for David Sohappy. But with the spring salmon run approaching, Severtson and Fields had to grasp whatever opportunities presented themselves and hope the evidence they needed to thoroughly entrap Sohappy would come along in due course. By the middle of April, they'd hammered together a buying shed next to Bruce Jim's place at Celilo. With bank accounts and an answering service linked to Advanced Marketing Research's phony Seattle address already in place, Severtson and Fields erected hidden cameras, donned wireless transmitters, and opened for business. Within days they were, as Special Agent Severtson put it, "inundated" by fish and—since they had to resell the fish to maintain their cover—they were also awash in profits: Advanced Marketing Research was earning the NMFS a windfall that would quickly mount to six figures.

On April 28, Wilbur Slockish, Jr., turned up at Celilo. He now headed a household of a dozen people and he had fish to convert to the cash he needed to support them. In the last two years, he'd remade his life free from alcohol and the numb despair of the reservation, and he'd done it by fishing and by the Washat faith. He started going to the Yakima tribal council and arguing with them about their regulations—about how the tribe shouldn't countenance fishing on Sunday, for example—and they sent him away: he was too young to talk, and where did he get off thinking he was the only one who needed or cared about fish?

That was no matter. Just a few weeks before, Wilbur had rein-augurated the first-salmon ceremony at Klikitat, where it had been moribund since his grandfather's death almost forty years before. He didn't hear that train talking to him in the night anymore. Now he was at Celilo with some fish to sell and Dick and Penny's tape was running. Dick told Wilbur he was "just tickled to death" to do business with him; Penny tittered and giggled, and handed Wilbur a nice big check. Wilbur came back twice more.

The fish rolled into the shed for five more days. Special Agents Severtson and Fields came back for another buying trip in the middle of May, and by then they figured they'd implicated close to eighty people in illegal activities of one kind or another. Then they were gone, suddenly, the way Lewis and Clark had passed through 175 years before—trading a little, handing out coins, buying dogs, and disappearing back to whatever place it was that made such people as they were.

❀

In late May, the NMFS arranged to have Cook's Landing pho-tographed from the air. Then, in the shattered landscape of the

Mount St. Helens "red zone" where public entry was still forbidden, they built a mock-up, down to the sheds and trailers and junked cars. They flew in agents from around the country, briefed them on the likelihood that they would be fired upon, and practiced until they got it right.

At a little before 6:00 A.M. on June 17, 1982, thirteen cars, a seaplane, and two dozen NMFS and state agents swept into Cook's Landing. They kicked down the door of David and Myra's shack, rushed into their bedroom, and held a pistol to David's head, telling him, "We've got a warrant here to search this place." Guns leveled at them, David and Myra were told to get dressed, slowly, with no unnecessary movements. Myra put her clothes on and sputtered imprecations at the white men who stood watching her. Outside, on the highway where the wind had blown the limbs of the big firs into contorted wings bent westward, NMFS director Wayne Lewis and Special Agent Severtson paced and shuffled.

Elsewhere at Cook's Landing, they pulled David's grandson roughly from his bed—rupturing stitches a doctor had just sewn in a wound to his hand—and locked him and eight other children in a camper shell. They were left there, unfed and in the dark, until 10:00 A.M. when, after four hours of searching, the agents were finished. What they hadn't hauled away—radios, appliances, manuals, keys, phone books, books, photos, cassettes, and David's black footlocker—they left a shambles. Then they took the Sohappys' family car and drove away.

Wayne Lewis had a news release ready in advance for the newspapers. For years, it said, "Cook's Landing has been the scene of confrontation, violence, and a source of danger to law enforcement officials." It was the home of the "criminal element" behind the poaching ring that was responsible for thirty thousand or more missing salmon each year and that was endangering the Columbia River's entire run. However, highly trained, crack covert agents had "penetrated" the ring, which had culminated in today's lightning raid. Indictments would be forthcoming.

❀

On the afternoon of October 21, 1982, assistant United States attorney Stephen Schroeder and Lisa Hemmer from the Justice Department in Washington, D.C., were secreted with a federal grand jury in Seattle. No one got to talk whom they didn't want to talk; no one got to listen whom they didn't want to listen. That was the way justice worked.

They had special agent Penelope Fields testify for three hours. The jurors had heard every detail of every transaction; seen the thousands of dollars of checks; looked at the photographs; and listened to the surveillance tapes. But some of the jurors wondered if there were issues that weren't getting addressed. One asked:

> Did you run into the idea that you're in the middle of one of the Indians' most traditional fishing grounds and it was all theirs for years and years and years and years, and they lost Celilo Falls? I remember Celilo Falls very well, and we often stopped there, and that caused a very hostile situation, which has, as far as I know, never gone away. They feel it's theirs.

Special Agent Fields responded:

> Well, I think that, in fact, exactly what you're saying is true. They did suffer a loss and, of course, their traditional argument has been that the run of the Columbia River has been depleted by the dam situation and by the lumber situation, the timber situation, and I think that's a valid argument. We have to acknowledge that and agree to it.
>
> I think the concern that we have to look at now is that, yes, all of that is true and, yes, they are Indians who have a cultural and traditional history and right to that fishery, and that has to be recognized and protected.

Fields added that, of course, the Indians she had been investigating were an egregious and greedy bunch who exploited their own traditions for gain and were destroying the fishery in the process.

Schroeder and Hemmer steered the presentation back to money and the Indians' contempt for the law, but some of the jurors kept returning to something that was bothering them:

> David Sohappy, Sr., is just as old as I am, and if I remember the Celilo Falls fishing, he must remember it more than I do. . . . They figure they got taken [and] sure, it's true.

Schroeder broke in:

> I'm not sure, but perhaps you don't understand the context of these laws. . . . What we are concerned with here is people who are fishing outside of those established treaty rights, people who are fishing outside the authority of their tribes and outside the authority of the federal court decisions.

A juror retorted:

> That's what I mean. It doesn't mean all the Indians went for the treaty. There was a split in the tribes over this thing. . . . You're existing in a hostile atmosphere here about fish. That doesn't mean they all went for it or they ever will.

Schroeder interrupted:

> It's like the laws of the United States are binding on all the people of the United States. The laws of the Yakima tribe are binding on tribal members. The laws of the Warm Springs are binding on their tribal members, and you never get 100 percent of the agreement with the laws. . . . Other members are equally irate about the violation of the laws.

The juror commented, rather disconsolately, "Not everybody here has lived long enough to know."

At the end of the day, the grand jury indicted nineteen persons for violation of the Lacey Act, among them David Sohappy, Sr., Myra Sohappy, David Sohappy, Jr., Bruce Jim, and Wilbur Slockish, Jr., as well as an orphan named Matthew McConville and a Vietnam veteran named Leroy Yocash, both of whom lived with the Sohappys at Cook's Landing. The indictment named David Sohappy, Sr., as "the central figure in the illegal operation":

He introduced fishermen involved in illegal fishing to special agents operating undercover as purchasers of illegally caught fish. He provided the conspirators with a center of operations at his home, which included equipment for the delivery and transfer of fish. He provided radio and visual surveillance for the purpose of avoiding detection by law enforcement officials. Because of his notoriety as a poacher, he was able to maintain his position as an influential contact figure and a commissioned broker for illegal fishermen. In addition, he operated his own fishing crews which delivered and sold fish to undercover agents on his behalf.

At all times material hereto, David Sohappy, Jr., worked closely with his father, David Sohappy, Sr., in all phases of the operation. He participated in fishing on behalf of his father as well as independently by operating fishing crews, and in brokering sales of other persons' fish in return for a commission.

At all times material hereto, Myra Sohappy monitored radio scanning equipment and alerted conspirators as to law enforcement activities. She operated a subsistence fish-drying room which provided a legitimate appearing guise for the illegal fish-buying operation. She knowingly acted as a conduit for communication between the co-conspirators and the agents.

Altogether about ninety people were indicted: nineteen by the federal grand jury in Seattle, thirty-one in Washington State, and twenty-four in Oregon, with another twenty-five indictments under consideration. Down at Cook's Landing, David Sohappy, Sr., told a reporter, "I'll be showing up in court. I've been ready for this for ten years."

Wilbur Slockish read about his indictment in the newspaper. He went to see a lawyer who called the U.S. attorney's office in

Seattle to see what they ought to do. Nobody there knew anything about it. But then marshals came and took him and the others to Seattle to be arraigned. When the judge asked them to surrender their passports, Wilbur told him, "We haven't got any—we haven't got any place else to go. You might say we're from here."

The judge who would hear their cases—to be tried in three lots for convenience' sake—was Jack Tanner, a black attorney appointed to the federal bench by President Jimmy Carter in 1978. He'd grown up around prizefighters and longshoremen in Tacoma, Washington, and he cursed like a stevedore and swaggered like a lumberjack. Tanner helped defend Muhammad Ali when he refused to go to Vietnam and he'd been the chief counsel for Robert Satiacum, a renowned Puget Sound Indian fishing activist with an unfortunate penchant for racketeering and violence. Trial lawyers dreaded appearing before Tanner: he routinely topped polls as the worst judge in the state, and was known to be rude, capricious, intemperate, and prejudiced. By his own lights, he was one tough bastard.

As Robert Satiacum's lawyer, Tanner had played a major role in the cases that eventually resulted in the Boldt decision. But despite or perhaps because of that connection, Tanner was almost pitiless in his handling of the Indians who were now known as the "salmonscam" defendants. None of them were financially equipped to pay for expert legal help, nor were the lawyers who had helped them in the past equipped to handle a major federal trial. In the end, David Sohappy was defended by Jack Schwartz, a political activist from Portland, and Tom Hillier of the Seattle federal public defender's office.

Neither had much experience in the courtroom, and virtually none with high-profile, complex prosecutions of this kind. Schroeder had the full resources of the United States Justice Department behind him, and he sensed how ill prepared and ill equipped the defense was. He pressed for an early trial, and during the time Schwartz and Hillier should have been constructing their case, he diverted their attention from it by laying a stream of motions before Judge Tanner: Shouldn't Schwartz be cited for contempt for remarks he made to the press in Portland? Were the defendants truly poor enough to deserve legal aid? Schroeder was only asking in the interest of protecting the taxpayers from abuse.

In February 1983, Tanner decided the trial should be moved away from the publicity that surrounded it in the Northwest. When the judge selected Los Angeles as the new venue, Schroeder wondered if public funds really ought to be used to transport the defendants to California and to maintain them there. Weren't they, after all, rather comfortably off as a result of their criminal activities? When they got to Los Angeles, the defendants were lodged in an abandoned motel.

Schwartz and Hillier petitioned Tanner to delay the trial so they could adequately prepare, but Tanner refused. On April 4, 1983, Stephen Schroeder and Lisa Hemmer presented the first of six days of testimony. Schroeder called game agents, fisheries' biologists, radio surveillance experts, and finished his presentation with Special Agents Severtson and Fields. In his cross-examination, Hillier, who conducted the bulk of the courtroom defense, did the best he could. He asked the biologists if the number of fish being taken out of season by Indian fishers was really a threat to the river fishery in comparison to dams, deforestation, or the commercial ocean-fishing industry. They confessed it was a drop in the bucket. He asked Severtson and Fields if David Sohappy had ever been less than clear and truthful with them about his beliefs, activities, and intentions. They confessed he had not.

But in putting its own case, the defense was severely circumscribed. Tanner refused to allow Hillier to offer testimony on either treaty rights or religion and culture. The judge strictly limited the defense to the question of whether the defendants had fished contrary to the Lacey Act, and when David took the stand, he had to admit that of course he had. Hillier tried to introduce other, larger considerations, but succeeded only by subterfuge.

When Yakima chief Levi George took the stand, ostensibly to talk about tribal fishing rules, he instead rolled his eyes heavenward and began to chant a Washat song. Schroeder leapt to his feet, braying "Objection!" Tanner was apoplectic.

In their closing statements on Thursday, April 14, Schwartz and Hillier tried to raise these issues again. The defendants had openly fished in accordance with their traditions, and those traditions were the larger issue. It was the government and its million-dollar sting operation designed to entrap the defendants that was surreptitious, conspiratorial, and suspicious. What possible merit did this entire prosecution—based on speculation about thirty thousand "missing" fish in a sea of millions—have? If the prosecution was correct in alleging a conspiracy dealing in tens of thousands of dollars, where was the fortune that these Indians—who lived in shacks and trailers and drove broken-down cars—must have amassed? Hillier implored the jury to ignore the government's mean-spirited and fatuous persecution of these indigent, hapless river fishers and look to the larger truth.

Judge Tanner instructed the jury that the violations cited in the indictment were the only issue to be decided. The jury deliberated all day that Friday, and Tanner told them to work through Saturday. On Monday, April 18, they returned their verdict. There was no conspiracy, but David Sohappy, Sr., Bruce Jim, and David Sohappy, Jr., were guilty of illegal fish sales to Special Agents Severtson and Fields. Schroeder and Hemmer immediately moved to have the defendants' bail revoked. Hemmer told the judge that an informant had told authorities that a number of 30.06 semiautomatic rifles had been purchased by persons on the river: "The government has concern, as does the sheriff of Skamania County, Washington, that there may be an armed insurrection at Cook's Landing." Bruce Jim and the Sohappys spent the night in jail, but in the morning Schroeder and Hemmer were unable to adduce any evidence of an incipient uprising and the defendants were released pending sentencing.

The other groups of defendants were processed quickly. Most offered no defense at all, having been given the understanding that the court would be lenient. Judge Tanner issued his sentences back in Tacoma. As expected, Myra Sohappy was put on probation, and since they had effectively thrown themselves on the mercy of the court, Matthew McConville, Leroy Yocash, and Wilbur Slockish expected brief or suspended sentences and fines at worst. But Judge Tanner sentenced McConville to one year in prison for having sold 21 illegal fish, Leroy Yocash to two years for 78, and Wilbur Slockish to three years for 63. Tanner sentenced David Sohappy, Sr., to five years in prison for the sale of 295 fish. His son David Sohappy, Jr., also received five years, although he was convicted of selling only 28 fish. Bruce Jim, the only person the government had been able to show might have participated in anything that could be described as a "ring"—the ring in question being the NMFS's own "Advanced Marketing Research"—also received five years.

A few weeks after the sentences were handed down, a secret NMFS report was uncovered by a reporter in Portland: There were no thirty thousand "missing" fish after all, and no evidence that Indian "poaching" was harming the Columbia River salmon run. The fish in question had been diverted from their usual run by pollution discharged into the river from an aluminum mill. The story received little attention.

Tom Hillier immediately began work on an appeal to the United States court of appeals, although it would not be heard for almost two years. Nor did others lose their interest in David Sohappy. Later in 1983, after Judge Tanner had issued his sentences, Senator Slade Gorton, joined by his colleagues from Oregon, Robert Packwood and Mark Hatfield, wrote Secretary of the Interior James Watt, directing him to take action in a matter of mutual concern:

No permanent structures are to be permitted on the "in lieu" sites. B.I.A. [Bureau of Indian Affairs]'s inaction and failure to enforce its own regulations has led to the establishment of a permanent community on one "in lieu" site, Cook's Landing in Skamania County, Washington.

By the spring of 1984, the Portland office of the Bureau of Indian Affairs had posted eviction notices at Cook's Landing, and Jack Schwartz launched an administrative appeal. If nothing else, the notices refocused the attention of the press on the Indian fishers. The Los Angeles trial and Tanner's sentences had received virtually no coverage in the Northwest. But neither, until now, had the growing rift between "Book Indians" and "traditionals." The salmonscam defendants, after all, had defied tribal as well as state regulations; had denounced all recent negotiations and settlements between government and the tribes; and were placing the tribal councils in an awkward position over their occupation of "in lieu" sites. Now reporters were coming to interview David at Cook's again, and his comments seemed to underline his differences with Indian moderates:

> A long time ago people used to say "Never accept anything from the non-Indian. Pretty soon, they'll come to you with a piece of paper and a little law you have to live by. Pretty soon, they'll come to you with a big piece of paper and a whole lot of laws that you have to live by. And pretty soon, they'll move you out of the river."

There was nothing to do but wait for the various courts to act, and to fish. But when Wilbur went fishing, he caught salmon that had welts and sores on their flanks in a way he'd never seen before. Down at Cook's, David talked to more reporters in a manner they liked to describe as "apocalyptic":

> A long time ago people were more advanced than we are now. The dead would lie in state for five days and then come alive.

They'd tell us "Here's what I heard. Here's what I've seen. Here's what's going to happen." Now they get cut up and embalmed and we've lost touch.

Your government will spend billions of dollars on weather-related things until the Indians get things the way they should be. Like Mount St. Helens, ice storms, winds. Your scientists can't explain this El Niño current, can they? Why the ocean fish don't come back? This is nature's way of making people pay.

In August, when the fall chinook should have been running and he should have been on the river, Wilbur started hearing the train again. It came down the track and killed his youngest brother, Paul, that very month. Maybe it was coming for him.

Hillier brought the defendants' appeal before the Ninth Circuit Court of Appeals on February 5, 1985. He argued that Tanner's insistence on focusing narrowly on the specific violations overlooked three vital issues: whether the Lacey Act applies equally to Indians and non-Indians; whether the government proved that violations of tribal law occurred in tribal jurisdictions; and whether the government proved that the state regulations being enforced under the Lacey Act were in fact valid.

During the summer, the Sohappys continued to fight their eviction from Cook's Landing. David spoke of his religion and his traditions, and of the agreements the government had made and reneged on about "in lieu" sites. Myra's comments tended to be more pointed: "They'll have to drag me out." The months passed in a torpid agony, as though real life were being lived just out of reach, clearly visible behind a wall of glass.

On September 4, the court of appeals upheld Tanner's convictions. The Lacey Act was valid: Congress had the right to override Indian treaties through legislation, a view that did not much surprise the Sohappys. The court did allow that the government may not have dealt adequately with the validity of the state regulations, and Hillier immediately filed for a rehearing on this matter. His petition was denied, and Hillier began work on an appeal to the United States Supreme Court. He reduced the case to one question: "Does the Lacey Act, 16 U.S.C. 3371 et seq., confer on the federal government authority to prosecute Indians for violating tribal laws relating to treaty-preserved fishing rights, when those violations occur at 'usual and accustomed' fishing sites?" The appeal was filed on March 21, 1986.

Meanwhile, in Portland, Jack Schwartz filed a suit to block the Cook's Landing evictions. In June, the court threw it out. And at the beginning of July, the Supreme Court refused to hear Hillier's appeal. Back in Tacoma, Judge Tanner wasted no time. He ordered the five defendants still facing jail sentences—David Sohappy, Sr., David Sohappy, Jr., Wilbur Slockish, Leroy Yocash, and Matthew McConville—to report to the Federal Penitentiary at Lompoc, California, by noon on August 8.

Wilbur Slockish was in New York City giving a talk to an Indian rights group when he heard about the Supreme Court's decision. The people running the group were solicitous: Was there anything they could do? Would he like to be alone? Wilbur thought about it, and told them what he'd like to do was go see Coney Island. They rode the subway, reeling and screeching underground, through the rusting iron bones of the city. They got off and walked a few blocks and there was the ocean. It wasn't blue like the Pacific. It was like a sheet of hammered lead, the color of stone, like the river.

This was the water the *suyapo*s crossed when they came looking for the river, the water Columbus thought he was bearing his Christ over. But he wasn't carrying him, he was looking for him, like a hunter. God had come among the *suyapo*s once, and for his trouble they killed him. Ever since, they'd been trying to find him, pursuing him across the face of the world, over the waters, into the forests. And when they found him, they killed him. They hunted him down to Nch'i-Wana, and named it for Columbus, the Christ-bearer who was really a hunter. They must have known God was in the river, because over the next two hundred years, they drowned it.

It is always this way. The *suyapo* is a hunter, and he is always going into the forest. But there is never enough game for him. He is a captive of his hunger. He wants his God to come back and he hunts him, but when he finds him, he kills him. His prey never fills him, so he never thanks it; he honors it no more than the rapist honors the ravished. The truth is, he hates it, because it doesn't love him. And always he goes on hunting, to get his God's love back. He thinks he is free in the woods, the master of the hunt. But he is forever the captive of his longing.

Only one thing stood between the five remaining defendants and jail, and that was the Yakima Nation. The tribal government was not necessarily in sympathy with the defendants, but it was reluctant to give up any sovereignty it might have in their case: since the defendants had been convicted of violating not only state laws but tribal regulations, shouldn't the tribe have the right to try them?

For their part, the defendants were suspicious of the Yakima Nation, which had done very little to defend them against what they believed were blatant attacks on treaty rights. But they were willing to take whatever remaining course was open to them, and trial in the Yakima tribal court was the only one available. On August 7, 1986, the day before they were due to report to federal prison, David Sohappy, Sr., David Sohappy, Jr., Wilbur Slockish, Leroy Yocash, and Matthew McConville went to Toppenish on the Yakima Reservation and turned themselves over to tribal police. The following day they were arraigned before tribal judge David Ward on violations of Yakima fishing regulations. Tribal lawyer Jack Fiander was appointed special prosecutor. The defendants were told not to leave the reservation. They sheltered in the longhouse.

In Tacoma, Judge Tanner was incensed. He issued bench warrants for all five defendants ordering them to be taken into federal custody. Judge Ward was unwilling to give the defendants up to federal marshals, but neither did he want a confrontation with Tanner. Prosecutor Fiander proposed that they be incarcerated in the tribal jail as an accommodation to the federal authorities until the matter could be resolved. On August 15, the two Sohappys moved from the longhouse to the jail, but McConville, Yocash, and Slockish disappeared into the backcountry of the 1.3-million-acre reservation.

Within a week, activists and supporters had formed a vigil outside the jail in Toppenish. Federal marshals waited outside, too, sitting in their cars, neither entering to take custody of the prisoners nor driving away. On August 27, Matthew McConville surrendered and joined the Sohappys. No one—judges, police, attorneys, or defendants—was sure what would happen next. Because Tom Hillier was a federal public defender, the defendants' case was no longer in his purview. Jack Schwartz, whom many now believed was more adept at publicity than procedure, was leaving for London to bring the case to the attention of Amnesty International. They were effectively without counsel.

Tom Keefe was a Seattle attorney who had worked in Washington for Senator Warren Magnuson and returned home to practice law. He was both idealistic and combative, and as a child in Seattle he had rooted for the Indians at the Saturday movie matinees he frequented. As an adult, he had married a Native American and now took an active interest in their concerns. He'd been contacted to act on behalf of Wilbur Slockish, but by the beginning of September he found himself representing the Sohappys as well.

On September 6, Keefe sat in the jail with the elder Sohappy and David and talked for several hours. David wasn't feeling so well. He was used to eating salmon every day, but in the jail you could have fish only on Friday for some crazy reason. The Irish-Catholic Keefe explained the source of the custom. As usual, Sohappy said, the whites had things backwards. They laughed. By the end of the day, when David had told him the story of his life, the life of Smohalla and the Wanapum, and the life of the river, Keefe felt he'd met another Gandhi or Martin Luther King. Sohappy had $105.24 to his name. It would be a pro bono case and that was fine. The injustice, racism, and sheer folly of this prosecution made him color when he thought about it.

Elsewhere in Washington, other Lacey Act violators were being prosecuted. The NMFS sued two California companies for smuggling 3.8 million pounds of illegal Columbia salmon to Japan, thirty-five hundred times the amount of fish involved in the salmonscam. The NMFS wanted some stiff fines levied, but wasn't asking for jail time or anything extreme. The defendants would be represented by Senator Slade Gorton's old law firm.

Jack Schwartz had returned from London, having made an impression on Amnesty International, which asked the U.S. attorney general for a report on the salmonscam case. But from here on, Tom Keefe would be the attorney for the defendants, or at least those presently in custody. The Indians in custody were actually becoming a source of anxiety to Yakima tribal officials, who were finding they had little stomach for the continuing standoff with the federal marshals in Toppenish. Seeking to resolve their dilemma without seeming to yield any legal sovereignty to the federal courts, one of the tribal attorneys had a suggestion: Couldn't it be said that if the tribe brought the defendants to trial, it would be placing them in double jeopardy, since they had already been tried on the same charges by the federal court? If the charges were dismissed on those grounds, the defendants could be handed over to the marshals without the tribe losing face legally.

Judge Ward found the argument compelling, and on September 18 dismissed the charges against the Sohappys and McConville. By the time Tom Keefe heard about it, tribal police chief David Washines was already arranging their transfer out of his jurisdiction. By 3:00 A.M., the prisoners had been moved to the Yakima County jail and were held incommunicado in a room furnished only with a steel bench; by 6:00 A.M., they had been put in handcuffs, waist chains, and leg irons by federal marshals and were being driven to Tacoma.

Keefe rushed to Toppenish the next morning and found himself making an unusual motion to Judge Ward: that the court withdraw its dismissal of the charges against the defendants pending another hearing. At the end of the day, Keefe made his way back over to western Washington, where he was told he could meet his clients the following morning at the Pierce County jail in Tacoma. When he arrived shortly after dawn, he was informed the prisoners had been put in a van at 6:00 A.M. and were being driven to Lompoc by way of Sacramento, California. On September 21, having been manacled and strip-searched a half-dozen times, the Sohappys and Matthew McConville were taken into Lompoc prison and processed yet again. This time they took away the feather David Sohappy, Sr., carried with him everywhere, telling him, "You won't be needing this anymore."

The prisoners thought their journey had ended at Lompoc, but the federal authorities had decided that a higher security, more spartan facility was in order. They were awakened at dawn, stripped and manacled, and flown to Oklahoma City; then taken by bus to El Reno, Oklahoma; thence north to the federal prison at Leavenworth, Kansas; on to a federal facility at Rochester, Minnesota; and at last, in early October, to Sandstone Federal Penitentiary in northern Minnesota.

On October 6, Keefe at last succeeded in getting the charges against the Sohappys and McConville reinstated, and ten days later the Yakima Nation formally asked the federal government to extradite the prisoners to them. Six weeks later, federal officials agreed to release them into tribal custody provided the Yakima understood that their trial was essentially a pro forma exercise: that it could have no effect on the defendants' existing convictions and prison sentences. The tribe accepted the government's terms and scheduled the trial for January 13, 1987.

During this time, Wilbur Slockish and Leroy Yocash reckoned they had traveled five thousand miles within the boundaries of the Yakima Reservation. They found themselves living as their people of old had lived: they haunted the forests and meadows on the slopes of Mount Adams during the elk-hunting time and the berry time; and when the weather turned cold, they descended into the valleys, traces, and draws while the world gathered itself into winter. By day the sun blazed their path and at night the moon washed away their tracks. When the snow came, they moved among the homes of friends and kin. Sometimes they even forgot their legal situation entirely and wondered if, even at the best of times, there was much difference between being a fugitive and being an Indian.

Slockish and Yocash found ways to communicate with Tom Keefe, and even with the press. They gave an extensive interview complete with photos to a reporter from the *Seattle Times*, the same reporter who had been responsible for the original thirty-thousand-missing-fish story in the *Vancouver Columbian* in 1982. They told him they planned to be in court on January 13, but until then they'd continue to hide out. Tom Keefe was displeased with their recklessness: "You just printed 400,000 wanted posters," he told them.

Ten days before the trial was to begin, the assistant warden of Sandstone prison released a statement announcing that the Sohappys and Matthew McConville would not be released after all due to "the potential for development of a confrontation with federal law-enforcement officials." In Seattle, Stephen Schroeder pointed out that in the past demonstrators had held vigils in Toppenish. To deter violence "would require quite a few men on the marshal's part." He added, "To have this media blitz portraying us as attacking the poor Indian is really unfair. I don't think we're the bad guys in this."

The Yakima leadership was furious. Tribal chairman Mel Sampson flew to Washington, D.C., and asked Senators Brock Adams and Dan Evans to intervene. On a tour of the Washington State Indians' reservations, Senator Daniel Inouye was briefed on the Sohappy case and promised to look into the matter. Myra Sohappy was invited to address the United Nations Commission on Human Rights in Geneva and told them, "Our family has been constantly harassed and bullied by the state of Washington fish and game officials for over 20 years." Her husband, meanwhile, sat in Sandstone prison. David was sixty-two years old now, a grandfather among young convicts who couldn't imagine what he had done to pull down hard time in a place like Sandstone. He missed his traditional foods and his health was declining: he'd lost eleven pounds and burst a blood vessel in his left eye. At least he was getting credit on his five-year sentence for the 295 fish. He'd heard how two white men in Seattle received thirty days in jail and a $1,000 fine respectively for selling $20,000 worth of illegal salmon.

On February 14, 1987, during the Presidents' Day weekend, with no warning or explanation, the Sohappys and Matthew Mc-Conville were flown by private chartered jet from Sandstone to Toppenish. They arrived at 11:00 P.M. and Yakima Police Chief Washines hustled them into the jail, forbidding them to speak to the press or supporters. On February 20, Judge Ward refused Tom Keefe's motion to release the prisoners pending trial, agreeing with Prosecutor Fiander that to allow them bail would antagonize the federal authorities. The trial was set for April 13.

Fiander and Keefe went to work on their cases. Fiander was in an impossible position, having been charged with conducting a prosecution that no one wanted him to win. But he made an effort. In March he attempted to get the entire case thrown out since Keefe hadn't paid the correct filing fee. He and Keefe fired

motions at one another in the tribal courtroom between arraign-
ments and hearings that were themselves a mosaic of the miseries
of reservation life: drunkenness, assault, petty theft, vandalism,
child and spouse battering. In the first of a series of remarks that
would characterize their relationship, Keefe declared Fiander's
motion to dismiss "beneath contempt."

For the rest of the month the two Sohappys and McConville
waited in jail. Wilbur Slockish and Leroy Yocash were still at large
somewhere on the reservation. Slockish was sorely tempted to
leave the reservation boundaries, even if only for a day. His father, Wilbur Slockish, Sr., was due to be installed as chief of the
Klikitat on April 5 at the first-salmon ceremony. The chieftancy
had remained vacant ever since Slockish's grandfather had died,
more than forty years ago. But Slockish couldn't risk traveling off
the reservation. The day after his father's inauguration, the police
tracked down Leroy Yocash and put him in the Yakima County
jail. On April 10, after half a year in hiding, Slockish surrendered
to the Yakima tribal police. They led him past the drummers outside the jail, and inside there was David in a green prison jump-
suit, a red headband tied around his silver hair.

The trial began on Monday, April 13, 1987, and the twenty-
by-thirty-foot courtroom was crowded with the families of the
defendants, their supporters, and the press. Outside, Indian and
white activists, police, and a drumbeating Buddhist nun milled
around. David had received letters of support from around the
world—"I am sad you are in jail. I want to live close to Mother
Earth," wrote a child in the Netherlands—and singers Jackson
Browne and Bonnie Raitt had volunteered to perform a benefit
concert in Seattle.

But in other respects the trial promised to be a repetition of the
arguments heard four years before in Los Angeles. Jack Fiander
planned to present a case confined strictly to specific violations of

the laws in question; Tom Keefe would do just the opposite, arguing that the jury not only needed to consider the spirit rather than the letter of the law, but needed to do so in light of thousands of years of tradition and 150 years of Indian–white relations.

Fiander, a slight, thirty-four-year-old Yakima, was as soft-spoken and bland as Keefe was edgy and vitriolic. He called a succession of game officers and quietly asked them to recite the chapter and verse of the law. He introduced canceled checks from "Advanced Marketing Research" into evidence. He read testimony into the record from the Los Angeles trial in which the defendants admitted they had fished out of season. He was done on Wednesday. In his closing statement, he said it was clear that the defendants not only had fished out of season but had done so for profit—they'd admitted the first charge, and the checks made the second irrefutable. The Yakima people might not like the idea of having the NMFS enforce their laws for them, but that didn't change the fact that the defendants had broken them.

On Thursday morning, Tom Keefe made his opening statement:

> In 1981, at the request of the Washington Department of Fisheries, a federal agent came to the big river with a pocketful of money, with a heart full of malice, and with a mouth full of lies. What he learned was something that was learned by two other federal men named Lewis and Clark when they came down the big river in 1805: That there are Columbia River Indians who have lived there since time immemorial who fish and live on the river, who subsist off the river, and if they trust you and if you're showing them respect, they will share that resource from the river with you—they will trade, barter, and sell that resource.

It was that simple. What was more complex and bitter was history and the nexus of law and language that underlay it:

> At the treaty time, written words changed the lives of the tribes and bands of the Northwest forever. The tribes and bands who

make up the Yakima Indian Nation gave up nine million acres of the sixteen thousand square miles that they occupied. It was an act of sovereignty that ceded those nine million acres and which reserved the right to fish.

Wilbur Slockish's great-great-grandfather Sla-Kish was the last of the chiefs to bite his lip and sign the paper; David Sohappy's great-grandfather Sohappy died because he refused to fight the war the treaty brought about. And since the Dawes Act of 1887—which began to unravel the title Indians held to their reservation lands—there had been one hundred years of "unremitting assault on the rights that were guaranteed by that treaty."

Keefe reviewed the various Supreme Court decisions that had upheld Indian fishing rights and the government's bad faith of recent years. Then he called Myra Sohappy as his first witness. She said, "We honor the salmon. It's our life." There wasn't much else to say. He called Wilbur Slockish's father. He asked him about his grandfather, Tommy Thompson, and about how Indians had fished the river when he ran Celilo. In the course of the next two days, Keefe called a dozen relatives and acquaintances of the defendants, asking each of them three basic questions: Were the defendants traditional Indians? Did they honor the salmon? Was it permissible for traditional Indians to barter and sell salmon? The answers were always yes.

On cross-examination, Jack Fiander tried to show that Keefe's witnesses were prejudiced—"These are your friends on trial, aren't they?"—and that they were also inconsistent. Didn't members of the tribe, benefiting as they did from tribal subsidies and other services, have an obligation to obey tribal laws, including fishing regulations? Some said, angrily or sheepishly, that they did; others, that they didn't know; and still others, that the old ways represented a higher law. Perhaps Fiander's cross-examination revealed some inconsistency or even hypocrisy in Keefe's witnesses, but it also exposed contradictions in modern Indian life that were manifest to some extent in practically every person in the courtroom. When Fiander asked one of the defense witnesses if, despite his support for the defendants' defiance of tribal law, he had accepted his cash subsidy from the tribe that year, Keefe rose to object: "Irrelevant— Every person in this tribe is automatically entitled to that. Like just about everyone here, I assume your honor received his. I even hope that you, Mr. Fiander, got yours."

Interspersed with these character witnesses, Keefe began to call the defendants, starting with Slockish. Each talked about his childhood, the people who'd taught him to fish and live in the old ways, and the importance of the Washat religion in his life. In his cross-examinations, Fiander concentrated on baser issues. He asked Slockish, "Did you sign a form saying you'd comply with tribal regulations?"

Slockish didn't respond.

"Would it refresh your memory if I showed it to you?"

Fiander fetched a paper and a canceled check. After Slockish confirmed that it was his signature on the paper, the prosecutor handed the check to Slockish.

"Who's it made out to?" Fiander asked.

"Me," Slockish said.

"What's the date?"

"April 28, 1982."

"The season was closed then by the Yakima, wasn't it?"

Slockish answered in a whisper, "Yeah, I guess it was."

"I have nothing further."

Keefe hustled over to the witness stand.

"Which is your higher obligation—traditional laws or tribal regulation?"

"Tradition."

"Wilbur, do you ever sell fish?"

"Yes."

"Is that how you put food on the table for 12 children?"

"Yes."

"That's all, Wilbur," Keefe concluded.

When Keefe called Matthew McConville, Leroy Yocash, and David Sohappy, Jr., the same pattern of testimony and cross-examination followed: Keefe portraying the defendants as decent, even high-minded traditional Indians; Fiander portraying them as greedy, opportunistic hypocrites. Between defendants, Keefe called tribal council members and officers in an effort to show that even at the highest levels of the Yakima Nation there was tremendous ambivalence about fishing rights and regulations. None was willing to condemn the defendants, and a number tacitly condoned their actions. Some tribal councillors openly sided with them, arguing that it was Yakima moderates who had forgotten the old ways and were responsible for the decline of the river fishery, not David Sohappy. "If you go against the Creator's law, you will be punished," said one. "I see the punishment happening to us."

Fiander, in a rare display of emotion, finally objected to Keefe calling any more such witnesses on the grounds of separation of powers: "Your honor, I was appointed to prosecute this case. It's frustrating for me to have one tribal witness after another come in here and undermine the prosecution." But Judge Ward overruled him, and the witnesses kept coming and Fiander did the best he could. In cross-examination, he'd show them the canceled checks and ask those who spoke of defending tradition, "Are these traditional checks?" He put the question to them without so much as a trace of irony in his voice, but perhaps that was because he was growing tired. At times, he called witnesses by the wrong name or made objections whose grounds seemed circular even to laypersons.

On Wednesday, April 22, Keefe called his final two witnesses.

"I call Richard Severtson." No one moved or came forward.

Keefe continued: "He's been supoenaed to this court, and I'd like him to come forward right now." Keefe let the silence hang in the air awhile longer.

"In the absence of Mr. Severtson's testimony, I'd ask that his affidavit be filed as adverse testimony." Keefe handed a copy of "Dick King's" original 1982 grand jury affidavit to the clerk, and let what he hoped the jury would see as the high-handed contempt of the white justice system for an Indian court sink in. Then he called David Sohappy, Sr.

The next six hours were not so much testimony as a story spun out in all directions, incorporating every aspect of Wanapum history, culture, and religion; the lives of David, his ancestors, and his children; and the epic and myth of the river and its salmon—how it had been, how it was, and how it must be. Keefe brought out a map and walked David around it: from Priest Rapids to Celilo to Cook's and across this very reservation and back to White Bluffs. Sometimes both Keefe's questions and David's responses seemed random, as though together they'd flung a net off the bow of the witness stand, hauled it in, and were sorting through whatever they found there. But David talked for forty-five minutes at a time without interruption, and for all the jury and the onlookers knew, the hands on the clock on the courtroom wall might have been spinning backwards.

In other trials and other courtrooms, Sohappy said, "I tried to explain to them what was in our dreams." Now he was having his chance at last. His voice was slow and soft, neither monotonous nor strident; there were no emphases, no perorations, no accents, no risings and lowerings—he wasn't selling anything. It was steady and went on and on, like a voice in your pillow, like a voice in a dream, like someone stroking your hair and telling you all the things you would do when you grew up.

So people were listening, forgetting themselves, because David had made his story into their story—the story of every Indian in that courtroom; had made them remember themselves. He was a voice that spoke their name, and yet all he ever claimed to do was wait and watch and keep the things he must in his mind. When he spoke about the salmon, he could have been talking about fish or himself or the end of the world, and his voice was like something rising from the bottom of the river:

The salmon is always coming, coming up now, always coming up; waiting in some deep pool, waiting, waiting for the right time. I've been on the river a long time. I know when they're coming, where they're going.

❀

The next morning, Thursday, Fiander began his cross-examination. He approached David with a pile of checks and instructed him to read the date, payee, and amount of each one. Keefe objected, was overruled, and with each subsequent check, objected again and was again overruled. When that was done, Fiander flipped them over and asked David if each endorsing signature on each check was his. Keefe began another litany of objections. Then Fiander brought out a stack of fishing violation citations and asked David to identify each one. Fiander explained, "I know it's painful, but the jury is entitled to know." Keefe broke in furiously: "It's not painful, it's ludicrous. If you're trying to prove my clients fished illegally, they'd be happy to plead guilty and save us all a lot of time."

Fiander continued guiding David through the roster of citations, asking him if he recognized his name on them, and David responded to them in batches: "Yes, yes, yes, yes, yes, yes." Keefe interrupted: "Your honor, that answers the next six questions. Can counsel move on now?" Keefe then threatened "to call every member of this tribe and ask each one if they've ever fished out of season." Judge Ward warned Keefe to settle down: "The defense does not need to instruct the plaintiff how to cross." "No," shot back Keefe, "but I would hope your honor would." When Fiander pressed David further on his finances, Keefe sighed and said, "You ought to be ashamed of yourself."

When Fiander was finished, Keefe tried to undo whatever damage the prosecution had done: he had David testify that the Sohappys had never owned a new car, never been on a vacation, never owed money or had money in the bank either, and at various times had supported an extended family of twenty-five. When

Keefe was done, David was perhaps no longer the same person he had seemed the previous afternoon, but he was something else that was equally valuable to the defense: an Indian like other Indians, capable of being humiliated in a courtroom, and outside of one inclined to be poor, luckless, sometimes foolish, and sometimes wise.

In his closing statement the following Monday, Fiander charged that David Sohappy indeed did not want to change: "He wants his tribe to change. He wants to be more sovereign than the Yakima Nation. Go through these checks and decide if this was a business or a religion. How many fish are enough? It's like *Jaws*."

Tom Keefe spoke for almost an hour. He said this case was about the old Indian law versus the new *suyapo* law; it was about greed, hypocrisy, and perfidy at the highest levels of American business and government versus tradition and faith. Keefe didn't so much make an argument as tell a tale into which was enfolded a prophecy. He read a story from David's great-uncle Smohalla:

> Once the world was all water and God lived alone. He was lonesome, but he had no place to put his foot, so he scratched up sand from the bottom and he made land. And he made rocks and made trees and he made a man. And the man had wings and he could go anywhere. The man was lonesome and God made a woman. They ate fish from the water, and God made the deer and other animals, and he sent the man to hunt, and told the woman to cook the meat and dress the skins.
>
> More men and women grew up, and they lived on the banks of a great river whose water was full of salmon. The mountains contained much game and there were buffalo on the plains. There were so many people that the stronger ones sometimes oppressed the weak, and drove them from the best fisheries, which they claimed as their own. They fought and nearly all were killed, and their bones are to be seen in the hills yet.
>
> God was very angry at this and he took away their wings, and he commanded that the land and the fishery were to be held in common by those who lived upon them, that they were

never to be marked off or divided, but that the people should enjoy the fruit that God had planted in the land. God said he was the father, and the earth was the mother of mankind; that nature is the law, that the animals and the plants and the fish obeyed nature, and that man only was sinful.

This is the old law.

After eight hours of deliberation, the jury found the defendants innocent of all charges on the grounds that they had been entrapped by the government. There was no jubilation. David Sohappy, Sr., shuffled back to his cell in the tribal jail, saying only, "I'm tired." The U.S. attorney in Yakima told reporters that the government wanted its prisoners back. Tom Keefe said the prisoners shouldn't be returned: their original conviction had been invalid and the sentences barbaric. Even Jack Fiander—whose thankless job had made him the object of epithets such as "pig" and, worse, "Slade Gorton" from his fellow Yakima—admitted that had Judge Tanner's sentences not been so harsh, the entire divisive spectacle he had just participated in might have been unnecessary.

On April 30, 1987, the day after the verdict, the Yakima tribal council began two days of closed meetings to decide what to do. There was arguing and shouting, but the final vote was unanimous: the council would seek a pardon for all five defendants. It drafted a letter to President Reagan on May 1.

The United States Department of Justice did nothing for two weeks and then formally asked for the defendants' return to federal custody. The Yakima Nation refused and asked for a "face to face, government to government" meeting with the Justice Department.

The Justice Department didn't reply. Instead, phone calls were placed from the Interior Department to tribal officials saying that unless the Yakima complied with the Justice Department's request, government funding to the tribe would be cut off. On May 28, the council agreed to turn over the defendants, subject to certain conditions: the time served in the Yakima jail would count toward the defendants' federal sentences; the defendants would be jailed in Washington State; the federal government would acknowledge that the Yakima Nation did have jurisdiction in the case; and a White House liaison would be appointed to deal with the tribe in the future.

On June 4, the defendants were handed over to federal marshals, once again without Tom Keefe being notified. Matthew McConville's sentence was already complete and he was paroled. The Sohappys were taken to a low-security federal facility called Geiger Camp near Spokane. Leroy Yocash and Wilbur Slockish were loaded and unloaded from buses and vans; shackled and searched and shackled again; and driven around the country in the night and dawn hours until they were back in Sandstone prison. The conditions the Yakima had attached to the defendants' release to the Justice Department were not honored.

On August 25, David Sohappy, Sr., felt a numbness in his left arm and hand. Over the next two days the sensation spread until he couldn't move his left side. His lips felt heavy and he couldn't speak easily. Three days later his jailers took him to a hospital in Spokane. He'd had a stroke, and he also had diabetes, a common affliction among Native Americans deprived of their traditional diets.

The hospital kept him until the end of the month, and released him with the recommendation that "this patient be sent home to be with his family and with his congregation of the Feather Religion. There is therapy with this religion that he believes will help him and certainly not contraindicated medically." Prison officials ignored this advice, and when Tom Keefe applied for a medical furlough on David's behalf, it, too, was refused. Their only concession was to allow David Sohappy, Jr., to share a cell with his father and look after him.

Despairing of reaching any accommodation with the Department of Justice, the Yakima Nation and Tom Keefe turned to Senators Dan Evans and Daniel Inouye, who in turn contacted former senator and White House chief of staff Howard Baker. Baker wrote them back two months later to assure them he would look into the matter. Nothing happened. Winter came in Spokane, and David shuffled through the snow on his son's arm. His eyes looked distracted and childlike, as though amused by things other people couldn't see, and his talk rambled and circled itself. He was an old man now, though he was scarcely sixty-three years of age.

Keefe, the Yakima council, and Senators Evans and Inouye were convinced that pardon or parole was imminent: the injustice of the defendants' situation was clear to anyone, and even a conservative Republican administration would want to avoid being associated with the incarceration of a sick old Indian over some out-of-season fish. On December 9, however, the Justice Department announced that, far from releasing them, it planned to move the Sohappys to the high-security penitentiary at Terminal Island, California.

Tom Keefe managed to get an injunction in federal court in Spokane while Inouye and Evans again wrote to Howard Baker. A few days later federal judge McNichols in Spokane decided he could not stop the transfer, although he could delay it pending a neurological examination that David Sohappy, Sr., was scheduled to receive. That same week, a federal judge in Portland upheld the eviction notices posted at Cook's Landing: if David were allowed to go home, it was increasingly unlikely it would be to Cook's.

On December 18, Senators Evans and Inouye were at last granted a meeting with Howard Baker and the attorney general, Edwin Meese, at the White House. Afterwards, Inouye told Yakima chairman Mel Sampson, "This is not for public attribution, but I can tell you that the Yakima fishermen are going to have a very merry Christmas." Six days later, on Christmas Eve, an attorney for the Yakima Nation called Tom Keefe. He had received the details of the government's clemency offer from a Justice Department lawyer named Donald Carr. Keefe knew Carr's reputation: he had argued on the government's behalf in 1981 when the Yakima tribe sued the Commerce Department for its fair share of the salmon fishery. Keefe believed that salmonscam had always been in part a retaliation against the river Indians for that suit.

Carr's conditions were as follows: only David Sohappy, Sr., would be released—David Sohappy, Jr., Leroy Yocash, and Wilbur Slockish would remain in prison; the leaders of the Yakima Nation must swear an affidavit undertaking to enforce all government fishing regulations; and David Sohappy, Sr., would have to sign a statement of contrition. "You can tell Carr to shove it!" Keefe howled into the phone. When he had calmed down, Keefe said he'd call David in Spokane and tell him what the government had offered.

When Keefe reached David, he told him it was bad news. You had to speak slowly to David these days. Keefe said, "They'll let you out, but they want an affidavit from you indicating contrition." David asked, "What's that?" Keefe told him, "That means you have to say you're sorry for what you did."

Keefe's words sank into David's befuddlement and took a while to settle. Then, in the voice he used to have, David said, "No way."

By Christmas 1987, Leroy Yocash and Wilbur Slockish had been back in Sandstone for four months. Slockish was inmate number 12858-086, and every ninety days he'd have an evaluation interview with a counselor. Every ninety days they'd ask him what he planned to do when he got out of prison and every ninety days he'd tell them, "Go fishing." They told him that his file said he was an alcoholic, and he could do himself some good—maybe help with his parole even—if he'd go to AA meetings. Slockish said he didn't want to go to AA meetings, but he'd sure like to set up some Washat ceremonies with the other Indians in Sandstone. That wasn't allowed, they told him.

They offered Slockish a job making work gloves in the prison factory, but he said he didn't want it. They asked him if it wouldn't be wise for him to learn to work a forty-hour week like normal people, so when he got out he wouldn't return to his "criminal activities." He told them that if he had to, he'd work eighty hours a week to avoid working a forty-hour week. They didn't understand that. He did tell them he had changed his mind about the AA meetings, provided they could be Indian only. Pleased to have made a dent in Slockish's incorrigible demeanor, the prison officials told him that would be fine. At the meetings, once the door was closed, he and the other Indians did Washat.

To the people who ran the prison, Slockish wasn't so much rebellious as opaque. They couldn't read him or his intentions, not that he had any intentions other than to go fishing. But he'd been a fugitive from federal justice, so he was kept under constant surveillance. At night the guard's flashlight beam would sweep through his cell at random hours, feathering his face and arcing across the wall and the ceiling like the headlight of a locomotive.

At the beginning of 1988, the Bureau of Prisons decided it would not move the Sohappys to Terminal Island Penitentiary after all. Then, on February 22, Senators Evans and Inouye announced they had been successful in persuading the Justice Department to present a motion to Judge Tanner asking that the Sohappys' sentences be reduced to the amount of time they had already served:

> We are very pleased to learn that the Department of Justice has agreed to seek the release of David Sohappy Sr. and his son. The sentences these men received were grossly disproportionate to the crimes of which they were convicted. The events which gave rise to the present situation are merely the symptoms of a much bigger problem. David Sohappy and his son are not the reasons for conflict on the Columbia River. Instead

the problems are a lack of river access for Indians and non-Indians alike and the confused jurisdiction over the activities of Indian fishermen.

Evans's staff had also prepared a speech for the senator to read on the Senate floor on March 4, the day after the motion was to be filed:

Mr. President, inscribed on the marble facade of the west front of the United States Supreme Court building are the words "Equal Justice Under Law." No phrase better embodies the promise of America. Yet for two Indian fishermen who are members of the Yakima Tribe of Washington state, that promise has rung hollow—at least until today.

But neither Evans nor his staff had reckoned on Jack Tanner. The afternoon of March 3—after Evans's office in Washington, D.C., had already closed—Tanner denied the motion without explanation. It had been taken to his court in Tacoma by assistant U.S. attorney Stephen Schroeder. Schroeder neither queried Tanner about his action nor felt any urgency to notify his superiors in the east: "It wasn't my motion. I was the delivery boy who carried the document for an associate deputy attorney in Washington, D.C."

Evans learned of Tanner's action at noon the next day. "I am shocked and saddened by Judge Tanner's intransigence," he said. "The sentences he gave these men were extremely harsh given the circumstances. I cannot and do not understand Judge Tanner's rationale for their continued suffering." Senator Inouye was livid: "I could sell heroin to a child and I would get less than three years." He vowed to haul Judge Tanner before the Senate Judiciary Committee to explain himself. Inouye then flew to Spokane and spoke to David Sohappy, Sr., in his cell, before continuing on to Olympia, where he castigated Tanner in a speech to the Washington State Legislature.

Evans and Inouye again considered appealing to the White

House to circumvent Tanner. But by now it was clear that President Reagan was unwilling to commute the sentences of renegade Indians whose persecution had been set in motion by his own administration. Another stratagem was found: the United States Parole Board determined that it could move the Sohappys' parole dates forward to the middle of May, now only two months off.

In the interim, Evans and Inouye held hearings on Indian fishing rights on the Columbia River. David Sohappy, Sr., sent them testimony in a forthright letter:

> My old grandfather Smohalla said, "It is a bad word that comes from Washington. It is a bad law, and my people cannot obey it. I want my people to stay with me. All the dead men will come to life again. We must wait here in the homes of our fathers and be ready to meet them in the bosom of the mother." This Lacey Act was a bad law for Indians on the Columbia River. . . .

On May 17, 1988, at 6:00 A.M., David shuffled out of the Spokane prison's gate. Myra held his arm. There were TV cameras and a crowd of supporters, but he couldn't think of any words in English. The wind whipped at the reporters' microphones and jangled the chain-link fence. He tried to speak in the language of the Wanapum, but all he could seem to say was "Nch'i-Wana"— "Great River"—"Wanapum"—"river people." That was all he could say—the name of all that he was and had ever wanted to be—and then his tears crested his eyes and flooded down his cheeks and he cried like a lost child.

They let David Sohappy, Jr., out the day after his father, and two weeks later the prison authorities told Wilbur Slockish and Leroy Yocash that they were being transferred to Spokane. The prison chaplain arranged a party for them, and they and the other Indians at Sandstone who had substituted the Seven Drums for the Twelve Steps got to watch a video called *Mystic Warrior*, a sort of Native American martial arts film—"Sioux Kung Fu," somebody said. Then Slockish and Yocash each got a cardboard box for their belongings, and they were flown to Spokane.

They let Leroy Yocash out of prison on October 3, 1988, and then Slockish was the last of the salmonscam defendants doing time. Judge Tanner would have wanted it that way: Slockish had a mouth on him, and his eyes, the way he carried his body like a sleepy bear, seemed to mock authority and the law. They finally let him out on December 17 with the understanding that for the next six months he would not leave his house except to work. He'd spent nearly two years in prison and seven months as a fugitive for catching and selling sixty-three fish.

He left Geiger at dawn and waited around the Spokane depot until he could get a bus for Biggs Junction, the closest stop to Celilo. It was 7:30 at night when he stepped down onto the pavement outside the restaurant in Biggs. It was cold, as though snow were coming, and the river lay off before him in the dark. The restaurant windows glowed yellow, and he went inside where his family was waiting. They sat him down, and he realized he hadn't eaten all day. He wanted some salmon.

When David Sohappy, Sr., came home to Cook's Landing, he was restless and distracted. He walked up and down the riverbank, and on the other side the wall of the gorge rose up, but it was as though he were looking through it; as though he were gazing out on the sea. His sons fished and got arrested for it sometimes. Andy Sohappy and his cousins Jeff and Tim went out of their way to get cited, and sometimes they'd have to ask the wardens to oblige them with a ticket. The states had lost their stomach for the fight, but the Sohappys hadn't. Myra was cited by the Yakima game warden for out-of-season fishing. She sat in the courtroom—behind her sunglasses, under the florid brim of her hat—

rigid with anger. The prosecutor asked her if she would promise to return for her trial. "This is my home. This is where I have lived and will live forever," she said coldly, and then she left. To no one in particular, she fumed, "Our troubles started with Columbus."

Meanwhile, the Sohappys fought to keep their home. In August 1990, the Ninth Circuit Court of Appeals reversed the federal district court in Portland's decision to uphold the Department of the Interior's eviction order. But the government was not going to give up. "I'm sure our original decision to evict has not changed," an official said.

David hobbled around that autumn using a golf putter as a cane, and sat inside the shack watching soap operas on television. Then he'd get up and walk around outside some more. Trains thundered down the track just behind the house, and Myra worried he'd get hit. His mind wasn't on the same path as his feet. A reporter came to see him, and David's voice seeped out rusty and slow, like water from under a stone: "The creator is angry now. Something could happen. A quake, maybe. A flood. Something bad." Then he'd look out to Nch'i-Wana: "If I prayed enough, I could stop this river and walk across. But I do not pray so much now. I have slipped."

5.

At night sometimes, Wilbur Slockish would think they were shining the flashlight into his cell at Sandstone, and he'd sit up out of a sound sleep. His wife, Suzy, would try to talk to him, but his mind was hard to reach. His youngest children didn't know who he was. When they'd called him "Inmate" at Sandstone, he'd joked back, "I'm not an inmate—I'm a hostage," but the truth was that they'd done a pretty good job of making him believe he was a criminal. When he'd go into a store, he'd get the feeling everyone was watching, whispering about him, or trying to catch him stealing. He'd wanted to come home all this time, but sometimes he felt home didn't want him.

So he fished. One day he was netting salmon from a platform on the river near the Cascades. Since he'd been away, there were more and more tourist boats on the rivers and windsurfers skidded down the gorge, like grasshoppers clutching kites. A tour went by, and Slockish heard the guide pointing him out to the passengers over the loudspeaker: "These Indians don't work. They sit there all day and make five dollars an hour catching your fish."

To Slockish, it seemed as easy to get branded a dirty, lazy Indian in 1990 as it had been when his father had come home from fighting the war in 1945. And there was a new edge to it: As long as the whites had been able to extract money from the land, particularly from the forests on the riverbanks, they were content to let the Indians have the fish. But now the fish were leaving, most of the old forests had been cut down, and Skamania County, where Slockish was fishing that day, was the poorest place in Washington. Being seen to pass the day in idleness and to get something for nothing in the bargain could provoke hostility on this part of the river. Stevenson, the county seat just up the road from Cook's Landing, was losing the last of its mills and the white loggers and mill workers felt besieged; haunted and hunted by bad luck, failure, and misapprehension as though by a pack of dogs. And then something happened in the forest.

In the new year, on January 26, 1991, a fifteen-year-old girl named Amy Dexter went to have her picture taken in Stevenson. She was a smiling, pretty girl with kind, fearful eyes. She brushed her long hair and put on an off-the-shoulder dress with little dots. She wore a ring on the third finger of her left hand as though she were married and she was lovely as a bride.

She was going to be sixteen soon, and she thought she'd get a driver's license and try out for cheerleading. She loved people, but she liked to be alone, too. She found a bag of kittens someone had thrown in the river and managed to save one of them and nurse it back to health. She liked to go up into the forest. She wanted to get a wolf puppy.

That evening she met a boy named Christopher Bradley. She knew him from Stevenson High. He'd been a senior last year, but now he worked in a timber mill, like nearly everyone else in his family; like nearly everybody else in Stevenson. Christopher had a pickup truck with four-wheel drive. He'd been hunting cougars in the mountains the day before. He asked Amy if she'd like to go up on the logging roads and into the woods with him. She said yes. It was Saturday night. Maybe she thought it would be fun. Maybe she had nothing to do. Maybe she kind of liked him. Maybe she had no reason at all for what she did. She was a child, and they were as children.

When they got into the forest, he wanted to touch her and then he wanted to touch her more—to be with her the way people in love were with one another. She didn't want him to, but he didn't care. He was a hunter and he had a knife in his hand. He pulled the clothes off her lower body like he was skinning a squirrel. While he was raping her, she didn't say anything and then when he was done she told him she was going to tell. He drove the knife into her neck and she gave a little sigh like a shift of wind in the trees.

Christopher buried Amy in the forest. It was winter and dark and the ground was hard and he couldn't dig very deep. He laid her on her right side like she was sleeping and covered her with dirt, leaves, and cones. Then he went home. In the morning people started looking for Amy. They couldn't find her. The police talked to Christopher. He told them his truck had broken down while they'd been driving around on the logging roads and Amy said she had to get home by curfew, so he gave her a flashlight and she walked off into the dark and that was the last time he saw her.

Everyone in Stevenson was afraid and alarmed. Nobody could find Amy and no one had ever disappeared in Stevenson before. On Wednesday it rained in the forest, and on Thursday a logger saw a patch of something white exposed in the duff. Amy had very white skin and it was her. The police talked to Christopher again, and this time he told them what really happened. Christopher couldn't explain why he'd done it. Neither could anyone else. People said he was a nice, easygoing sort of guy. And Amy was a sweet, generous girl.

The town cried for Amy and built a monument to her in the town park on the riverbank. And they puzzled over Christopher. The police kept pressing him to tell them more about everything he and Amy had done in the forest. In his own mind Christopher was trying to understand what had happened to him that night— what had gotten into him in the woods—and it made him think of hunting:

> It was a sudden impulse that came up out of the blue.
>
> *After* I shoot a deer, I just get bored. I think it's got something to do with the thrill. It's just the thrill of the hunt. After I pull the trigger it's gone. It's one of the biggest thrills I know, to go out and just stalk something and get right up to it.

The police asked Christopher if he felt that way with Amy, and he thought about it. He said, "Yeah, I almost did."

The afternoon they found Amy Dexter's body, David Sohappy had another stroke. It was the third since he'd come home, and Myra took him to the hospital. He couldn't move or talk, and the doctors told Myra he should have full-time medical care. He was moved to a nursing home in Hood River, halfway between Cook's Landing and Celilo. He never spoke again.

David mostly lay in his bed and dozed through the winter. At the end of March, the salmon started to come and David's nephew Jeff was ready to be arrested again. He built a platform at Willamette Falls where Dr. McLoughlin retired when the Hudson's Bay Company abandoned the river in 1846. Jeff dipnetted five times and got five warnings from the fish warden. Then they stopped him before he could catch anything. "He shouldn't have stopped me," Jeff said. "I was trying to put evidence on the table."

During the spring run, Jeff kept putting nets out up and down the river, but the authorities wouldn't give him any tickets. On May 5, he set his net out below Bonneville Dam, but no matter what he did no fish would come. It was Sunday. The next evening, David died at 10:55.

Myra wrapped him in blankets and laid him on a mat of tule reeds facing west, down the river. One hundred and fifty people came to the longhouse and they brought salmon, elk, roots, and berries. Tom Keefe read a letter from Senator Inouye and wept. Then the people who loved David Sohappy danced and sang songs around his body for hours.

Two mornings later, at 5:00 A.M., they buried him among his fathers and his sons near the place he was born. They sang and emptied handfuls of earth into the grave. The sun came up and colored the world a piece at a time, like water rising. The wind swelled and gusted west, and later the rain came.

There is a graveyard on the Klikitat River above the place where long ago a girl learned to weave baskets that could carry water without losing a drop. Among the headstones there are dolls, plates, cups, and garlands of foil. Each plot is set up like a place at the table for an honored guest. There are yellow and purple plastic flowers, and pinwheels stuck in the ground at the heads of the graves. The pinwheels spin in the wind, and it seems as though they are ticking off the running down of this world like clocks for the dead.

But perhaps they turn in some other course, like the propellers of ships, for what can save the world but persistence, the unceasing ebb and flood of winds and the descent of water? What else can set the world right, when death ensures that no one endures in it for long, and that for the living, loss is as daily as bread? Nor is death content to fill its stomach on the old; it stalks the young like a hunter. It seeks children in the woods and the river, where they are compelled to go. In the woods, children seek visions, love, and names; in the river, they try to master water, the stuff from which God made the world, and which was therefore before the world and to which the world must return.

The children put their feet in the river, run their hands through the water, trying to seize it before it seizes them, as though they could plunge their arms in and retrieve a fish formed of water, as clear and slippery as the river and solid as crystal. For children, the woods and the river are perilous. They go to them to assay dreams from the heart of the world, but sometimes they fetch back nightmares from the woods and drownings from the river. And sometimes there are travelers on the river, and sometimes people mistake them for children when they are something else, as did Slockish's great-grandfather's forbears when they sang and danced for "the children of the stars."

It is April 1992. The Klikitat children pass back and forth through the graveyard, the forest on one side, the river on the other. They slip into the woods like smoke; they race to the river's edge as though to a precipice. Next to the longhouse, the women prepare salmon and berries, bloodying their hands a venous blue. The elders begin to drum. In the distance, the Klikitat rumbles down toward Nch'i-Wana where the salmon are waiting until it is time for them to ascend. The current pushes west downriver, the fish orient themselves upstream, eastward against it, beating their tails just enough to remain suspended in the same spot above the river bottom that itself is being scoured deeper as the salmon wait. With enough water and time, the river might cut its gorge clean through the earth and split it in two, just as affliction—God's leaving, love's going—must rend every human heart.

The past year has been a bitter one. The people of Stevenson were visited by more violence, and in the autumn fires incinerated the forests, and the trees stood black and shorn, like charred bones.

At Cook's Landing, the Sohappys had finally won the right to keep their homes, if only during their immediate lifetimes. But a few weeks after David's death, his two-year-old grandson Gabriel Sohappy clambered onto the train tracks and was struck by a locomotive. He died a few hours later and was buried next to his grandfather.

Up the river a few miles, the home of the Klikitat subchief, Johnny Jackson, burned to the ground on July 25. Johnny thought it was arson and the authorities thought he might be right.

A month later, on August 24, a Klikitat named Gerald Tulee, whose forebear Sampson Tulee brought the suit *Tulee v. Washington* to the United States Supreme Court in 1939, was fishing in the river off Stevenson. Around noon he was pulling in his nets and the wind drove the water into larger and larger waves. He'd hauled in four of his five nets, and he was getting ready for his fifth when the boat was swamped. It took the police divers five hours to find the boat. It was forty feet under the water and Gerald Tulee was with it, swaddled in a net. He was seventeen.

It was ten years ago to the day in 1982 that Wilbur Slockish reinstituted the salmon ceremony in this place. That was also the time he caught the fish that made him a captive. But today has other purposes. The families that have endured death and hardship in the last year need to be honored and succored, their grief attended and named as much as the salmon. And other things must be thanked and remembered.

It is the day Wilbur will take his Indian name. His father will give it to him. The name is Sla-Kish, the name of his great-great-grandfather, the chief of the Klikitat in 1855, and the last to sign the treaty of Isaac Stevens, who brought the wars and the trains that run through the night. Wilbur's father radiates his pleasure as his son stands in the longhouse. He beams at Wilbur and says

"Praise the Lord" and "Say hello to old man Sla-Kish." The drums pound, deep and regular, like the beats of a heart enraptured with its own vitality. They go on and on, a kind of waiting and watching that never ends.

Wilbur's sons William and Lawren come and stand next to him. He didn't want them to wait until they were men for their names as he did. They will be called Schlauxun and Twinashut. Wilbur and his sons are robed in blankets and then more blankets are draped over their shoulders and arms: Pendleton blankets in purple and red, in the colors of Chief Joseph; white blankets with the red, green, and yellow stripes of the Hudson's Bay Company. Now Wilbur and his sons have their names and there must be a giveaway. Everyone, man, woman, and child, is called and receives something from the goods that are spread over the floor of the longhouse: stacks of blankets, heaps of crockery, pots, pans, cutlery, clothing, tools, and toys. These are the things people need to make a home in the world, and Wilbur stands among them. He is like an island in the river, and everything here flows around him. The words in the songs are like fish, and they beat their way home.

Then the Klikitat honor the salmon and the other foods, ringing a bell to call attention to each one, saying their names, thanking them. They have set a table for themselves, the living, at which their sorrows and their dead are made welcome and remembered together with the foods that sustain them. Without the remembering, the Klikitat's lives would be formless as water, so the first thing they say is the water's name, "*choos.*" And the water binds them to God as the river binds water to earth—water running west, bound with orange and yellow light.

Acknowledgments

I want to thank both Schuyler Ingle and Jessica Maxwell for independently suggesting on the same day that I write this book. I am grateful, as ever, to Sallie Gouverneur, agent, friend, and counselor, who found a home for it at HarperCollins West. Once there, my editor Joann Moschella, her assistant Beth Weber, and production editor Lisa Zuniga Carlsen capably steered it into print.

This book is also the beneficiary of materials and memories culled from individuals, libraries, and institutions. While any errors and foolishness contained in it are my own doing, I was utterly dependent on their kindness and cooperation and wish to express my thanks to them: Ralph Bennett, R. Cole Harris, Tom Hillier, Tom Keefe, Robert Mull, Bill Murlin, Robert Ruby, Steve Sanger, Wilbur Slockish, David Sohappy, Jr., Myra Sohappy, and Jim Strassmeier. I also want to thank the staffs of the Bonneville Power Administration, the Seattle office of the National Archives, the Multnomah County Library, the Oregon Historical Society, the Seattle Public Library, the University of British Columbia Library, the University of Washington Library, the Washington State University Library, and the Yakima Valley Regional Library.

Finally, my gratitude and love to three assiduous friends and readers, Peter Juvonen, Jeff Smith, and Lilly Tuholske; to my daughter Tessa Clark, whose curiosity, humor, and spirit are an inspiration to me; and to Caroline Johnson, who was with me every day and whose presence is in every page.

Sources

CHAPTER 1
OUT OF THE FLOOD

Allen, John E., and Marjorie Burns. *Cataclysms on the Columbia.*
Portland, OR: Timber Press, 1986.

Allen, John Logan. *Passage Through the Garden: Lewis and Clark
and the Image of the American Northwest.* Urbana: Univ. of Illinois Press, 1975.

Ames, Kenneth M., and Alan G. Marshall. "Villages, Demography and Subsistence Intensification on the South Columbia
Plateau." *North American Archeologist.* 2:25–52 (1980–81).

Beavert, Virginia. *The Way It Was: Anaku Iwacha—Yakima Indian
Legends.* Yakima, WA: Franklin, 1974.

Borden, Charles E. "Peopling and Early Cultures of the Pacific
Northwest." *Science* 203:963–70 (1979).

Bunnell, Clarence. *Legends of the Klikitats.* Portland, OR: Binfords
and Mort, 1933.

Chance, David H. *People of the Falls.* Colville, WA: Kettle Falls
Historical Center, 1986.

Childerhose, R. J., and Marjorie Trim. *Pacific Salmon and Steelhead
Trout.* Seattle: Univ. of Washington Press, 1979.

Condon, Thomas. *The Two Islands and What Came of Them.* Portland, OR, 1902.

Cressman, Luther. *Prehistory of the Far West: Homes of Vanished
Peoples.* Salt Lake City: Univ. of Utah Press, 1977.

Cressman, Luther, et al. "Cultural Sequences at The Dalles, Oregon." *American Philosophical Society Transactions* 50:10 (1960).

Curtis, Edward. *The North American Indian,* vols. 7 and 8. Reprint. New York: Johnson, 1970.

French, Peter J. *John Dee: The World of an Elizabethan Magus.* London: Routledge and Kegan Paul, 1972.

Goetzmann, William. *New Lands, New Men.* New York: Viking, 1986.

Goetzmann, William, and Glyndir Williams. *The Atlas of North American Exploration.* London: Swanston, 1992.

Greenblatt, Stephen. *Marvelous Possessions: The Wonder of the New World.* Chicago: Univ. of Chicago Press, 1991.

Gunther, Erna. "An Analysis of the First Salmon Ceremony." *American Anthropologist* 28:605–17 (1926).

Gunther, Erna. "A Further Analysis of the First Salmon Ceremony." *University of Washington Publications in Anthropology* 2:129–73 (1928).

Hakluyt, Richard. *Hakluyt's Voyages.* Edited by Irwin Blacker. New York: Viking, 1965.

Hezeta, Bruno de. *For Honor and Country.* Translated by Herbert K. Beals. Portland: Oregon Historical Society, 1985.

Hines, Donald. *Ghost Voices: Yakima Indian Myths, Legends, Humor, and Hunting Stories.* Issaquah, WA: Great Eagle, 1992.

Holbrook, Stewart. *The Columbia.* New York: Holt, 1956.

Howay, Frederic W., ed. *Voyages of the "Columbia" to the Northwest Coast: 1787-1790 and 1790-1793.* Portland: Oregon Historical Society, 1990.

Huhn, Eugene S. *Nch'i-Wana: Mid-Columbia Indians and Their Land.* Seattle: Univ. of Washington Press, 1990.

Jacobs, Melville. "Religion, Mythology, Northwest Sahaptian Text." *Columbia University Contributions to Anthropology,* vol. 19, pts. 1–2 (1934).

Jay, Tom. "The Salmon of the Heart." In *Working the Woods, Working the Sea,* edited by F. Wilcox and J. Gorsline. Port Townsend, WA: Empty Bowl, 1986.

Keyser, James. *Indian Rock Art of the Columbia Plateau.* Seattle: Univ. of Washington Press, 1992.

Kirk, Ruth, and Richard Daughtery. *Exploring Washington Archeology.* Seattle: Univ. of Washington Press, 1978.

Kuneki, Nettie, Elsie Thomas, and Marie Slockish. *The Heritage of Klickitat Basketry.* Portland: Oregon Historical Society, 1982.

Marshall, J. S., and C. Marshall. *Vancouver's Voyage.* Vancouver, BC: Mitchell, 1955.

McDonald, E. V., and A. J. Busacca. "Late Quaternary Stratigraphy of Loess in Channeled Scabland and Palouse Regions of Washington State." *Quaternary Research* 38:141–56 (1992).

Meinig, D. W. *The Great Columbia Plain.* Seattle: Univ. of Washington Press, 1968.

Meinig, D. W. *The Shaping of America.* Vol. 1, *Atlantic America, 1492–1800.* New Haven: Yale Univ. Press, 1986.

Miller, Christopher. *Prophetic Worlds: Indians and Whites on the Columbia Plateau.* New Brunswick, NJ: Rutgers Univ. Press, 1985.

Morrison, Samuel Elliot. *The European Discovery of America: The Northern Voyages.* New York: Oxford Univ. Press, 1971.

Moulton, Gary E., ed. *The Journals of the Lewis and Clark Expedition, Volumes 5, 6, and 7.* Lincoln: Univ. of Nebraska Press, 1988–91.

Polk, Dora. *The Island of California: A History of a Myth.* Spokane, WA: Arthur Clark, 1991.

Purchas, Samuel. *Hakluytus posthumus, or Purchas his Pilgrimes: contayning a history of the world in sea voyages and lande travells by Englishmen and others.* Glasgow: J. MacLehose and Sons, 1905–7.

Ramsey, Jarold. *Coyote Was Going There: Indian Literature of the Oregon Country.* Seattle: Univ. of Washington Press, 1977.

Sapir, Edward. *Wishram Texts 2.* Washington, DC: American Ethnology Society, 1909.

Schwantes, Carlos A. *The Pacific Northwest: An Interpretive History.* Lincoln: Univ. of Nebraska Press, 1989.

Smith, Courtland. *Salmon Fisheries of the Columbia.* Corvallis: Oregon State Univ. Press, 1979.

Speck, Gordon. *Myths and New World Explorations.* Fairfield, WA: Galleon, 1979.

Strong, Emory. *Stone Age on the Columbia River.* Portland, OR: Binfords and Mort, 1959.

Turner, Frederick. *Beyond Geography: The Western Spirit Against the Wilderness.* New York: Viking, 1980.

CHAPTER 2
THE ASTRONOMER

Chance, David. "Influences of the Hudson's Bay Company on the Native Cultures of the Colville District." *Northwest Anthropological Research Notes* 7(1), pt. 2 (1973).

Church of England. *Ayumehawe mussinahikun, mena ka isse makinanewukee kunache keche issetwawina, mena ateet kotuka issetwawina ayumehawinik, ka isse aputchetanewukee akayasewe ayumehawinik: ussitche David oo Nikumoona . . . A isse mussinahuk naheyowe isse keeswawinik, akayasewe mussinahikunik oche, the Ven. Archdeacon Hunter.* [The Book of Common Prayer, together with the Psalter, etc., translated by the Venerable Archdeacon Hunter]. London: Society for Promoting Christian Knowledge, 1877.

Coues, Elliott. *New Light on the History of the Greater North West: The Manuscript Journals of Alexander Henry and of David Thompson.* 3 vols. New York, 1897.

Elliott, T. C. "Journals of David Thompson." *Oregon Historical Quarterly* 15:39-123 (1914).

Elliott, T. C. "The Discovery of the Source of the Columbia River." *Oregon Historical Quarterly* 26:23–49 (1925).

Glover, Richard. "The Witness of David Thompson." *Canadian Historical Review* 31:25–38 (1950).

Glover, Richard, ed. *David Thompson's Narrative, 1784–1812.* Toronto: Champlain Society, 1962.

Howay, F. W. "David Thompson's Account of His First Attempt to Cross the Rocky Mountains." *Queen's Quarterly* 40:333–56 (1933).

Irving, Washington. *Astoria, or Anecdotes of an Enterprise Beyond the Rocky Mountains.* London, 1939.

Mackenzie, Alexander. *Voyages from Montreal, on the River St. Lawrence, Through the Continent of North America, to the Frozen and Pacific Oceans; In the Years 1789 and 1793.* London, 1801.

Masson, Louis-François. *Les Bourgeois de la Compagnie Nord-ouest; Recits de Voyages.* Letres, Quebec, 1889–90.

Morton, A. S. "The Columbia Enterprise and David Thompson." *Canadian Historical Review* 17:266-88 (1936).

Newman, Peter C. *Company of Adventurers.* New York: Viking, 1985.

Newman, Peter C. *Caesars of the Wilderness.* New York: Viking, 1987.

Rich, E. E. *Hudson's Bay Company, 1660–1870.* London: Hudson's Bay Record Society, 1959.

Ross, Alexander. *Adventures of the First Settlers on the Oregon or Columbia River, 1810–1813.* Lincoln: Univ. of Nebraska Press, 1986.

Schaeffer, Claude E. "The Kutenai Female Berdache: Courier, Guide, Prophetess, and Warrior." *Ethnohistory* 12:193–236 (1965).

Tyrell, J. B. *Hearne and Turnor Journals.* Toronto: Champlain Society, 1934.

Tyrell, J. B. "David Thompson and the Columbia River." *Canadian Historical Review* 18:13-18 (1937).

White, Catherine, ed. *David Thompson's Journals Relating to Montana and Adjacent Regions, 1808–1812.* Missoula: Univ. of Montana Press, 1950.

CHAPTER 3
CASTAWAYS

Clark, Robert C. "Military History of Oregon, 1849–59." *Pacific Northwest Quarterly* 36:14–59 (March 1945).

Davies, John. *Douglas of the Forests: The North American Journals of David Douglas.* Seattle: Univ. of Washington Press, 1980.

Douglas, David. "Sketch of a Journey to Northwestern Parts of the Continent of North America During the Years 1824–25–26–27." *Oregon Historical Quarterly* 5:230–71, 325–69 (1904); 6:76–97, 206–27 (1905).

Franklin, Jerry F., and C. T. Dyrness. *Natural Vegetation of Oregon and Washington.* Corvallis: Oregon State Univ. Press, 1988.

Green, J. S. "Extracts from the Report of an Exploring Tour on the North-West Coast of North America in 1829." *Missionary Herald* 27:33–39, 75–77, 105–7 (1831).

Harper, Russell, ed. *Paul Kane's Frontier.* Austin: Univ. of Texas Press, 1971.

Harrison, Robert Pogue. *Forests: The Shadow of Civilization.* Chicago: Univ. of Chicago Press, 1992.

Harvey, A. G. *Douglas of the Fir.* Cambridge, MA: Harvard Univ. Press, 1947.

Hulbert, A. B. *Where Rolls the Oregon: Prophet and Pessimist Look Northwest, 1825–30.* Colorado Springs and Denver, 1933.

Hulbert, A. B. *The Call of the Columbia: Iron Men and Saints Take the Oregon Trail, 1830–35.* Colorado Springs and Denver, 1934.

Irving, Washington. *The Adventures of Captain Bonneville.* New York, 1843.

Jeffrey, Julie Roy. *Converting the West: A Biography of Narcissa Whitman.* Norman: Univ. of Oklahoma Press, 1991.

Jesset, Thomas, ed. *Reports and Letters of Herbert Beaver, 1836–1838.* Portland, OR: Champoeg Press, 1959.

Kane, Paul. *Wanderings of an Artist Among the Indians of North America.* Toronto: Radisson Society, 1925.

Kane, Paul. *Sketch Pad.* Toronto: Royal Ontario Museum, 1969.

Lavender, David, ed. *The Oregon Journals of David Douglas.* Ashland: Oregon Book Society, 1972.

Parker, Samuel. *An Exploring Tour Beyond the Rocky Mountains.* Dublin, 1840.

Powell, Fred Wilbur. "Hall Jackson Kelley." *Oregon Historical Quarterly* 18:177-189 (March–December 1917).

Powell, Fred Wilbur. *Hall J. Kelley on Oregon.* Princeton, NJ: Princeton University Press, 1932.

Taylor, H. C., and L. L. Hoaglin. "The Intermittent Fever Epidemic of the 1830s on the Lower Columbia River." *Ethnohistory* 9:160–78 (1978).

Whitman, Narcissa. *My Journal, 1836.* Edited by Lawrence L. Dodd. Fairfield, WA: Galleon, 1982.

Whitman, Narcissa. *The Letters of Narcissa Whitman.* Fairfield, WA: Galleon, 1986.

Young, F. G., ed. *Sources of the History of Oregon.* Vol. 1, *The Correspondence and Journals of Captain Nathaniel J. Wyeth, 1831-6.* Eugene: Univ. of Oregon Press, 1899.

CHAPTER 4
PRIESTS

Bureau of Indian Affairs. *Report on Indians Taxed and Not Taxed in the United States at the Eleventh Census.* Washington, DC, 1894.

Chief Joseph. "An Indian's Views of Indian Affairs." *North American Review,* April 1879.

Doty, James. *A True Copy of the Record of the Official Proceedings at the Council in the Walla Walla Valley, Held Jointly by Isaac I. Stevens and Joel Palmer on the Part of the United States with the Tribes of Indians Named in the Treaties Made at That Council, June 9 and 11, 1855.* Microfilm, Oregon Historical Society, Portland.

Garth, Thomas R. "Wailatpu After the Massacre." *Pacific Northwest Quarterly* 38:315–18 (1947).

Gogol, J. M. "Columbia River Indian Basketry." *American Indian Basketry* 1:4–9 (1979).

Grassi, Reverend Urban. "Indian Memoirs." *Woodstock Letters* 3 (1874); 7 (1878).

Gwydir, Richard. "A Record of the San Poil Indians." *Washington Historical Quarterly* 8 (October 1917).

Haskell, Daniel C., ed. *On Reconnaissance for the Great Northern: Letters of C. F. B. Haskell, 1889–91*. New York, 1948.

Huggins, E. L. "Smohalla, the Prophet of Priest Rapids." *Overland Monthly*, 2d ser., 17:208–15 (1891).

Josephy, Alvin M., Jr. *The Nez Perce Indians and the Opening of the Northwest*. New Haven: Yale Univ. Press, 1965.

Kemble, E. C. Notes of a Council Held with Dreamer Indians, at Wallula, Washington Territory, September 22, 1873. National Archives, Washington, DC.

Lavender, David. *Let Me Be Free: The Nez Perce Tragedy*. New York: HarperCollins, 1992.

MacMurray, J. W. "The Dreamers of the Columbia Valley in Washington Territory." *Transactions of the Albany Institute* 11:240–48 (1887).

Meacham, A. B. *Wigwam and Warpath; or The Royal Chief in Chains*. Boston, 1875.

Milroy, Robert Huston. MS. 2520. Milroy Papers. Oregon Historical Society, Portland.

Mooney, James. "The Ghost Dance Religion." *Annual Report of the Bureau of American Ethnology* 14:641-1110 (1896).

O'Donnell, Terrence. *An Arrow in the Earth: General Joel Palmer and the Indians of Oregon*. Portland: Oregon Historical Society, 1991.

Oregon Superintendency of Indian Affairs. Letters Received 1848–72. National Archives, Washington, DC.

Ray, Verne F. "The Kolaskin Cult: A Prophet Movement of 1870 in Northeastern Washington." *American Anthropologist*, n.s., 38 (1936).

Ray, Verne F. "Native Villages and Groupings of the Columbia Basin." *Pacific Northwest Quarterly* 27:99–152 (1936).

Relander, Click. Interview with George Sohappy, February 14, 1952. Relander Papers. Yakima Valley Regional Library, Yakima, WA.

Relander, Click. *Drummers and Dreamers.* Caldwell, ID: Caxton, 1956.

Rockwell, Cleveland. "The Columbia River." *Harpers Monthly* 66:3–14 (1882).

Ross, John Alan. "Political Conflict on the Colville Reservation." *Northwest Anthropological Notes* 2:29–91 (1968).

Ruby, Robert, and John A. Brown. *Half Sun on the Columbia: A Biography of Chief Moses.* Norman: Univ. of Oklahoma Press, 1965.

Schuster, Helen. *The Yakima: A Critical Bibliography.* Bloomington: Indiana Univ. Press, 1982.

Spier, Leslie. *The Prophet Dance of the Northwest and Its Derivation.* General Series in Anthropology 1, Menasha, WI (1935).

Splawn, Andrew Jackson. *Ka-Mi-Akin: Last Hero of the Yakimas.* Portland, OR: Binfords and Mort, 1917.

Supreme Court of the State of Washington. "In re estate of John Enos, deceased. Susan Enos, appellant, v. Lawrence R. Hamilton." *Washington Reports* 79: Cases Determined in the Supreme Court of Washington, March 27, 1914-June 1, 1914.

Symons, Lt. Thomas W. *Report of an Examination of the Columbia River.* Washington, DC, 1882.

Trafzer, Clifford, and Margery Ann Beach. "Smohalla, the Washani, and Religion as a Factor in Northwestern History." *American Indian Quarterly* 9:309–24 (1985).

Trafzer, Clifford E., ed. *American Indian Prophets.* Newcastle, CA: Sierra Oaks, 1986.

United States Department of War. *Annual Report of the Secretary of War, 1877.* Washington, DC, 1877.

Walker, Deward E. *Conflict and Schism in Nez Perce Acculturation.* Pullman: Washington State Univ. Press, 1968.

Winthrop, Theodore. *The Canoe and the Saddle.* New York: Dodd, Mead, 1862.

Wood, Charles Erskine Scott. "Private Journal, 1879." *Oregon Historical Quarterly* 70 (June 1969).

The Union, 1871–83. Walla Walla, WA.

CHAPTER 5
EMIGRANTS

Bennett, Ralph. Interview. Oregon Historical Society oral history recording by J. Strassmaier, June 8, 1991.

Blanchard, John. *Caravans to the Northwest.* Boston: Houghton Mifflin, 1940.

Bonneville Power Administration. *Hydro!* and *The Columbia* (films), 1940, 1948.

Case, Robert. "Eighth Wonder of the World." *Saturday Evening Post,* July 13, 1936, p. 23.

Chase, Stewart. "Great Dam." *Atlantic,* November 1938, p. 593; condensed in *Reader's Digest,* January 1939.

Chiles, James. "Engineers Versus Eons." *Smithsonian,* March 1984.

Davenport, Walter. "Power in the Wilderness." *Colliers,* September 21, 1935, p. 593.

Foster, Richard F. Some Effects of Pile Area Effluent Water on Young Chinook Salmon and Steelhead Trout. Battelle Pacific Northwest Laboratories, File No. 7-4759, August 31, 1946.

Foster, Richard F. *Effects of Hanford Reactors on Columbia River and Adjacent Land Areas.* Report to State of Washington Ecological Commission, Richland, December 15, 1970.

Gamboa, Erasmo. *Mexican Labor and World War II: Braceros in the Pacific Northwest, 1942–1947.* Austin: Univ. of Texas Press, 1990.

Gerber, Michelle. *On the Home Front: The Cold War Legacy of the Hanford Nuclear Site.* Lincoln: Univ. of Nebraska Press, 1992.

Guthrie, Woody. Letter to Loring Family, July 9, 1948. Oregon Historical Society, MS. 1500.

Guthrie, Woody. *Pastures of Plenty: A Self-Portrait.* Edited by Dave Marsh and Harold Leventhal. New York: HarperCollins, 1990.

Holbrook, Stewart. "The Mythmakers." *New Yorker,* July 31, 1948, pp. 35–36.

"Irrigation Makes the Northwest Land Bloom." *Life,* June 5, 1939, pp. 15, 36.

Klein, Joe. *Woody Guthrie: A Life*. New York: Knopf, 1980.

Lange, Dorothea. *An American Exodus*. New York: Reynal and Hitchcock, 1939.

Lowitt, Richard. *The New Deal and the American West*. Bloomington: Univ. of Indiana Press, 1984.

Maben, Manly. *Vanport*. Portland: Oregon Historical Society, 1887.

Mattila, Walter. "Death of a War Orphan." *Oregon Journal*, May 29, 1949.

McKinley, Charles. *Uncle Sam in the Pacific Northwest*. Berkeley: Univ. of California Press, 1952.

Mezey, Phil. "The Real Vanport Disaster." *New Republic*, July 5, 1948.

Mull, Robert. *Something to Win the War* (film). Seattle, 1985.

Neuberger, Richard. "Roosevelt Builds the Biggest Dam." *Life*, October 11, 1937, p. 34.

Neuberger, Richard L. *Our Promised Land*. New York: Macmillan, 1938.

Neuberger, Richard. "Miracle in Concrete." *Nation*, June 1940.

Neuberger, Richard L. "One of Our Cities Is Missing." *Nation*, June 12, 1948, p. 652.

Rice, David G. *Archeological Investigations at WPPSS Nuclear Plants on the Hanford Reservation, Washington*. Richland: Washington Public Power Supply System, 1983.

Rice, David G. *Cultural Resources at Hanford*. Richland, WA: U.S. Department of Energy, WPPSS, 1983.

Rogers, John R. *Free Land: The Remedy for Involuntary Poverty, Social Unrest and the Woes of Labor*. Tacoma, WA: The Morning Union, 1897.

Rogers, John R. *The Inalienable Rights of Man*. Olympia, WA, 1900.

Rorty, J. "Grand Coulee." *Nation*, March 20, 1935, p. 329; April 17, 1935, p. 446; July 24, 1935, p. 101.

Sanger, S. L. *Hanford and the Bomb*. Seattle: Living History Press, 1989.

Schwarz, Jordan. *The New Dealers: Power Brokers in the Age of Roosevelt.* New York: Knopf, 1993.

Snell, Arthur. "Graveyard Shift, Hanford, 28 September 1944— Henry W. Newson." *American Journal of Physics,* 50(4) April 1982: 43–48.

Thompson, Margaret. *Space for Living: A Novel of the Grand Coulee and Columbia Basin.* Portland, OR: Binfords and Mort, 1944.

Tollefson, Gene. *BPA and the Struggle for Power at Cost.* Portland, OR: Bonneville Power Administration, 1987.

United States Land Policy Review. *The Migrants.* Washington, DC: United States Land Policy Review, 1940.

United States Resettlement Administration. *Suggestions to Prospective Settlers in Idaho, Washington, and Oregon.* Washington, DC: GPO, 1940.

Van Arsdol, Ted. *Hanford, the Big Secret.* Richland, WA: Columbia Basin News, 1958; reprinted by author, Vancouver, WA, 1992.

CHAPTER 6
CAPTIVES

American Friends Service Committee. *Uncommon Controversy: Fishing Rights of the Muckleshoot, Puyallup, and Nisqually Indians.* Seattle: Univ. of Washington Press, 1970.

Argus, 1939, 1961. Seattle.

Becker, C. D. *Aquatic Bioenvironmental Studies: The Hanford Experience, 1944–84.* Amsterdam: Elsevier, 1990.

Churchill, Sam. "The Day Celilo Falls Died." *Oregon Farmer,* April 6, 1961.

Columbian, 1981. Vancouver, WA.

Cressman, Luther. *A Golden Journey: Memoirs of an Archeologist.* Salt Lake City: Univ. of Utah Press, 1988.

Dalles Chronicle, 1949. The Dalles, OR.

Dalles Optimist, 1945. The Dalles, OR.

Federal Grand Jury for the Western District of Washington at Seattle. Testimony of Penelope Fields, October 21, 1982. Hillier Papers. In the possession of Thomas Hillier, Seattle, WA.

Galt, Phyllis. "We Are the Last of the Wanapum." *Oregonian, Northwest Magazine,* March 10, 1968, p. 12.

Keefe, Tom. Taped interview with David Sohappy. Keefe Papers. In the possession of Thomas Keefe, Washington, DC.

Little White Salmon Indian Settlement News, Northwest Indian News, November 1972.

McWhorter, Lucullus. *The Crime Against the Yakimas.* Yakima, WA, 1913.

McWhorter, L. V. "Paiute Vision of First Wolf People." McWhorter Collection, Washington State Univ. Press.

National Marine Fisheries Service. Cook's Landing search warrant. Keefe Papers.

National Marine Fisheries Service. Inventory from Cook's Landing raid. Keefe Papers.

National Marine Fisheries Service. Tape of salmonscam undercover operations. Keefe Papers.

Neuberger, Richard L. *The Columbia.* New York: Holiday, 1949.

Oregon Historical Society. Oral history interview with Flora Thompson, Portland, 1975.

Oregonian, 1925–91. Portland.

Oregon Journal, 1920–70. Portland.

Seattle Post Intelligencer, 1945–92. Seattle.

Seattle Public Library. Scrapbooks C58 (Columbia Basin), DO8 (Dams), I9 (Irrigation), and I58 (Indians).

Seattle Public Library. Uncataloged Northwest Material, Box 29.

Seattle Times, 1941–91. Seattle.

Severtson, Richard. Affidavit. Keefe Papers.

Skamania County Pioneer, 1981–92. Skamania, WA.

Smithsonian Institution. *An Appraisal of the Archeological Resources of the Dalles Reservoir.* Washington, DC: Smithsonian, 1952.

Sohappy, David. Holograph autobiography. Keefe Papers.

Sohappy, David. Papers and letters. Hillier Papers.

Spokesman-Review, 1950–57, 1973. Spokane, WA.

United States District Court, Tacoma, Washington. Indictment, *United States of America v. David Sohappy, Sr., et al.* Hillier Papers.

United States Federal Court. Testimony from *David Sohappy et al. v. United States of America.* Keefe Papers.

Wenatchee World, 1940–59. Wenatchee, WA.

Yakima Nation. Tape of *Yakima Nation v. Sohappy et al.* Keefe Papers.